ROSE IS ROSE
RUNNING ON ALTER EGO

PAT BRADY

**Andrews McMeel
Publishing®**

Kansas City · Sydney · London

Rose is Rose is distributed internationally by Universal Uclick.

Andrews McMeel Publishing, LLC
an Andrews McMeel Universal company
1130 Walnut Street, Kansas City, Missouri 64106

www.andrewsmcmeel.com

ISBN: 978-0-7407-5127-1

Library of Congress Control Number: 2004114454

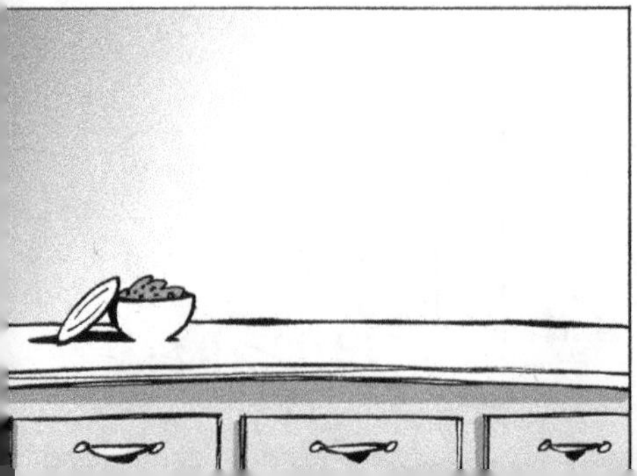

Other *Rose is Rose* books by Pat Brady
from Andrews McMeel Publishing

She's a Momma, Not a Movie Star

License to Dream

Rose is Rose 15th Anniversary Collection

The Irresistible Rose is Rose

High-Spirited Rose is Rose

Rose is Rose Right on the Lips

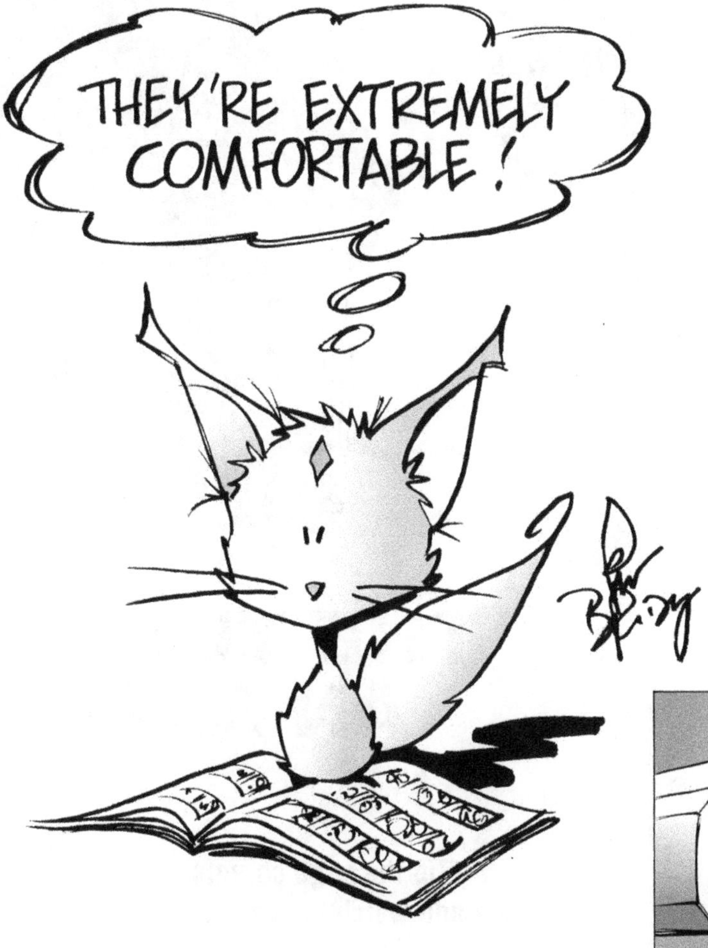
THEY'RE EXTREMELY COMFORTABLE!

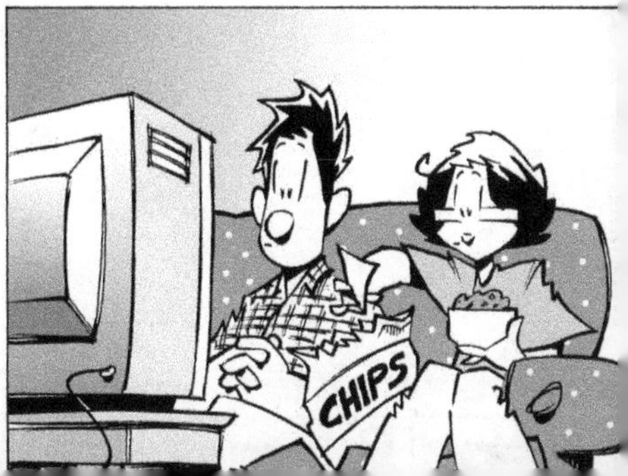
CHIPS

WHEN THE GOING GETS TOUGH...

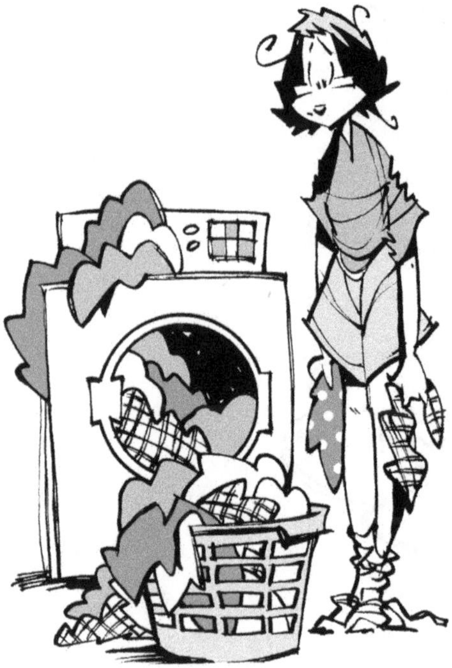

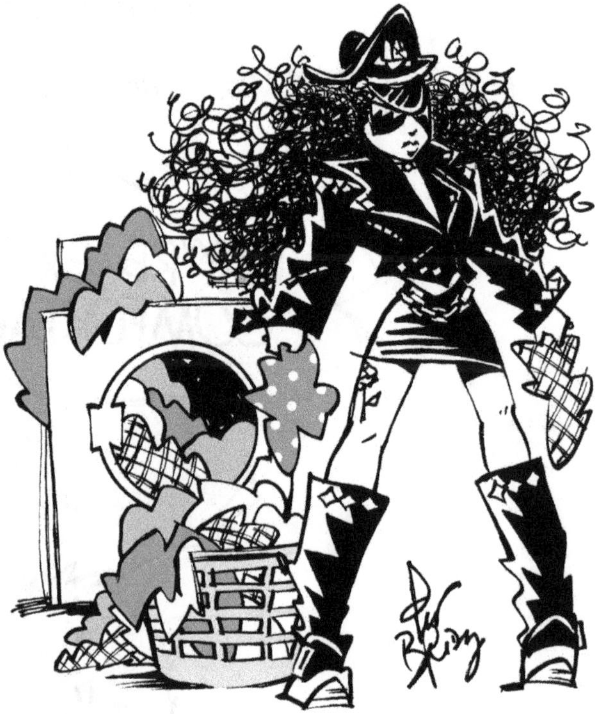

THE TOUGH GET AN ALTER EGO

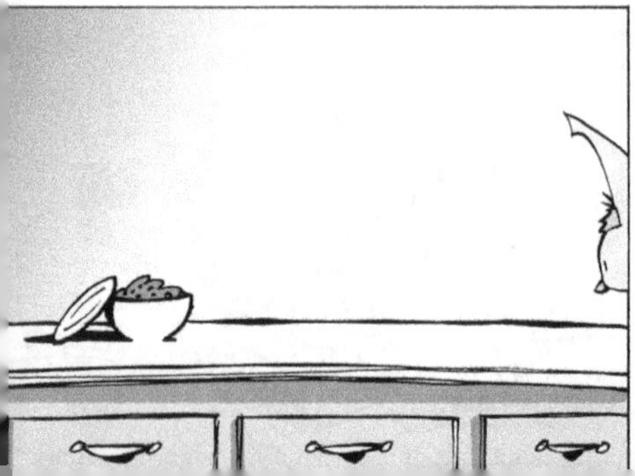

Flip the page corners and watch both sides!

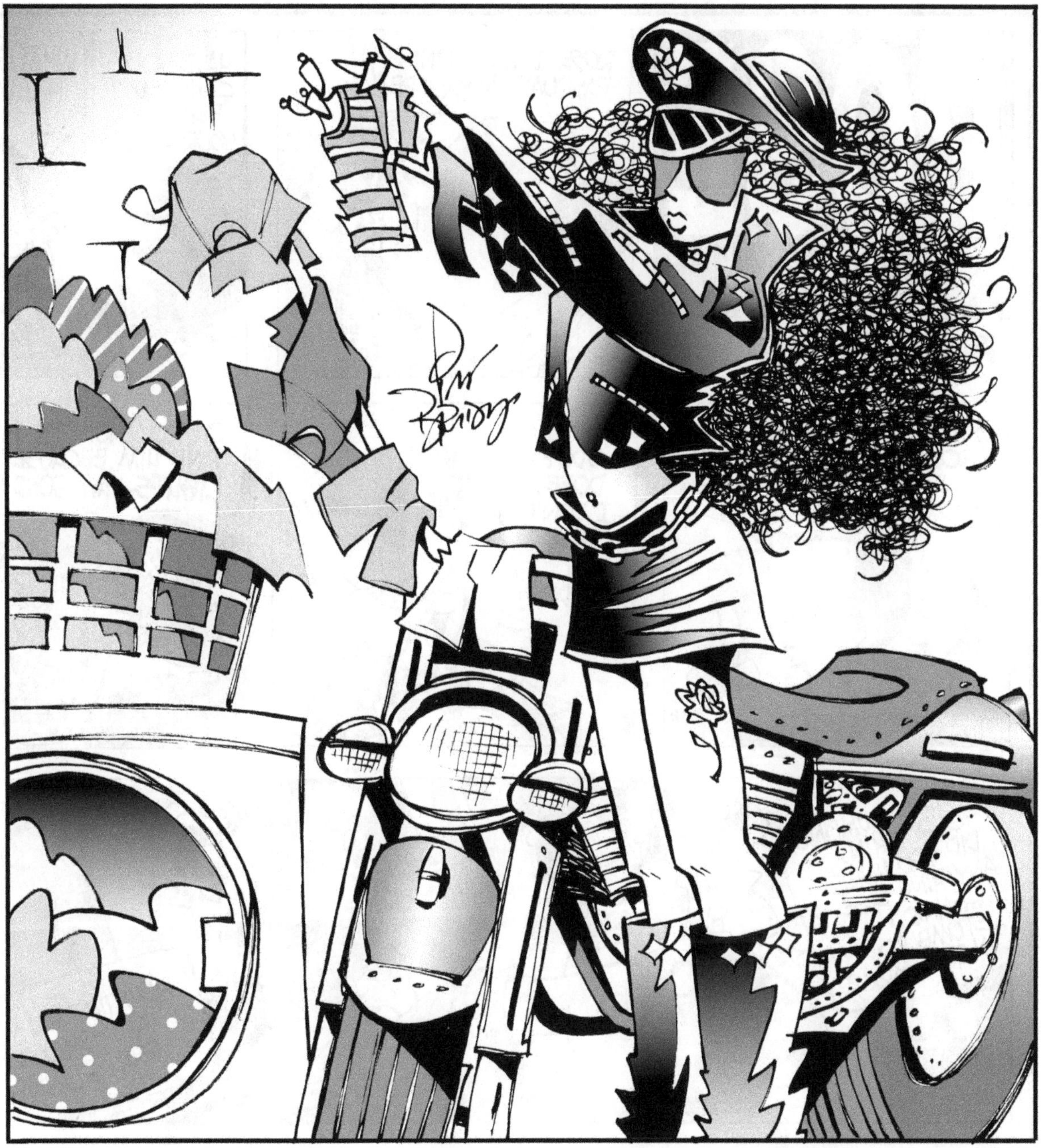

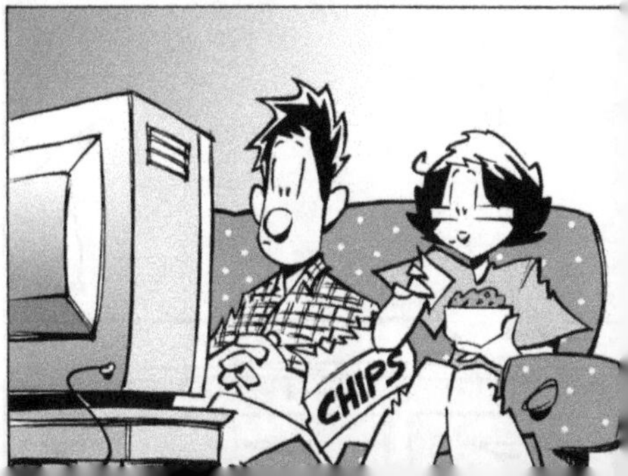
CHIPS

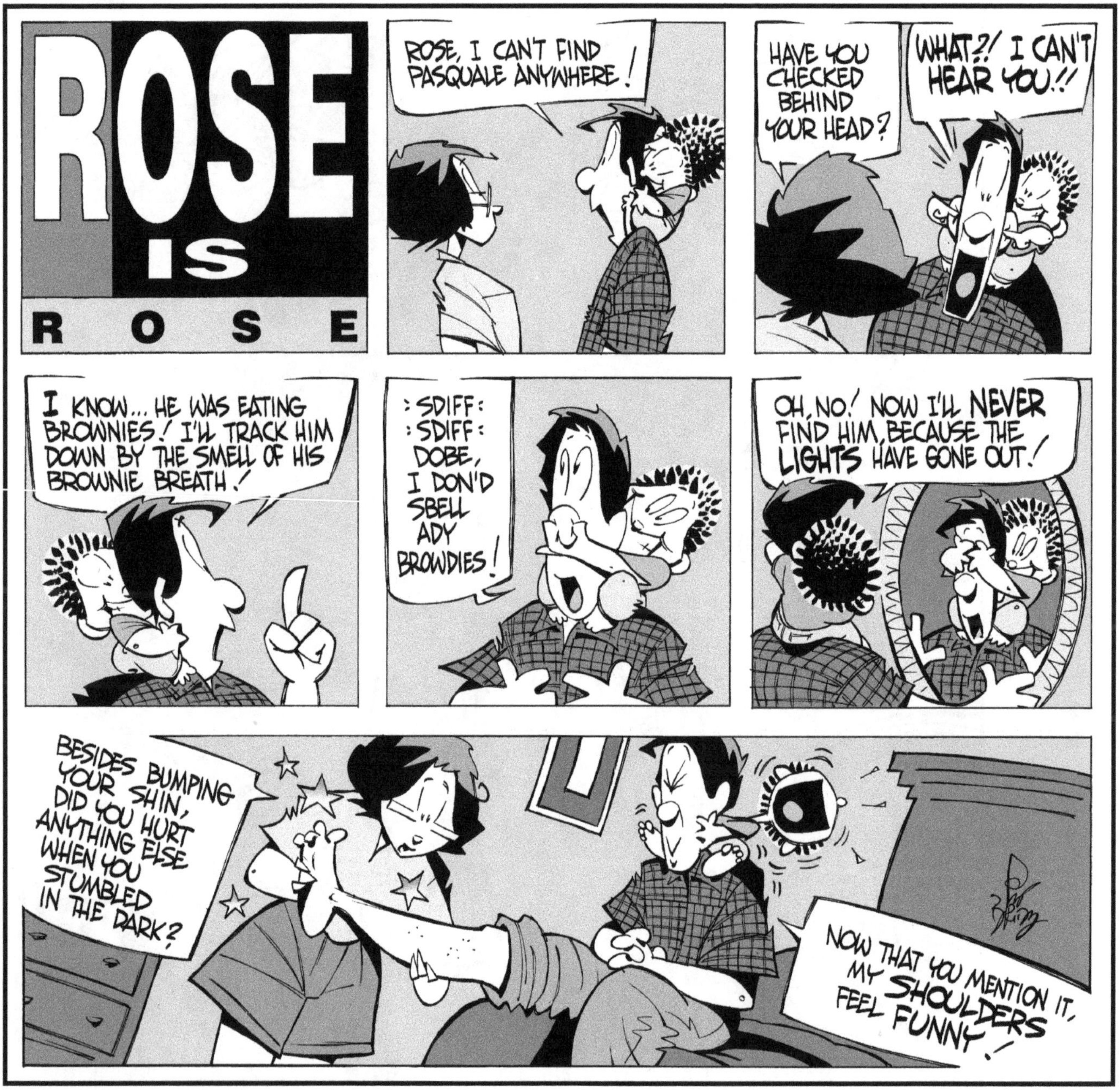
ROSE IS ROSE
ROSE, I CAN'T FIND PASQUALE ANYWHERE!
HAVE YOU CHECKED BEHIND YOUR HEAD?
WHAT?! I CAN'T HEAR YOU!!
I KNOW... HE WAS EATING BROWNIES! I'LL TRACK HIM DOWN BY THE SMELL OF HIS BROWNIE BREATH!
:SDIFF: :SDIFF: DOBE, I DON'D SBELL ADY BROWDIES!
OH, NO! NOW I'LL NEVER FIND HIM, BECAUSE THE LIGHTS HAVE GONE OUT!
BESIDES BUMPING YOUR SHIN, DID YOU HURT ANYTHING ELSE WHEN YOU STUMBLED IN THE DARK?
NOW THAT YOU MENTION IT, MY SHOULDERS FEEL FUNNY!

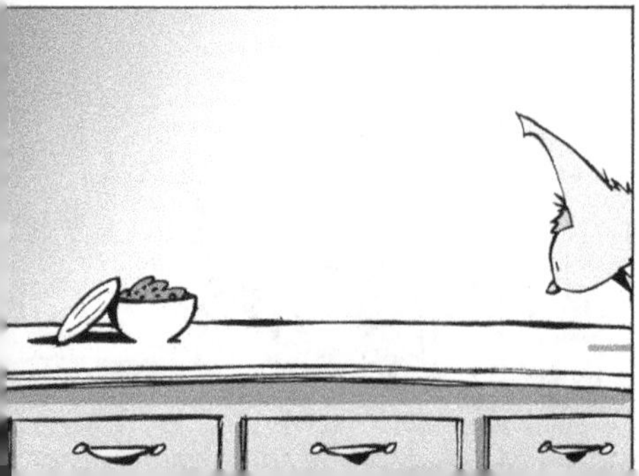

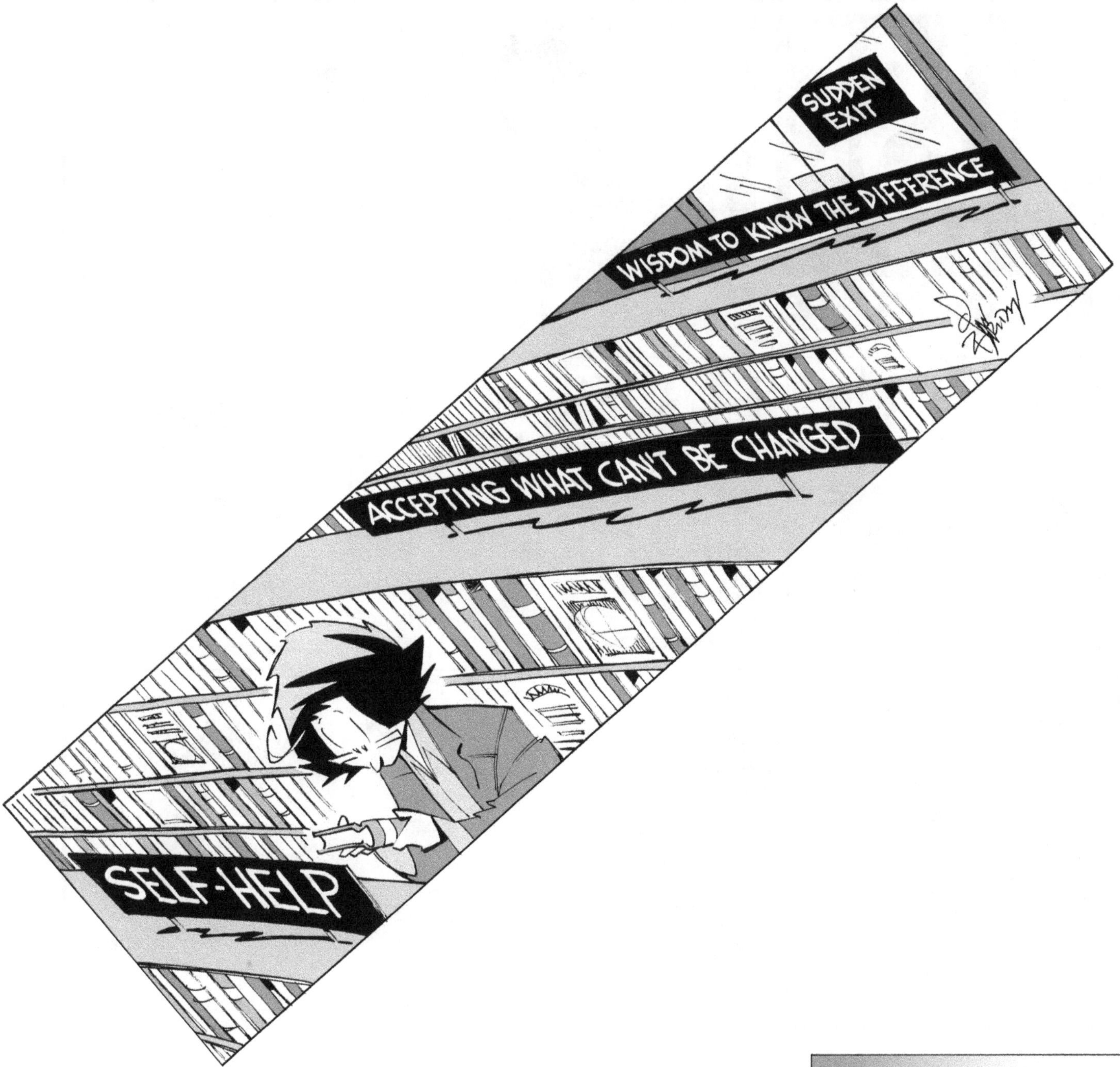
SUDDEN EXIT
WISDOM TO KNOW THE DIFFERENCE
ACCEPTING WHAT CAN'T BE CHANGED
SELF-HELP

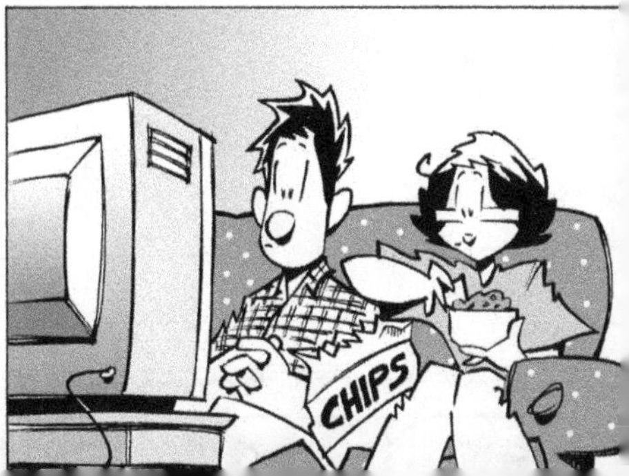
CHIPS

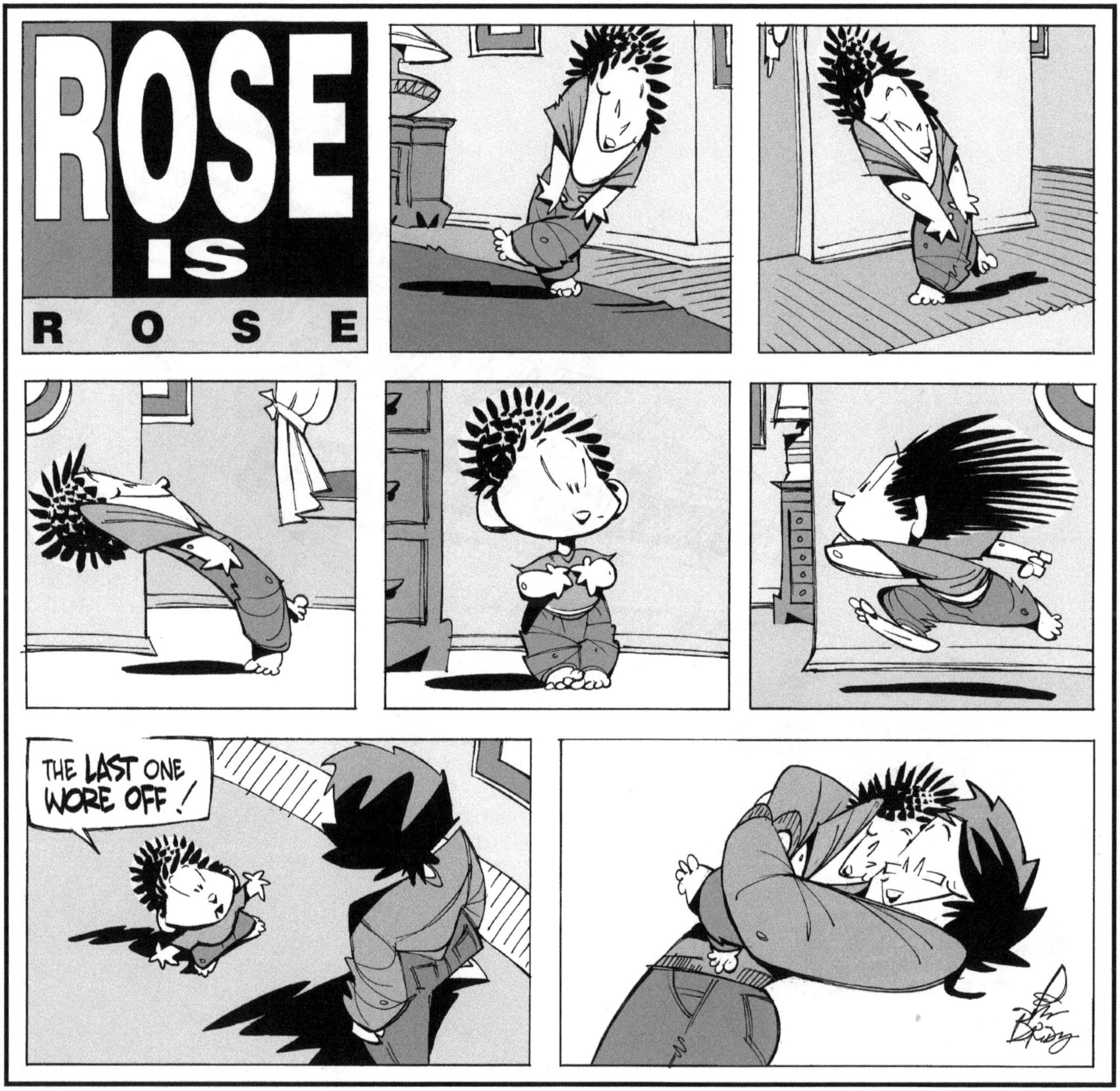
ROSE IS ROSE
THE LAST ONE WORE OFF!

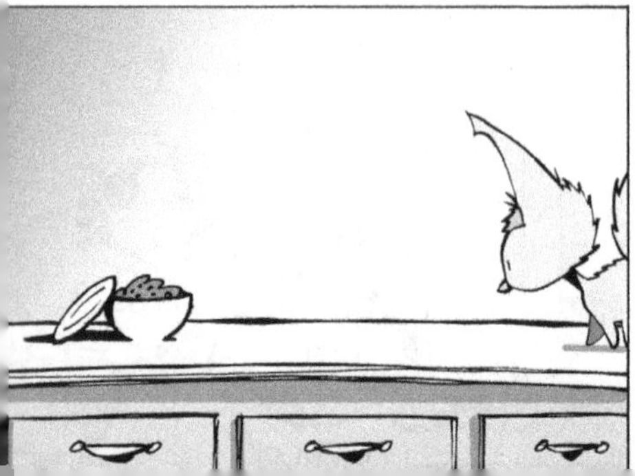

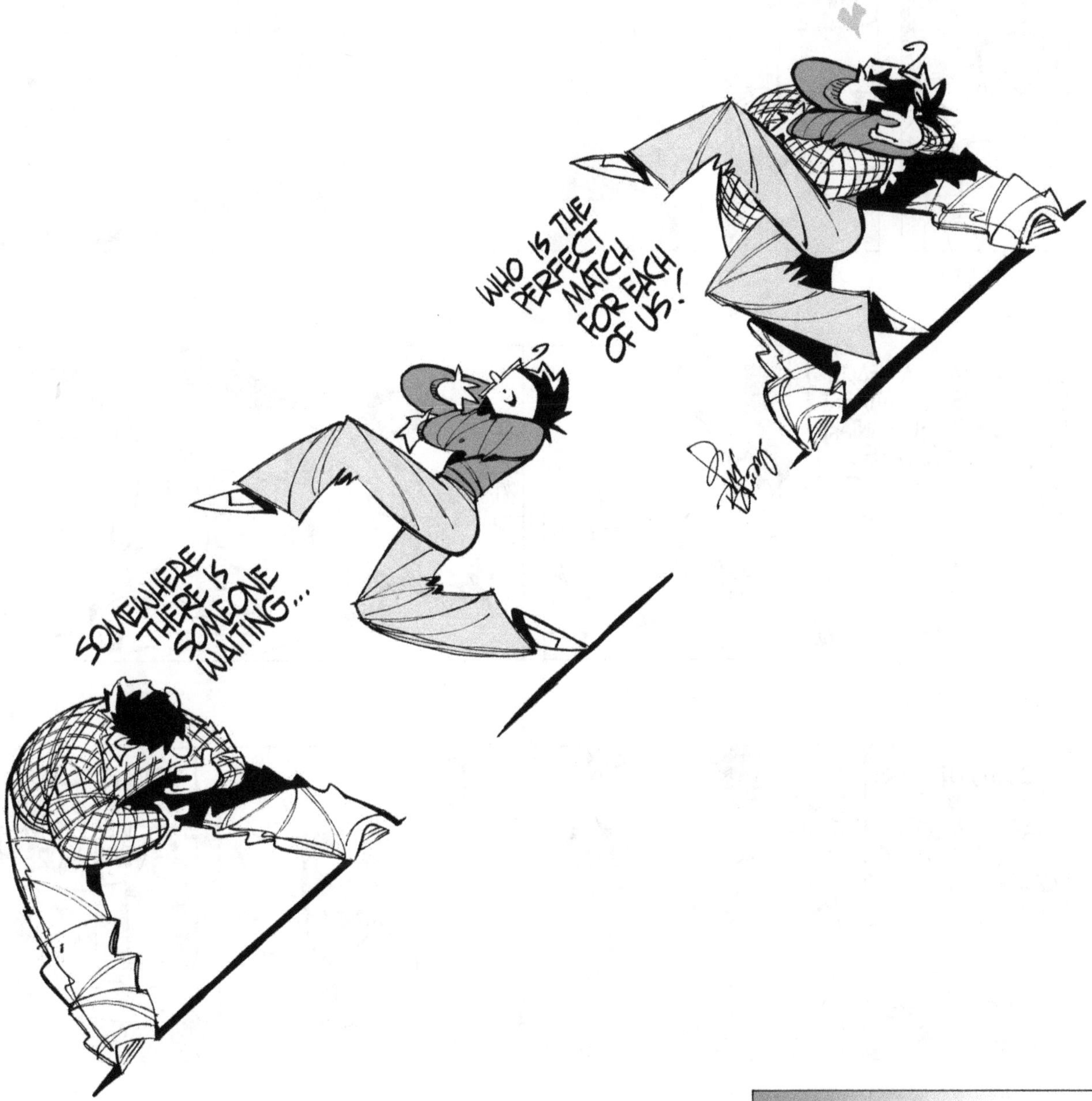
SOMEWHERE THERE IS SOMEONE WAITING...
WHO IS THE PERFECT MATCH FOR EACH OF US!

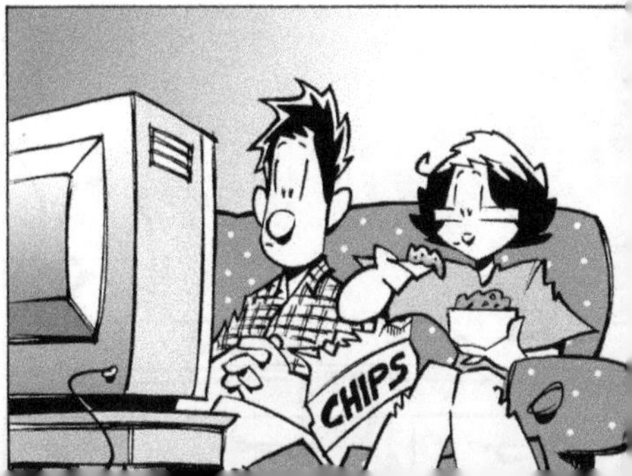
CHIPS

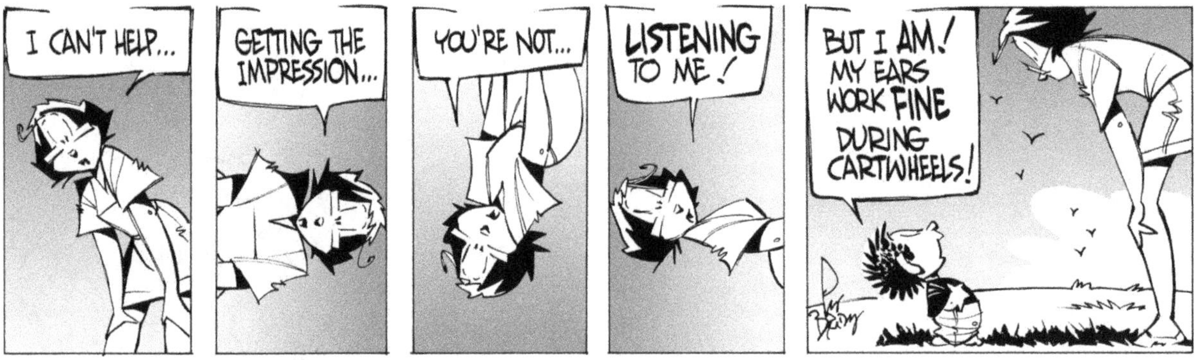
I CAN'T HELP...
GETTING THE IMPRESSION...
YOU'RE NOT...
LISTENING TO ME!
BUT I AM! MY EARS WORK FINE DURING CARTWHEELS!

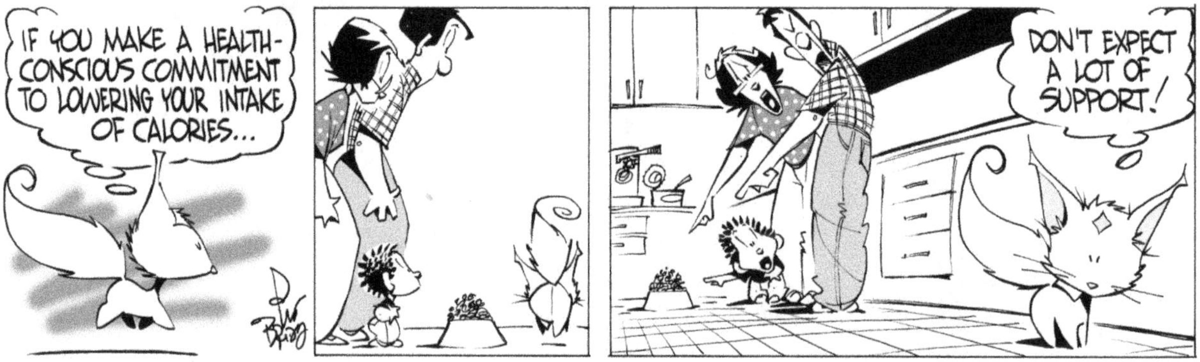
IF YOU MAKE A HEALTH-CONSCIOUS COMMITMENT TO LOWERING YOUR INTAKE OF CALORIES...
DON'T EXPECT A LOT OF SUPPORT!

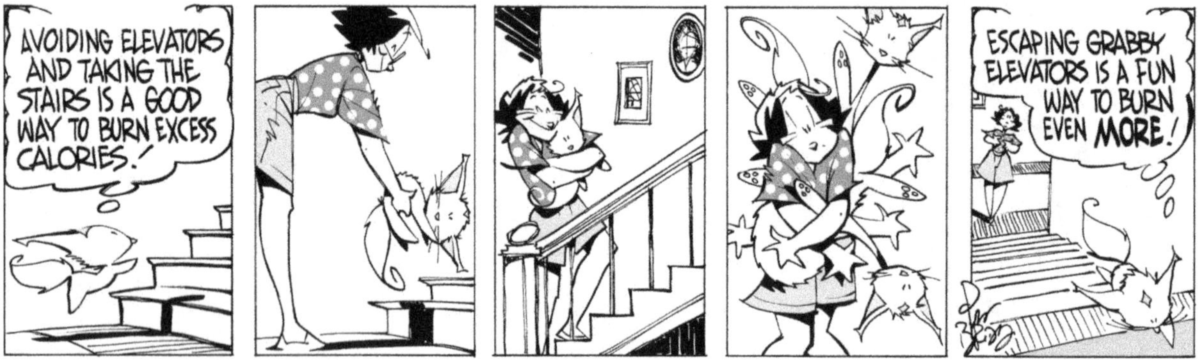
AVOIDING ELEVATORS AND TAKING THE STAIRS IS A GOOD WAY TO BURN EXCESS CALORIES!
ESCAPING GRABBY ELEVATORS IS A FUN WAY TO BURN EVEN MORE!

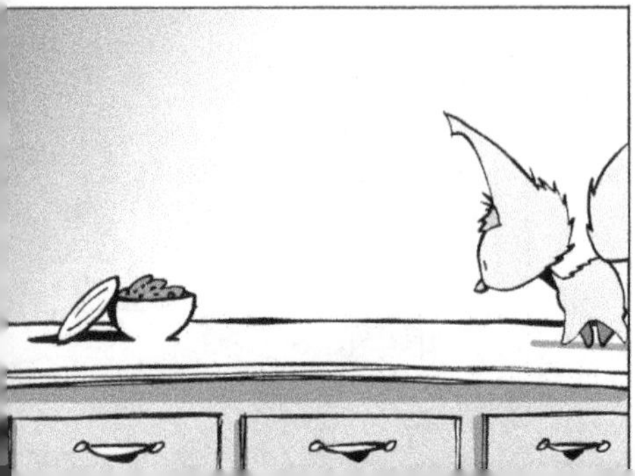

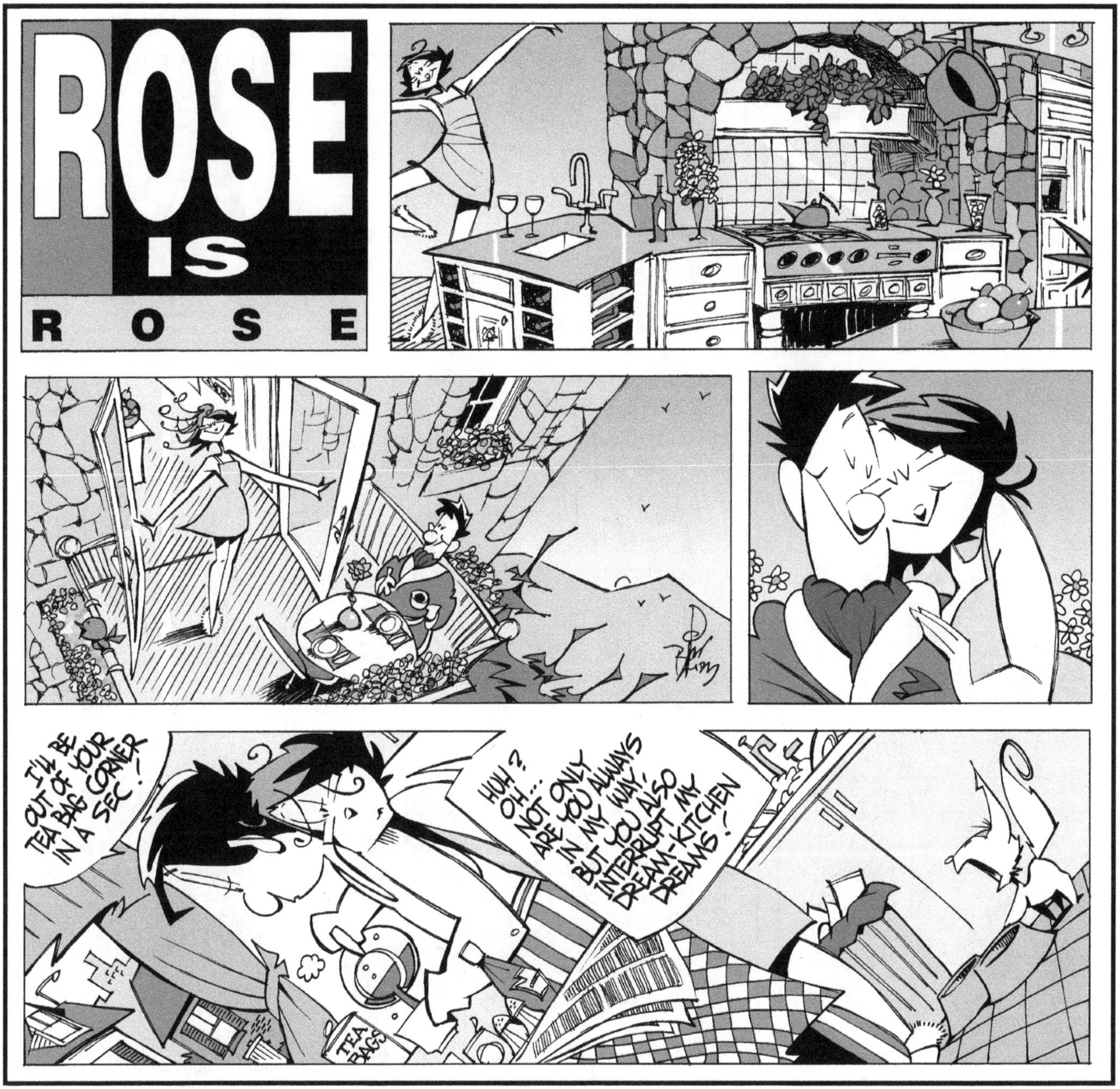
ROSE IS ROSE
I'LL BE OUT OF YOUR TEA BAG CORNER IN A SEC!
HUH? OH... NOT ONLY ARE YOU ALWAYS IN MY WAY, BUT YOU ALSO INTERRUPT MY DREAM-KITCHEN DREAMS!
TEA BAGS

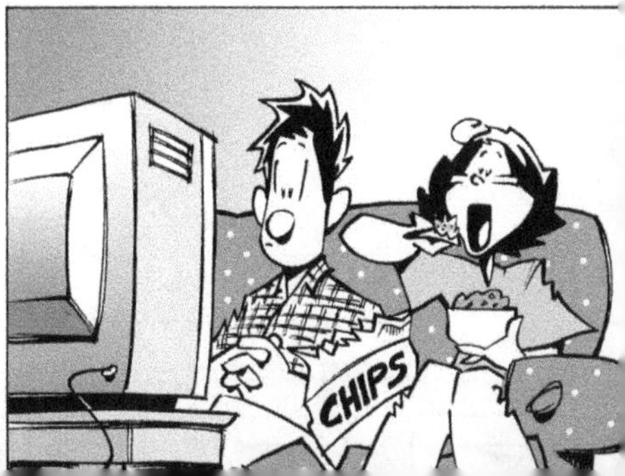
CHIPS

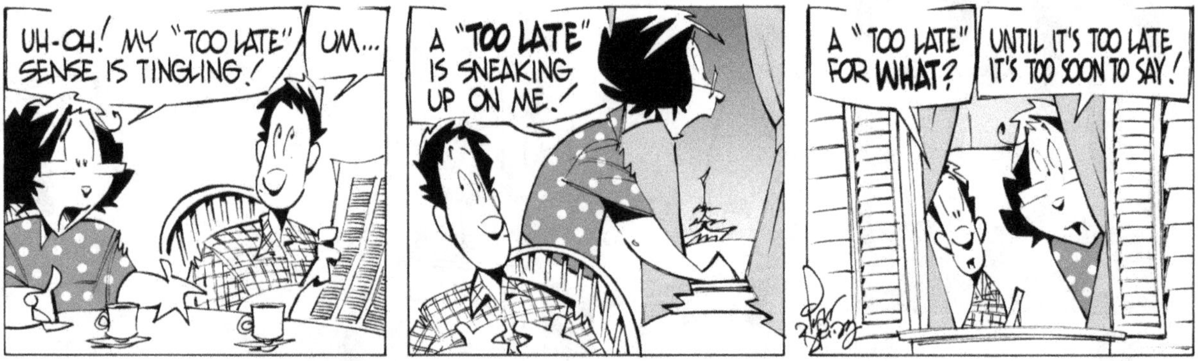
UH-OH! MY "TOO LATE" SENSE IS TINGLING!
UM...
A "TOO LATE" IS SNEAKING UP ON ME!
A "TOO LATE" FOR WHAT?
UNTIL IT'S TOO LATE IT'S TOO SOON TO SAY!

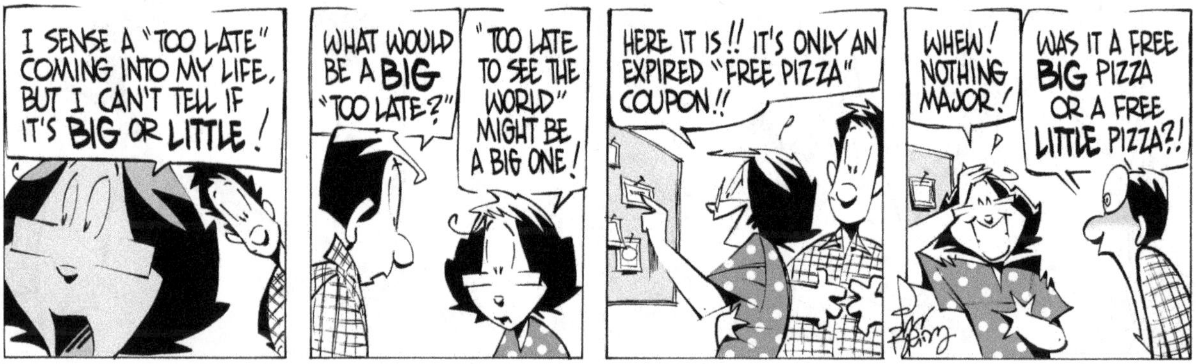
I SENSE A "TOO LATE" COMING INTO MY LIFE, BUT I CAN'T TELL IF IT'S BIG OR LITTLE!
WHAT WOULD BE A BIG "TOO LATE"?
"TOO LATE TO SEE THE WORLD" MIGHT BE A BIG ONE!
HERE IT IS!! IT'S ONLY AN EXPIRED "FREE PIZZA" COUPON!!
WHEW! NOTHING MAJOR!
WAS IT A FREE BIG PIZZA OR A FREE LITTLE PIZZA?!

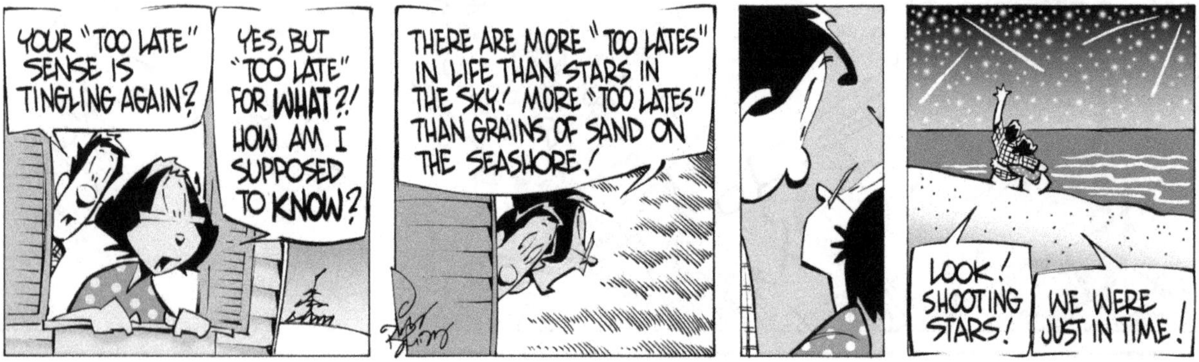
YOUR "TOO LATE" SENSE IS TINGLING AGAIN?
YES, BUT "TOO LATE" FOR WHAT?! HOW AM I SUPPOSED TO KNOW?
THERE ARE MORE "TOO LATES" IN LIFE THAN STARS IN THE SKY! MORE "TOO LATES" THAN GRAINS OF SAND ON THE SEASHORE!
LOOK! SHOOTING STARS!
WE WERE JUST IN TIME!

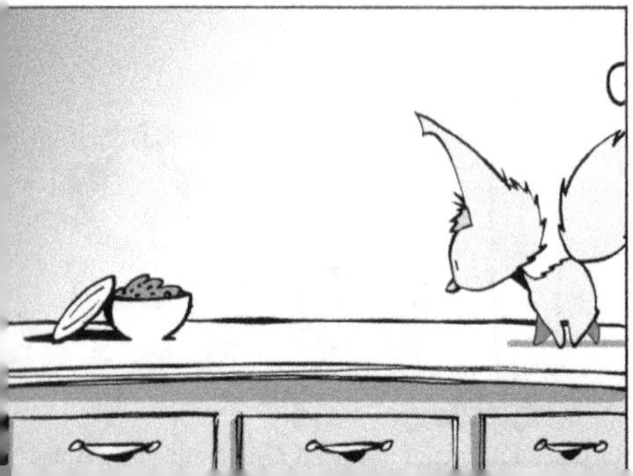

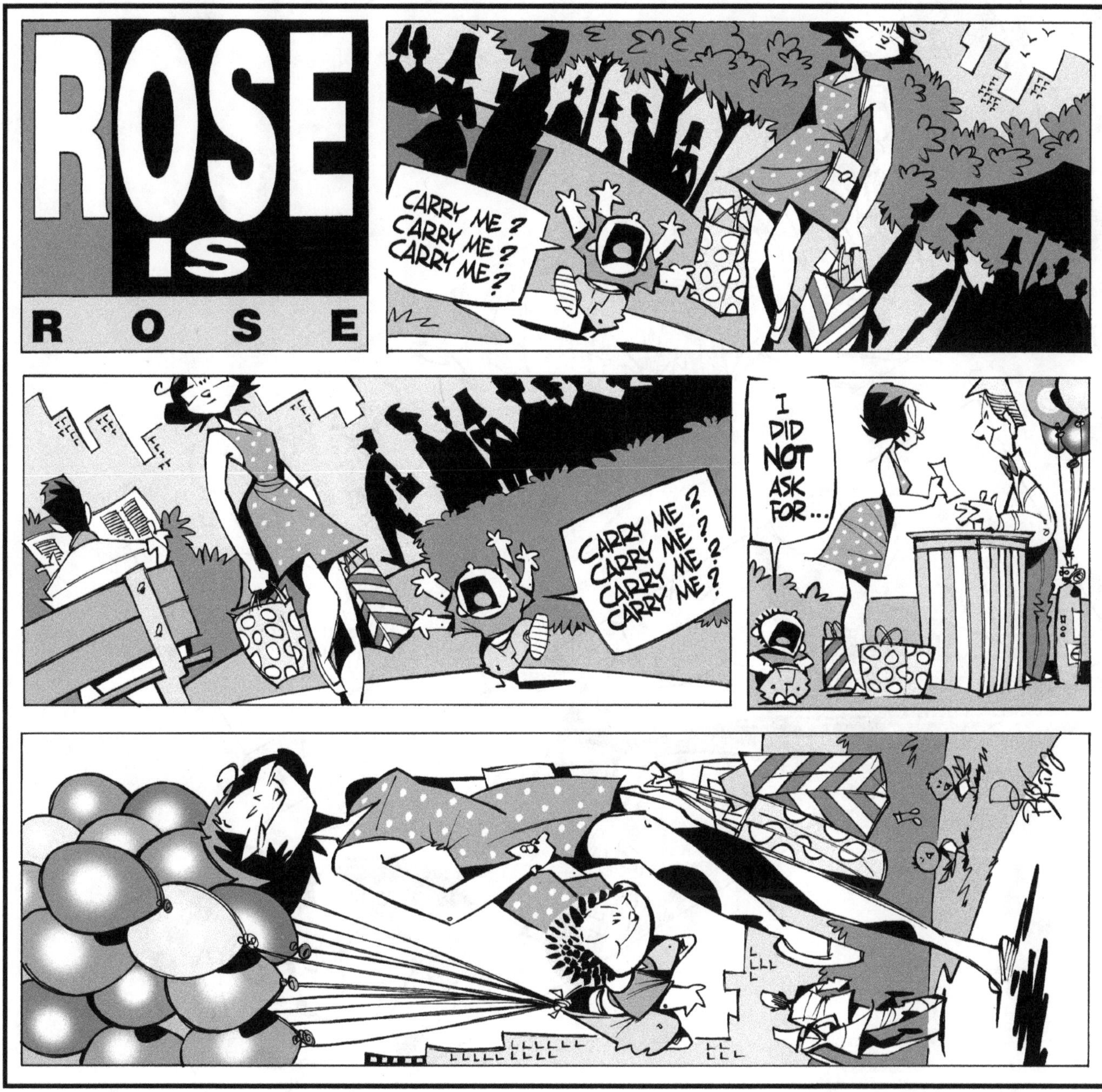
ROSE IS ROSE
CARRY ME? CARRY ME? CARRY ME?
CARRY ME? CARRY ME? CARRY ME? CARRY ME?
I DID NOT ASK FOR...

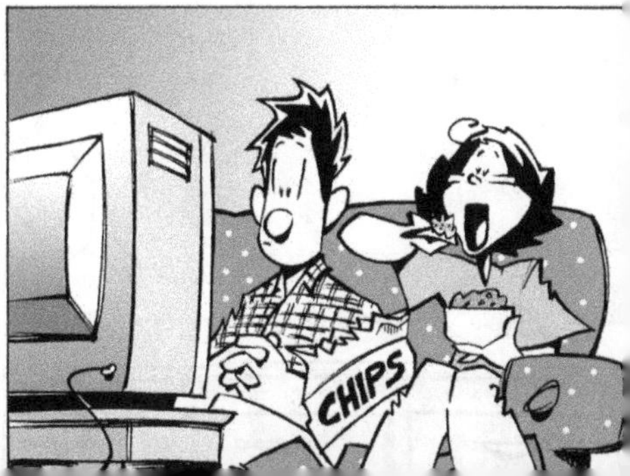
CHIPS

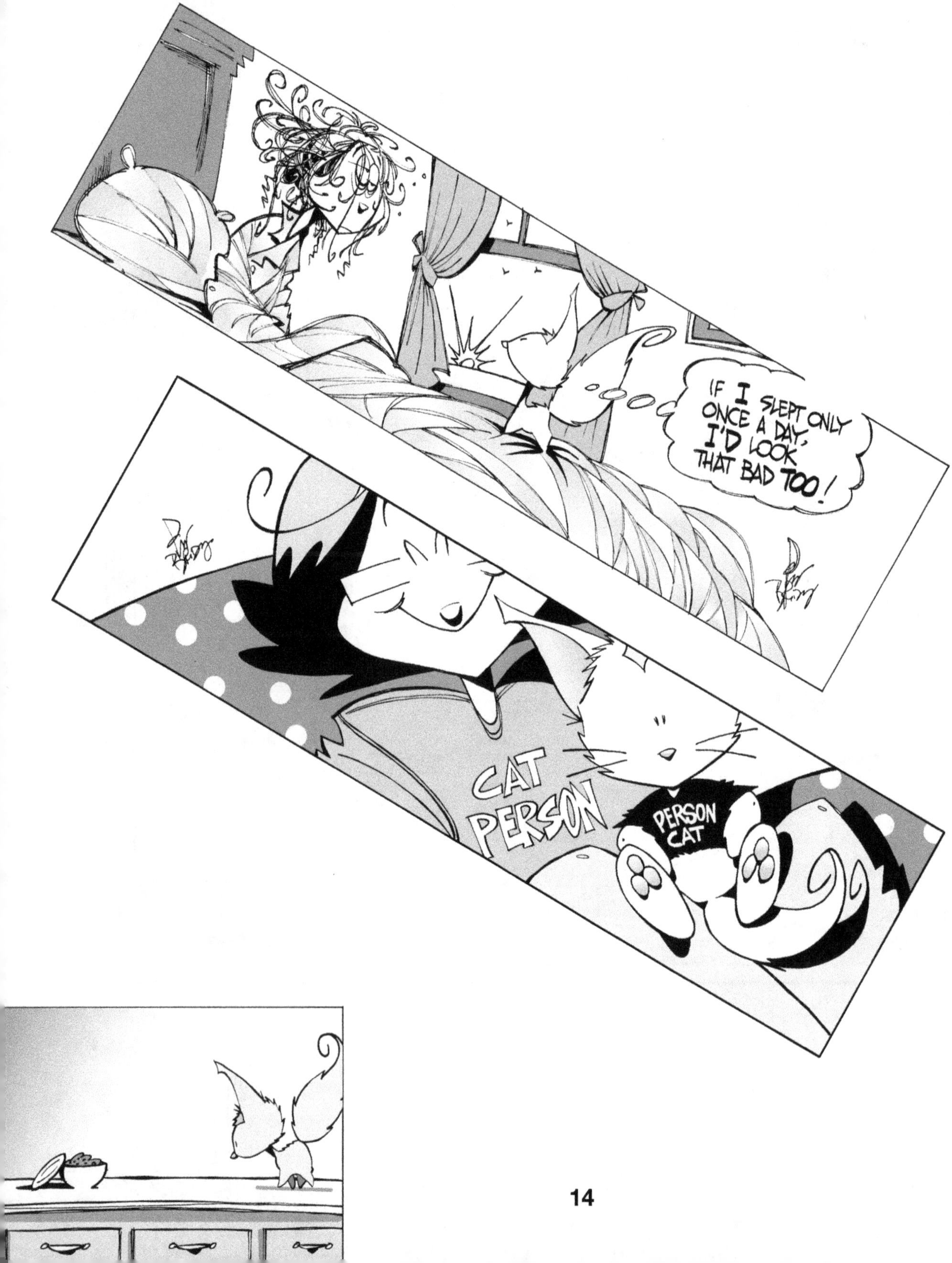
IF I SLEPT ONLY ONCE A DAY, I'D LOOK THAT BAD TOO!
CAT PERSON
PERSON CAT

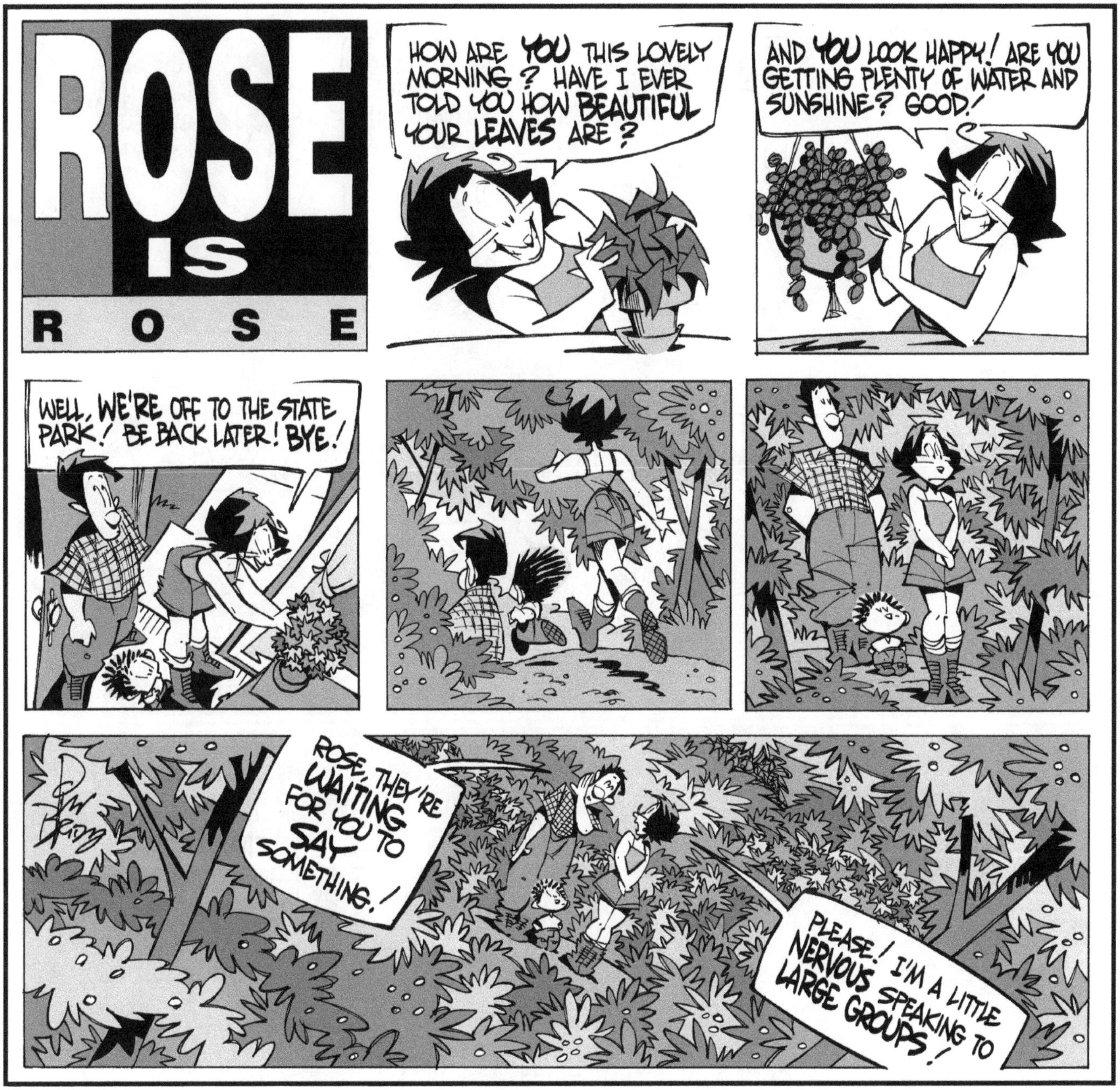
ROSE IS ROSE
HOW ARE YOU THIS LOVELY MORNING? HAVE I EVER TOLD YOU HOW BEAUTIFUL YOUR LEAVES ARE?
AND YOU LOOK HAPPY! ARE YOU GETTING PLENTY OF WATER AND SUNSHINE? GOOD!
WELL, WE'RE OFF TO THE STATE PARK! BE BACK LATER! BYE!
ROSE, THEY'RE WAITING FOR YOU TO SAY SOMETHING!
PLEASE! I'M A LITTLE NERVOUS SPEAKING TO LARGE GROUPS!

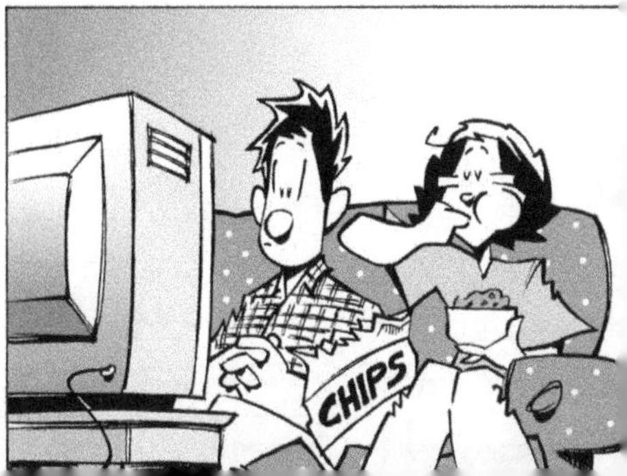
CHIPS

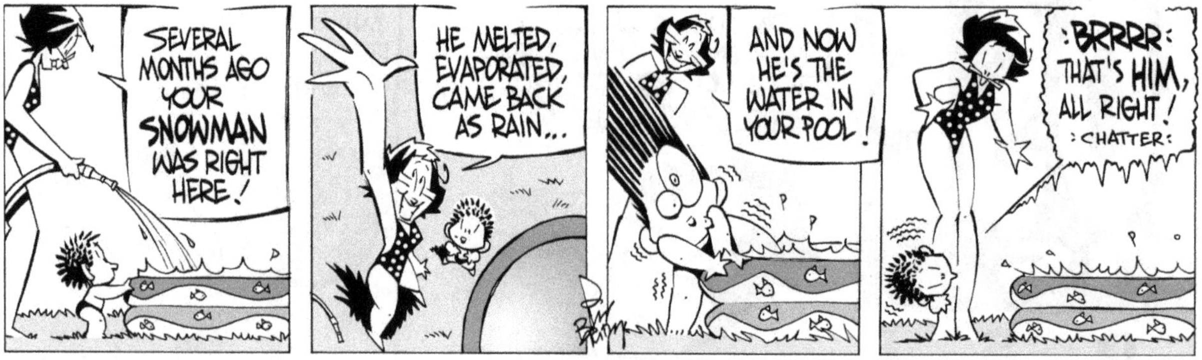
SEVERAL MONTHS AGO YOUR SNOWMAN WAS RIGHT HERE!
HE MELTED, EVAPORATED, CAME BACK AS RAIN...
AND NOW HE'S THE WATER IN YOUR POOL!
BRRRR THAT'S HIM, ALL RIGHT!
CHATTER

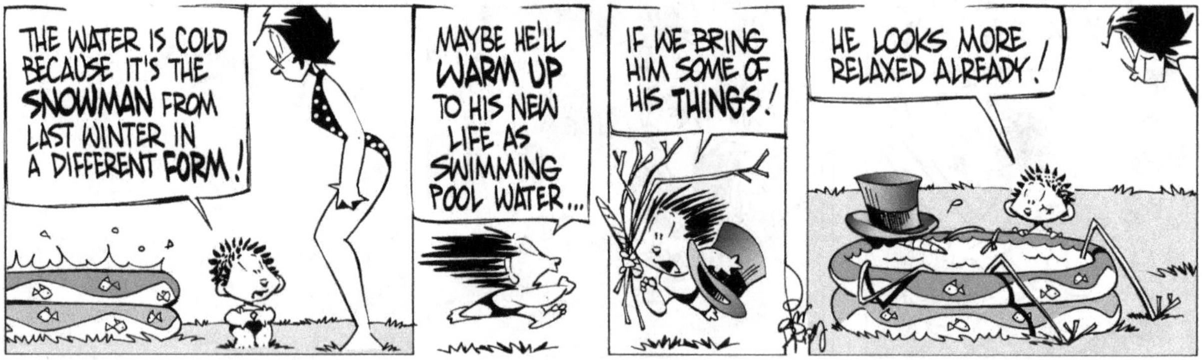
THE WATER IS COLD BECAUSE IT'S THE SNOWMAN FROM LAST WINTER IN A DIFFERENT FORM!
MAYBE HE'LL WARM UP TO HIS NEW LIFE AS SWIMMING POOL WATER...
IF WE BRING HIM SOME OF HIS THINGS!
HE LOOKS MORE RELAXED ALREADY!

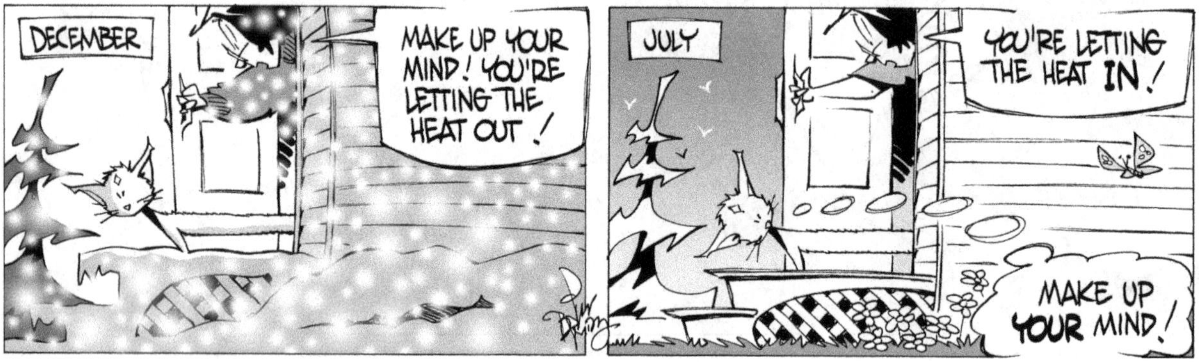
DECEMBER
MAKE UP YOUR MIND! YOU'RE LETTING THE HEAT OUT!
JULY
YOU'RE LETTING THE HEAT IN!
MAKE UP YOUR MIND!

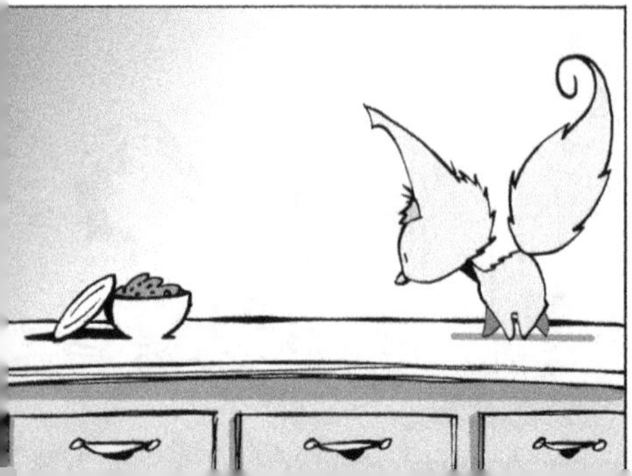

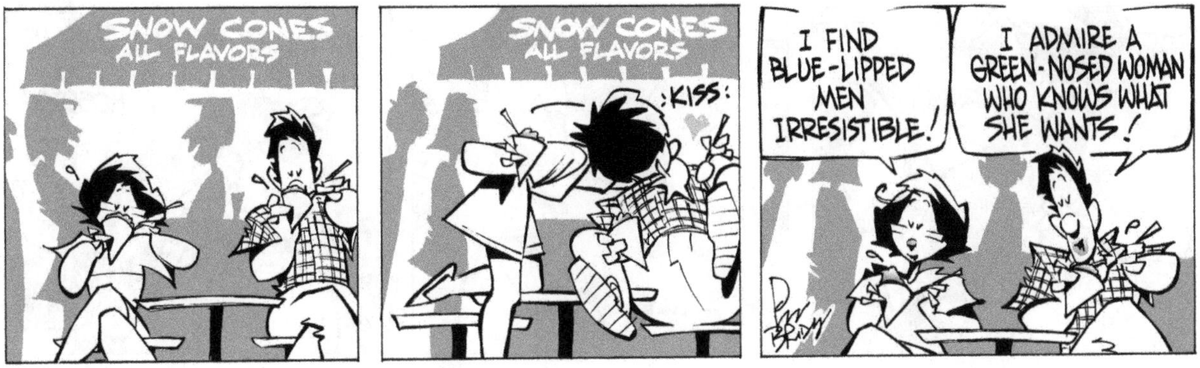
SNOW CONES
ALL FLAVORS
SNOW CONES
ALL FLAVORS
:KISS:
I FIND BLUE-LIPPED MEN IRRESISTIBLE!
I ADMIRE A GREEN-NOSED WOMAN WHO KNOWS WHAT SHE WANTS!

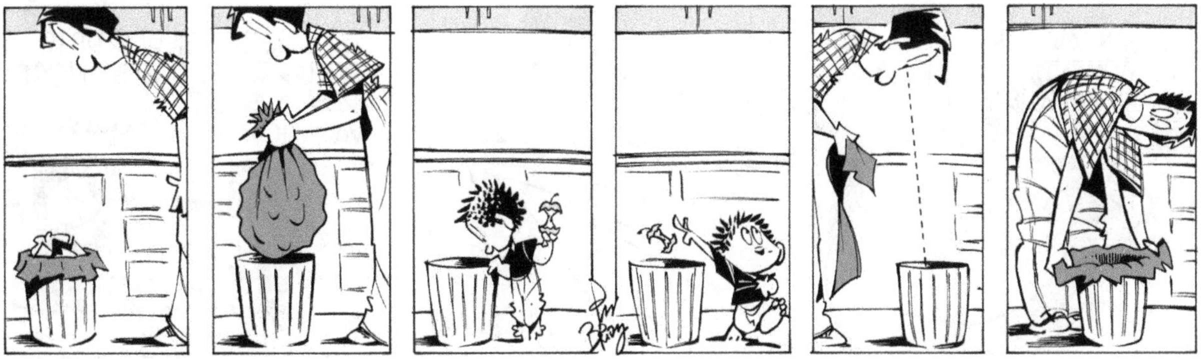

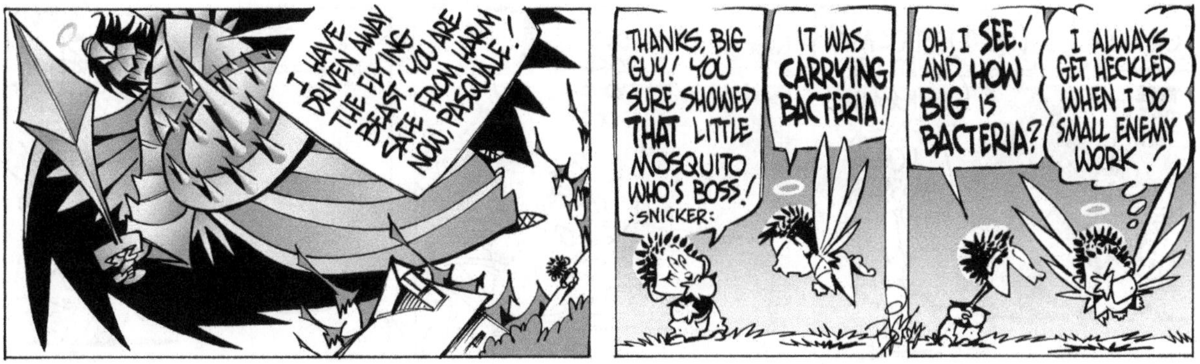
I HAVE DRIVEN AWAY THE FLYING BEAST! YOU ARE SAFE FROM HARM NOW, PASQUALE!
THANKS, BIG GUY! YOU SURE SHOWED THAT LITTLE MOSQUITO WHO'S BOSS!
:SNICKER:
IT WAS CARRYING BACTERIA!
OH, I SEE! AND HOW BIG IS BACTERIA?
I ALWAYS GET HECKLED WHEN I DO SMALL ENEMY WORK!

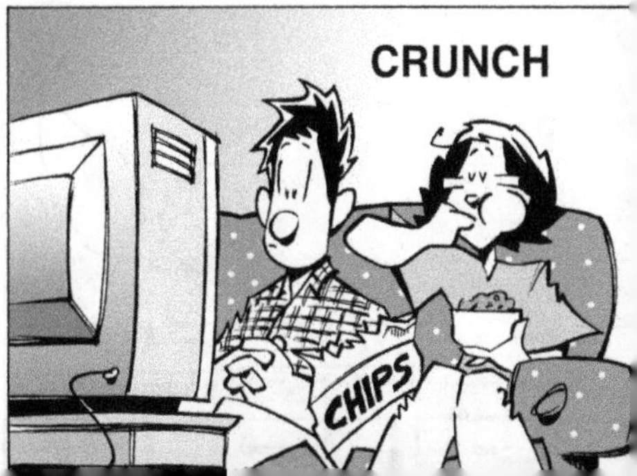
CRUNCH
CHIPS

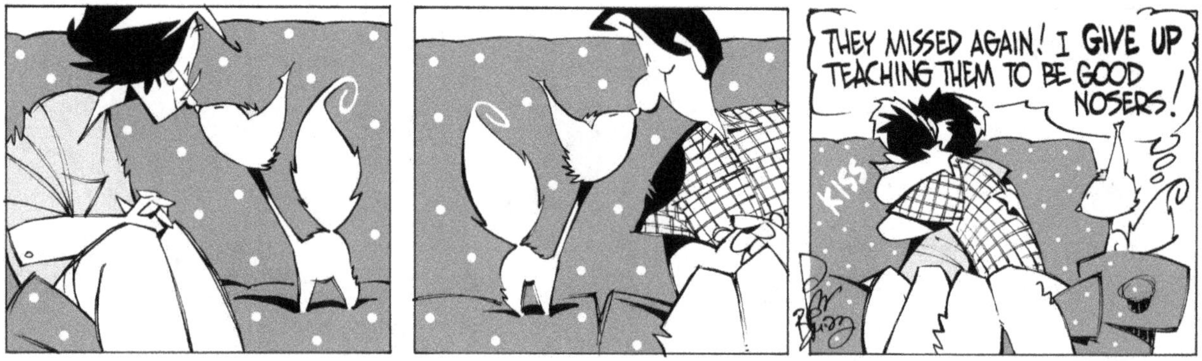
THEY MISSED AGAIN! I GIVE UP TEACHING THEM TO BE GOOD NOSERS!
KISS

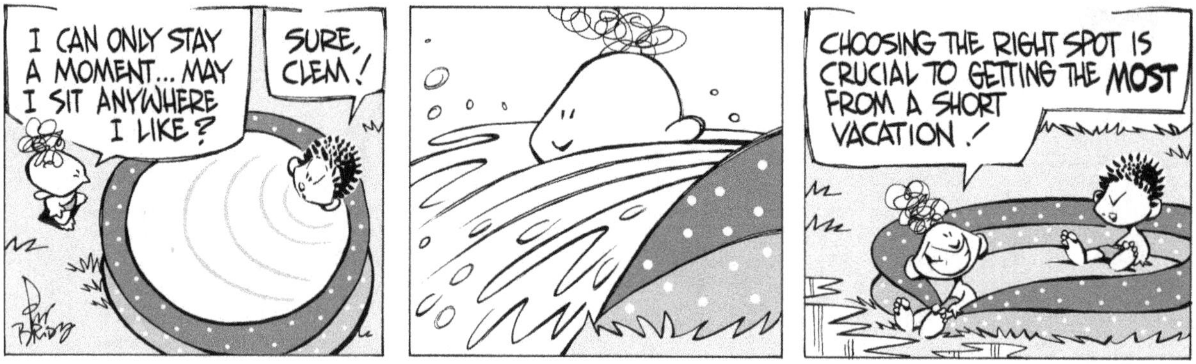
I CAN ONLY STAY A MOMENT... MAY I SIT ANYWHERE I LIKE?
SURE, CLEM!
CHOOSING THE RIGHT SPOT IS CRUCIAL TO GETTING THE MOST FROM A SHORT VACATION!

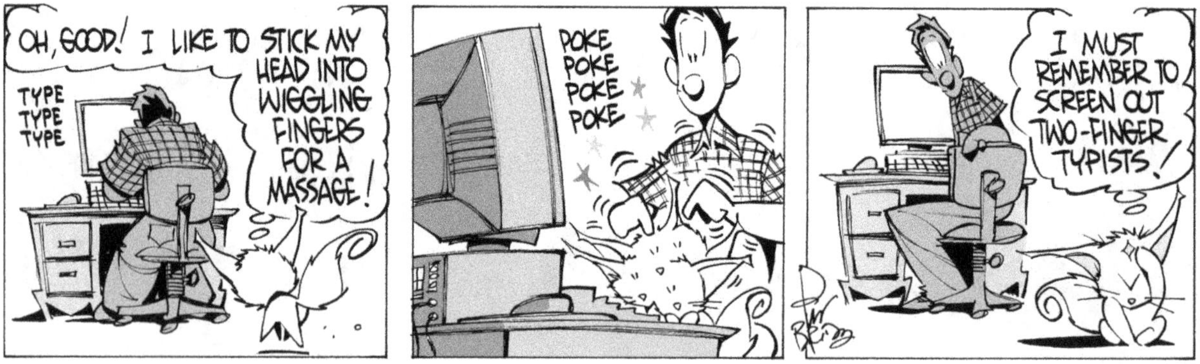
OH, GOOD! I LIKE TO STICK MY HEAD INTO WIGGLING FINGERS FOR A MASSAGE!
TYPE TYPE TYPE
POKE POKE POKE POKE
I MUST REMEMBER TO SCREEN OUT TWO-FINGER TYPISTS!

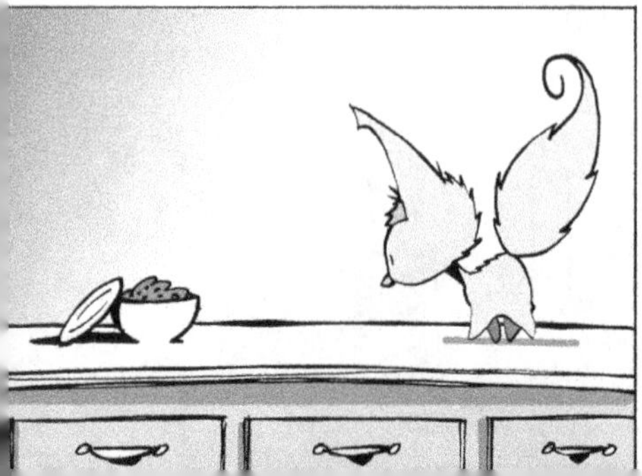

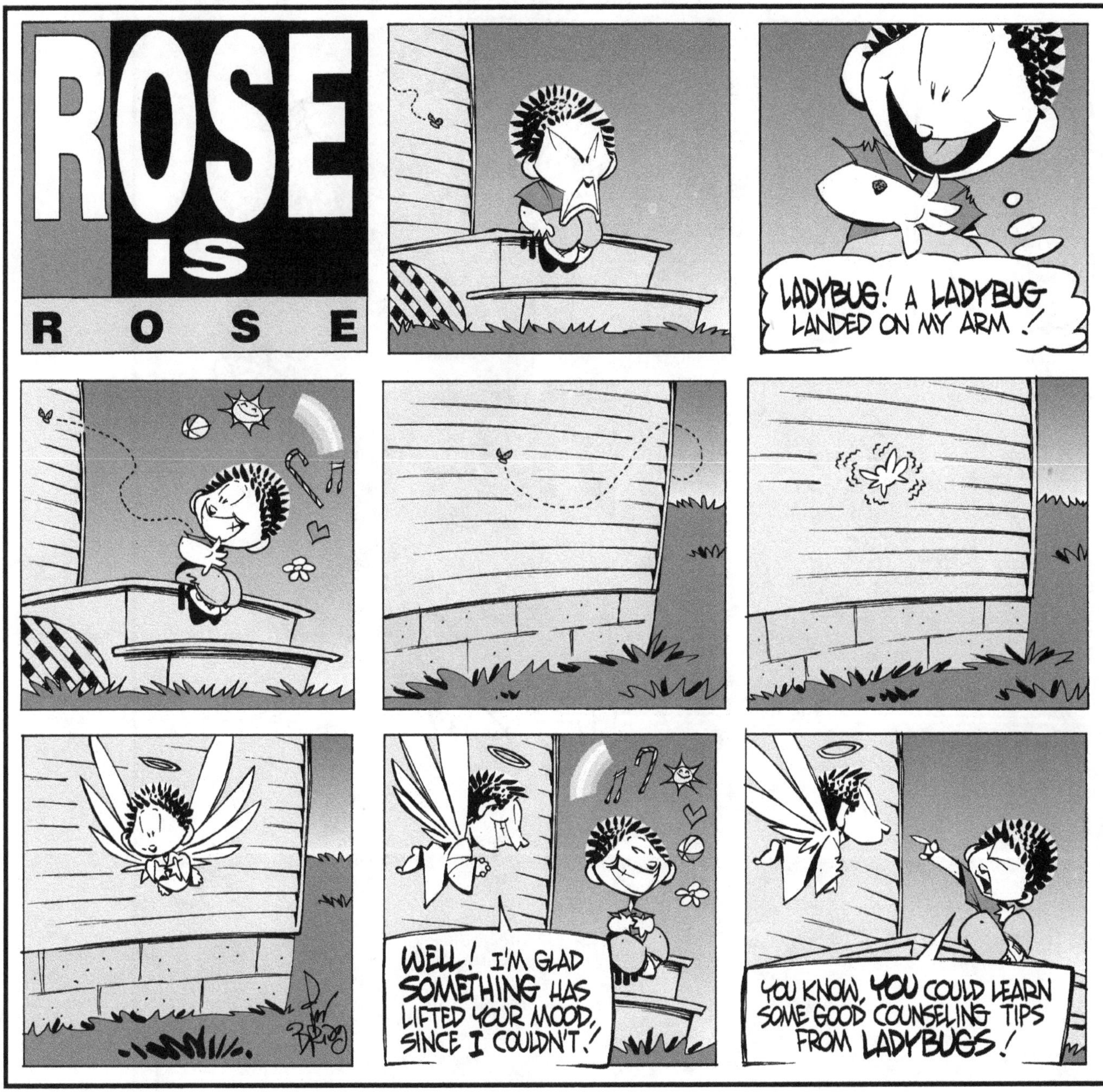
ROSE IS ROSE
LADYBUG! A LADYBUG LANDED ON MY ARM!
WELL! I'M GLAD SOMETHING HAS LIFTED YOUR MOOD, SINCE I COULDN'T!
YOU KNOW, YOU COULD LEARN SOME GOOD COUNSELING TIPS FROM LADYBUGS!

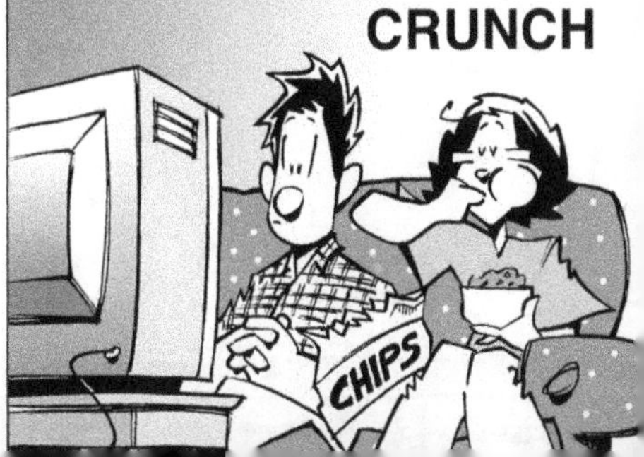
CRUNCH
CHIPS

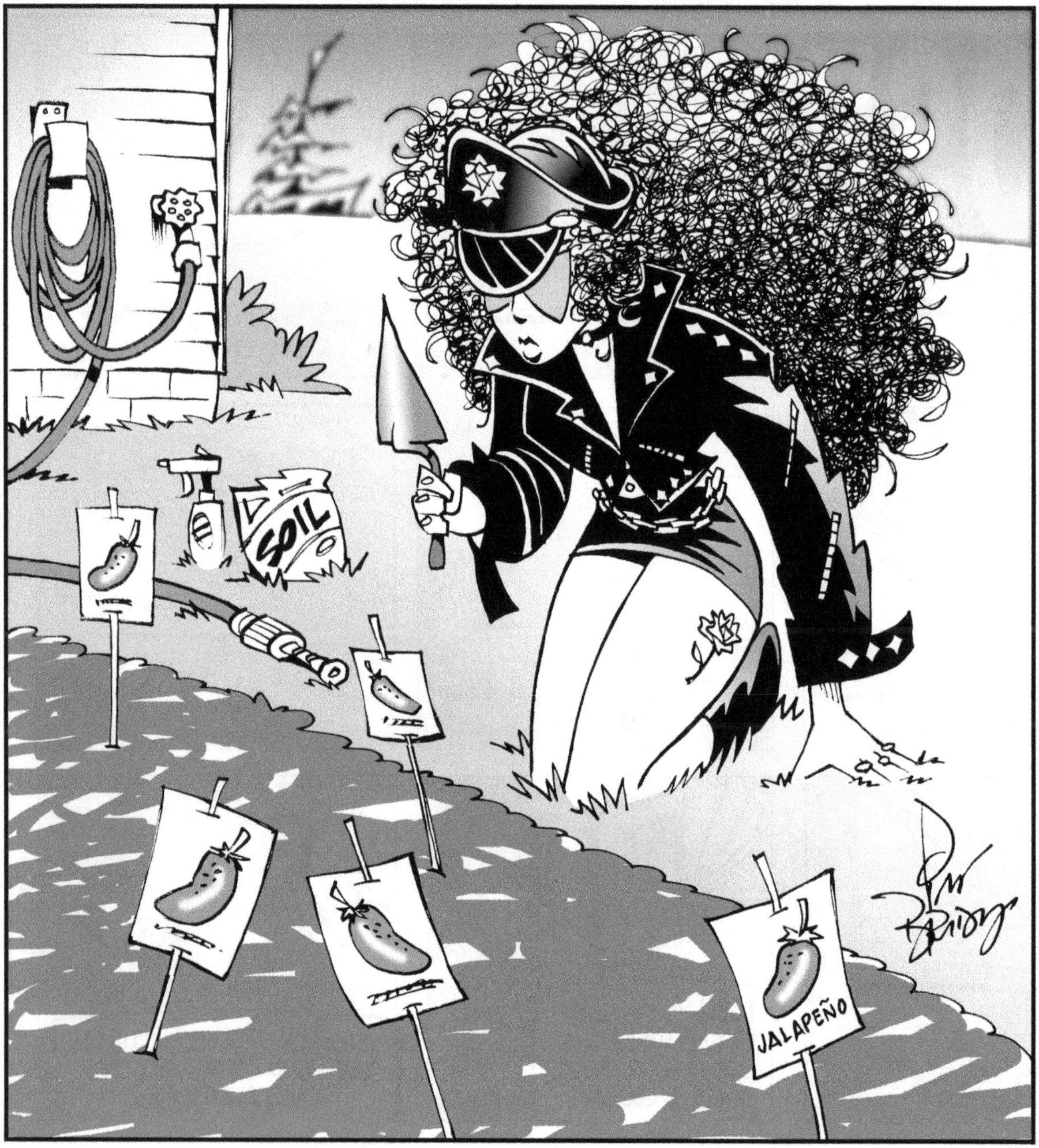
SOIL
JALAPEÑO

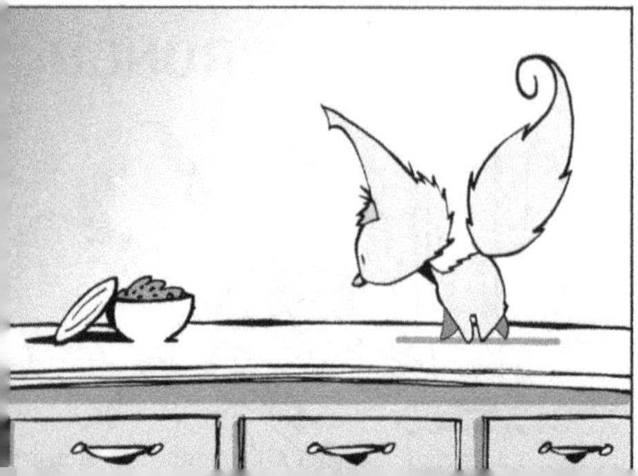

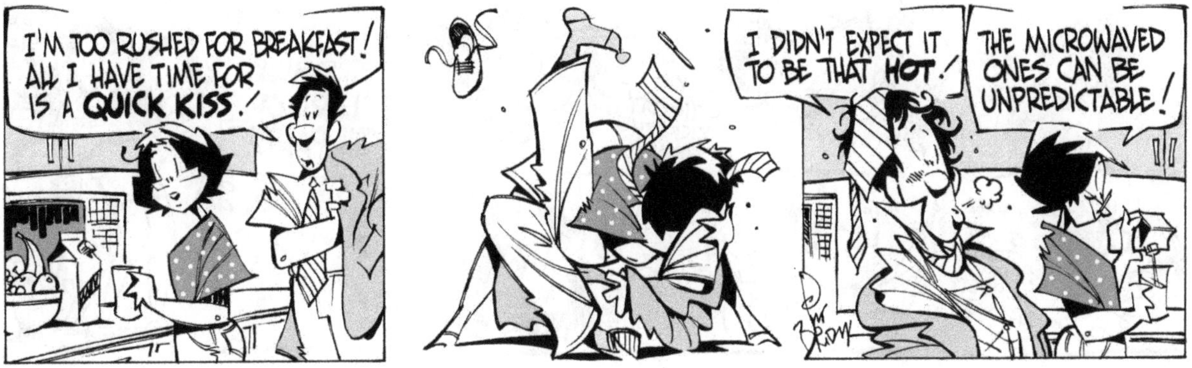
I'M TOO RUSHED FOR BREAKFAST! ALL I HAVE TIME FOR IS A **QUICK KISS**!
I DIDN'T EXPECT IT TO BE THAT **HOT**!
THE MICROWAVED ONES CAN BE UNPREDICTABLE!

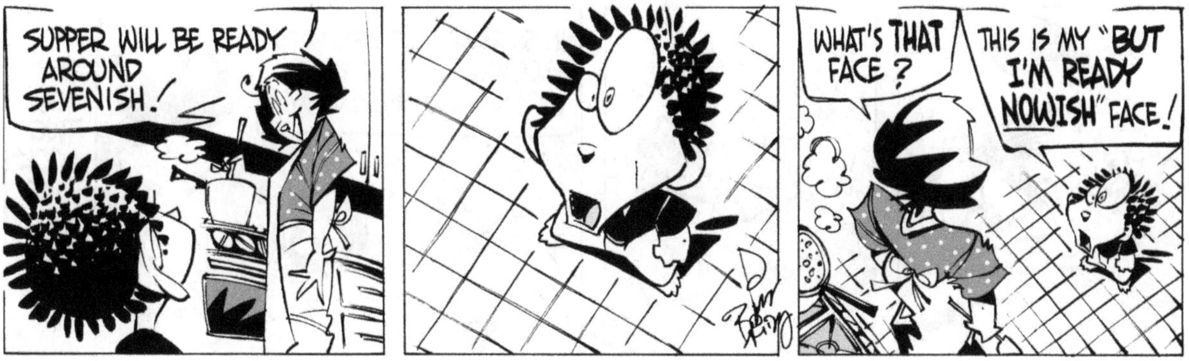
SUPPER WILL BE READY AROUND SEVENISH!
WHAT'S **THAT** FACE?
THIS IS MY "**BUT I'M READY NOWISH**" FACE!

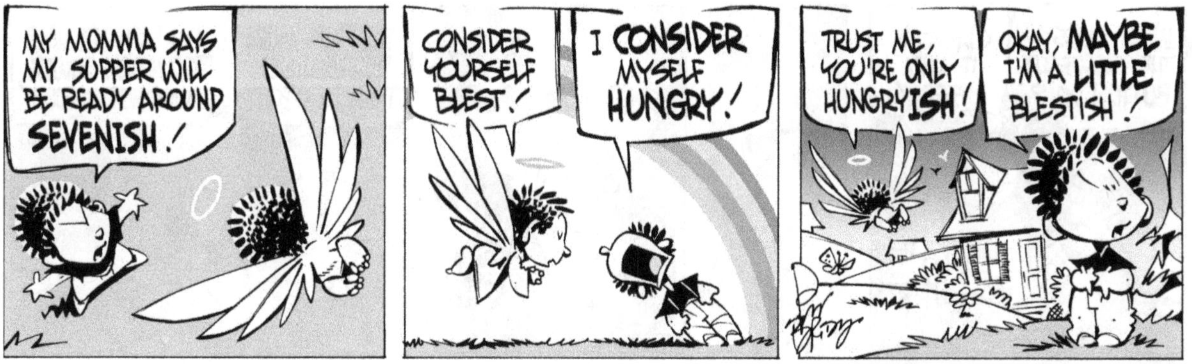
MY MOMMA SAYS MY SUPPER WILL BE READY AROUND **SEVENISH**!
CONSIDER YOURSELF BLEST!
I **CONSIDER** MYSELF **HUNGRY**!
TRUST ME, YOU'RE ONLY HUNGRY**ISH**!
OKAY, **MAYBE** I'M A **LITTLE** BLESTISH!

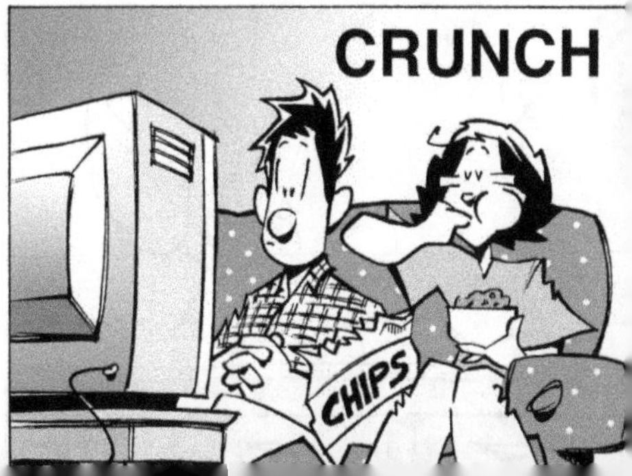
CRUNCH
CHIPS

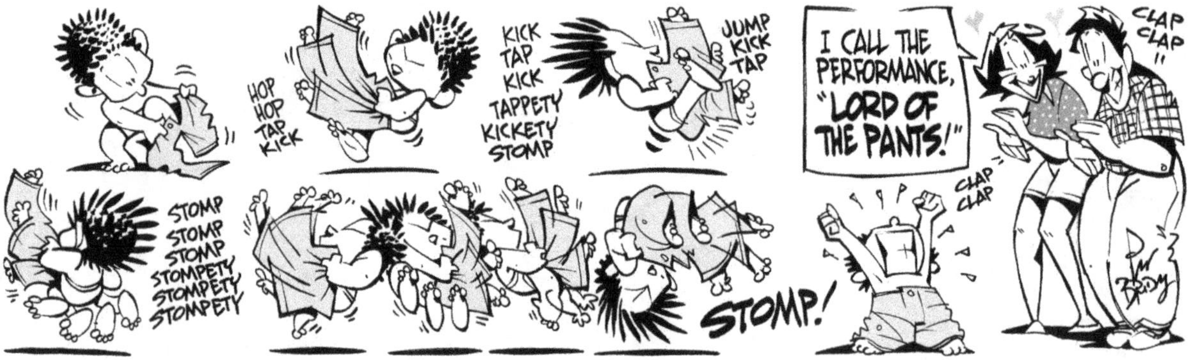
HOP HOP TAP KICK
KICK TAP KICK TAPPETY KICKETY STOMP
JUMP KICK TAP
STOMP STOMP STOMP STOMPETY STOMPETY STOMPETY
STOMP!
I CALL THE PERFORMANCE, "LORD OF THE PANTS!"
CLAP CLAP
CLAP CLAP

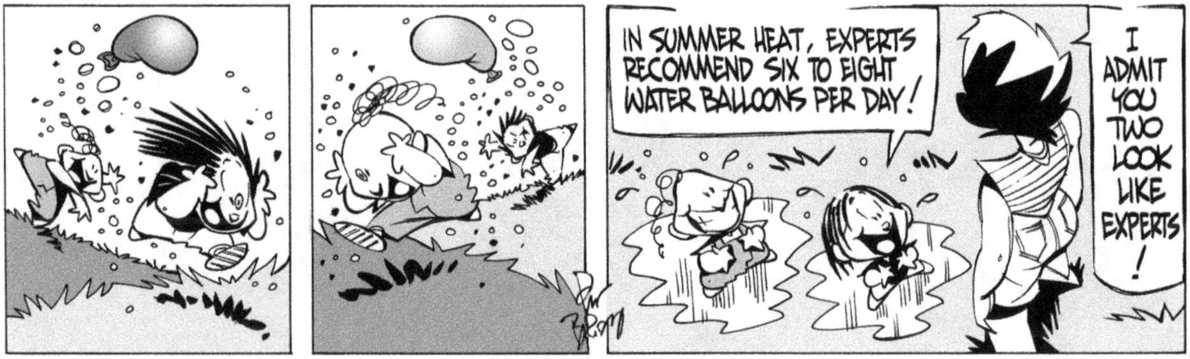
IN SUMMER HEAT, EXPERTS RECOMMEND SIX TO EIGHT WATER BALLOONS PER DAY!
I ADMIT YOU TWO LOOK LIKE EXPERTS!

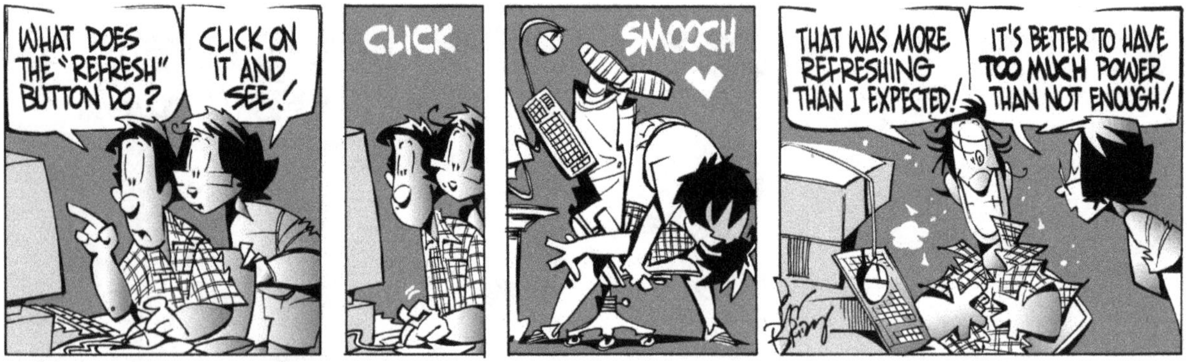
WHAT DOES THE "REFRESH" BUTTON DO?
CLICK ON IT AND SEE!
CLICK
SMOOCH
THAT WAS MORE REFRESHING THAN I EXPECTED!
IT'S BETTER TO HAVE TOO MUCH POWER THAN NOT ENOUGH!

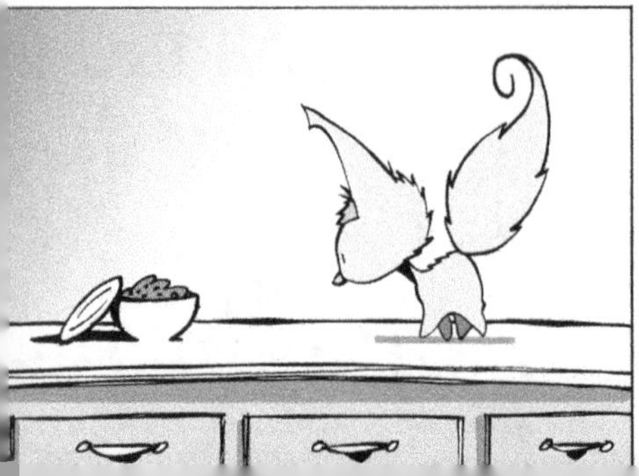

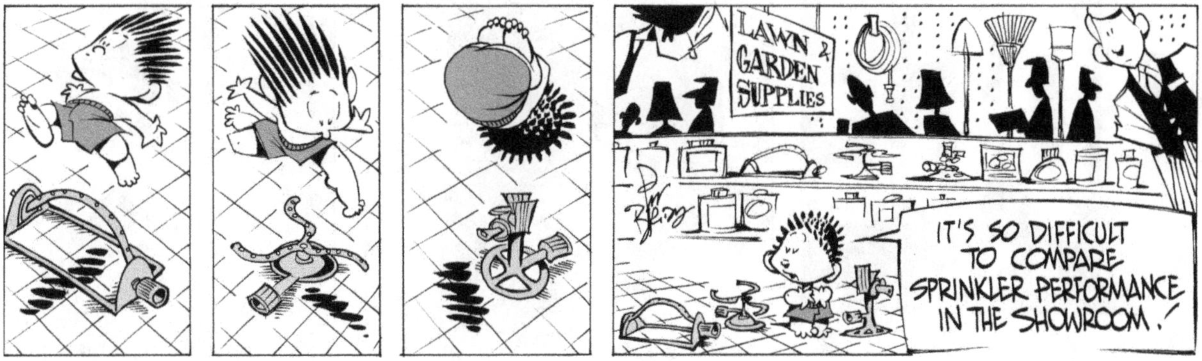
LAWN & GARDEN SUPPLIES
IT'S SO DIFFICULT TO COMPARE SPRINKLER PERFORMANCE IN THE SHOWROOM!

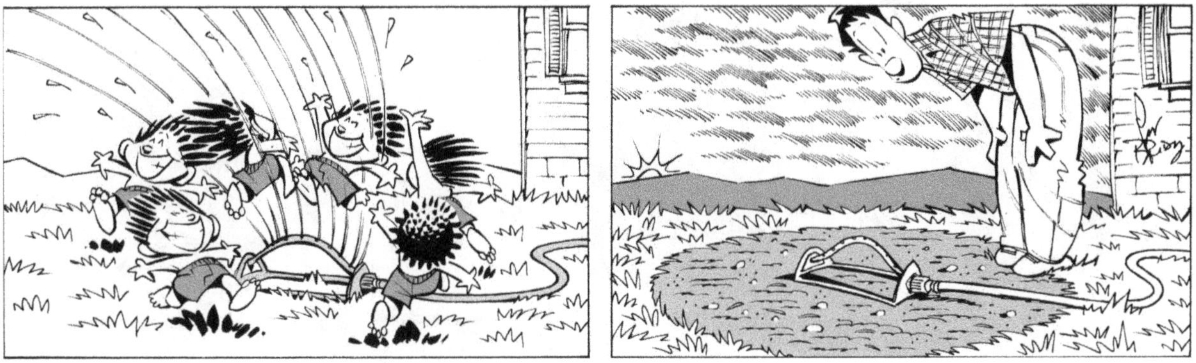

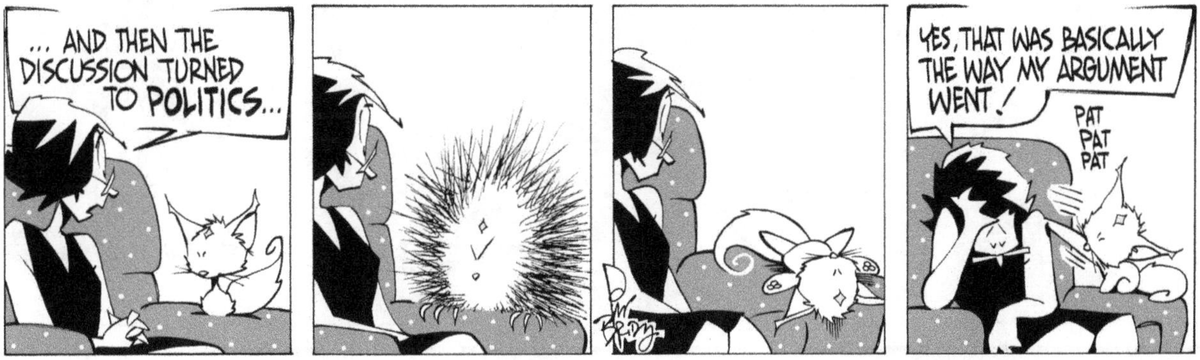
... AND THEN THE DISCUSSION TURNED TO POLITICS...
YES, THAT WAS BASICALLY THE WAY MY ARGUMENT WENT!
PAT PAT PAT

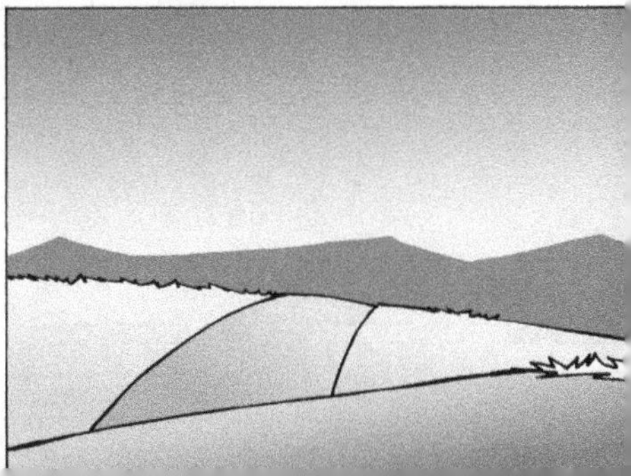

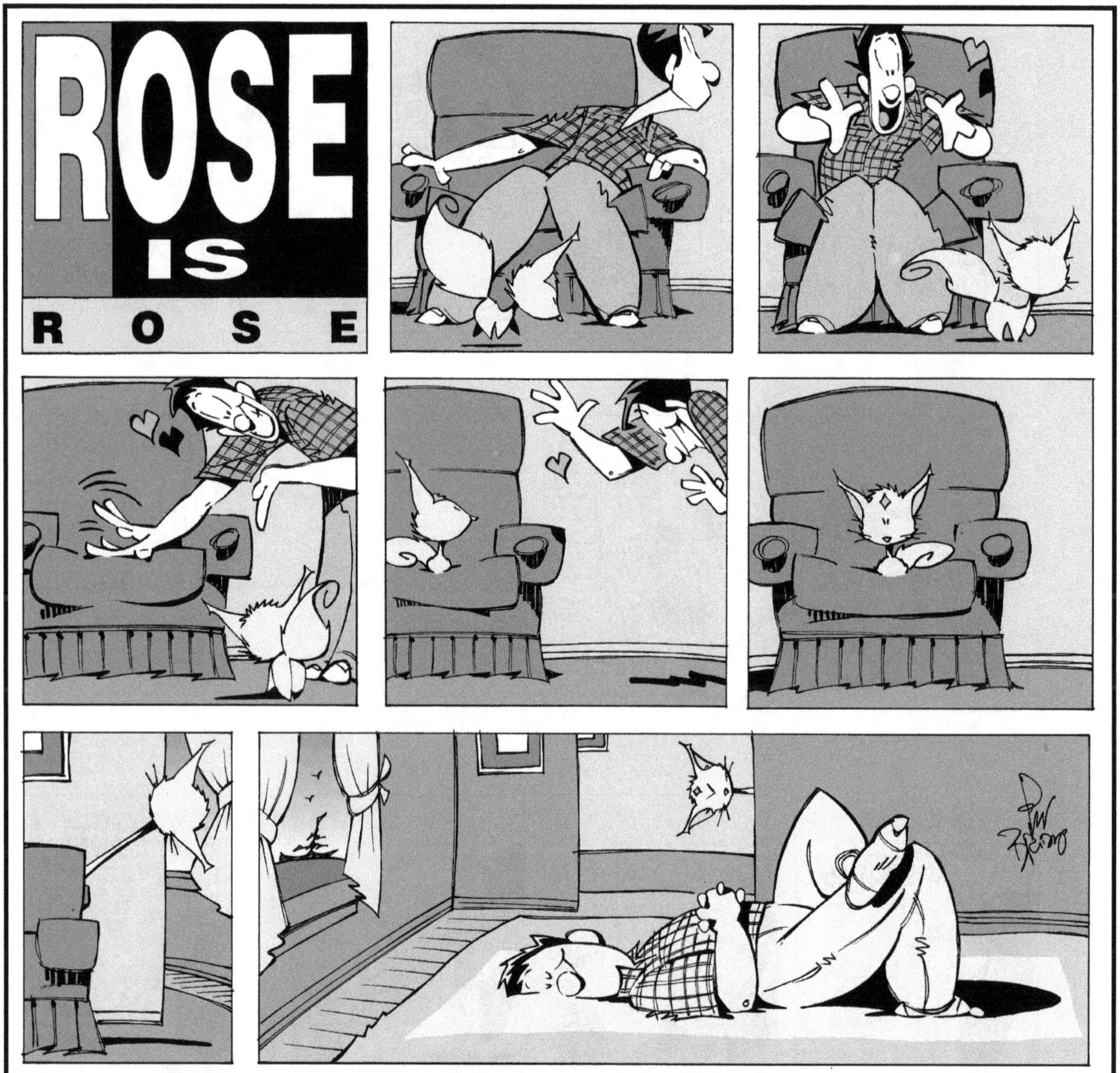
ROSE IS ROSE

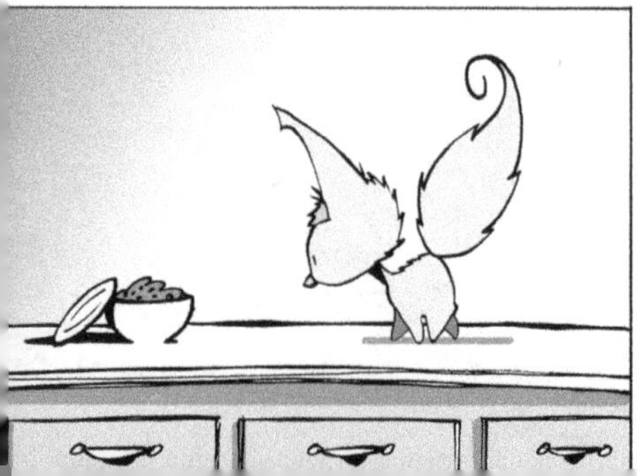

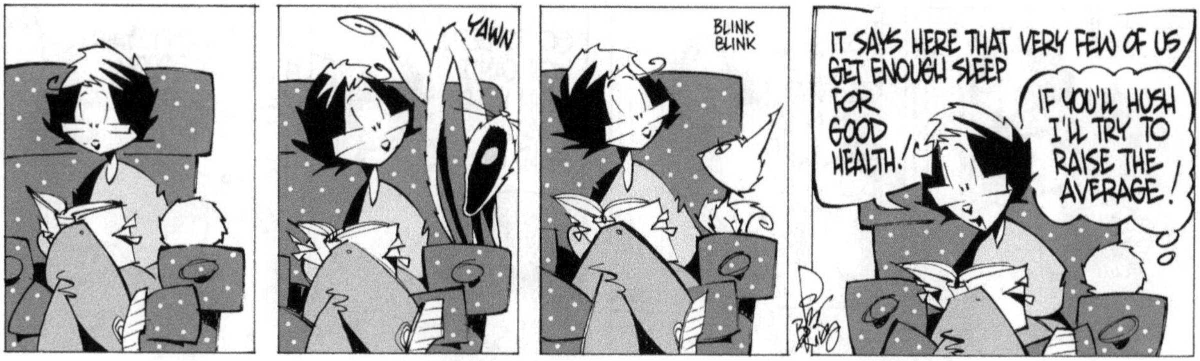
YAWN
BLINK BLINK
IT SAYS HERE THAT VERY FEW OF US GET ENOUGH SLEEP FOR GOOD HEALTH!
IF YOU'LL HUSH I'LL TRY TO RAISE THE AVERAGE!

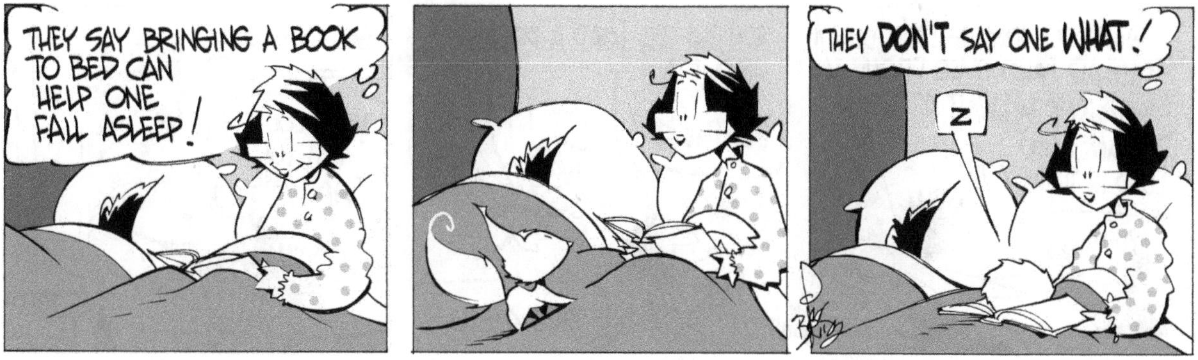
THEY SAY BRINGING A BOOK TO BED CAN HELP ONE FALL ASLEEP!
THEY DON'T SAY ONE WHAT!
Z

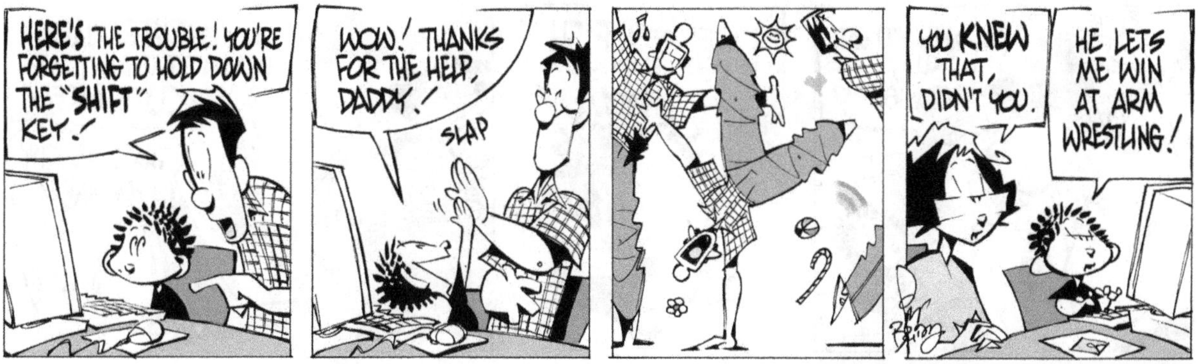
HERE'S THE TROUBLE! YOU'RE FORGETTING TO HOLD DOWN THE "SHIFT" KEY!
WOW! THANKS FOR THE HELP, DADDY!
SLAP
YOU KNEW THAT, DIDN'T YOU.
HE LETS ME WIN AT ARM WRESTLING!

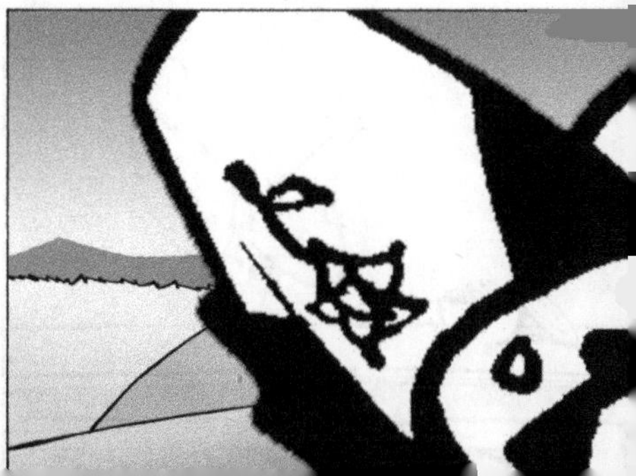

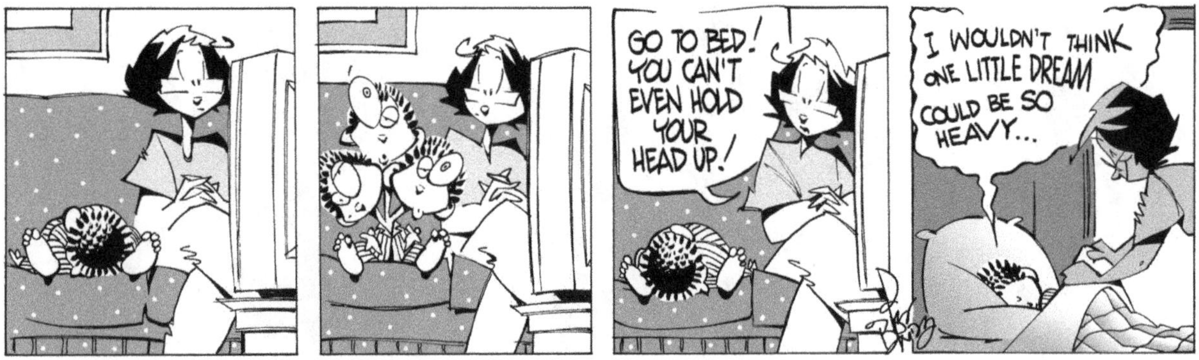
GO TO BED! YOU CAN'T EVEN HOLD YOUR HEAD UP!
I WOULDN'T THINK ONE LITTLE DREAM COULD BE SO HEAVY...

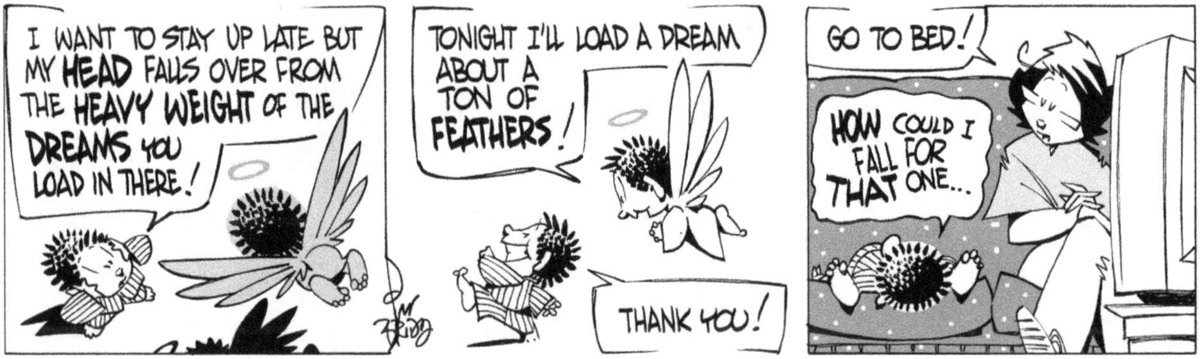
I WANT TO STAY UP LATE BUT MY HEAD FALLS OVER FROM THE HEAVY WEIGHT OF THE DREAMS YOU LOAD IN THERE!
TONIGHT I'LL LOAD A DREAM ABOUT A TON OF FEATHERS!
THANK YOU!
GO TO BED!
HOW COULD I FALL FOR THAT ONE...

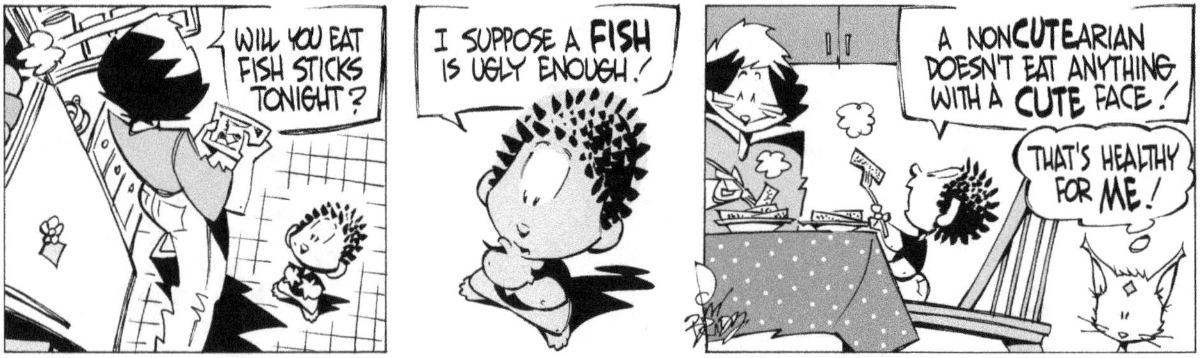
WILL YOU EAT FISH STICKS TONIGHT?
I SUPPOSE A FISH IS UGLY ENOUGH!
A NONCUTEARIAN DOESN'T EAT ANYTHING WITH A CUTE FACE!
THAT'S HEALTHY FOR ME!

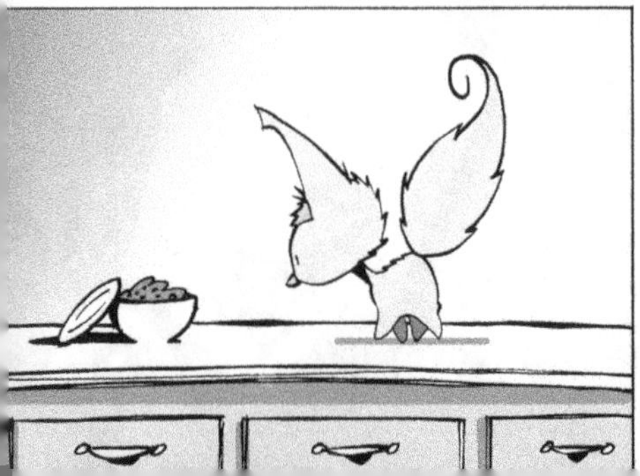

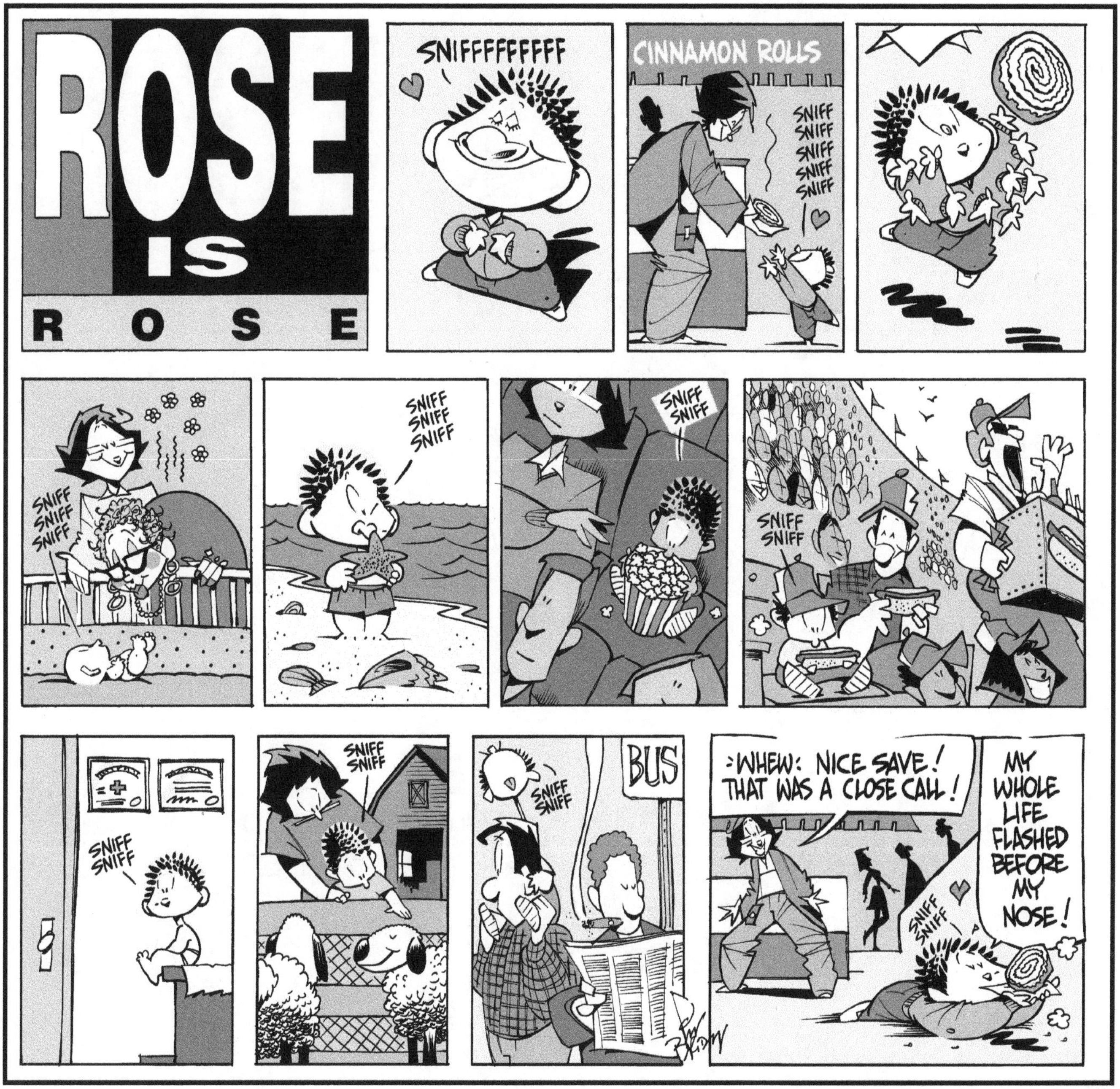
ROSE IS ROSE
SNIFFFFFFFFFF
CINNAMON ROLLS
SNIFF SNIFF SNIFF SNIFF SNIFF
SNIFF SNIFF SNIFF
SNIFF SNIFF SNIFF
SNIFF SNIFF
SNIFF SNIFF
SNIFF SNIFF
SNIFF SNIFF
BUS
SNIFF SNIFF
:WHEW: NICE SAVE! THAT WAS A CLOSE CALL!
MY WHOLE LIFE FLASHED BEFORE MY NOSE!
SNIFF SNIFF

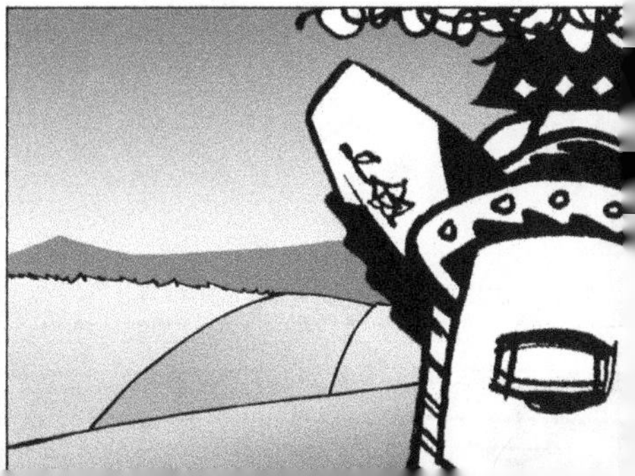

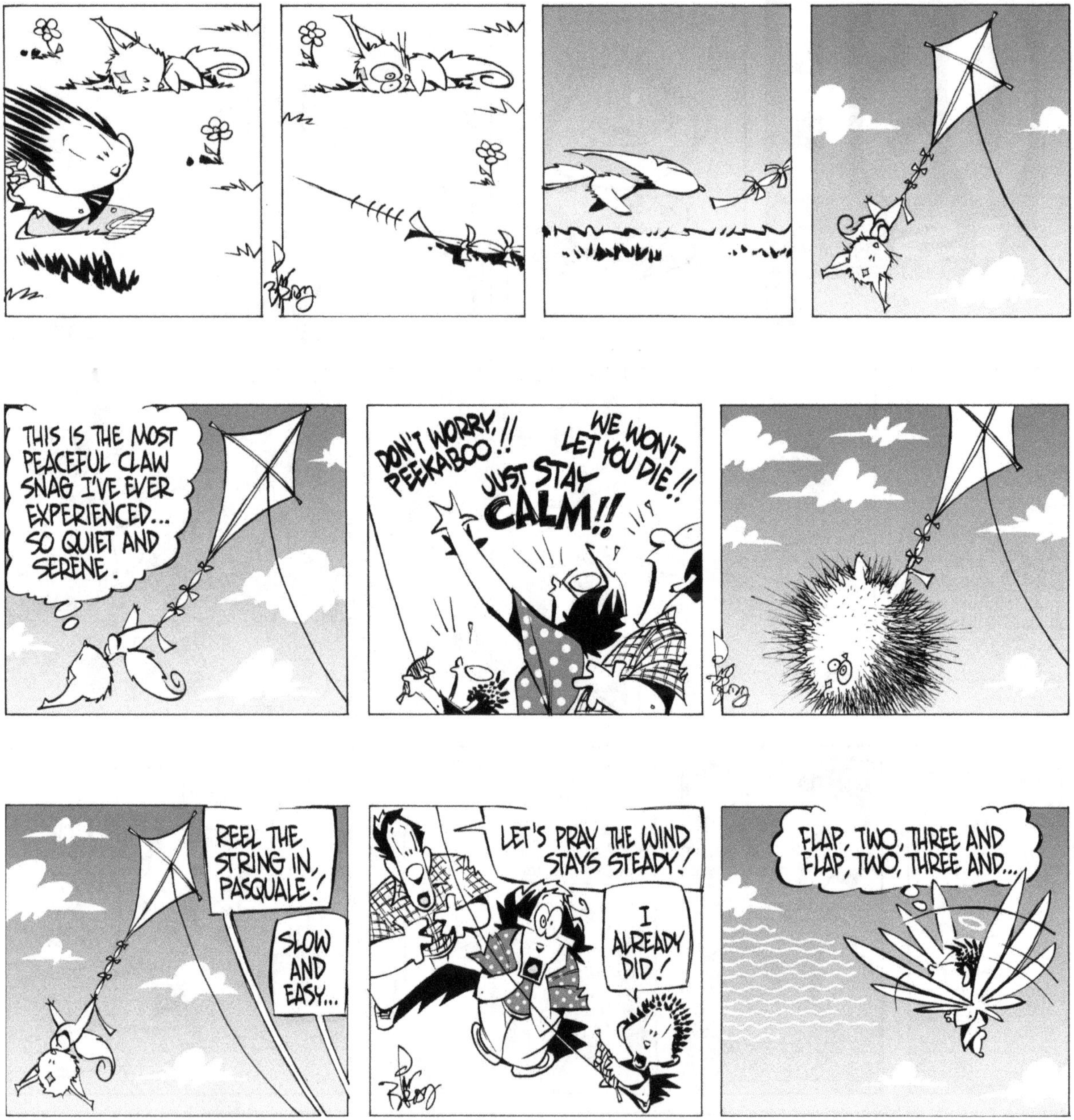
THIS IS THE MOST PEACEFUL CLAW SNAG I'VE EVER EXPERIENCED... SO QUIET AND SERENE.
DON'T WORRY, PEEKABOO!!
WE WON'T LET YOU DIE!!
JUST STAY CALM!!
REEL THE STRING IN, PASQUALE!
SLOW AND EASY...
LET'S PRAY THE WIND STAYS STEADY!
I ALREADY DID!
FLAP, TWO, THREE AND FLAP, TWO, THREE AND...

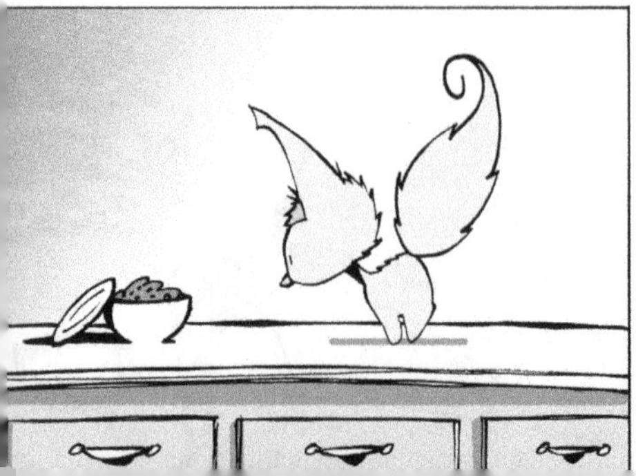

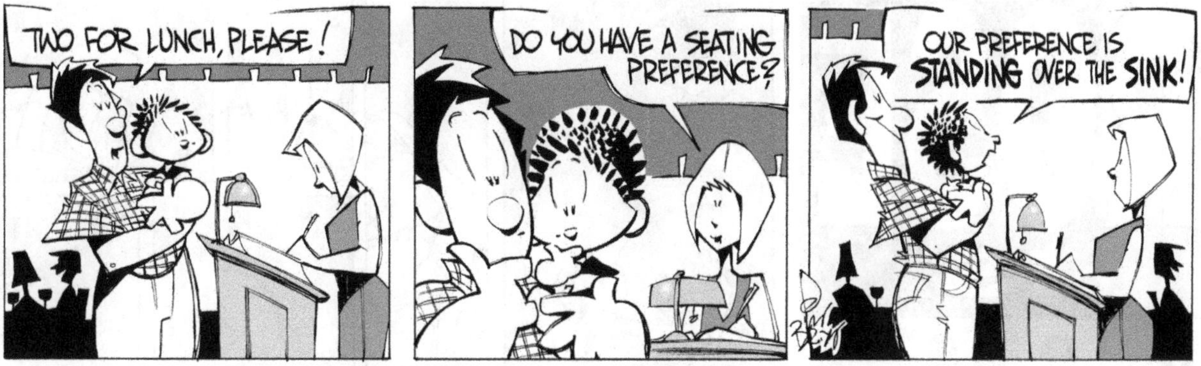
TWO FOR LUNCH, PLEASE!
DO YOU HAVE A SEATING PREFERENCE?
OUR PREFERENCE IS STANDING OVER THE SINK!

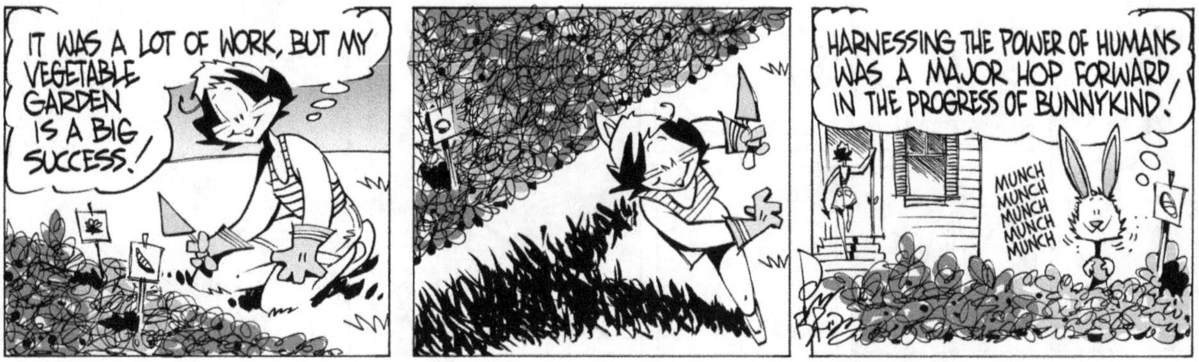
IT WAS A LOT OF WORK, BUT MY VEGETABLE GARDEN IS A BIG SUCCESS!
HARNESSING THE POWER OF HUMANS WAS A MAJOR HOP FORWARD IN THE PROGRESS OF BUNNYKIND!
MUNCH MUNCH MUNCH MUNCH MUNCH

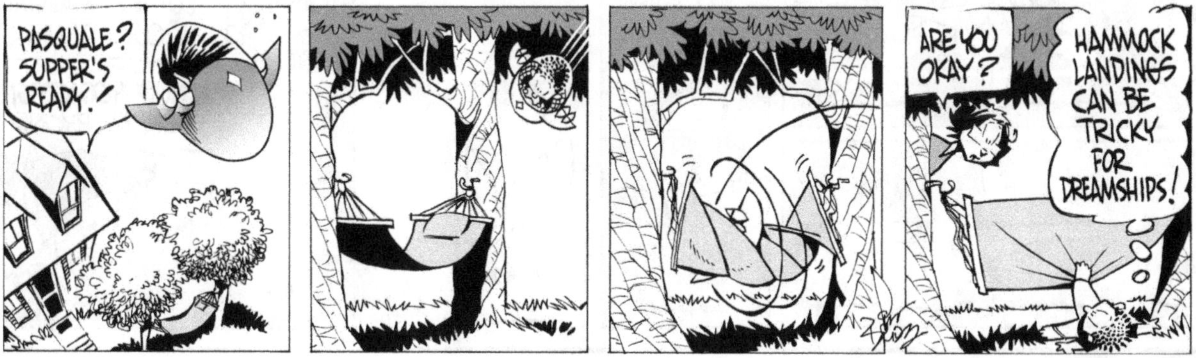
PASQUALE? SUPPER'S READY!
ARE YOU OKAY?
HAMMOCK LANDINGS CAN BE TRICKY FOR DREAMSHIPS!

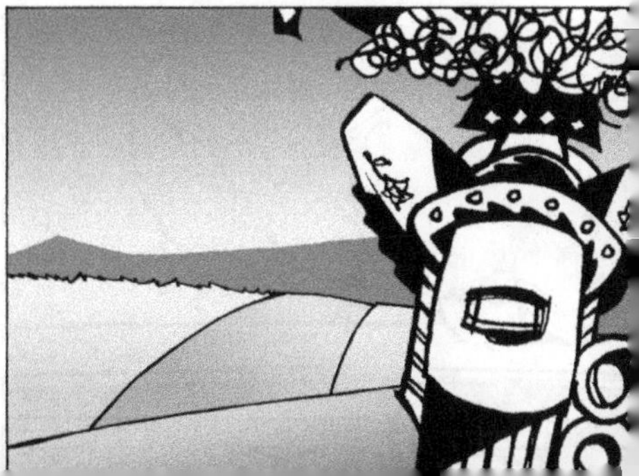

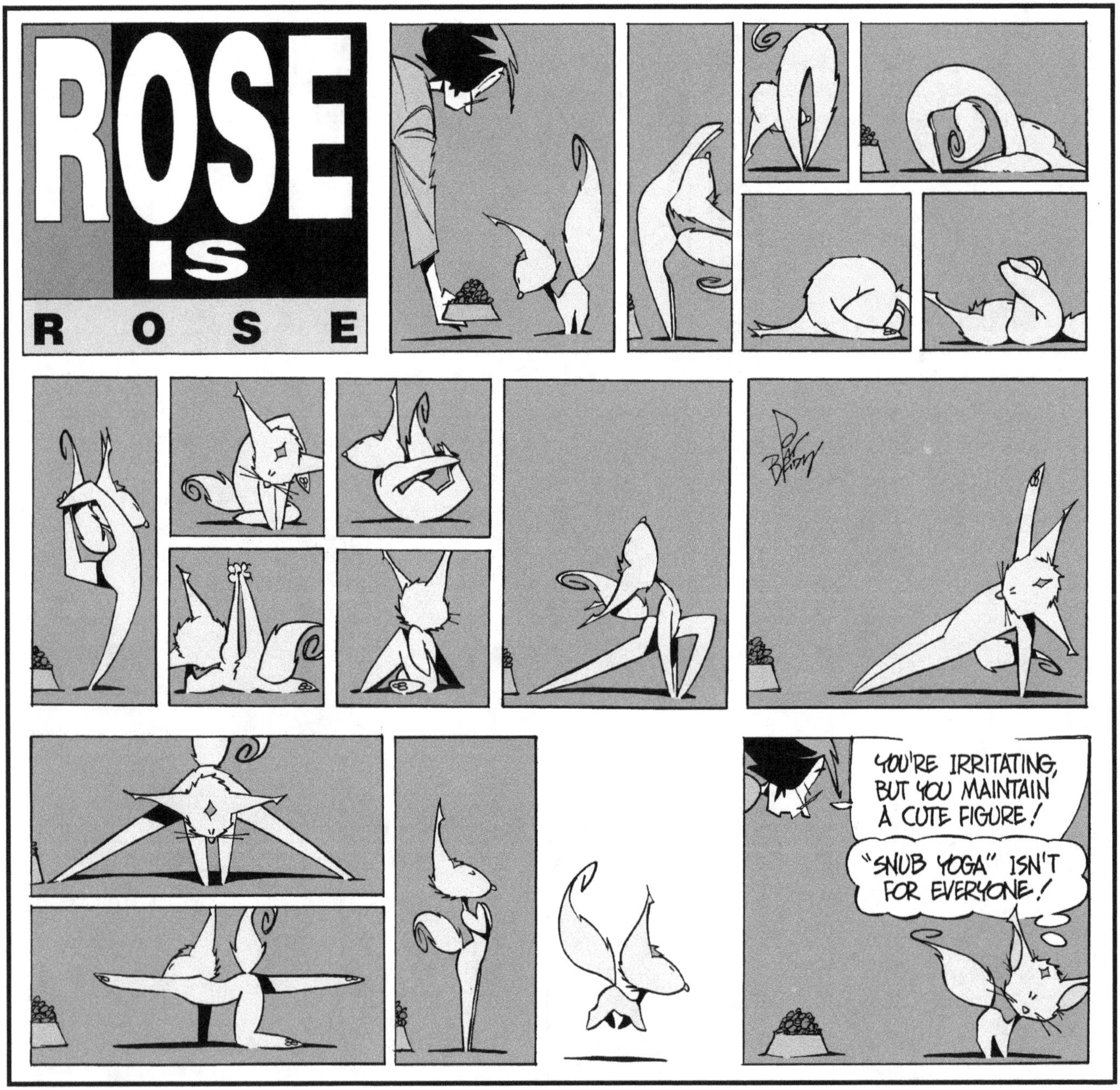
ROSE IS ROSE
YOU'RE IRRITATING, BUT YOU MAINTAIN A CUTE FIGURE!
"SNUB YOGA" ISN'T FOR EVERYONE!

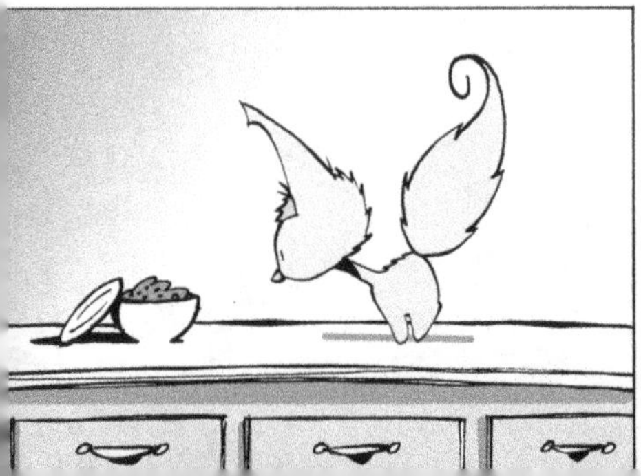

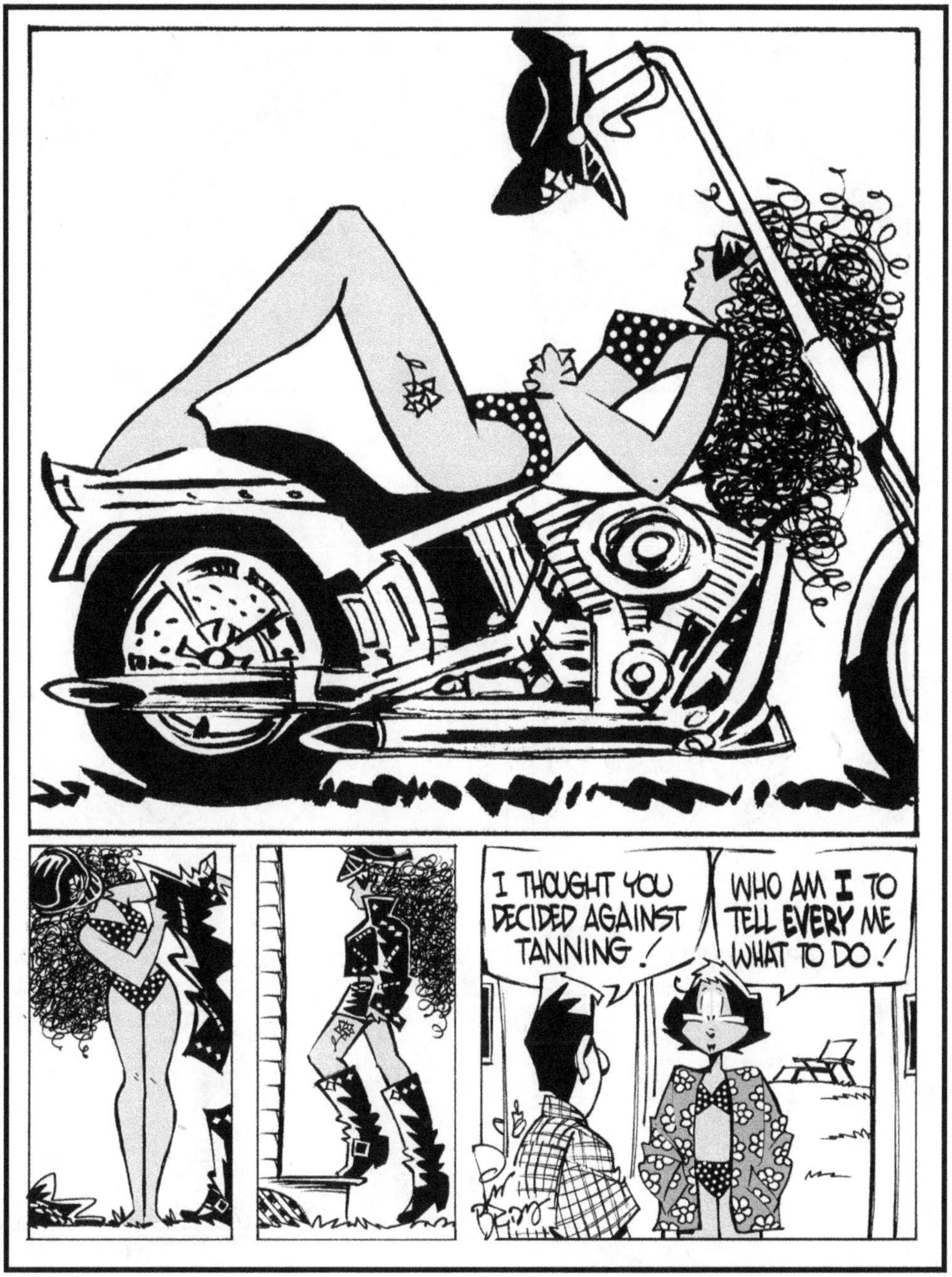
I THOUGHT YOU DECIDED AGAINST TANNING!
WHO AM I TO TELL EVERY ME WHAT TO DO!

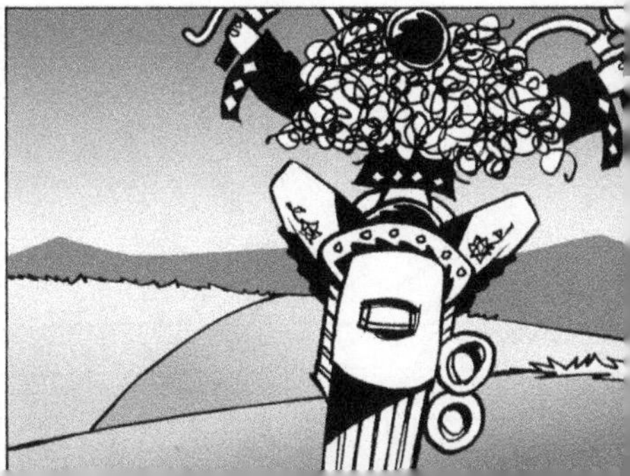

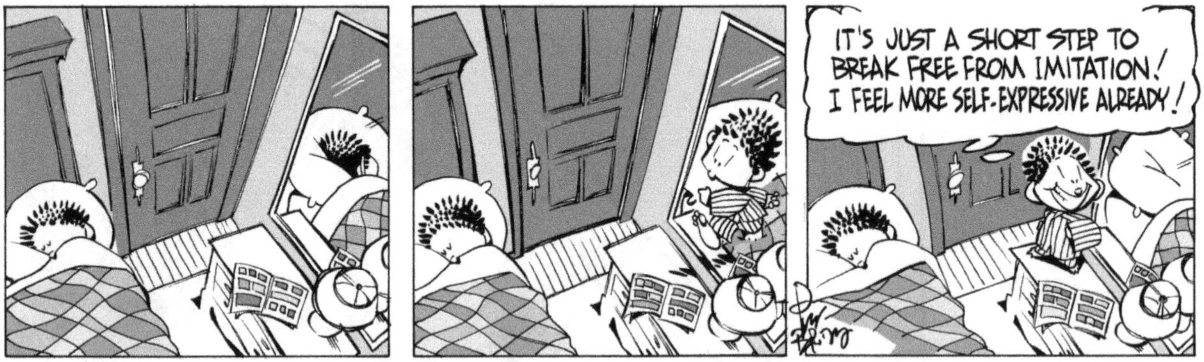
IT'S JUST A SHORT STEP TO BREAK FREE FROM IMITATION! I FEEL MORE SELF-EXPRESSIVE ALREADY!

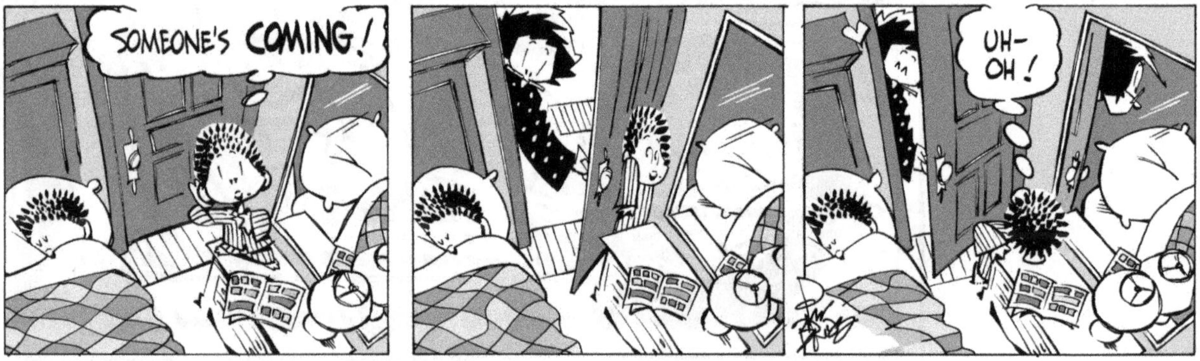
SOMEONE'S COMING!
UH-OH!

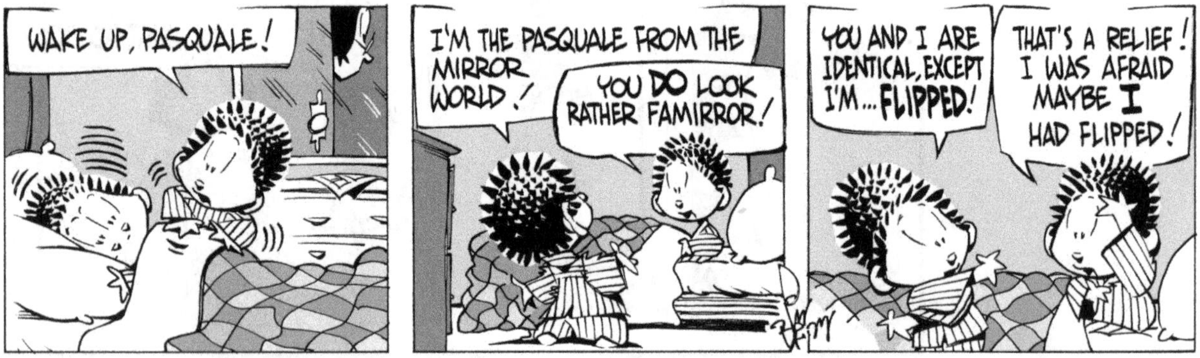
WAKE UP, PASQUALE!
I'M THE PASQUALE FROM THE MIRROR WORLD!
YOU DO LOOK RATHER FAMIRROR!
YOU AND I ARE IDENTICAL, EXCEPT I'M... FLIPPED!
THAT'S A RELIEF! I WAS AFRAID MAYBE I HAD FLIPPED!

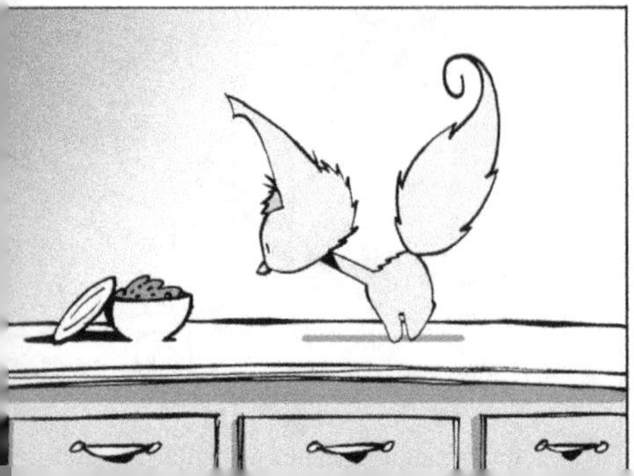

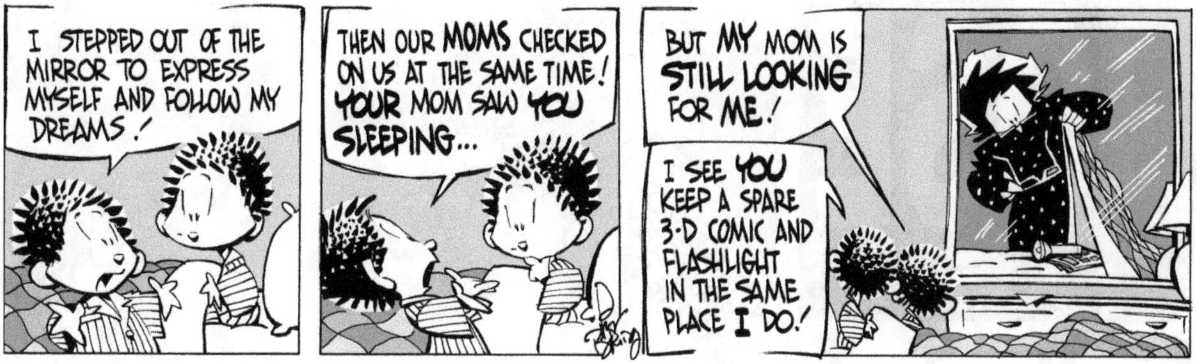
I STEPPED OUT OF THE MIRROR TO EXPRESS MYSELF AND FOLLOW MY DREAMS!
THEN OUR MOMS CHECKED ON US AT THE SAME TIME! YOUR MOM SAW YOU SLEEPING...
BUT MY MOM IS STILL LOOKING FOR ME!
I SEE YOU KEEP A SPARE 3-D COMIC AND FLASHLIGHT IN THE SAME PLACE I DO!

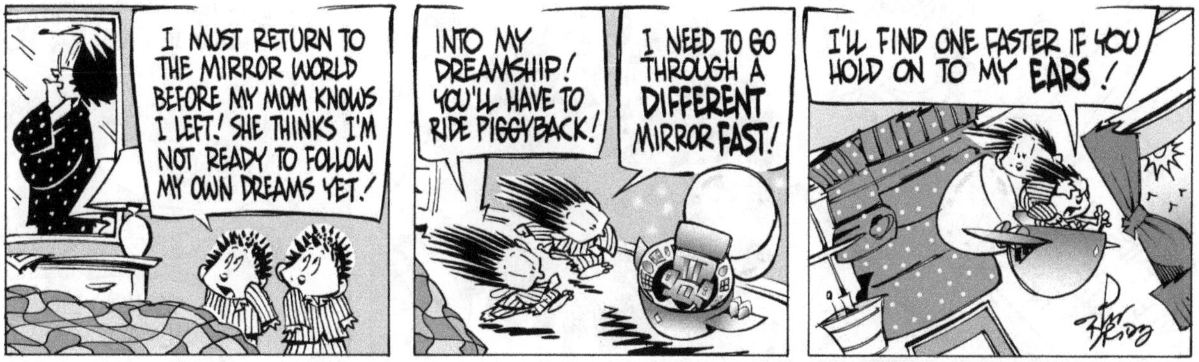
I MUST RETURN TO THE MIRROR WORLD BEFORE MY MOM KNOWS I LEFT! SHE THINKS I'M NOT READY TO FOLLOW MY OWN DREAMS YET!
INTO MY DREAMSHIP! YOU'LL HAVE TO RIDE PIGGYBACK!
I NEED TO GO THROUGH A DIFFERENT MIRROR FAST!
I'LL FIND ONE FASTER IF YOU HOLD ON TO MY EARS!

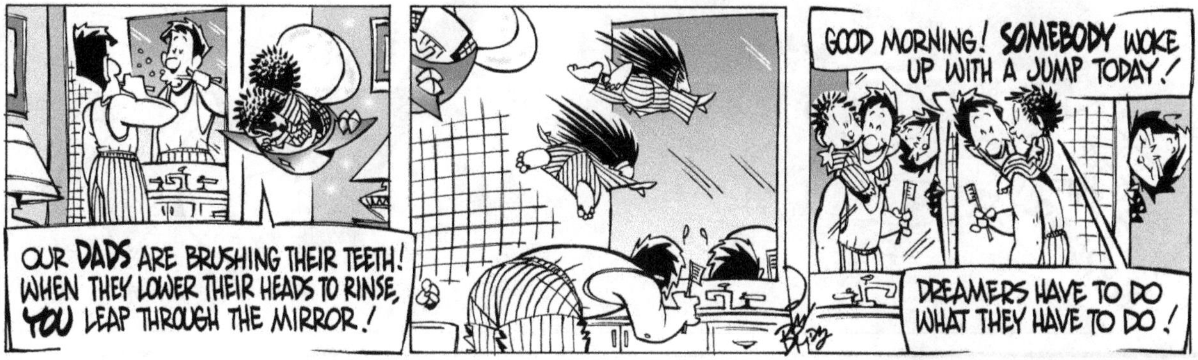
OUR DADS ARE BRUSHING THEIR TEETH! WHEN THEY LOWER THEIR HEADS TO RINSE, YOU LEAP THROUGH THE MIRROR!
GOOD MORNING! SOMEBODY WOKE UP WITH A JUMP TODAY!
DREAMERS HAVE TO DO WHAT THEY HAVE TO DO!

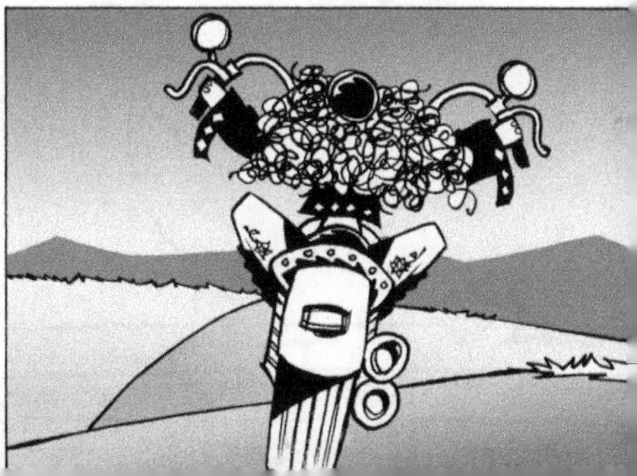

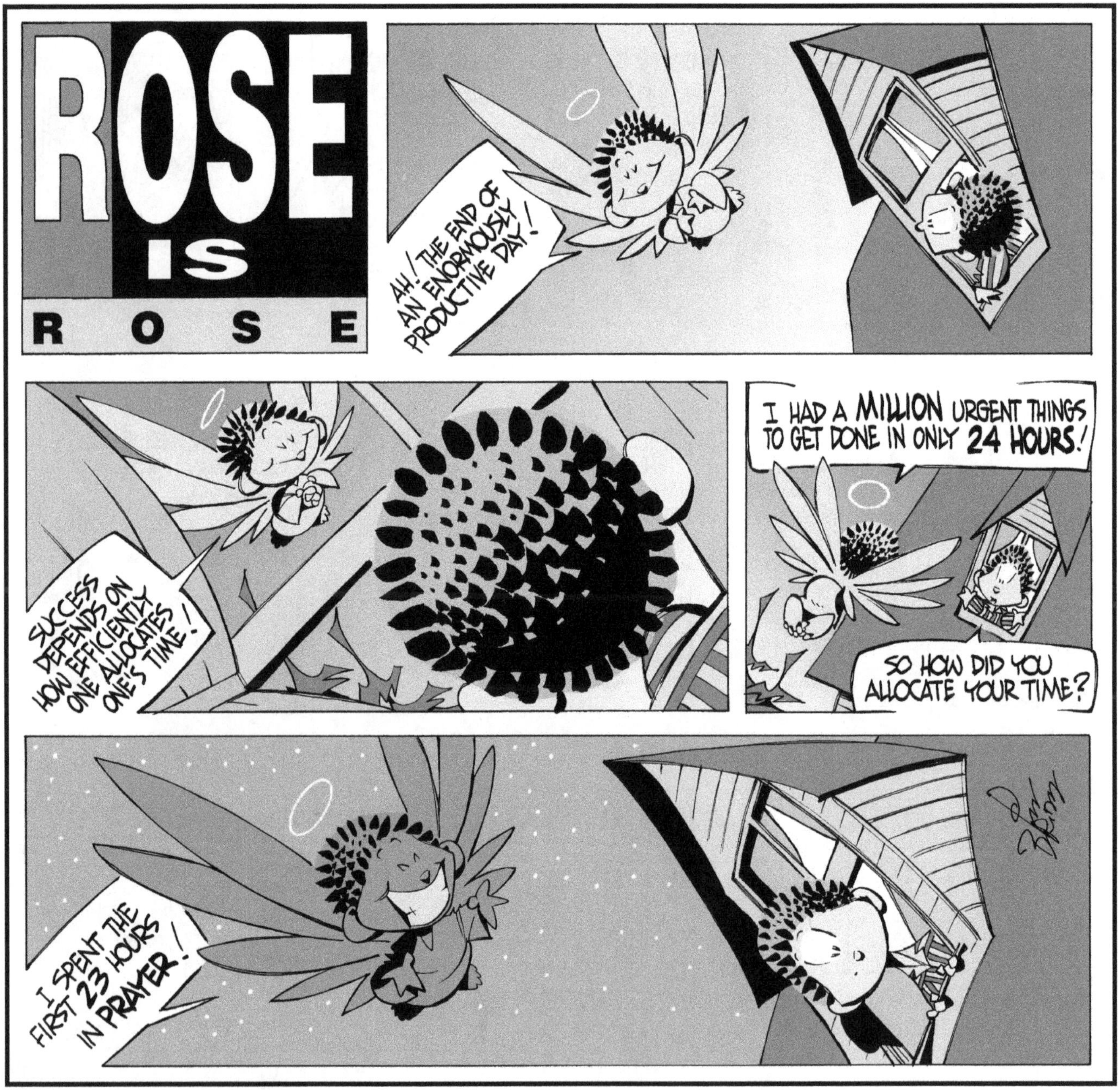
ROSE IS ROSE
AH! THE END OF AN ENORMOUSLY PRODUCTIVE DAY!
SUCCESS DEPENDS ON HOW EFFICIENTLY ONE ALLOCATES ONE'S TIME!
I HAD A MILLION URGENT THINGS TO GET DONE IN ONLY 24 HOURS!
SO HOW DID YOU ALLOCATE YOUR TIME?
I SPENT THE FIRST 23 HOURS IN PRAYER!

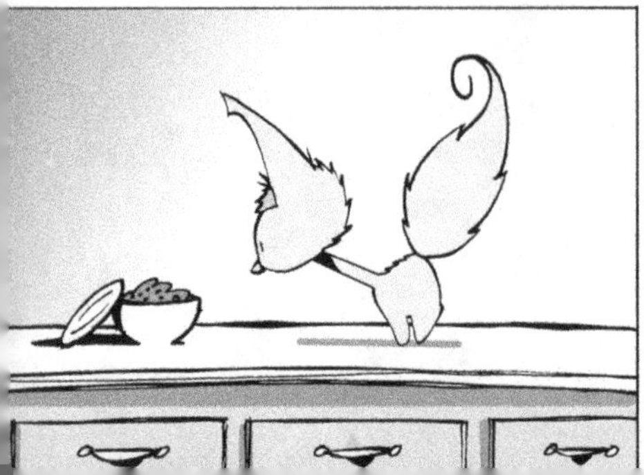

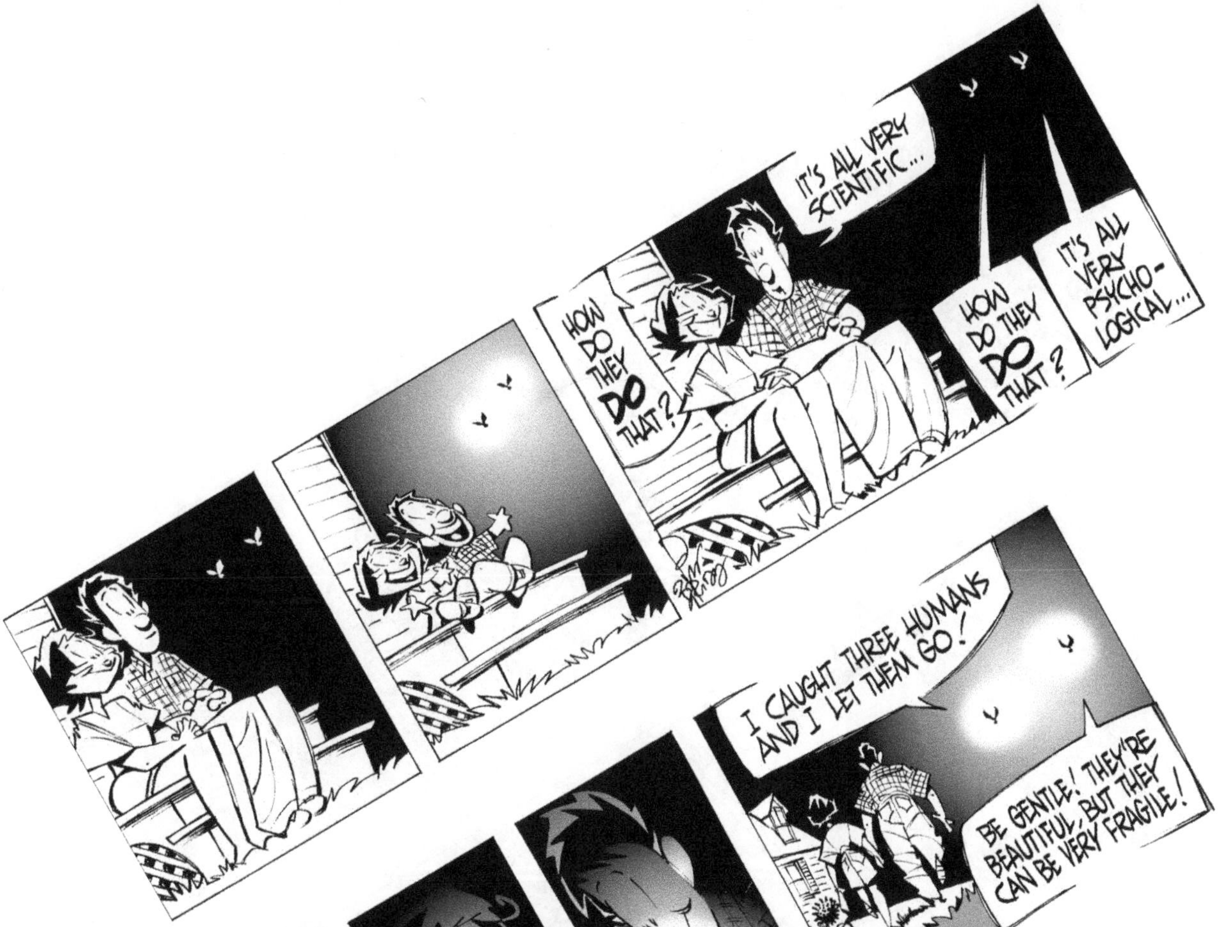
HOW DO THEY DO THAT?
IT'S ALL VERY SCIENTIFIC...
HOW DO THEY DO THAT?
IT'S ALL VERY PSYCHO-LOGICAL...

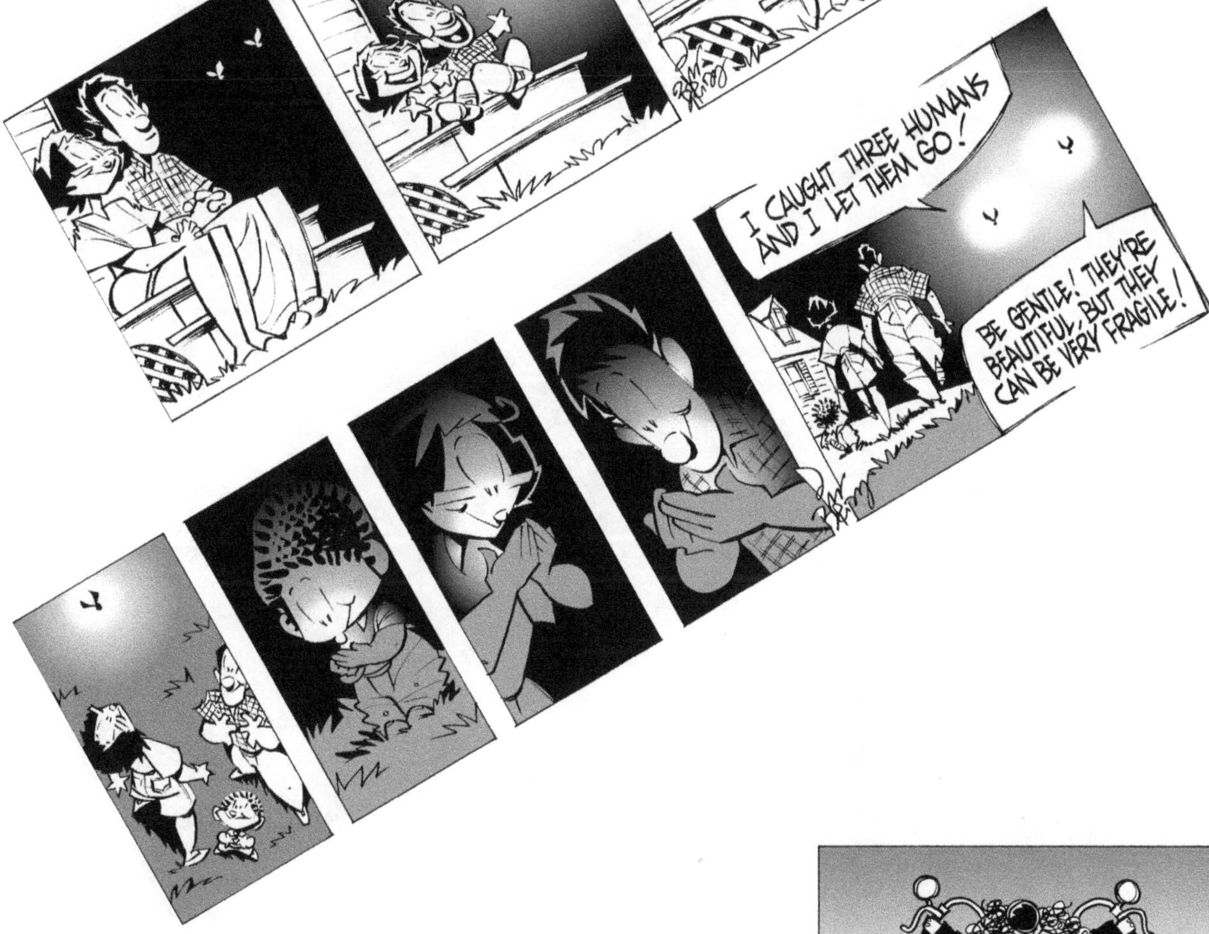
I CAUGHT THREE HUMANS AND I LET THEM GO!
BE GENTLE! THEY'RE BEAUTIFUL, BUT THEY CAN BE VERY FRAGILE!

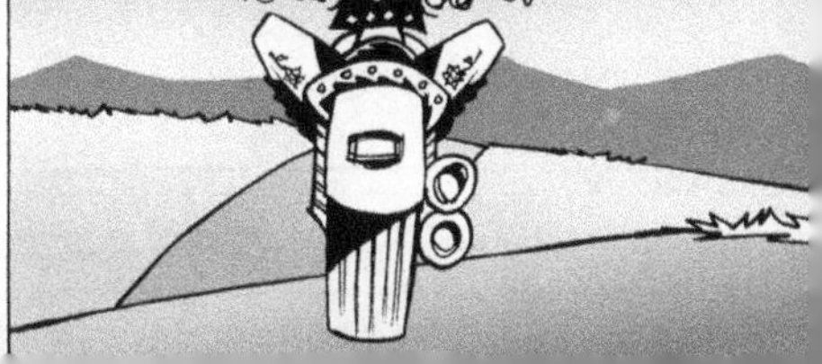

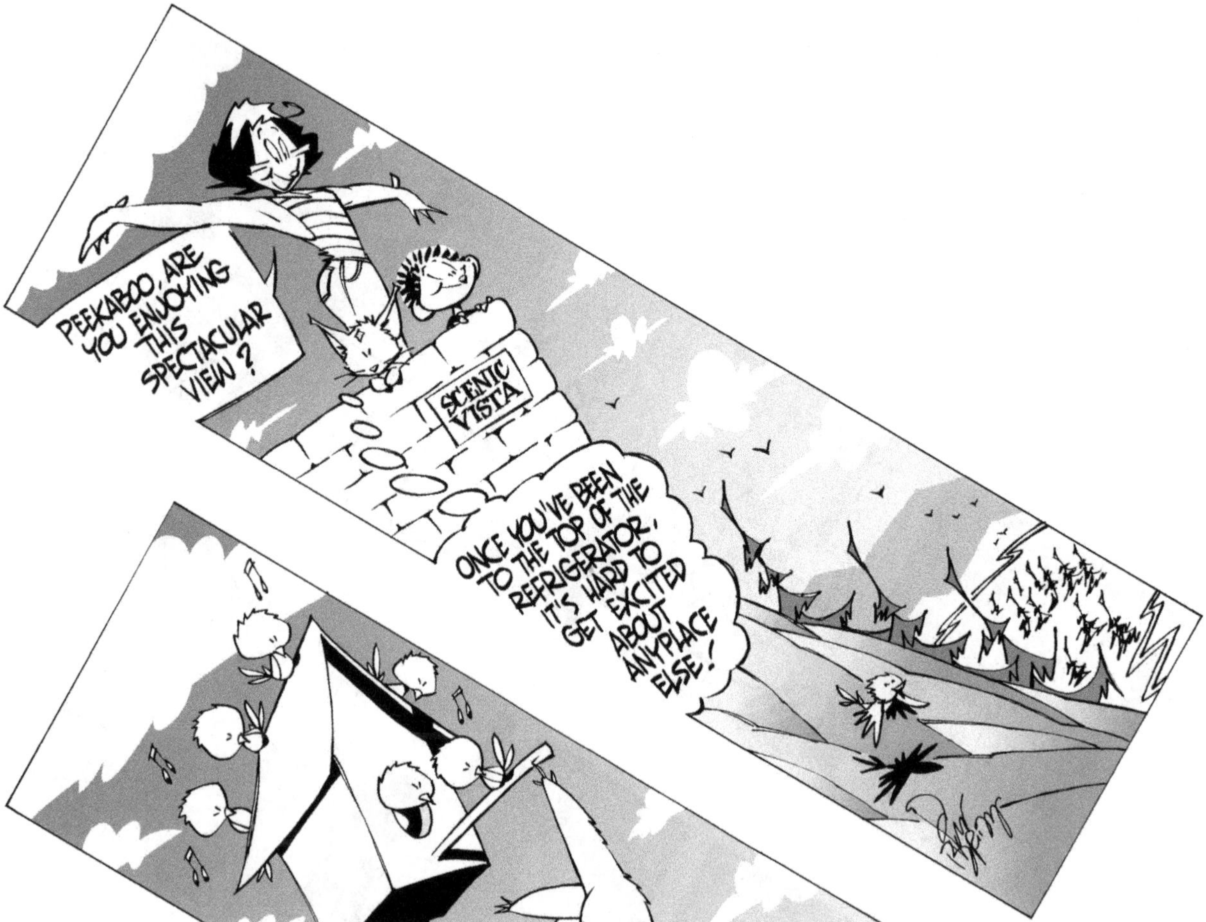
PEEKABOO, ARE YOU ENJOYING THIS SPECTACULAR VIEW?
SCENIC VISTA
ONCE YOU'VE BEEN TO THE TOP OF THE REFRIGERATOR, IT'S HARD TO GET EXCITED ABOUT ANYPLACE ELSE!

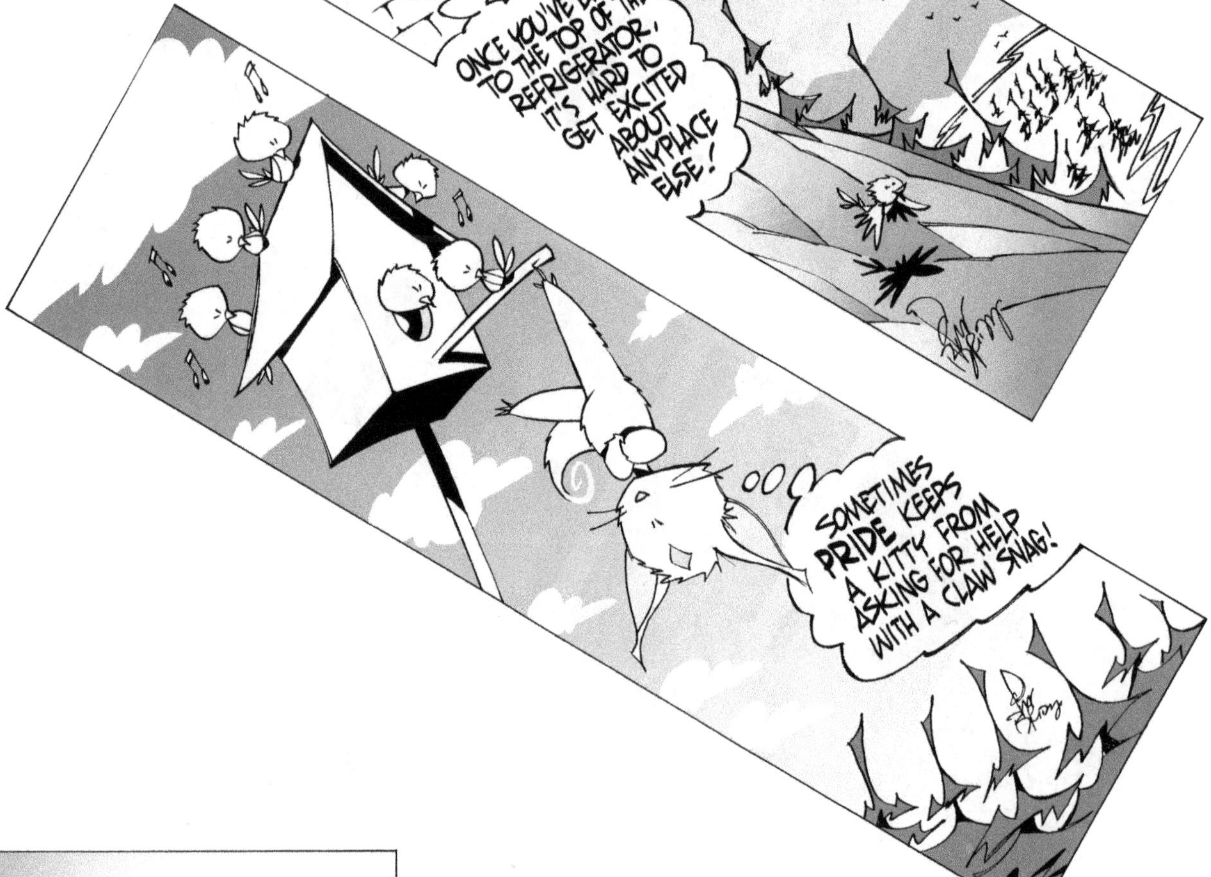
SOMETIMES PRIDE KEEPS A KITTY FROM ASKING FOR HELP WITH A CLAW SNAG!

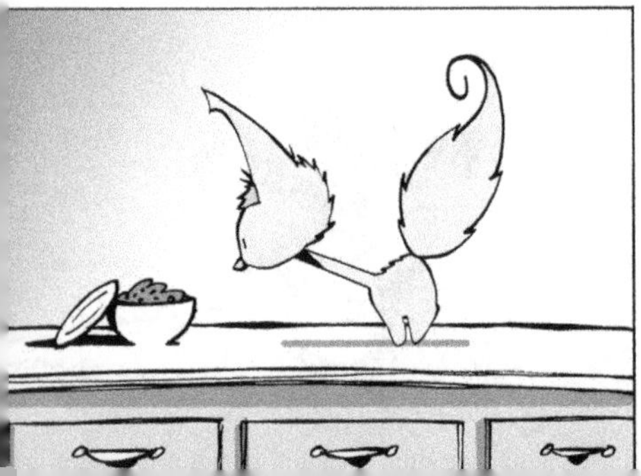

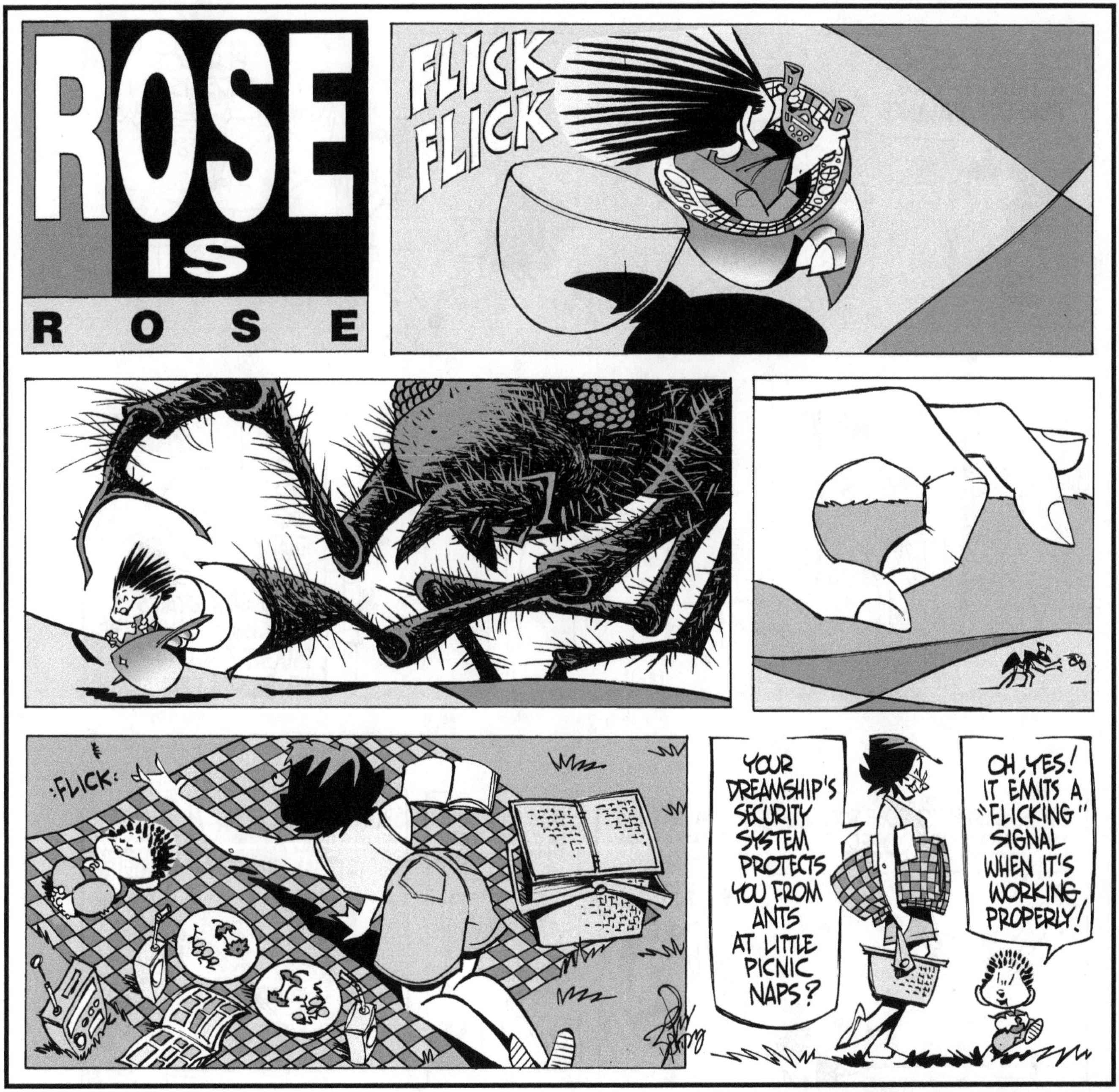
ROSE IS ROSE
FLICK FLICK
FLICK
YOUR DREAMSHIP'S SECURITY SYSTEM PROTECTS YOU FROM ANTS AT LITTLE PICNIC NAPS?
OH, YES! IT EMITS A "FLICKING" SIGNAL WHEN IT'S WORKING PROPERLY!

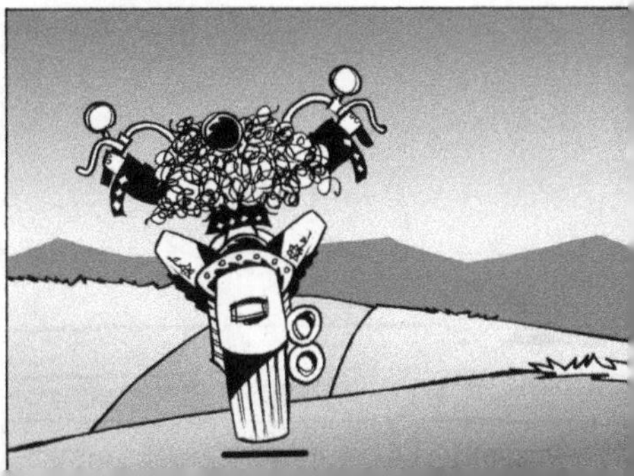

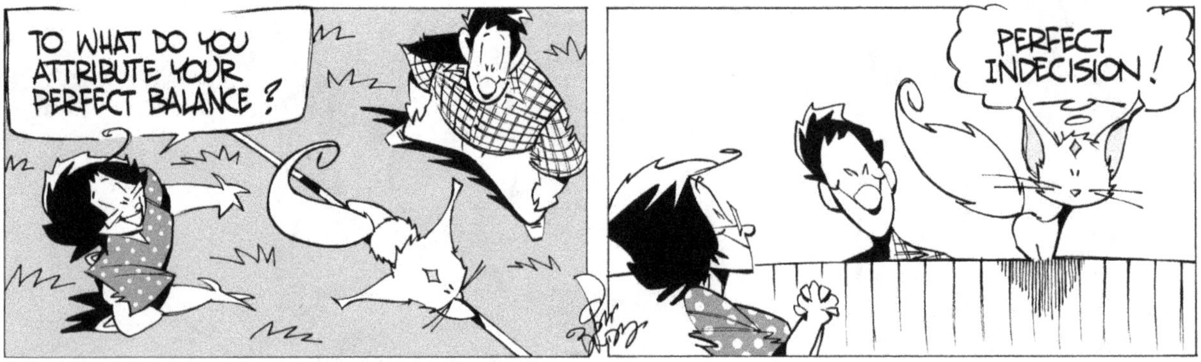

TO WHAT DO YOU ATTRIBUTE YOUR PERFECT BALANCE ?
PERFECT INDECISION !

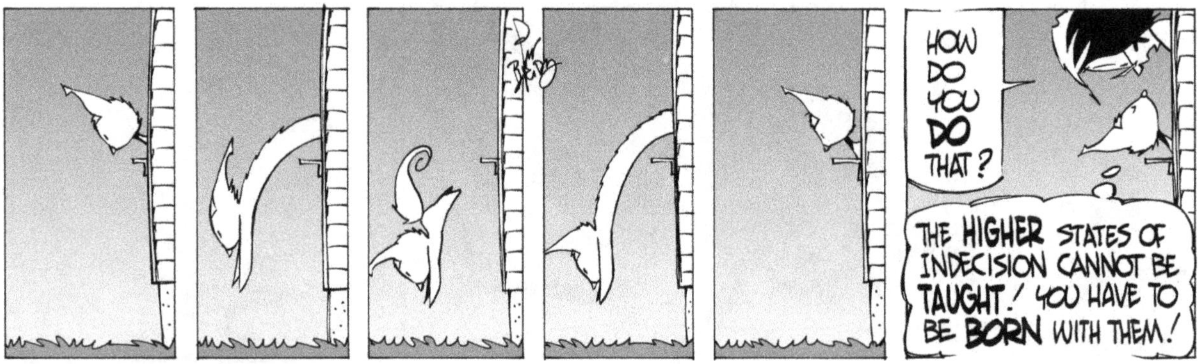

HOW DO YOU DO THAT ?
THE HIGHER STATES OF INDECISION CANNOT BE TAUGHT! YOU HAVE TO BE BORN WITH THEM!

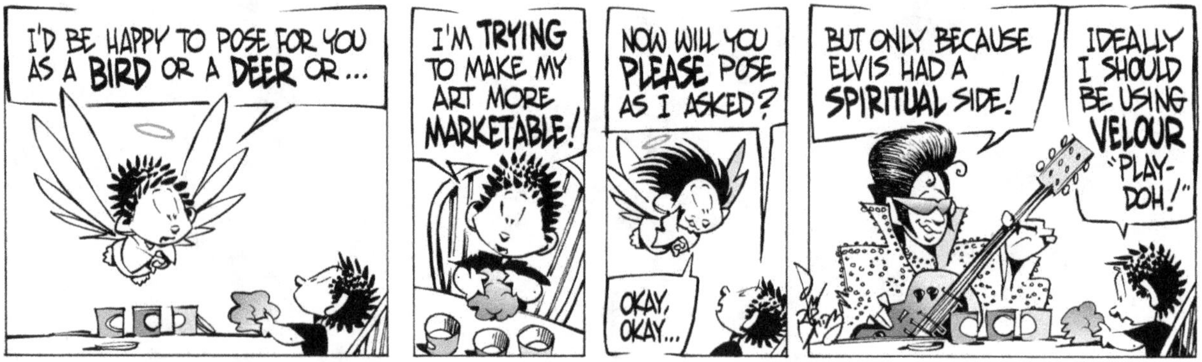

I'D BE HAPPY TO POSE FOR YOU AS A BIRD OR A DEER OR ...
I'M TRYING TO MAKE MY ART MORE MARKETABLE!
NOW WILL YOU PLEASE POSE AS I ASKED?
OKAY, OKAY...
BUT ONLY BECAUSE ELVIS HAD A SPIRITUAL SIDE!
IDEALLY I SHOULD BE USING VELOUR "PLAY-DOH!"

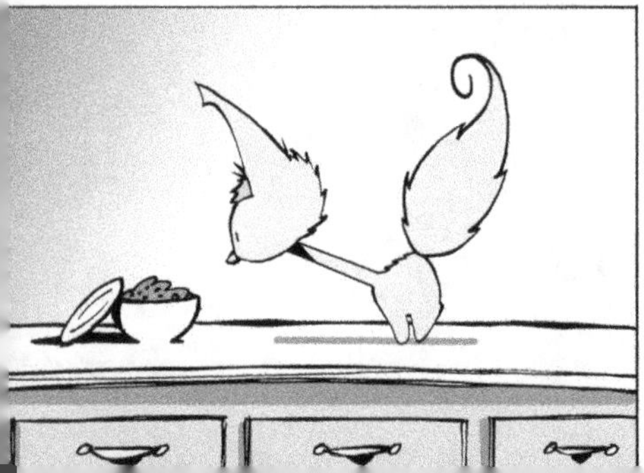

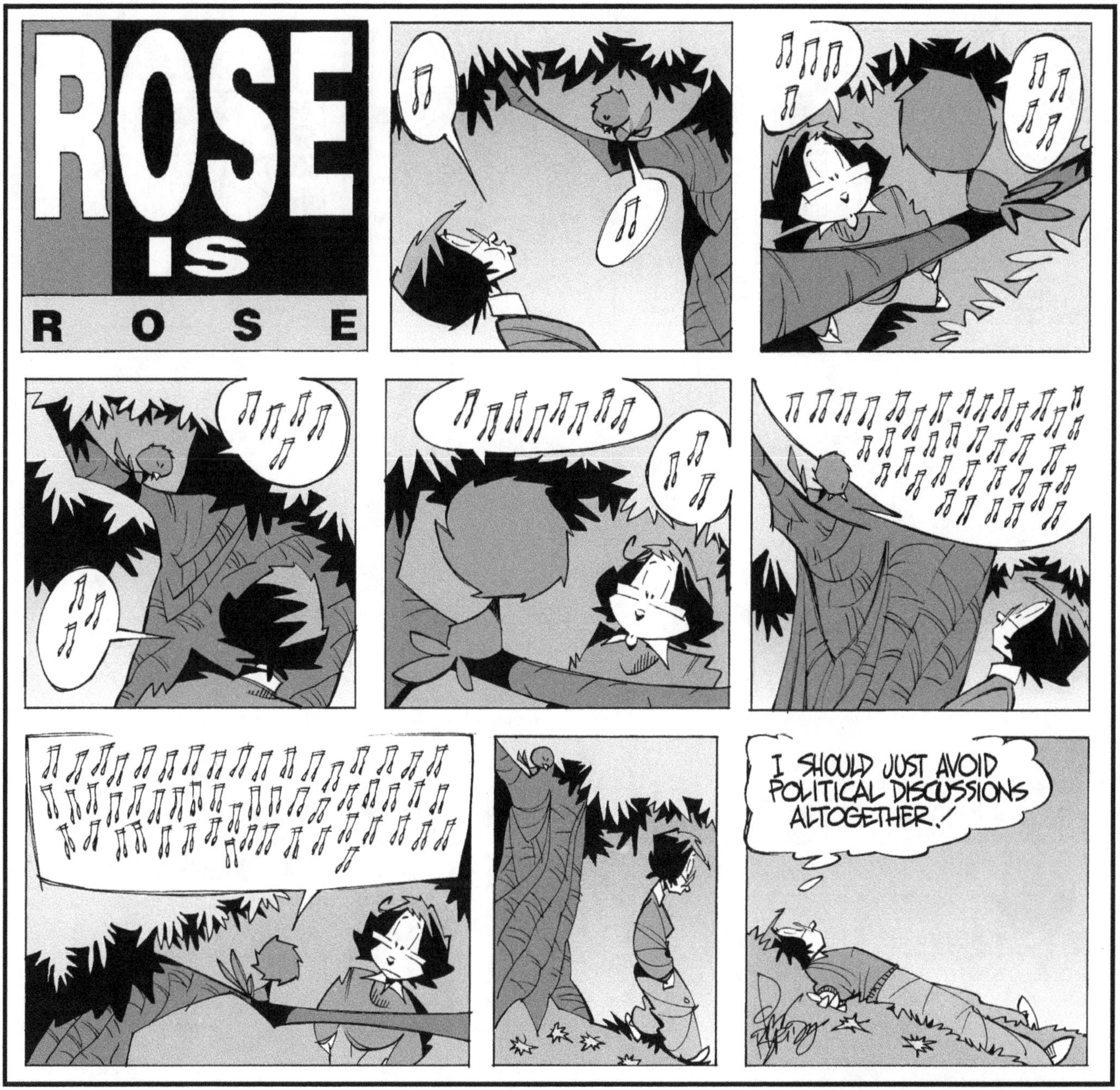
ROSE IS ROSE
I SHOULD JUST AVOID POLITICAL DISCUSSIONS ALTOGETHER.!

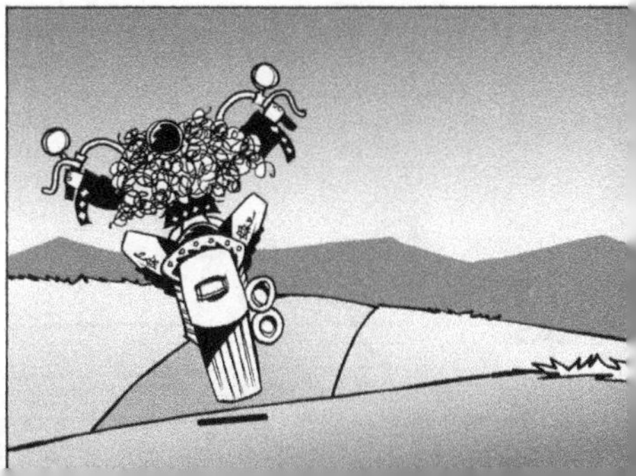

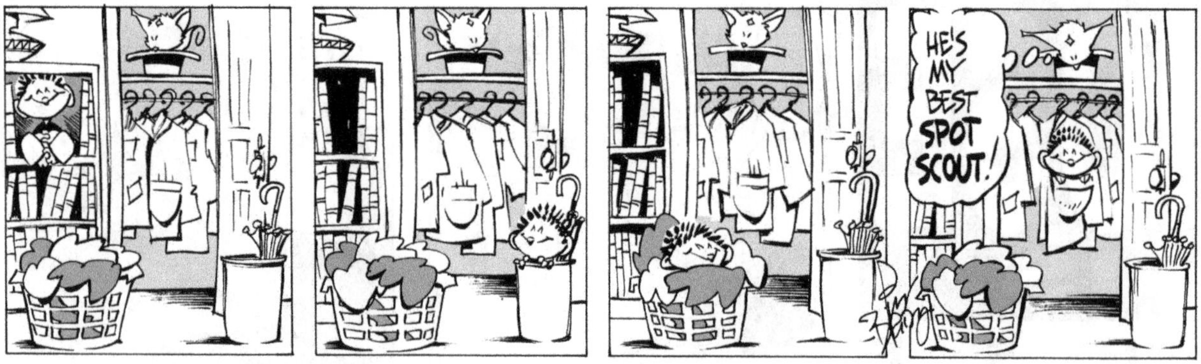
HE'S MY BEST SPOT SCOUT!

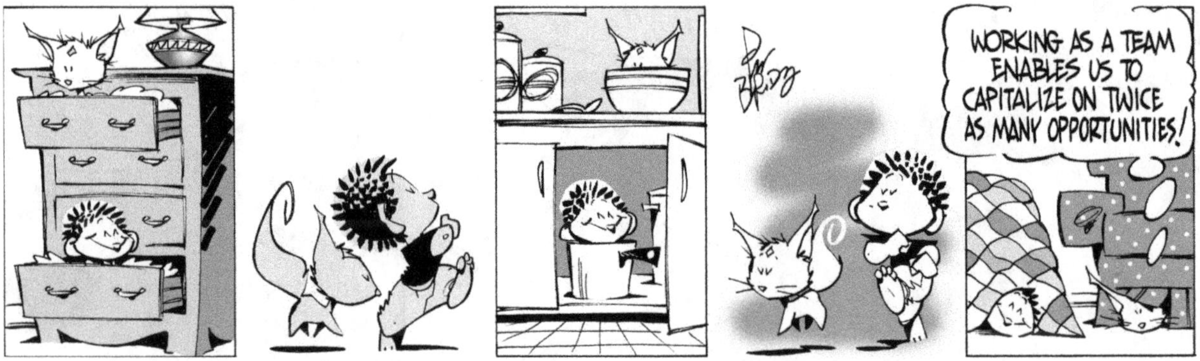
WORKING AS A TEAM ENABLES US TO CAPITALIZE ON TWICE AS MANY OPPORTUNITIES!

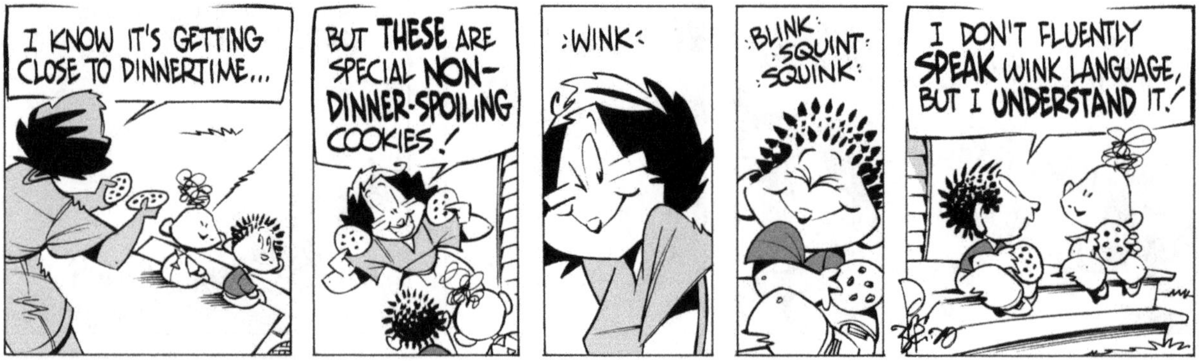
I KNOW IT'S GETTING CLOSE TO DINNERTIME...
BUT THESE ARE SPECIAL NON-DINNER-SPOILING COOKIES!
WINK
BLINK SQUINT SQUINK
I DON'T FLUENTLY SPEAK WINK LANGUAGE, BUT I UNDERSTAND IT!

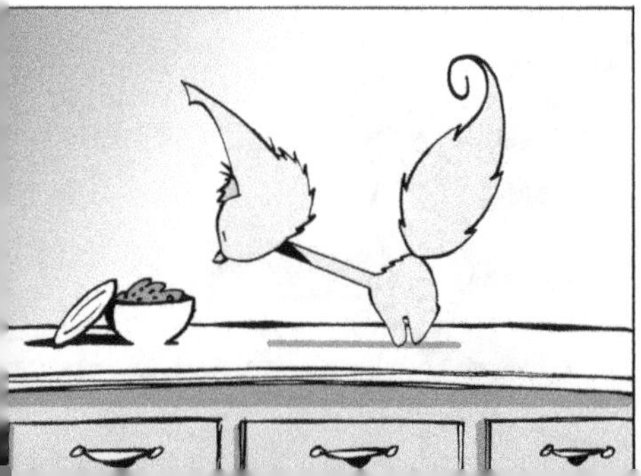

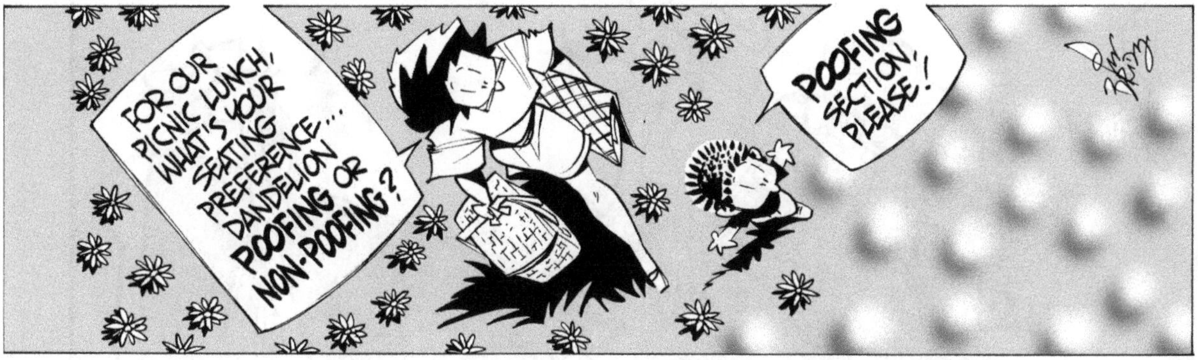
FOR OUR PICNIC LUNCH, WHAT'S YOUR SEATING PREFERENCE... DANDELION POOFING OR NON-POOFING?
POOFING SECTION, PLEASE!

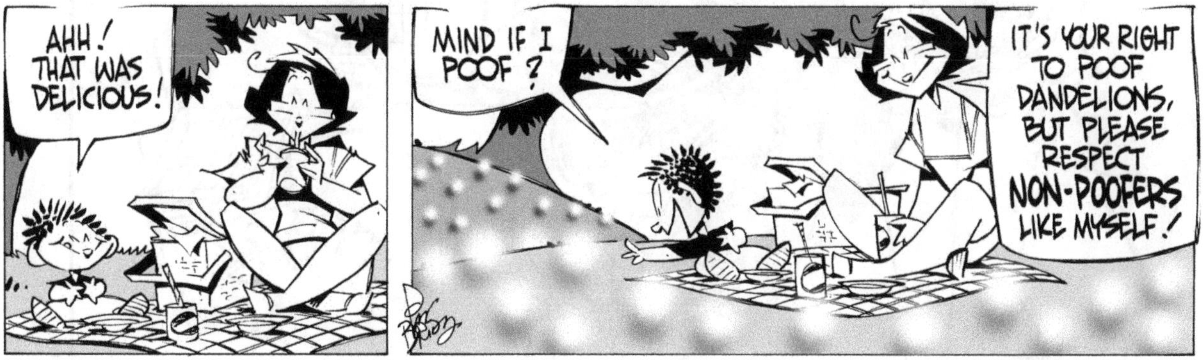
AHH! THAT WAS DELICIOUS!
MIND IF I POOF?
IT'S YOUR RIGHT TO POOF DANDELIONS, BUT PLEASE RESPECT NON-POOFERS LIKE MYSELF!

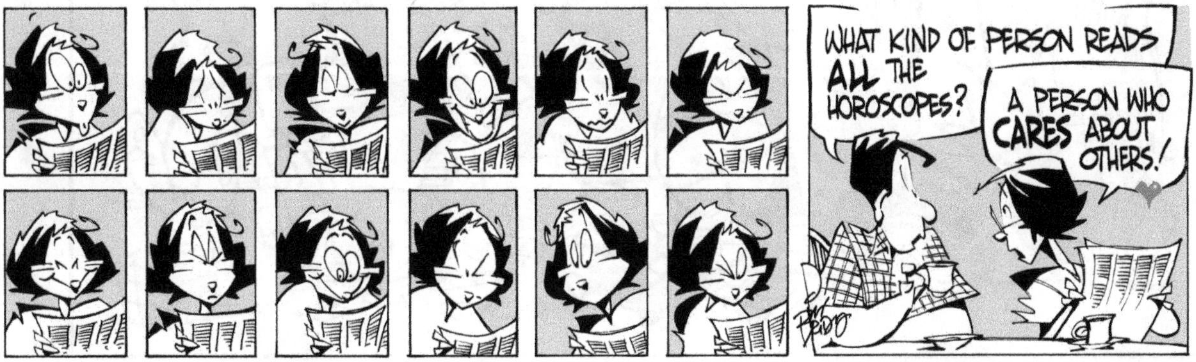
WHAT KIND OF PERSON READS ALL THE HOROSCOPES?
A PERSON WHO CARES ABOUT OTHERS!

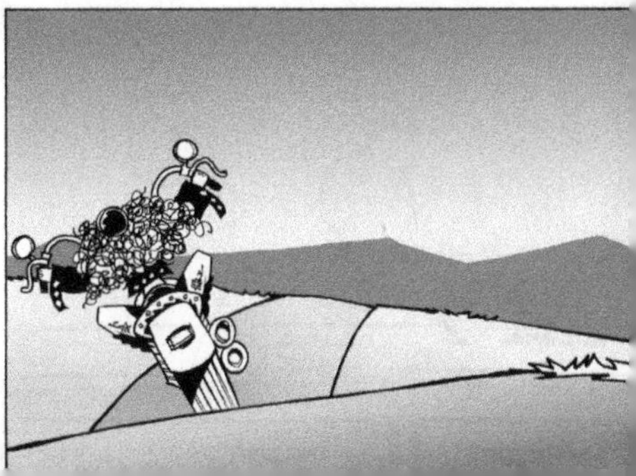

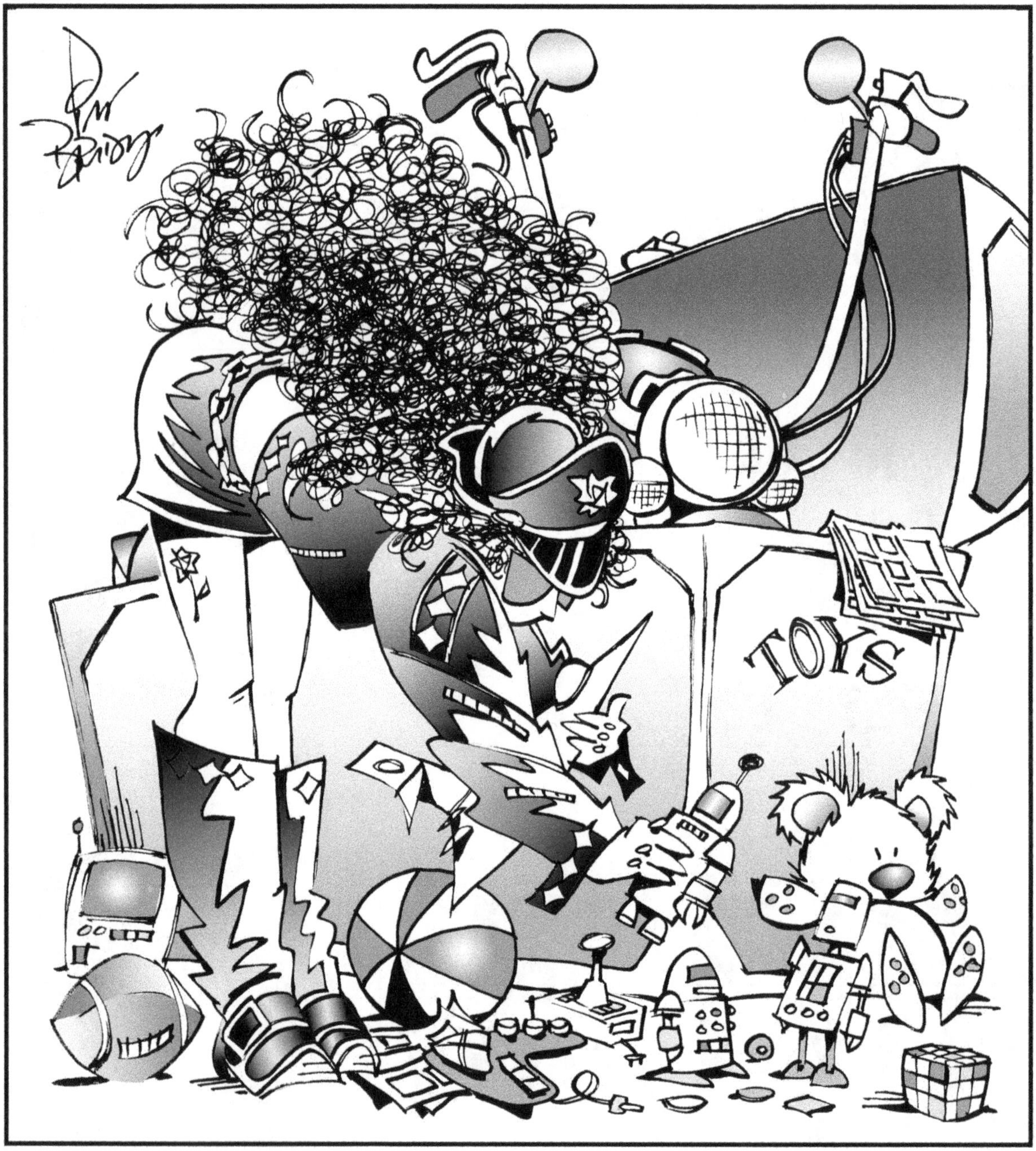
TOYS

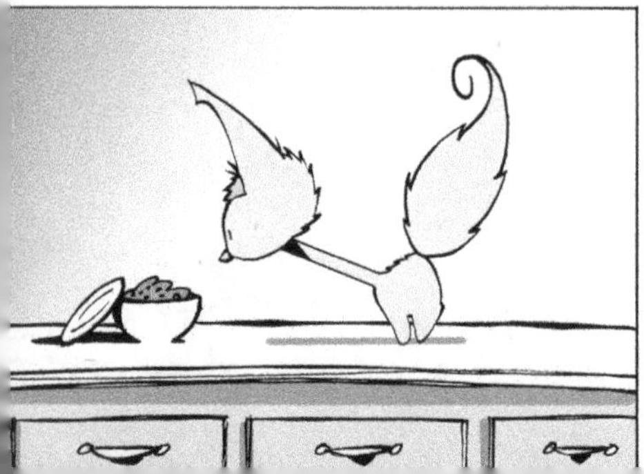

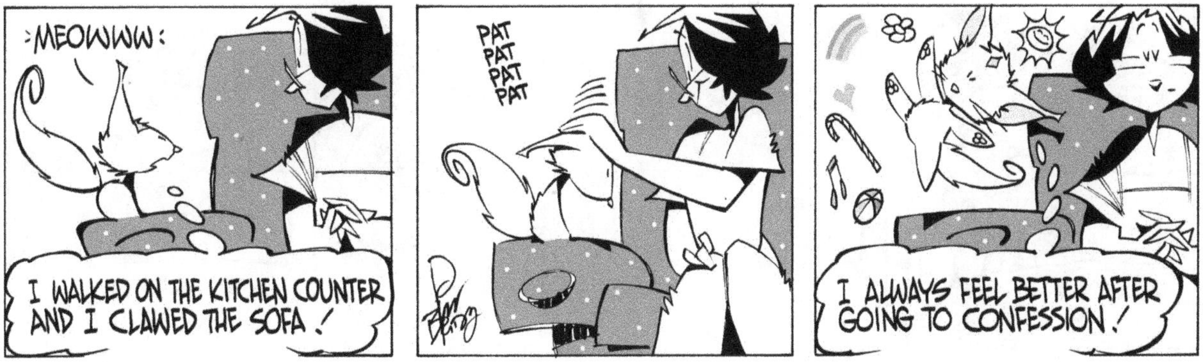
MEOWWW
I WALKED ON THE KITCHEN COUNTER AND I CLAWED THE SOFA!
PAT PAT PAT PAT
I ALWAYS FEEL BETTER AFTER GOING TO CONFESSION!

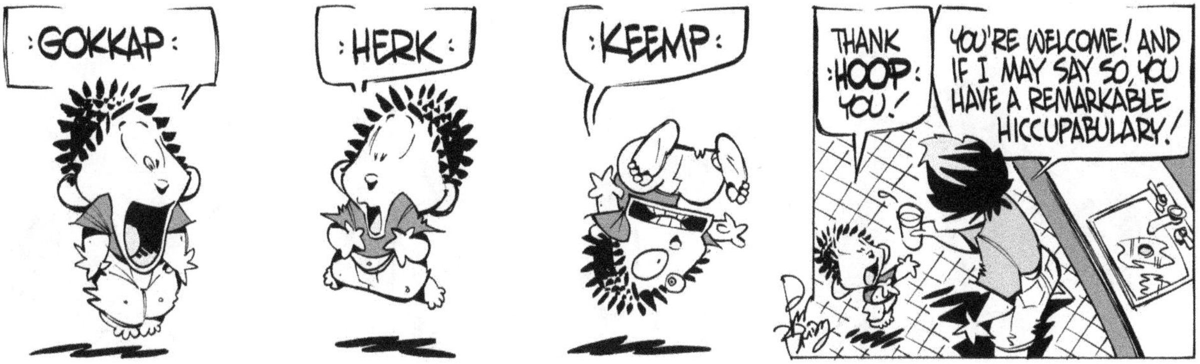
GOKKAP
HERK
KEEMP
THANK HOOP YOU!
YOU'RE WELCOME! AND IF I MAY SAY SO, YOU HAVE A REMARKABLE HICCUPABULARY!

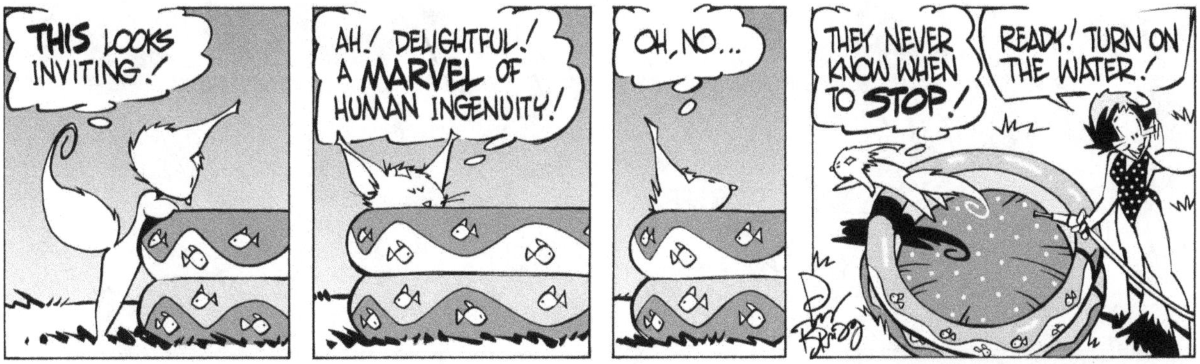
THIS LOOKS INVITING!
AH! DELIGHTFUL! A MARVEL OF HUMAN INGENUITY!
OH, NO...
THEY NEVER KNOW WHEN TO STOP!
READY! TURN ON THE WATER!

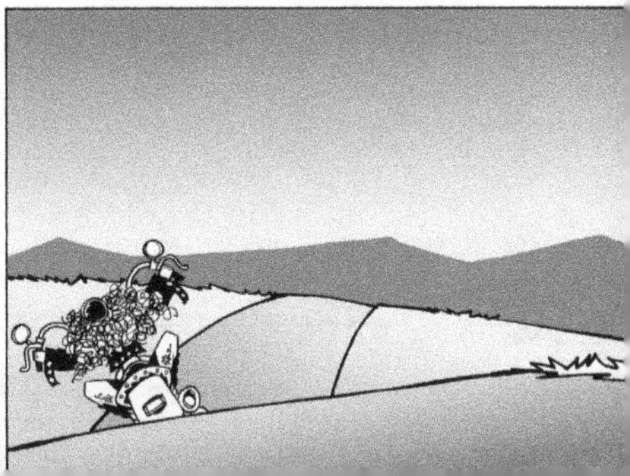

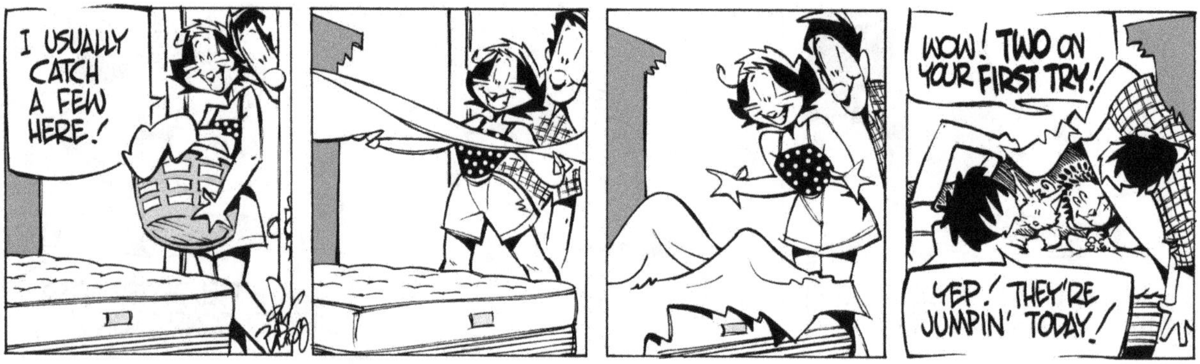
I USUALLY CATCH A FEW HERE!
WOW! TWO ON YOUR FIRST TRY!
YEP! THEY'RE JUMPIN' TODAY!

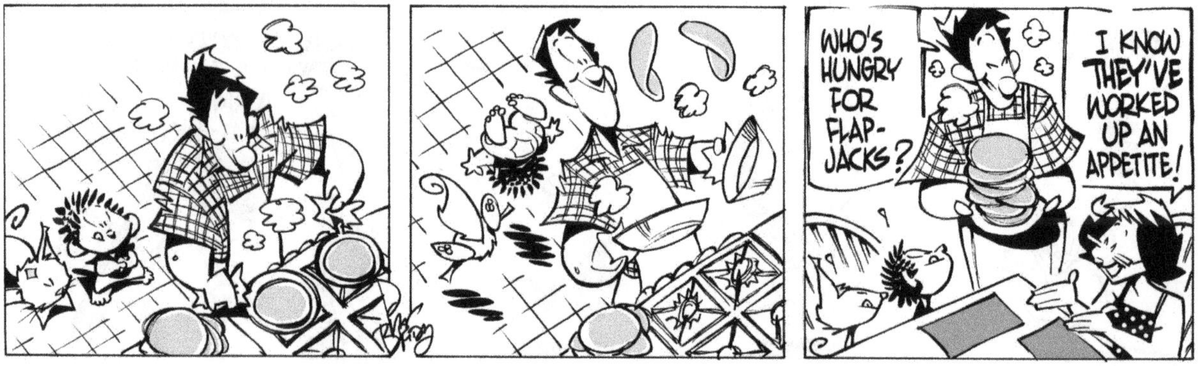
WHO'S HUNGRY FOR FLAP-JACKS?
I KNOW THEY'VE WORKED UP AN APPETITE!

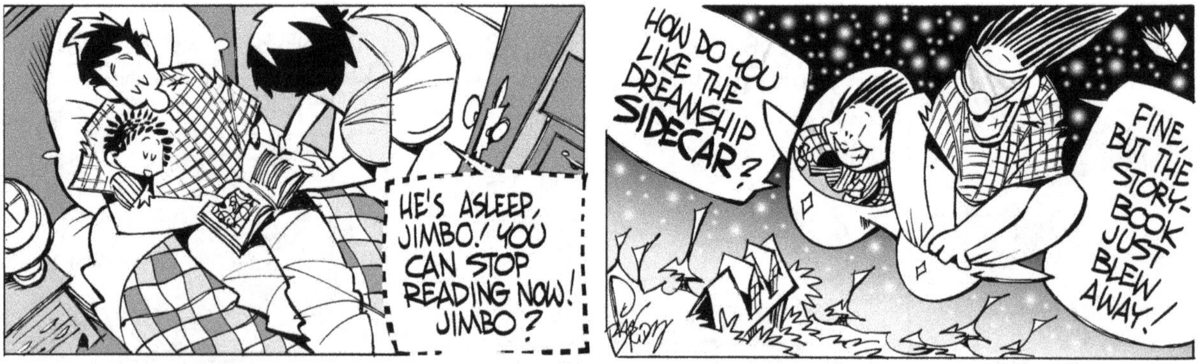
HE'S ASLEEP, JIMBO! YOU CAN STOP READING NOW! JIMBO?
HOW DO YOU LIKE THE DREAMSHIP SIDECAR?
FINE, BUT THE STORY-BOOK JUST BLEW AWAY!

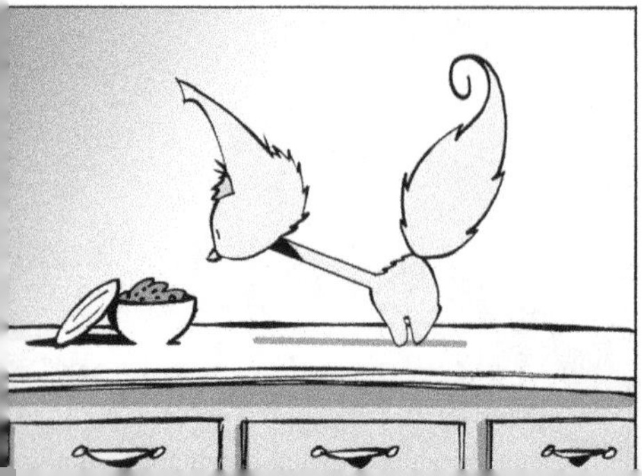

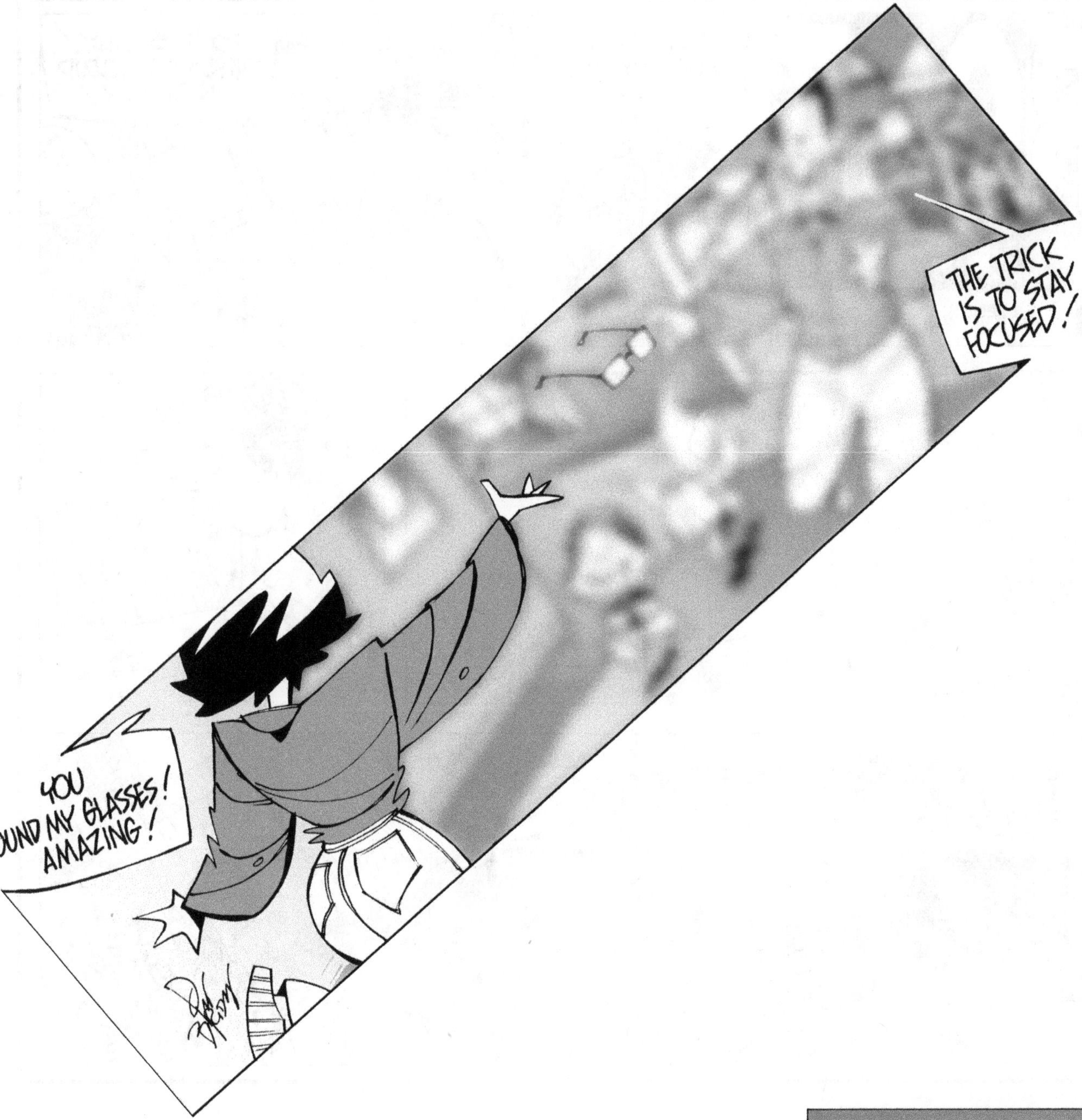
THE TRICK IS TO STAY FOCUSED!
YOU FOUND MY GLASSES! AMAZING!

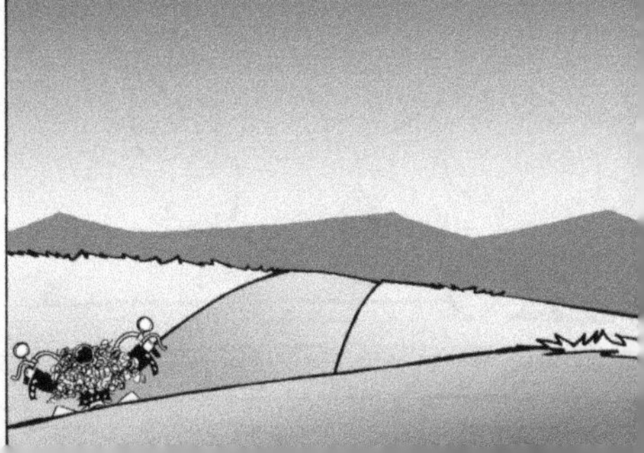

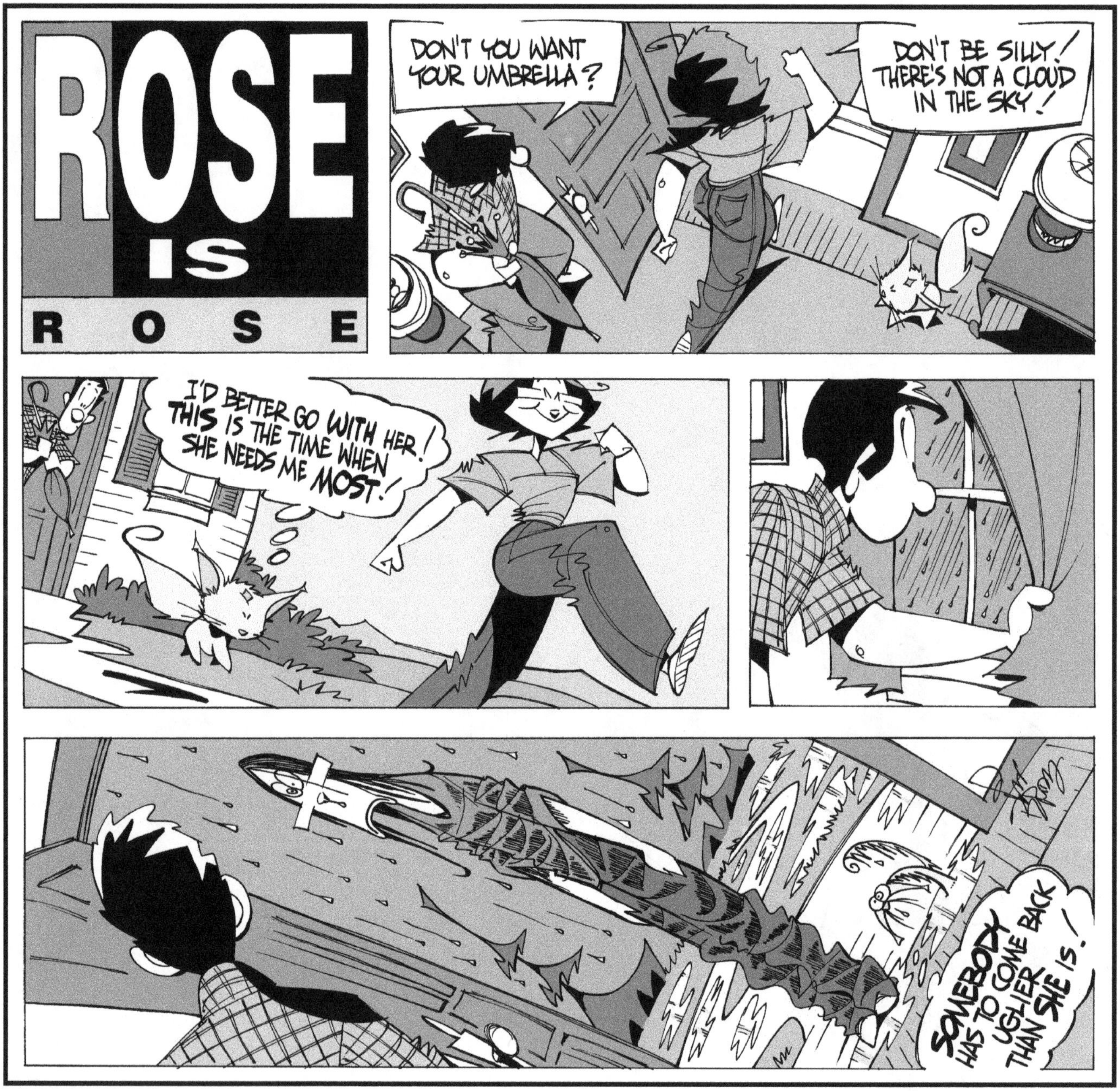
ROSE IS ROSE
DON'T YOU WANT YOUR UMBRELLA?
DON'T BE SILLY! THERE'S NOT A CLOUD IN THE SKY!
I'D BETTER GO WITH HER! THIS IS THE TIME WHEN SHE NEEDS ME MOST!
SOMEBODY HAS TO COME BACK UGLIER THAN SHE IS!

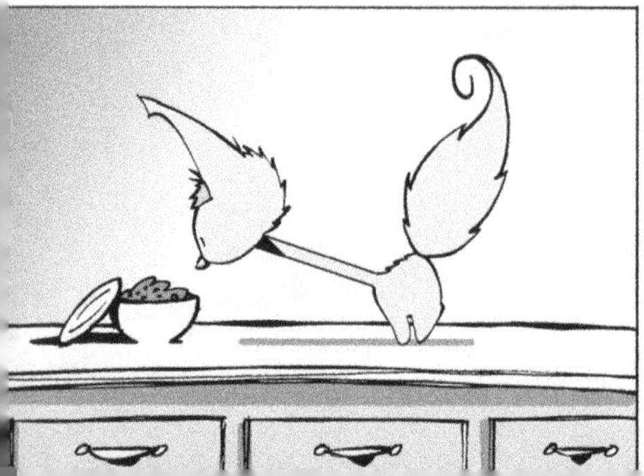

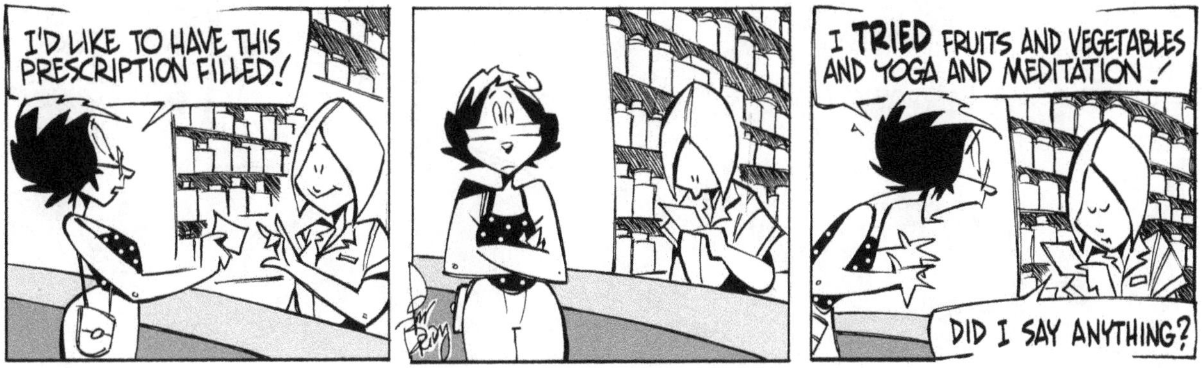
I'D LIKE TO HAVE THIS PRESCRIPTION FILLED!
I TRIED FRUITS AND VEGETABLES AND YOGA AND MEDITATION!
DID I SAY ANYTHING?

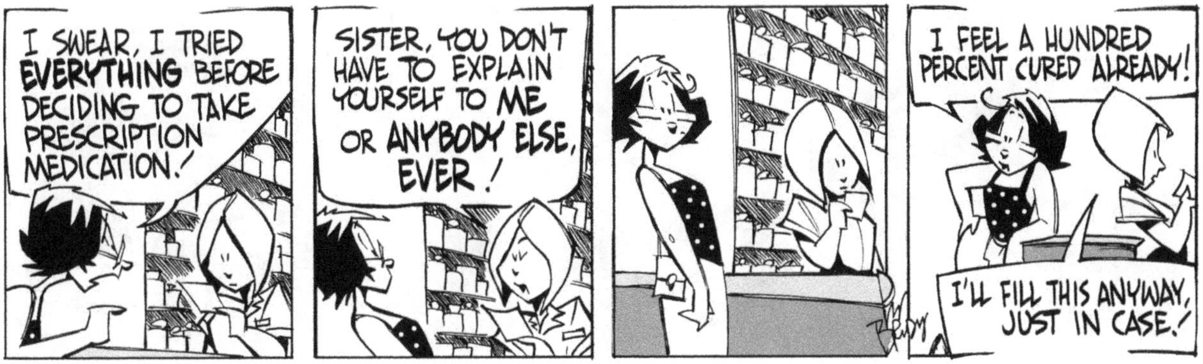
I SWEAR, I TRIED EVERYTHING BEFORE DECIDING TO TAKE PRESCRIPTION MEDICATION!
SISTER, YOU DON'T HAVE TO EXPLAIN YOURSELF TO ME OR ANYBODY ELSE, EVER!
I FEEL A HUNDRED PERCENT CURED ALREADY!
I'LL FILL THIS ANYWAY, JUST IN CASE!

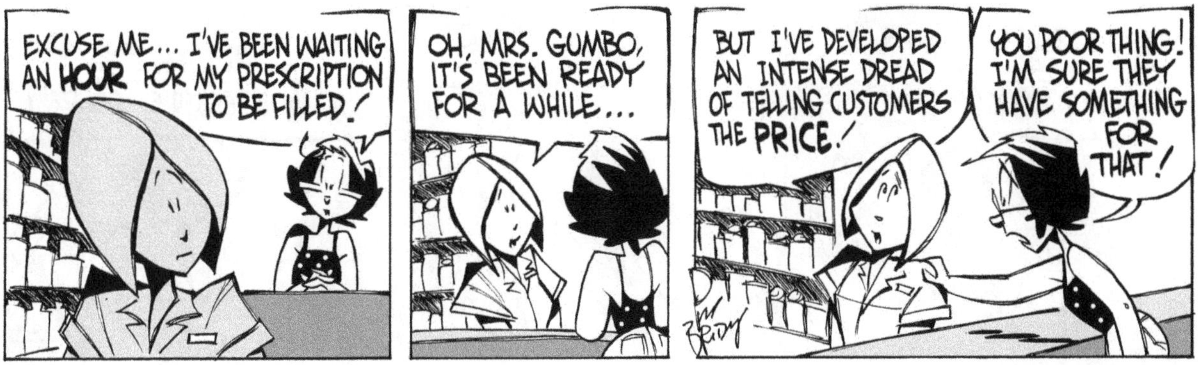
EXCUSE ME... I'VE BEEN WAITING AN HOUR FOR MY PRESCRIPTION TO BE FILLED!
OH, MRS. GUMBO, IT'S BEEN READY FOR A WHILE...
BUT I'VE DEVELOPED AN INTENSE DREAD OF TELLING CUSTOMERS THE PRICE!
YOU POOR THING! I'M SURE THEY HAVE SOMETHING FOR THAT!

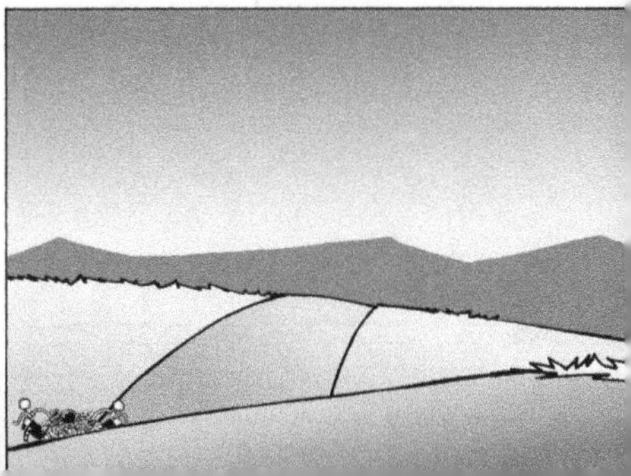

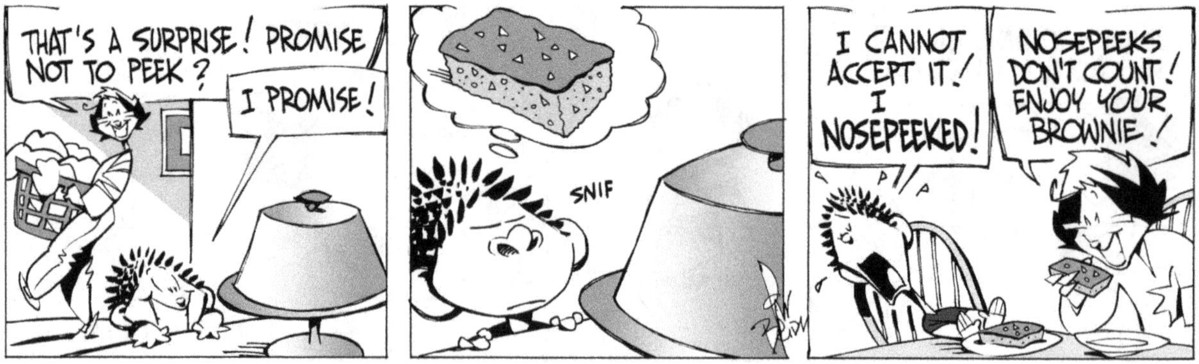
THAT'S A SURPRISE! PROMISE NOT TO PEEK?
I PROMISE!
SNIF
I CANNOT ACCEPT IT! I NOSEPEEKED!
NOSEPEEKS DON'T COUNT! ENJOY YOUR BROWNIE!

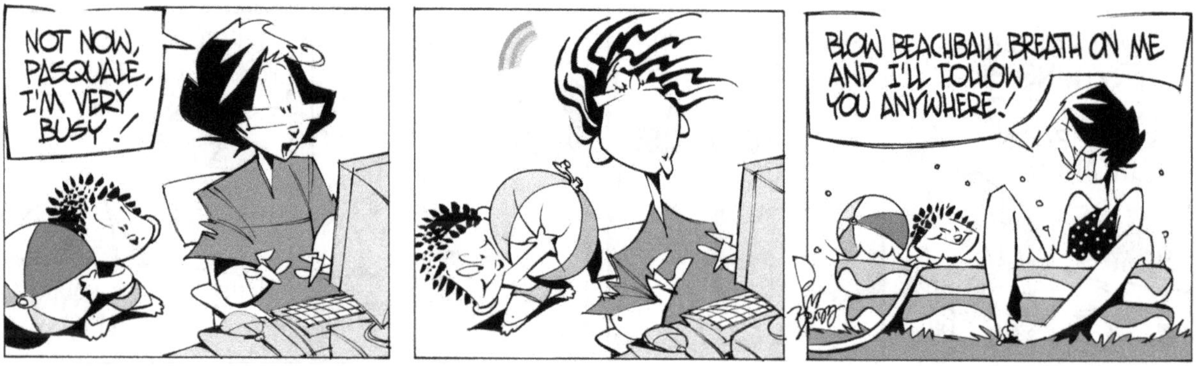
NOT NOW, PASQUALE, I'M VERY BUSY!
BLOW BEACHBALL BREATH ON ME AND I'LL FOLLOW YOU ANYWHERE!

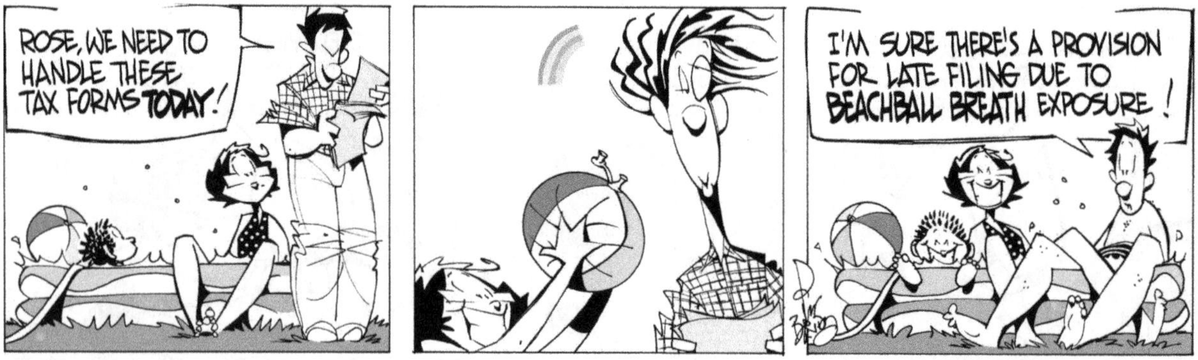
ROSE, WE NEED TO HANDLE THESE TAX FORMS TODAY!
I'M SURE THERE'S A PROVISION FOR LATE FILING DUE TO BEACHBALL BREATH EXPOSURE!

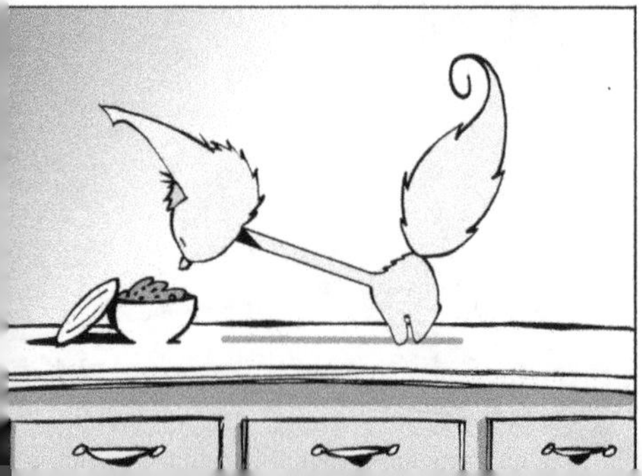

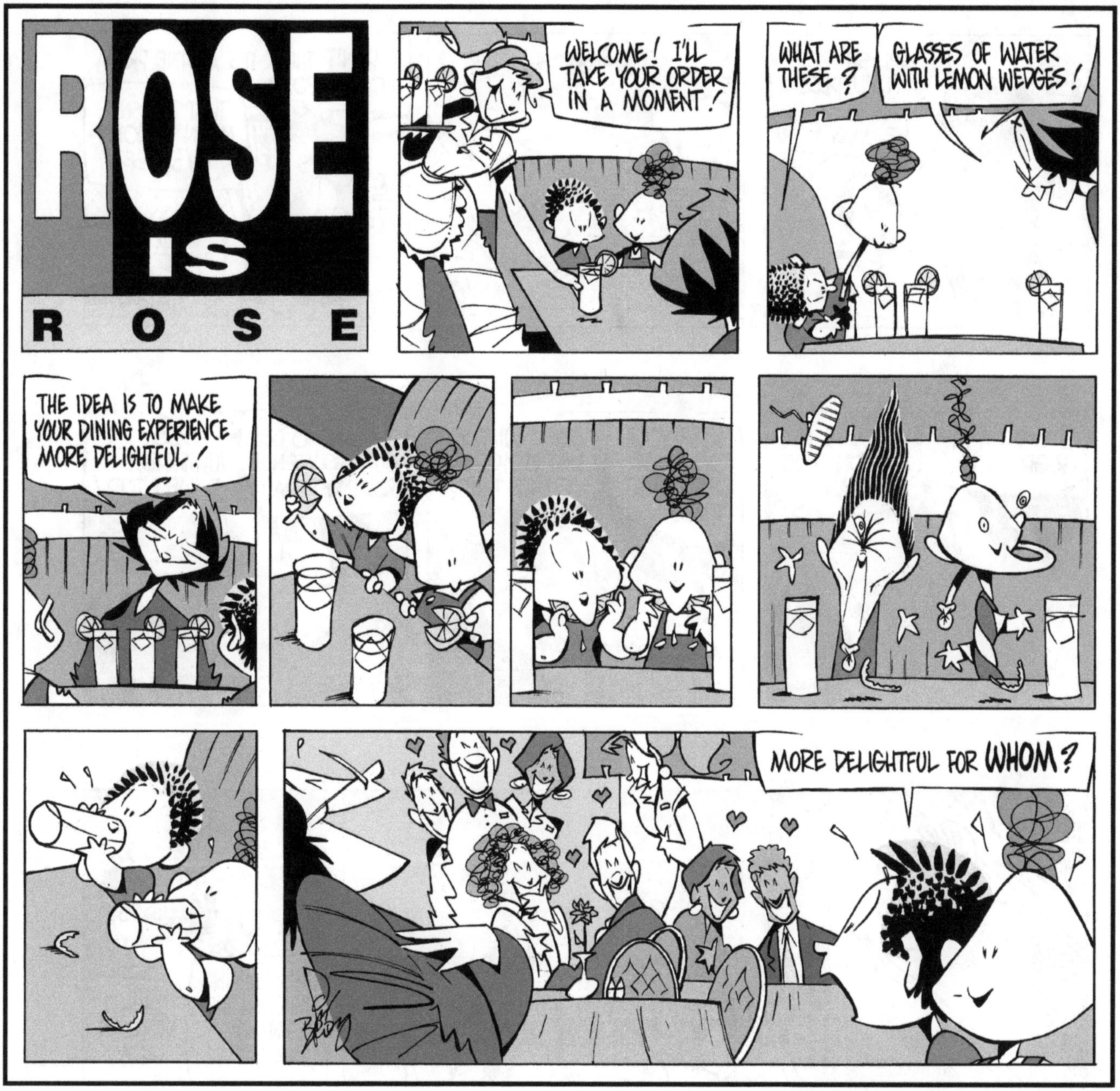
ROSE IS ROSE
WELCOME! I'LL TAKE YOUR ORDER IN A MOMENT!
WHAT ARE THESE?
GLASSES OF WATER WITH LEMON WEDGES!
THE IDEA IS TO MAKE YOUR DINING EXPERIENCE MORE DELIGHTFUL!
MORE DELIGHTFUL FOR WHOM?

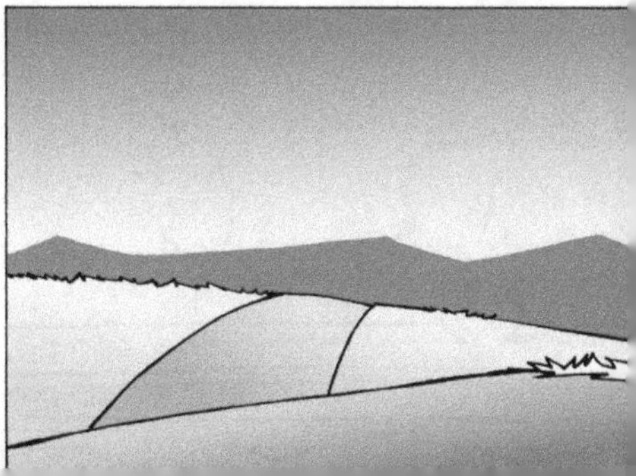

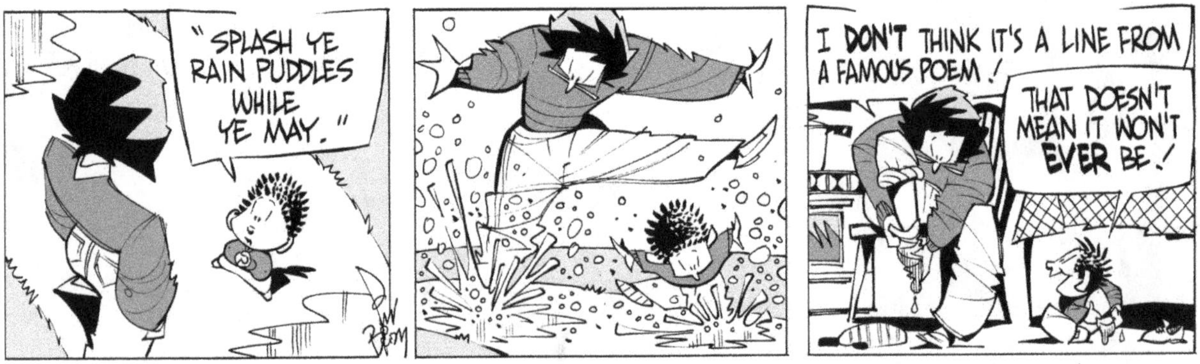
"SPLASH YE RAIN PUDDLES WHILE YE MAY."
I DON'T THINK IT'S A LINE FROM A FAMOUS POEM!
THAT DOESN'T MEAN IT WON'T EVER BE!

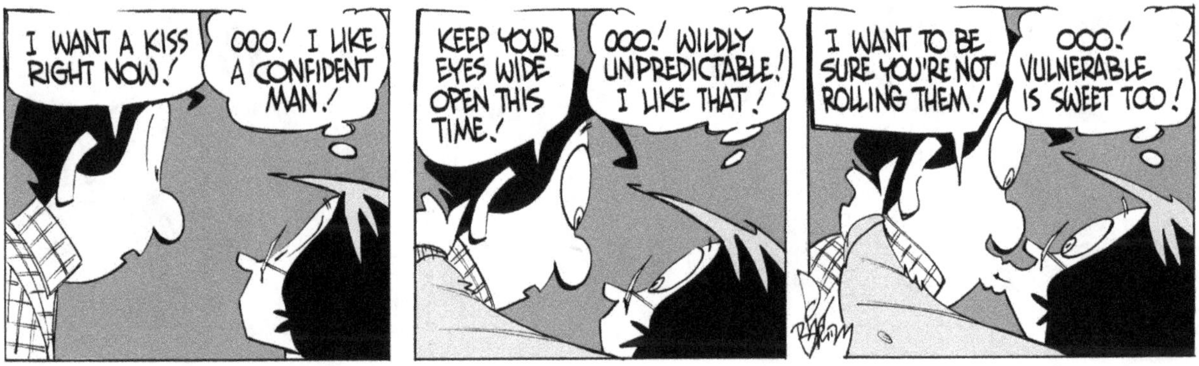
I WANT A KISS RIGHT NOW!
OOO! I LIKE A CONFIDENT MAN!
KEEP YOUR EYES WIDE OPEN THIS TIME!
OOO! WILDLY UNPREDICTABLE! I LIKE THAT!
I WANT TO BE SURE YOU'RE NOT ROLLING THEM!
OOO! VULNERABLE IS SWEET TOO!

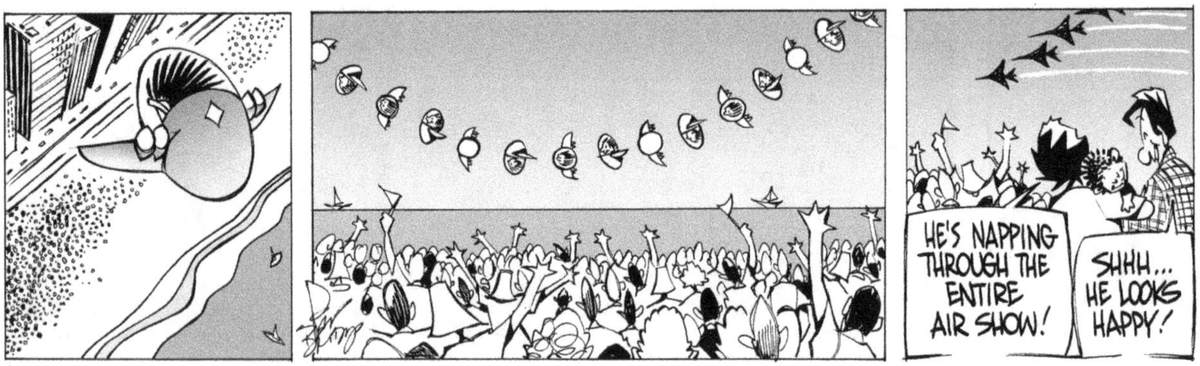
HE'S NAPPING THROUGH THE ENTIRE AIR SHOW!
SHHH... HE LOOKS HAPPY!

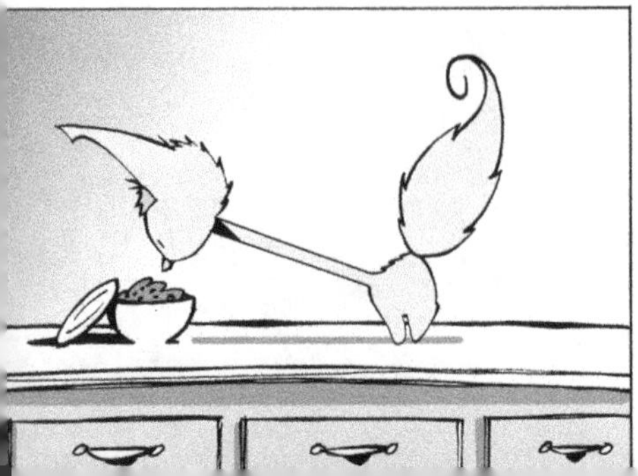

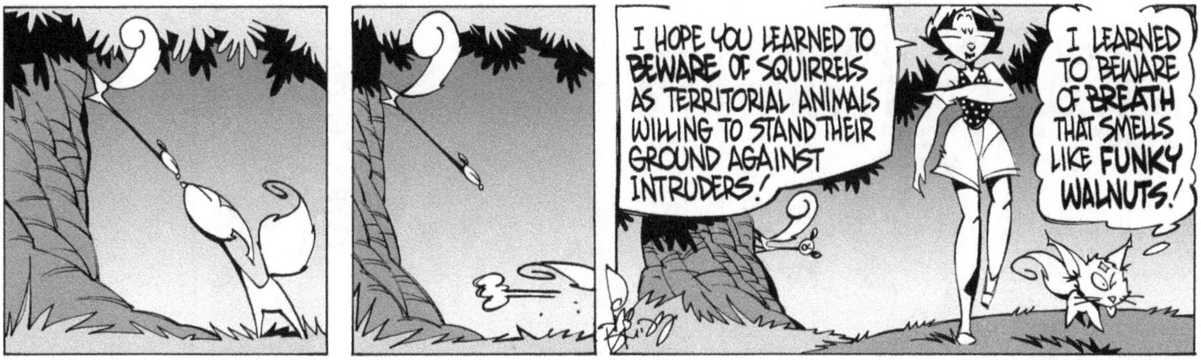
I HOPE YOU LEARNED TO BEWARE OF SQUIRRELS AS TERRITORIAL ANIMALS WILLING TO STAND THEIR GROUND AGAINST INTRUDERS!
I LEARNED TO BEWARE OF BREATH THAT SMELLS LIKE FUNKY WALNUTS!

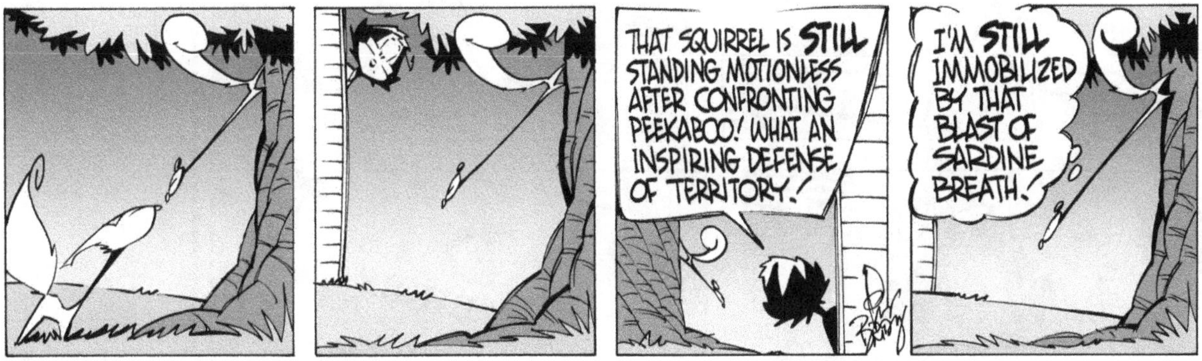
THAT SQUIRREL IS STILL STANDING MOTIONLESS AFTER CONFRONTING PEEKABOO! WHAT AN INSPIRING DEFENSE OF TERRITORY!
I'M STILL IMMOBILIZED BY THAT BLAST OF SARDINE BREATH!

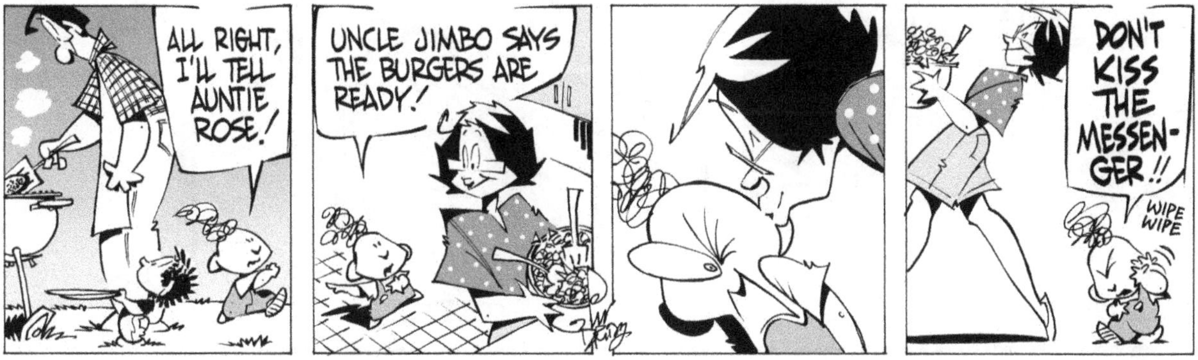
ALL RIGHT, I'LL TELL AUNTIE ROSE!
UNCLE JIMBO SAYS THE BURGERS ARE READY!
DON'T KISS THE MESSENGER!!
WIPE WIPE

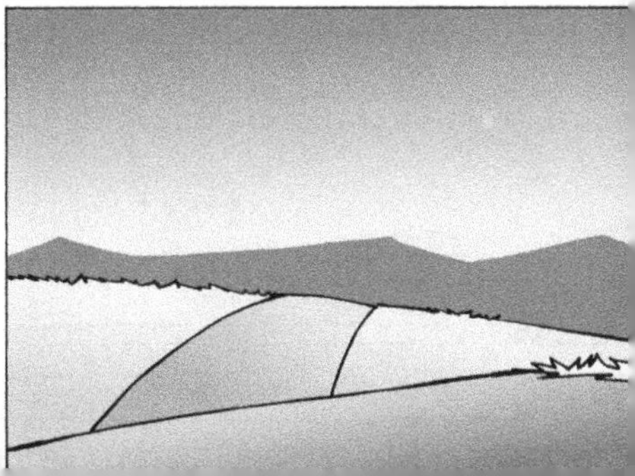

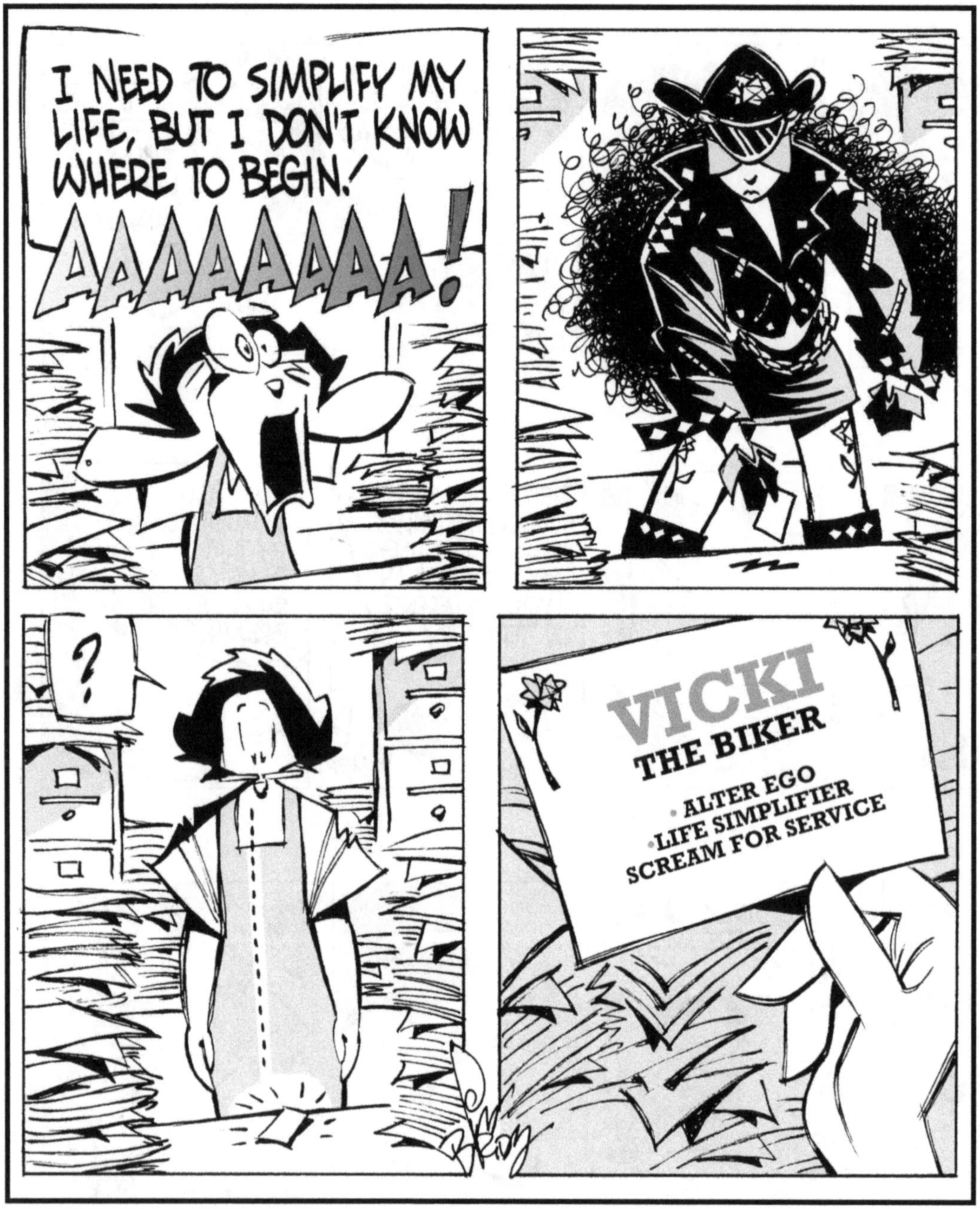
I NEED TO SIMPLIFY MY LIFE, BUT I DON'T KNOW WHERE TO BEGIN!
AAAAAAAA!
?
VICKI
THE BIKER
• ALTER EGO
• LIFE SIMPLIFIER
SCREAM FOR SERVICE

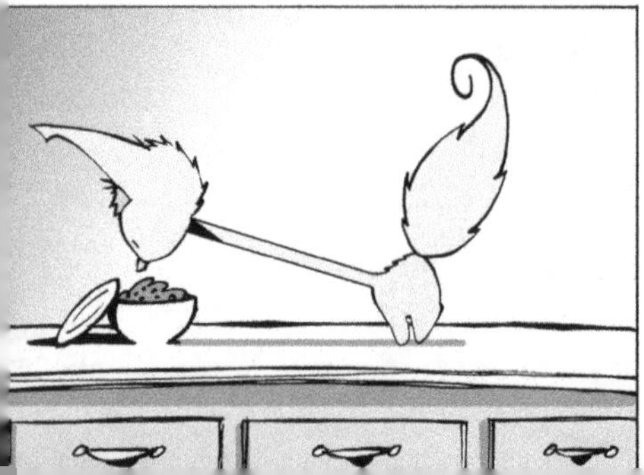

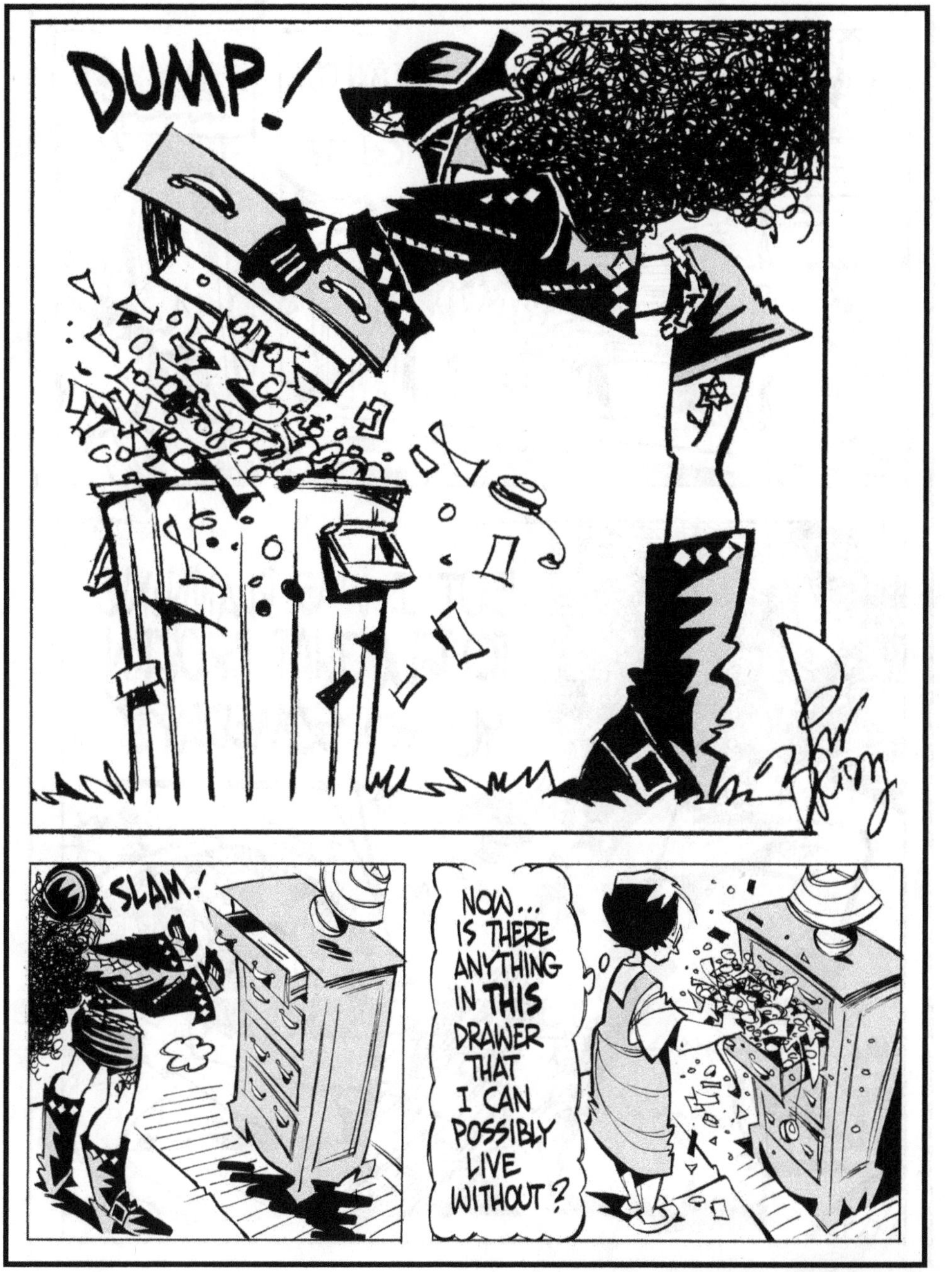
DUMP!
SLAM!
NOW... IS THERE ANYTHING IN THIS DRAWER THAT I CAN POSSIBLY LIVE WITHOUT?

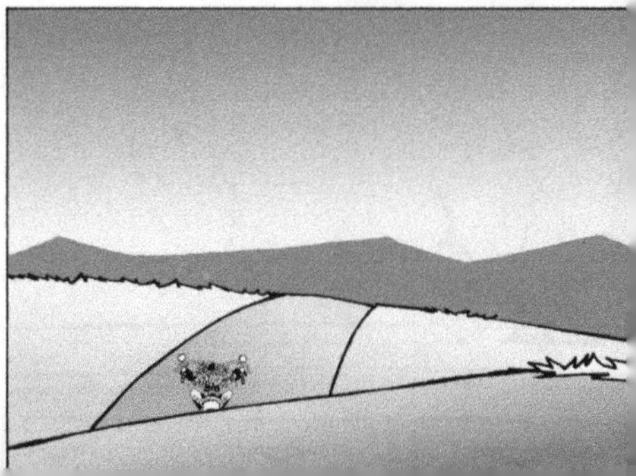

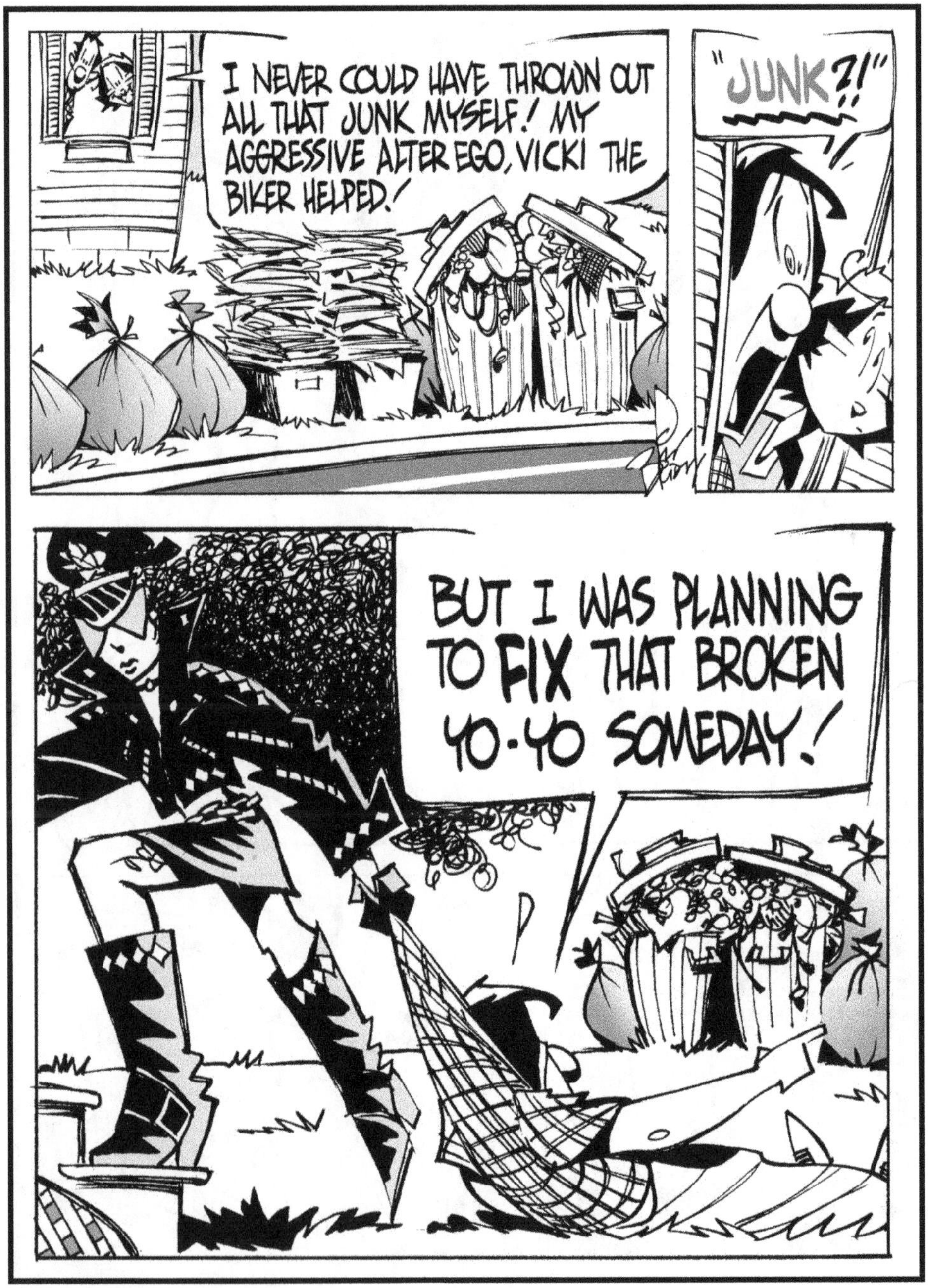
I NEVER COULD HAVE THROWN OUT ALL THAT JUNK MYSELF! MY AGGRESSIVE ALTER EGO, VICKI THE BIKER HELPED!
"JUNK?!"
BUT I WAS PLANNING TO FIX THAT BROKEN YO-YO SOMEDAY!

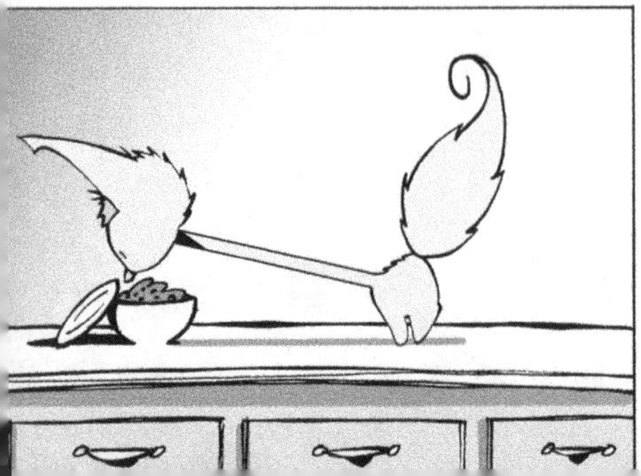

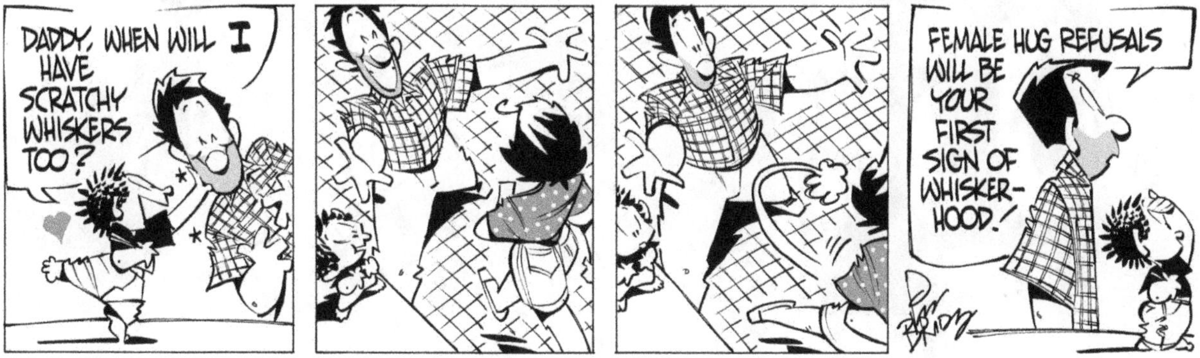
DADDY, WHEN WILL I HAVE SCRATCHY WHISKERS TOO?
FEMALE HUG REFUSALS WILL BE YOUR FIRST SIGN OF WHISKER-HOOD!

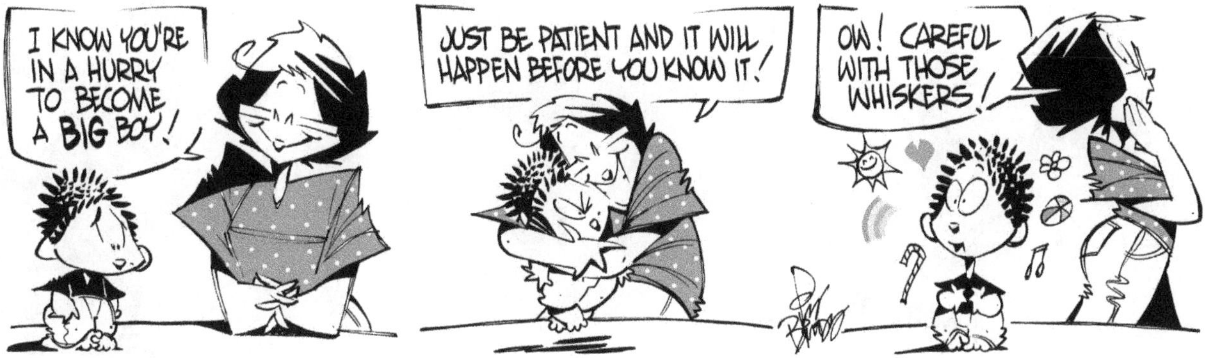
I KNOW YOU'RE IN A HURRY TO BECOME A BIG BOY!
JUST BE PATIENT AND IT WILL HAPPEN BEFORE YOU KNOW IT!
OW! CAREFUL WITH THOSE WHISKERS!

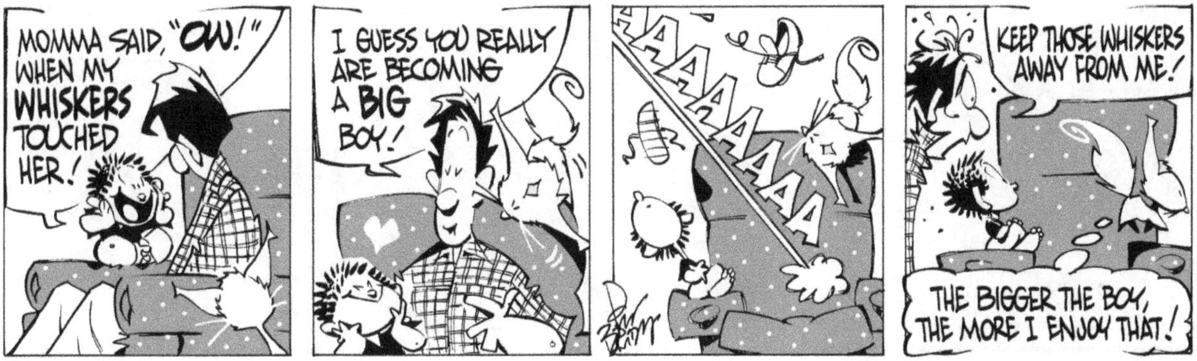
MOMMA SAID, "OW!" WHEN MY WHISKERS TOUCHED HER!
I GUESS YOU REALLY ARE BECOMING A BIG BOY!
AAAAAAAAA
KEEP THOSE WHISKERS AWAY FROM ME!
THE BIGGER THE BOY, THE MORE I ENJOY THAT!

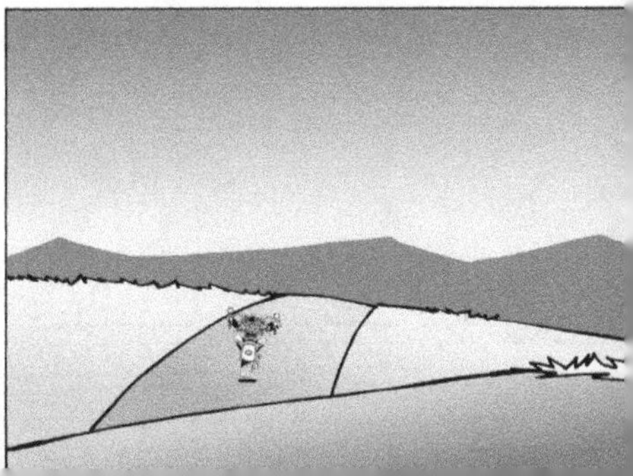

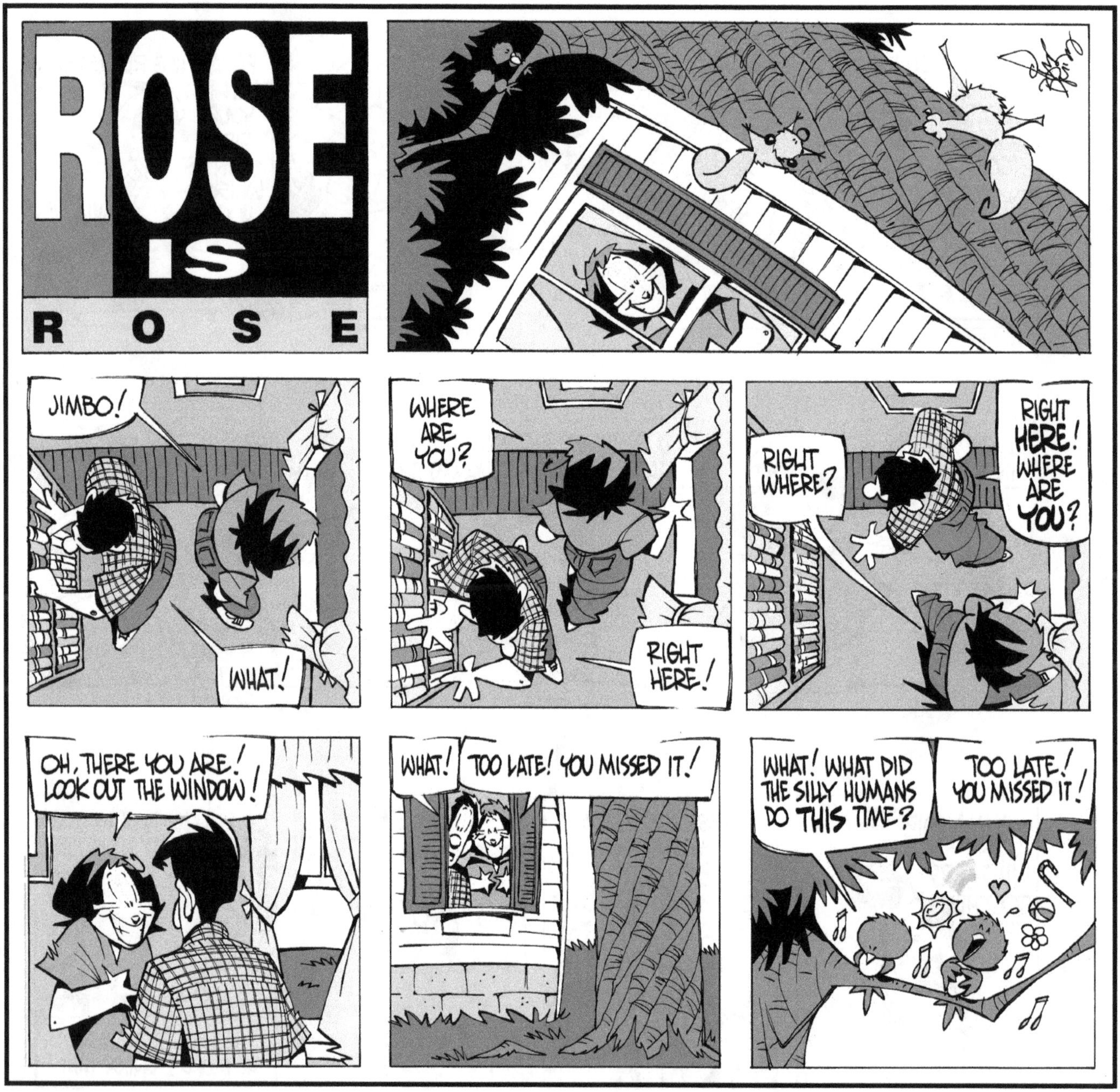

ROSE IS ROSE
JIMBO!
WHAT!
WHERE ARE YOU?
RIGHT HERE!
RIGHT WHERE?
RIGHT HERE! WHERE ARE YOU?
OH, THERE YOU ARE! LOOK OUT THE WINDOW!
WHAT!
TOO LATE! YOU MISSED IT!
WHAT! WHAT DID THE SILLY HUMANS DO THIS TIME?
TOO LATE! YOU MISSED IT!

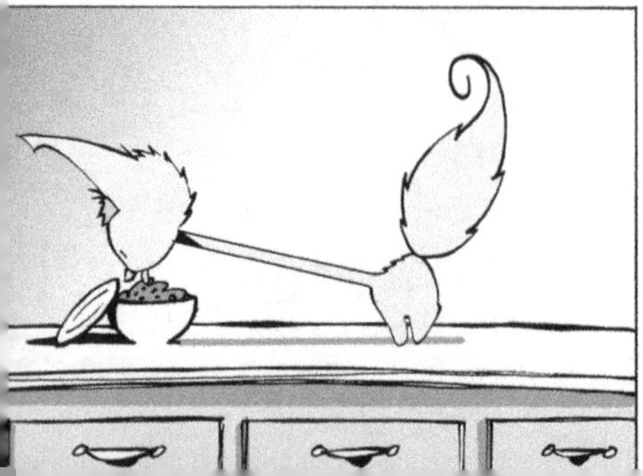

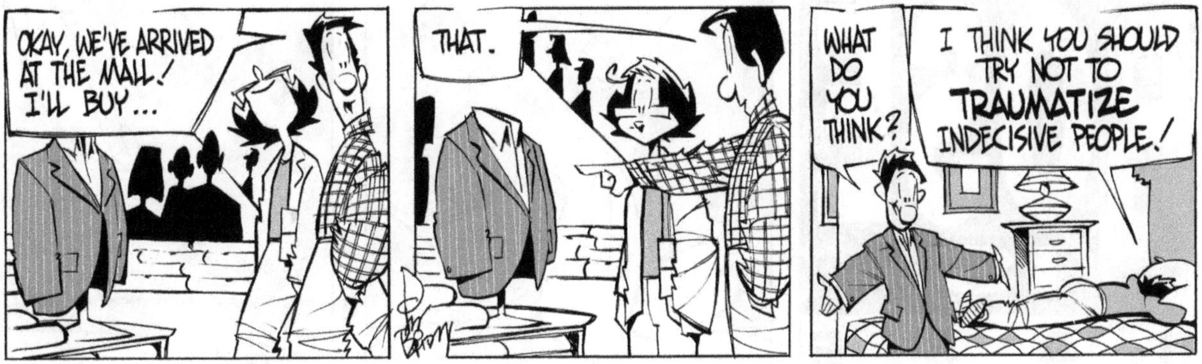
OKAY, WE'VE ARRIVED AT THE MALL! I'LL BUY...
THAT.
WHAT DO YOU THINK?
I THINK YOU SHOULD TRY NOT TO TRAUMATIZE INDECISIVE PEOPLE.!

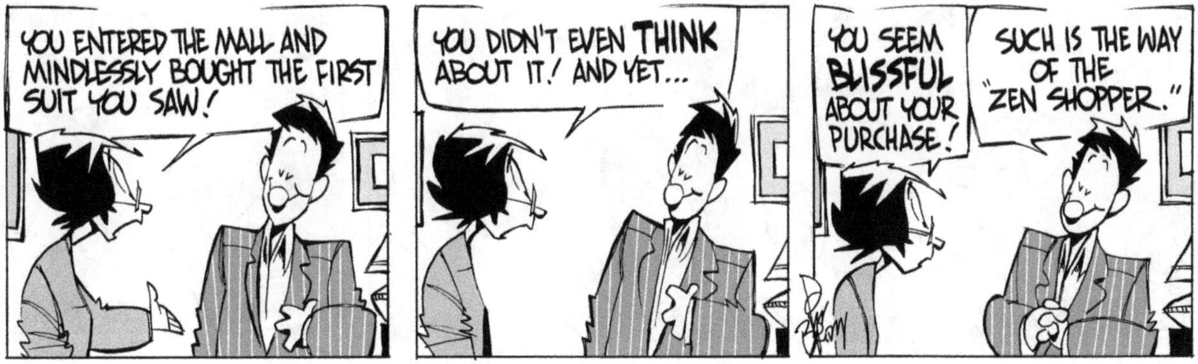
YOU ENTERED THE MALL AND MINDLESSLY BOUGHT THE FIRST SUIT YOU SAW!
YOU DIDN'T EVEN THINK ABOUT IT! AND YET...
YOU SEEM BLISSFUL ABOUT YOUR PURCHASE!
SUCH IS THE WAY OF THE "ZEN SHOPPER."

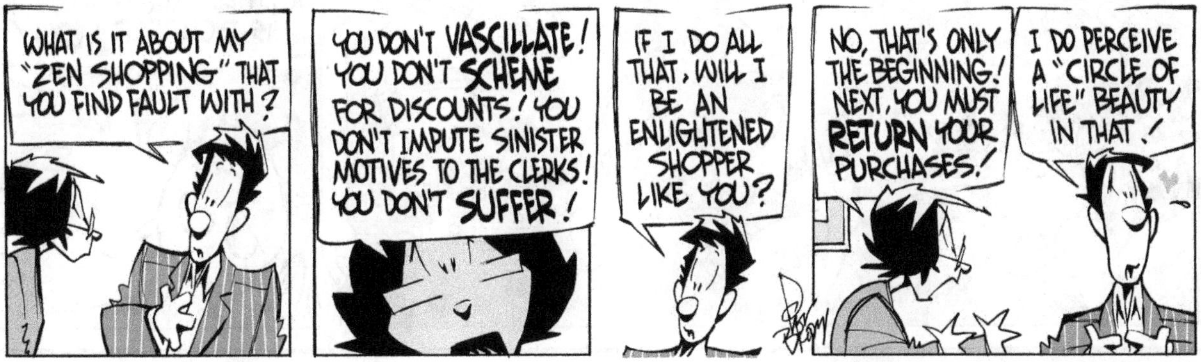
WHAT IS IT ABOUT MY "ZEN SHOPPING" THAT YOU FIND FAULT WITH?
YOU DON'T VASCILLATE! YOU DON'T SCHEME FOR DISCOUNTS! YOU DON'T IMPUTE SINISTER MOTIVES TO THE CLERKS! YOU DON'T SUFFER!
IF I DO ALL THAT, WILL I BE AN ENLIGHTENED SHOPPER LIKE YOU?
NO, THAT'S ONLY THE BEGINNING! NEXT, YOU MUST RETURN YOUR PURCHASES!
I DO PERCEIVE A "CIRCLE OF LIFE" BEAUTY IN THAT!

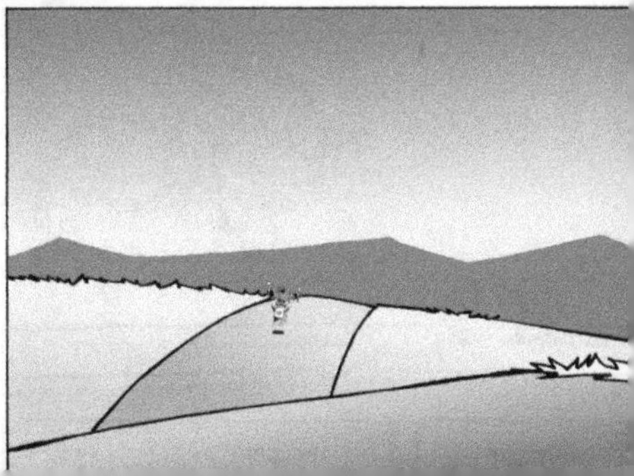

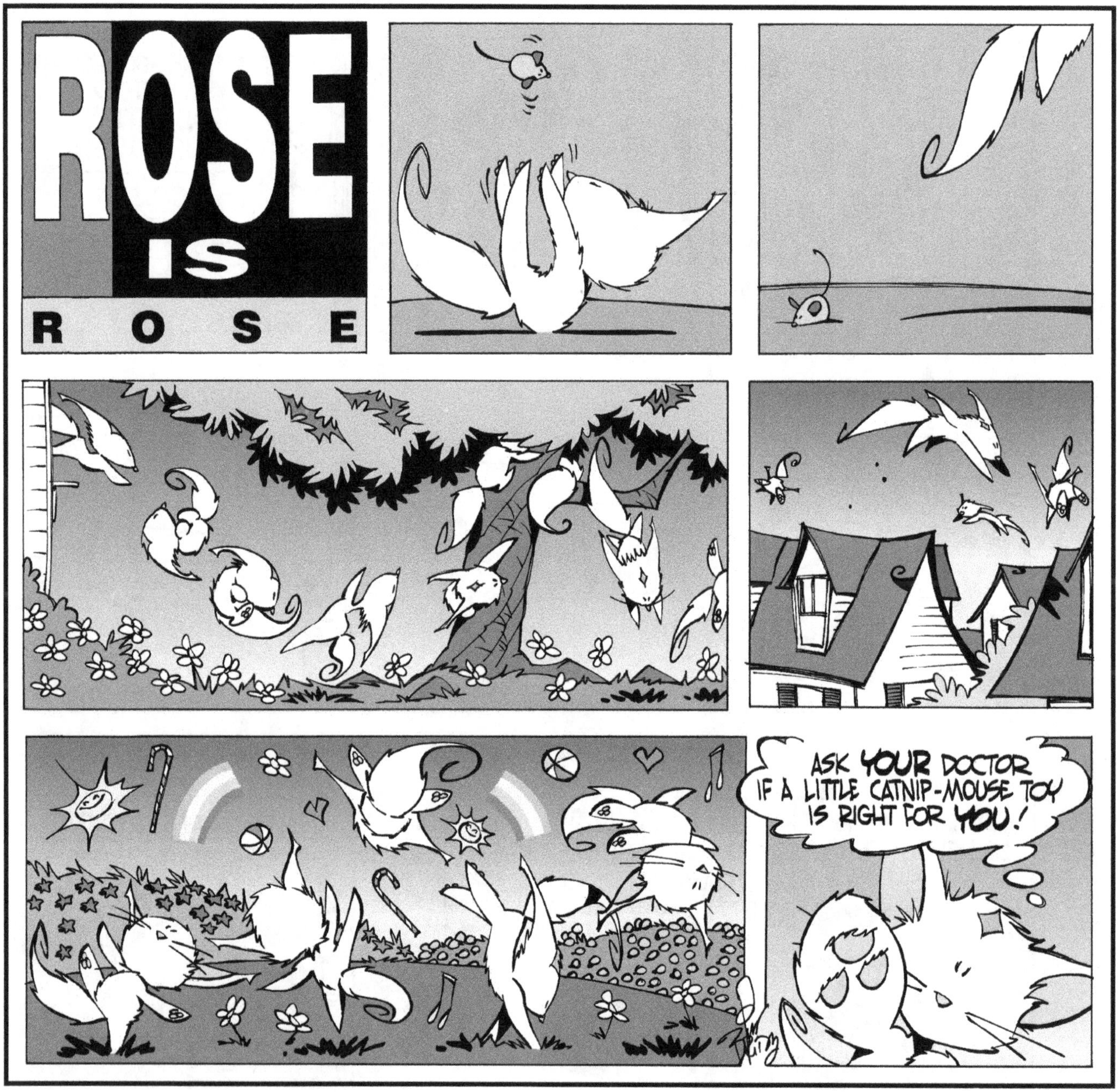
ROSE IS ROSE
ASK **YOUR** DOCTOR IF A LITTLE CATNIP-MOUSE TOY IS RIGHT FOR **YOU**!

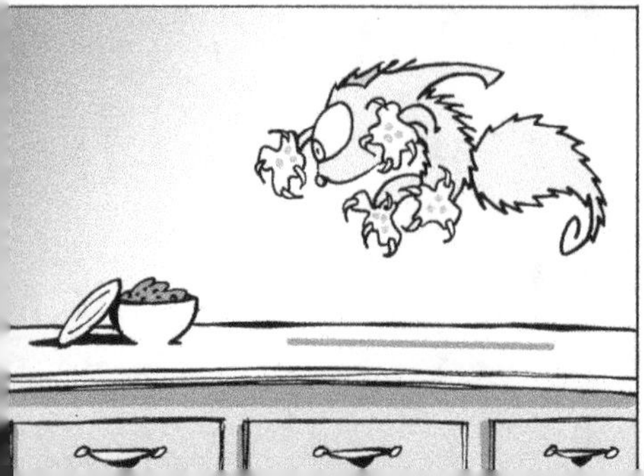

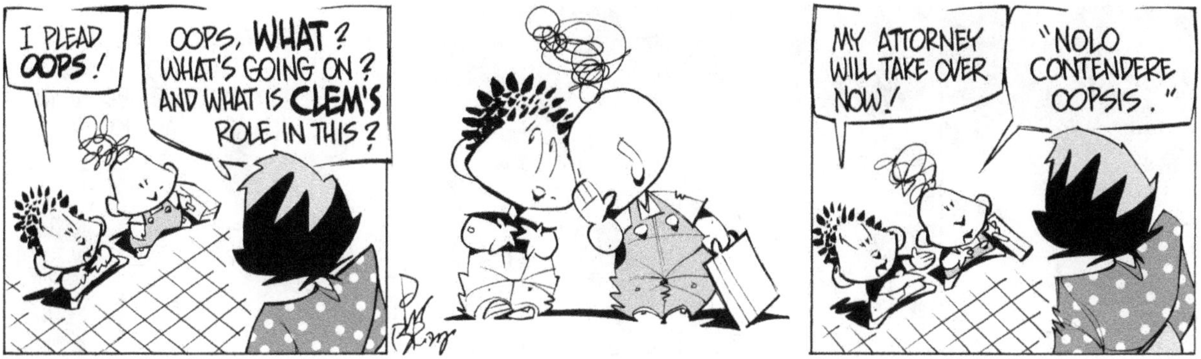
I PLEAD **OOPS**!
OOPS, **WHAT**? WHAT'S GOING ON? AND WHAT IS **CLEM'S** ROLE IN THIS?
MY ATTORNEY WILL TAKE OVER NOW!
"NOLO CONTENDERE OOPSIS."

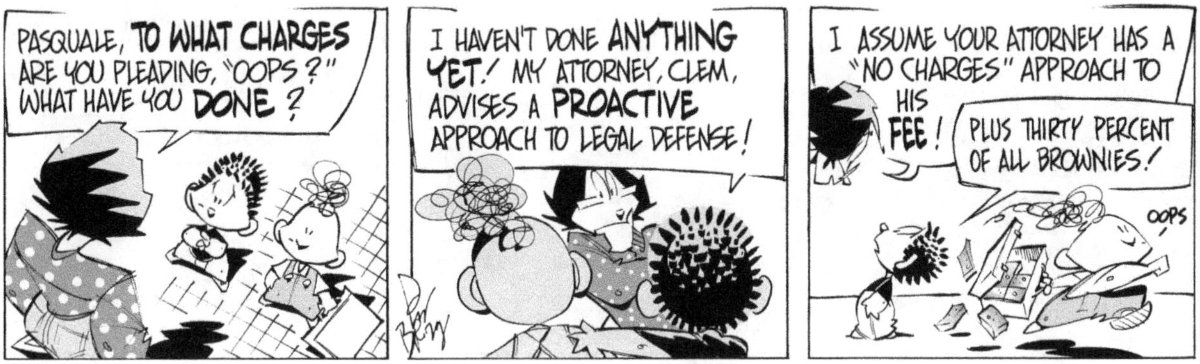
PASQUALE, **TO WHAT CHARGES** ARE YOU PLEADING, "OOPS?" WHAT HAVE YOU **DONE**?
I HAVEN'T DONE **ANYTHING YET**! MY ATTORNEY, CLEM, ADVISES A **PROACTIVE** APPROACH TO LEGAL DEFENSE!
I ASSUME YOUR ATTORNEY HAS A "NO CHARGES" APPROACH TO HIS **FEE**!
PLUS THIRTY PERCENT OF ALL BROWNIES!
OOPS

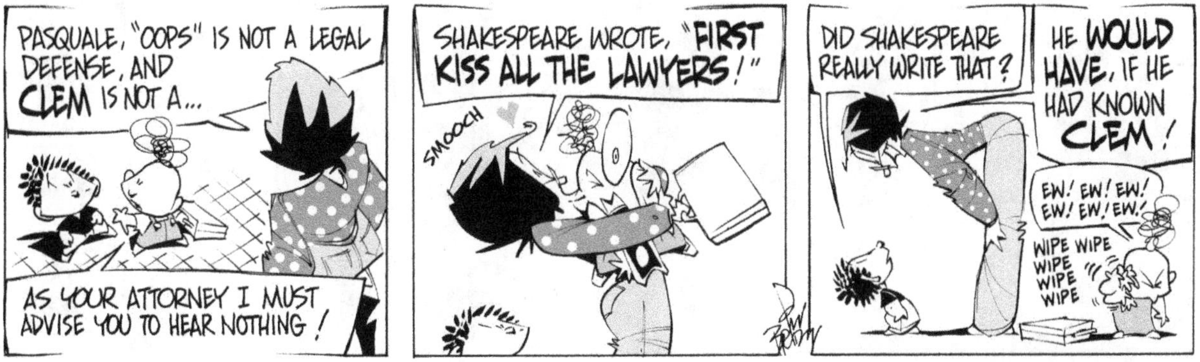
PASQUALE, "OOPS" IS NOT A LEGAL DEFENSE, AND **CLEM** IS NOT A...
AS YOUR ATTORNEY I MUST ADVISE YOU TO HEAR NOTHING!
SHAKESPEARE WROTE, "**FIRST KISS ALL THE LAWYERS**!"
SMOOCH
DID SHAKESPEARE REALLY WRITE THAT?
HE **WOULD HAVE**, IF HE HAD KNOWN **CLEM**!
EW! EW! EW! EW! EW! EW!
WIPE WIPE WIPE WIPE WIPE

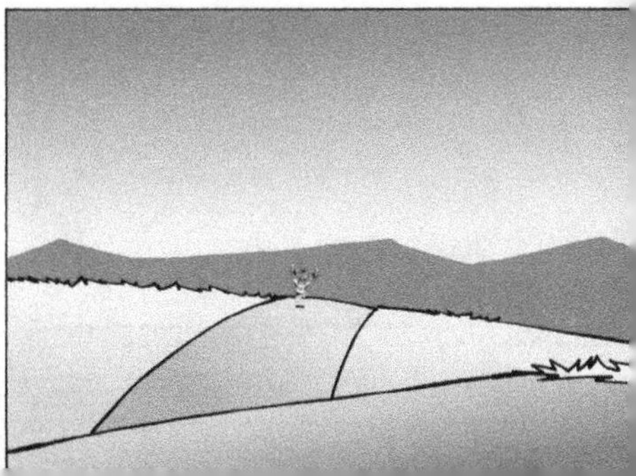

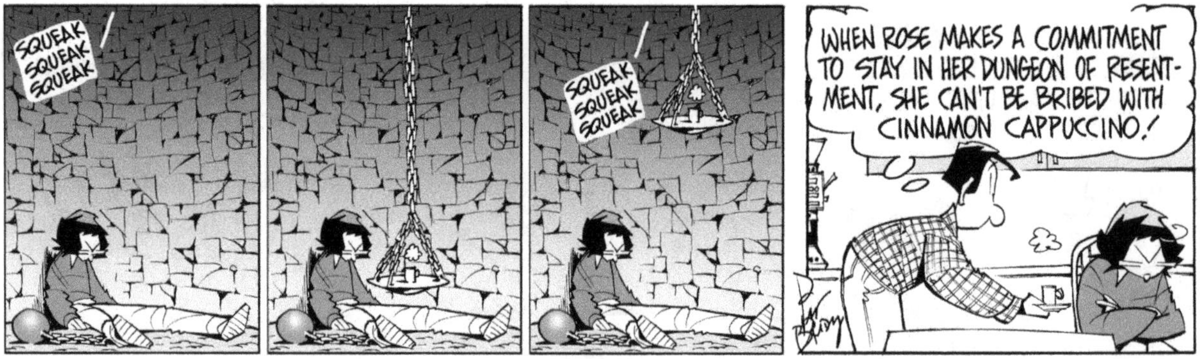
SQUEAK SQUEAK SQUEAK
SQUEAK SQUEAK SQUEAK
WHEN ROSE MAKES A COMMITMENT TO STAY IN HER DUNGEON OF RESENTMENT, SHE CAN'T BE BRIBED WITH CINNAMON CAPPUCCINO!

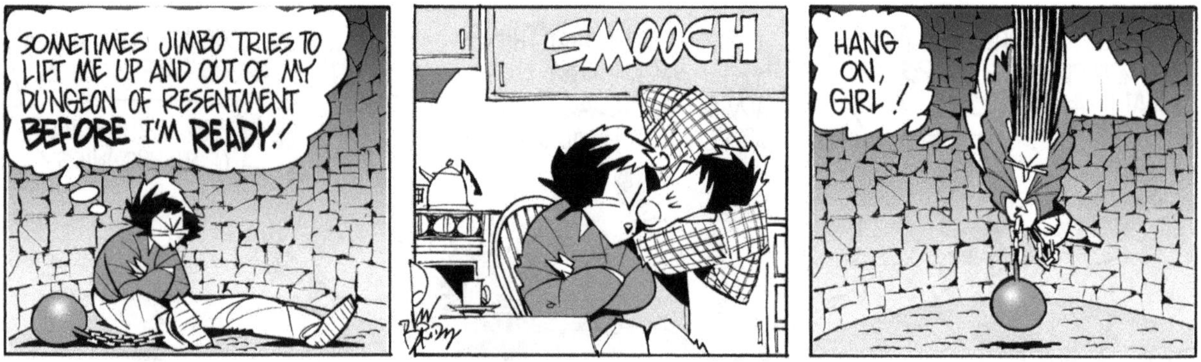
SOMETIMES JIMBO TRIES TO LIFT ME UP AND OUT OF MY DUNGEON OF RESENTMENT **BEFORE** I'M **READY**!
SMOOCH
HANG ON, GIRL!

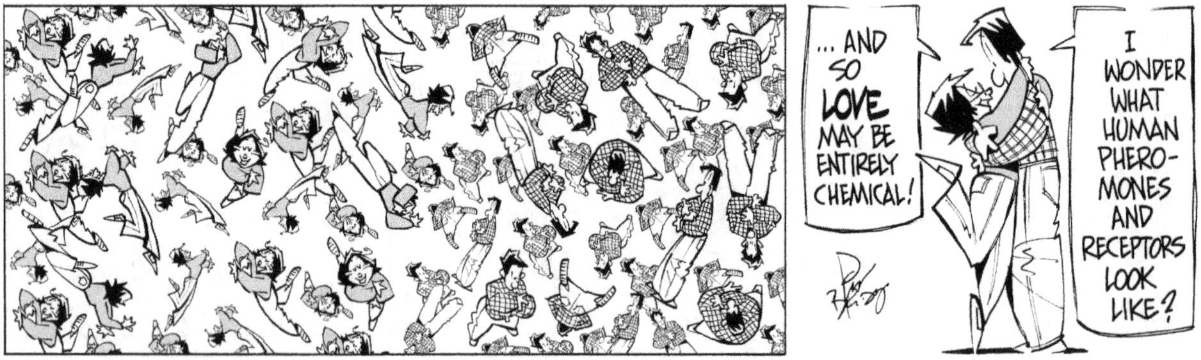
... AND SO **LOVE** MAY BE ENTIRELY CHEMICAL!
I WONDER WHAT HUMAN PHEROMONES AND RECEPTORS LOOK LIKE?

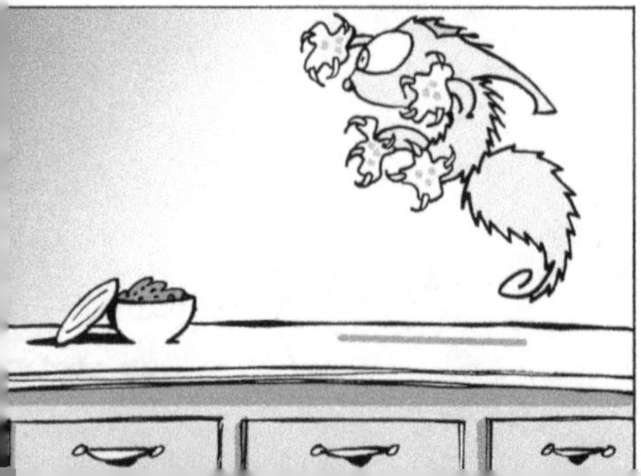

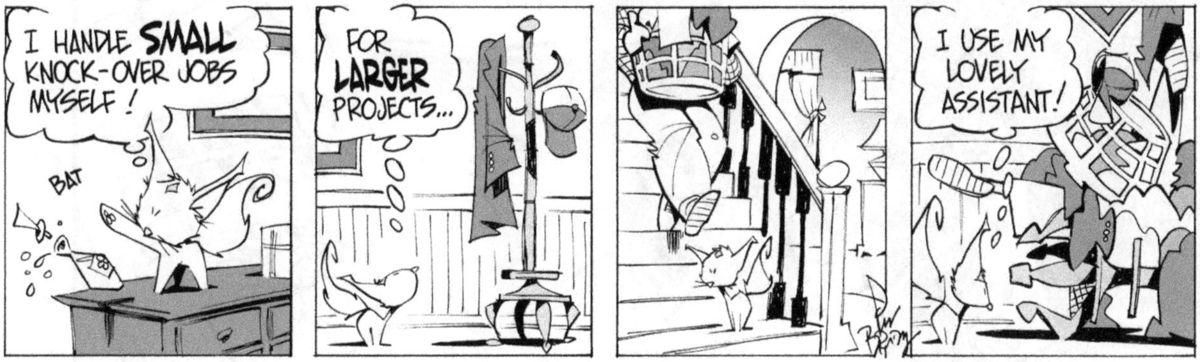
I HANDLE SMALL KNOCK-OVER JOBS MYSELF!
BAT
FOR LARGER PROJECTS...
I USE MY LOVELY ASSISTANT!

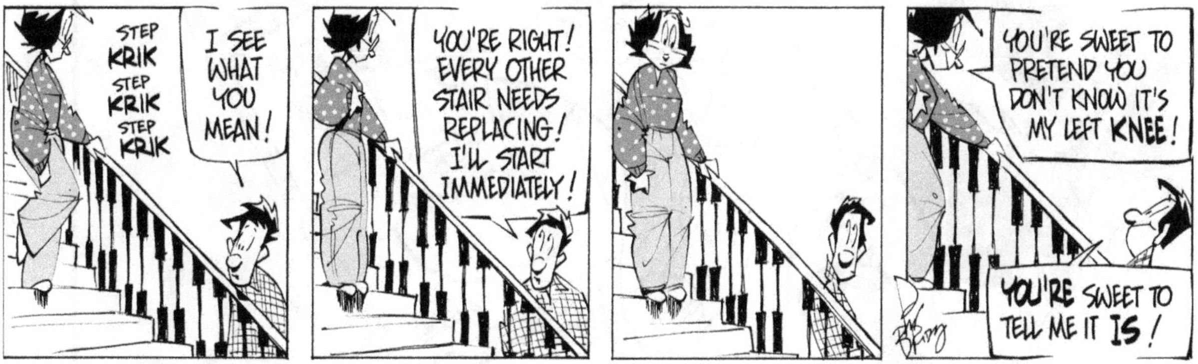
STEP KRIK STEP KRIK STEP KRIK
I SEE WHAT YOU MEAN!
YOU'RE RIGHT! EVERY OTHER STAIR NEEDS REPLACING! I'LL START IMMEDIATELY!
YOU'RE SWEET TO PRETEND YOU DON'T KNOW IT'S MY LEFT KNEE!
YOU'RE SWEET TO TELL ME IT IS!

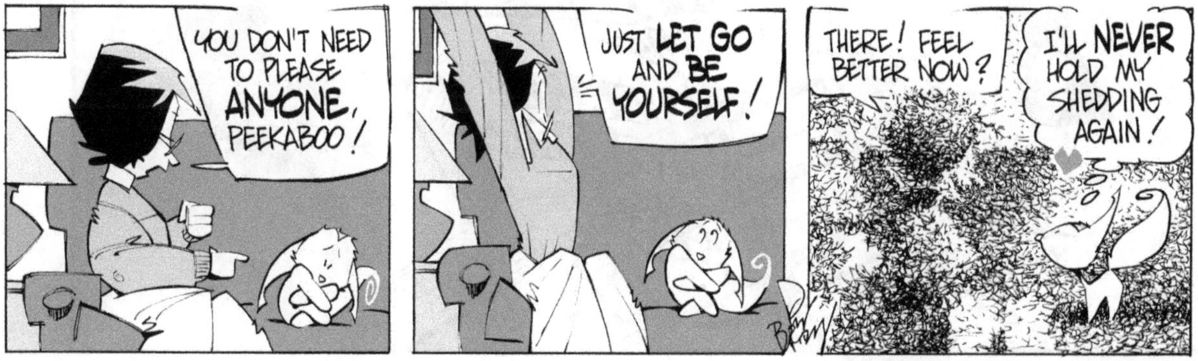
YOU DON'T NEED TO PLEASE ANYONE, PEEKABOO!
JUST LET GO AND BE YOURSELF!
THERE! FEEL BETTER NOW?
I'LL NEVER HOLD MY SHEDDING AGAIN!

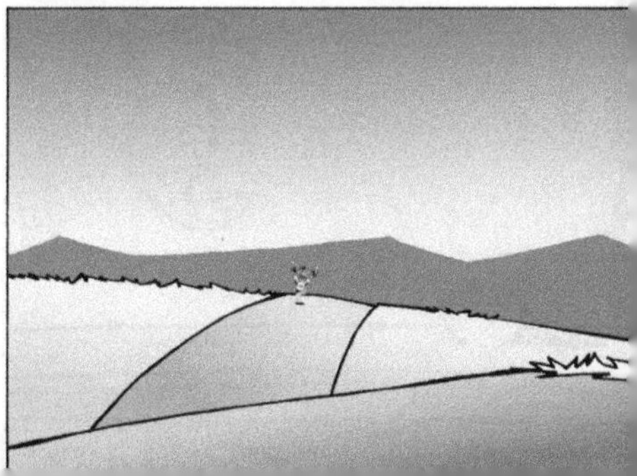

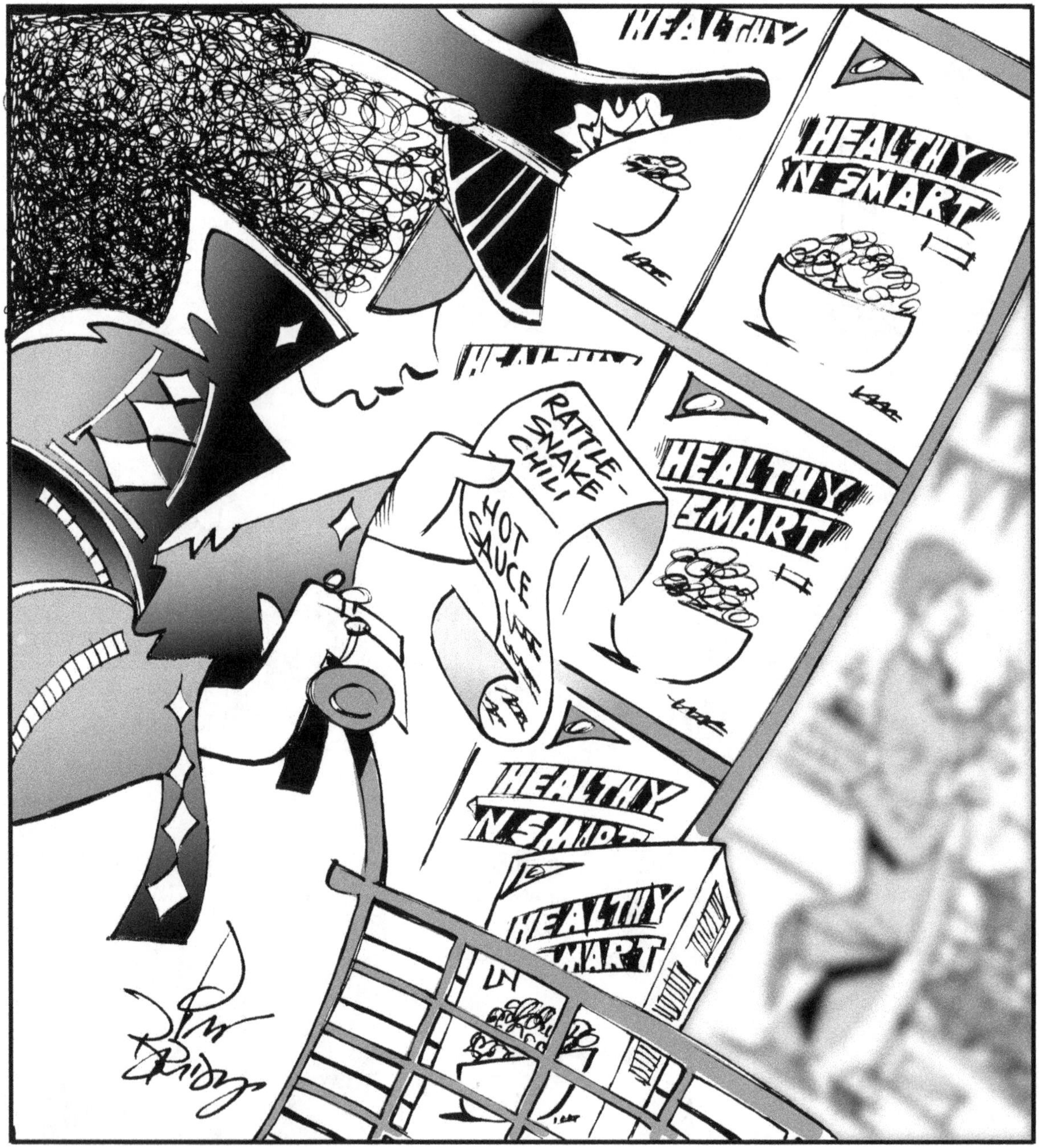
HEALTHY
HEALTHY 'N SMART
RATTLE-SNAKE CHILI
HOT SAUCE
HEALTHY SMART
HEALTHY 'N SMART
HEALTHY SMART

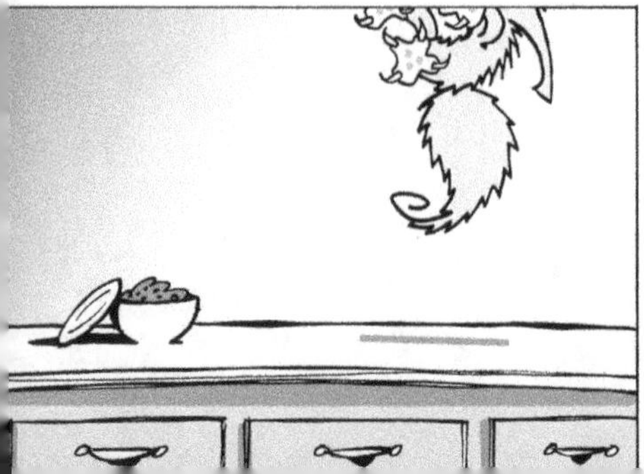

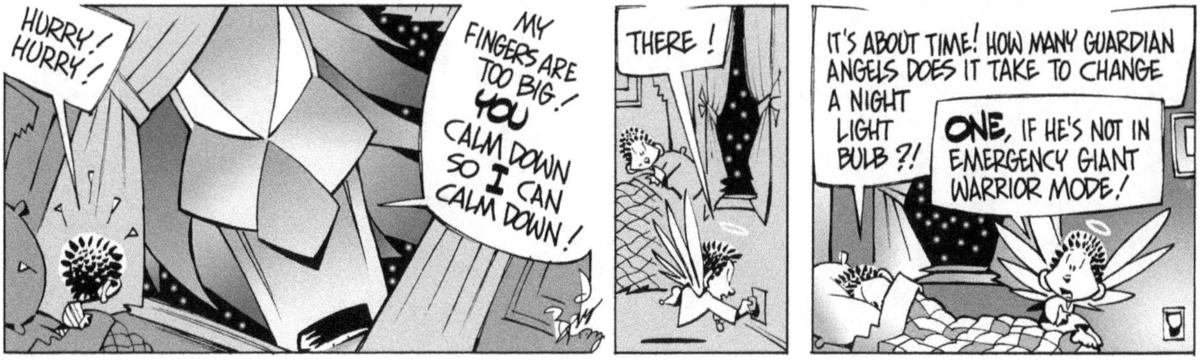
HURRY! HURRY!
MY FINGERS ARE TOO BIG! **YOU** CALM DOWN SO **I** CAN CALM DOWN!
THERE!
IT'S ABOUT TIME! HOW MANY GUARDIAN ANGELS DOES IT TAKE TO CHANGE A NIGHT LIGHT BULB ?!
ONE, IF HE'S NOT IN EMERGENCY GIANT WARRIOR MODE!

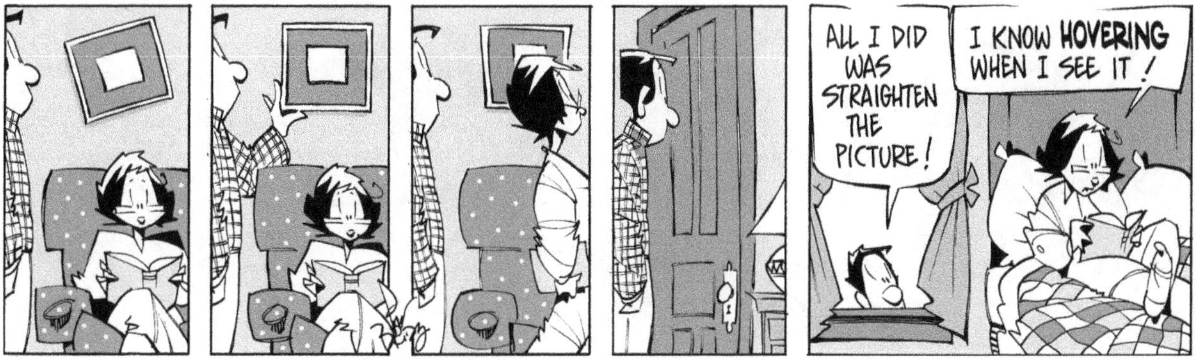
ALL I DID WAS STRAIGHTEN THE PICTURE!
I KNOW **HOVERING** WHEN I SEE IT!

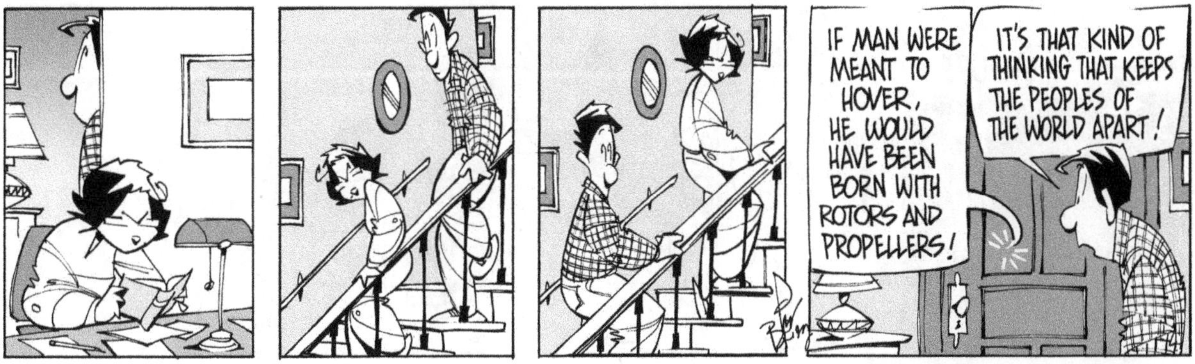
IF MAN WERE MEANT TO HOVER, HE WOULD HAVE BEEN BORN WITH ROTORS AND PROPELLERS!
IT'S THAT KIND OF THINKING THAT KEEPS THE PEOPLES OF THE WORLD APART!

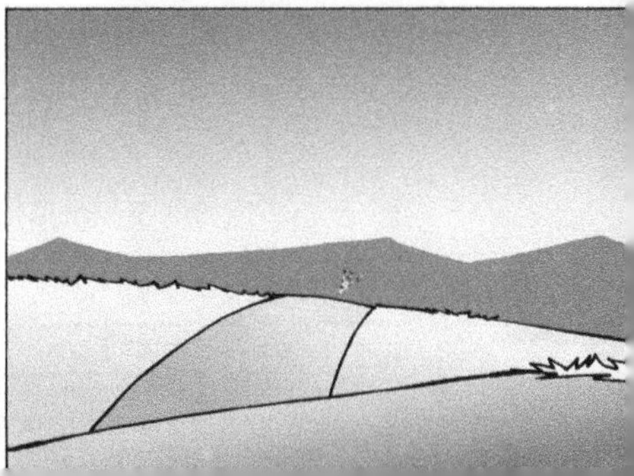

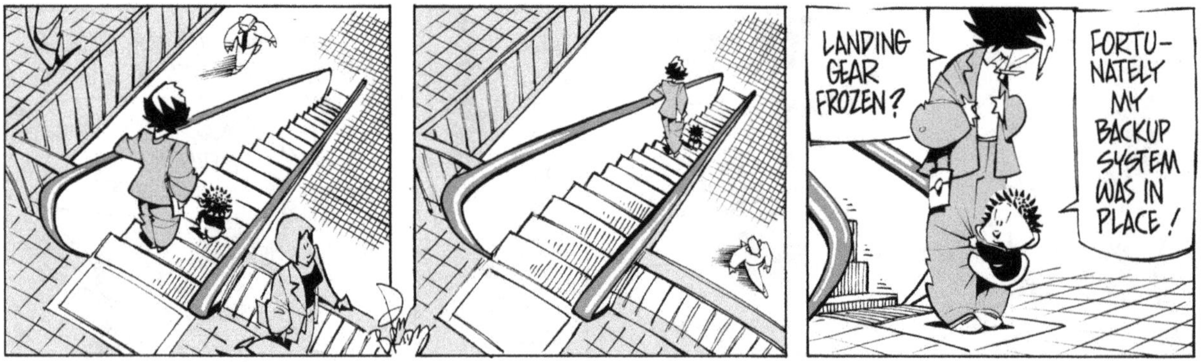
LANDING GEAR FROZEN?
FORTU-NATELY MY BACKUP SYSTEM WAS IN PLACE!

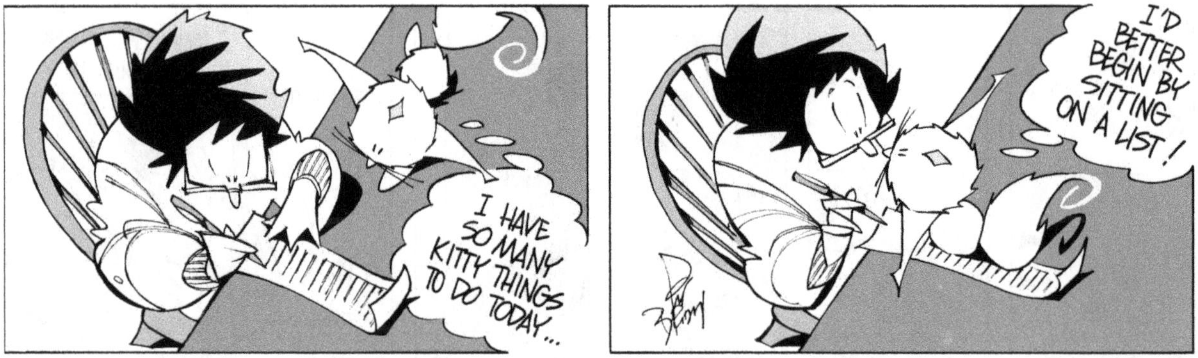
I HAVE SO MANY KITTY THINGS TO DO TODAY...
I'D BETTER BEGIN BY SITTING ON A LIST!

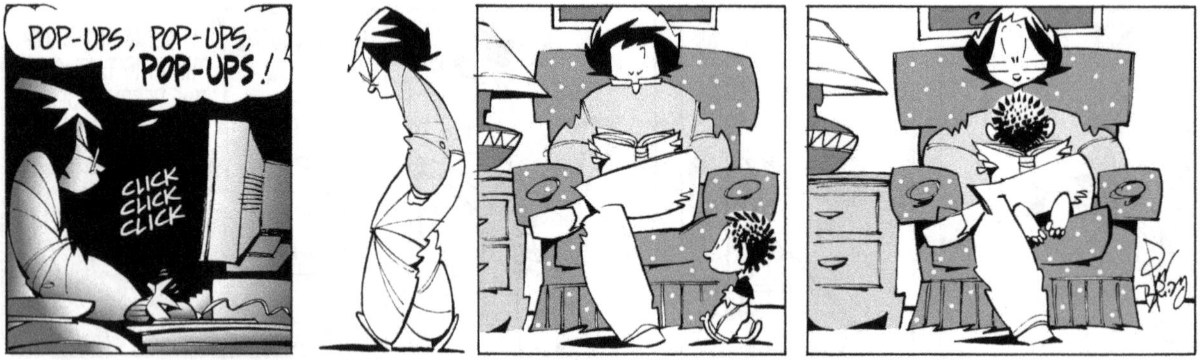
POP-UPS, POP-UPS, POP-UPS!
CLICK CLICK CLICK

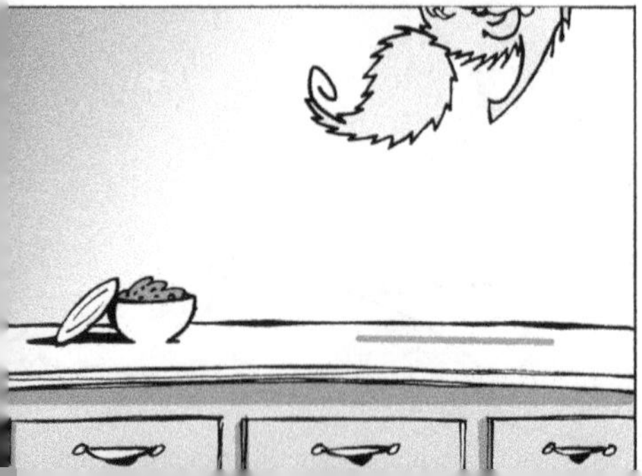

ROSE IS ROSE
HIS NAVIGATION IS IMPROVING!
IT'S NOT EASY DOCKING A DREAMSHIP IN A SPACE STATION RESTROOM FACILITY WITHOUT ANY ACCIDENTS!
Z

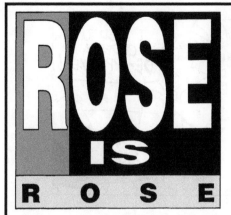

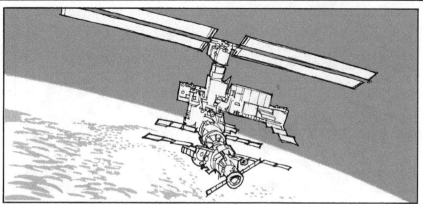

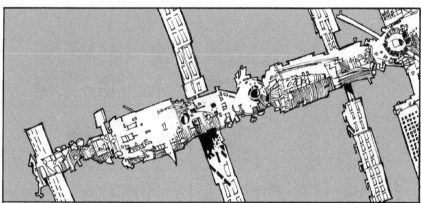

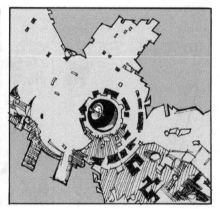

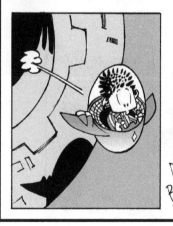

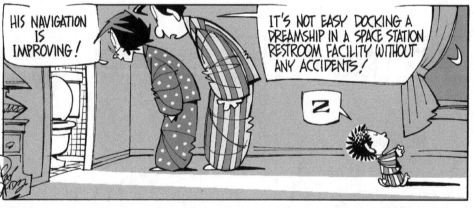

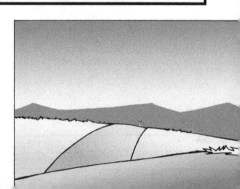

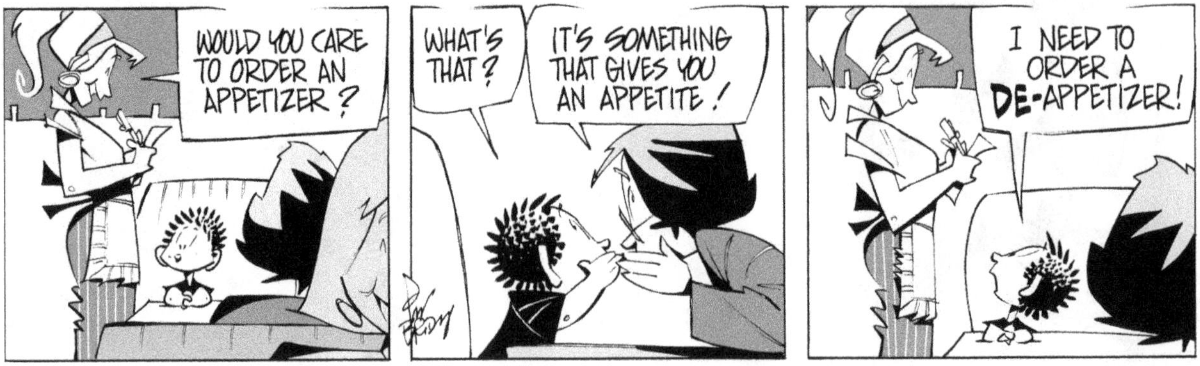
WOULD YOU CARE TO ORDER AN APPETIZER?
WHAT'S THAT?
IT'S SOMETHING THAT GIVES YOU AN APPETITE!
I NEED TO ORDER A DE-APPETIZER!

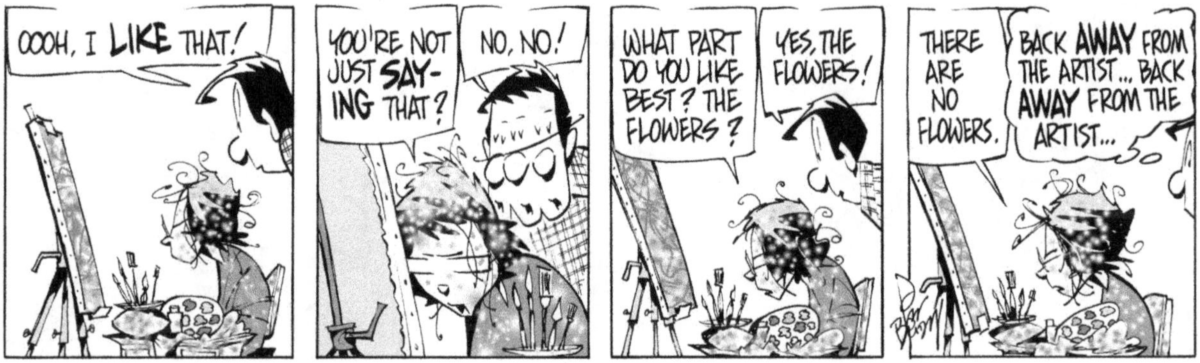
OOOH, I LIKE THAT!
YOU'RE NOT JUST SAYING THAT?
NO, NO!
WHAT PART DO YOU LIKE BEST? THE FLOWERS?
YES, THE FLOWERS!
THERE ARE NO FLOWERS.
BACK AWAY FROM THE ARTIST... BACK AWAY FROM THE ARTIST...

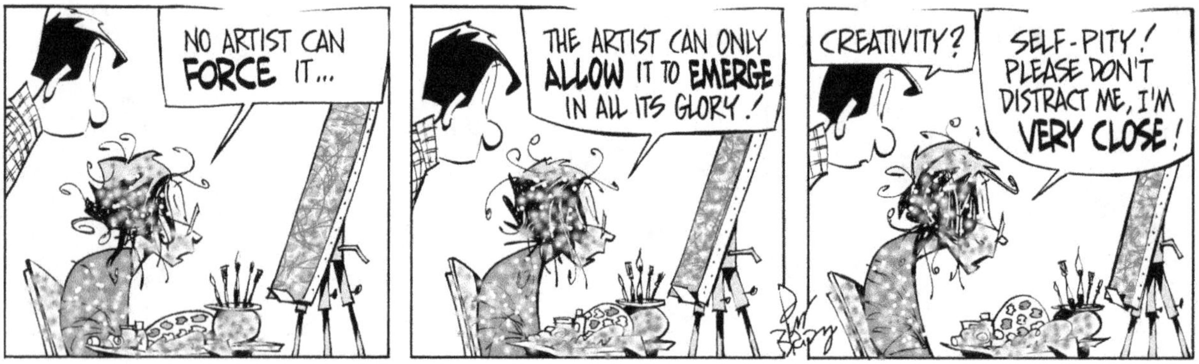
NO ARTIST CAN FORCE IT...
THE ARTIST CAN ONLY ALLOW IT TO EMERGE IN ALL ITS GLORY!
CREATIVITY?
SELF-PITY! PLEASE DON'T DISTRACT ME, I'M VERY CLOSE!

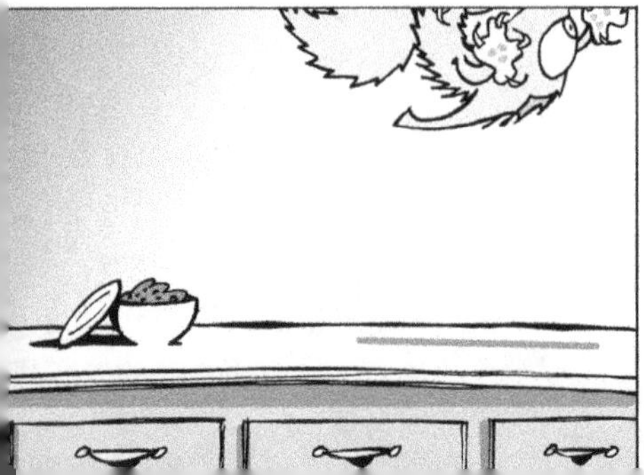

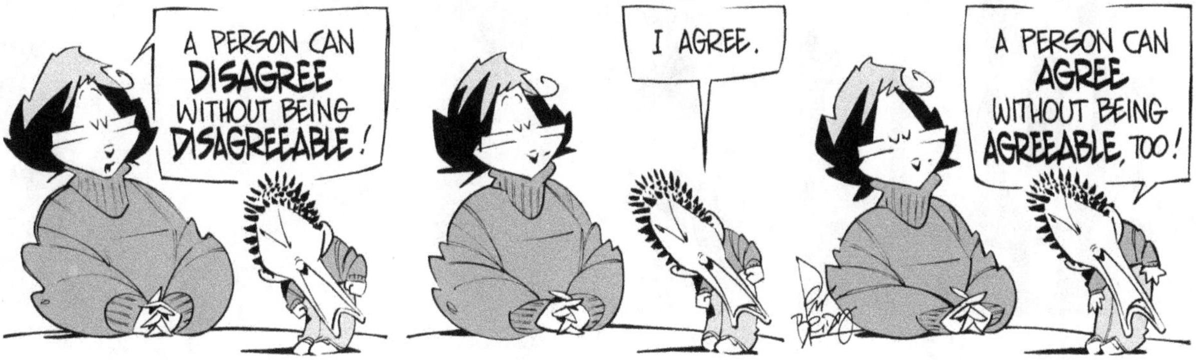
A PERSON CAN DISAGREE WITHOUT BEING DISAGREEABLE!
I AGREE.
A PERSON CAN AGREE WITHOUT BEING AGREEABLE, TOO!

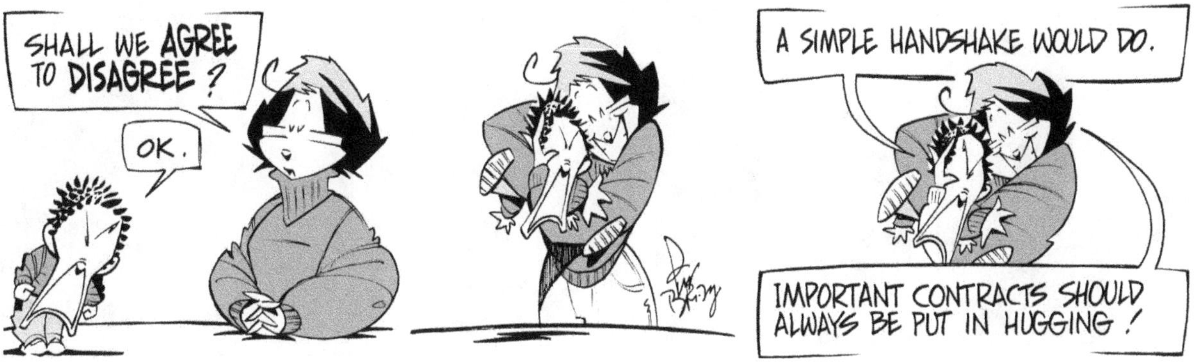
SHALL WE AGREE TO DISAGREE?
OK.
A SIMPLE HANDSHAKE WOULD DO.
IMPORTANT CONTRACTS SHOULD ALWAYS BE PUT IN HUGGING!

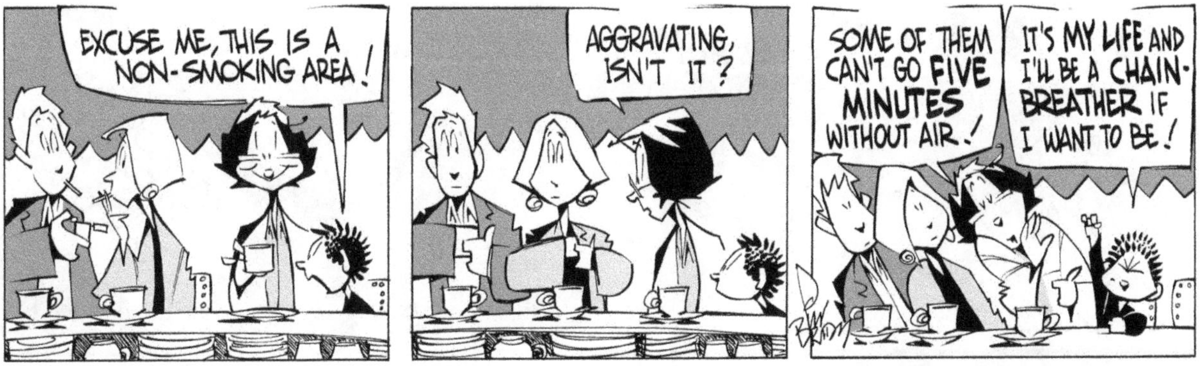
EXCUSE ME, THIS IS A NON-SMOKING AREA!
AGGRAVATING, ISN'T IT?
SOME OF THEM CAN'T GO FIVE MINUTES WITHOUT AIR!
IT'S MY LIFE AND I'LL BE A CHAIN-BREATHER IF I WANT TO BE!

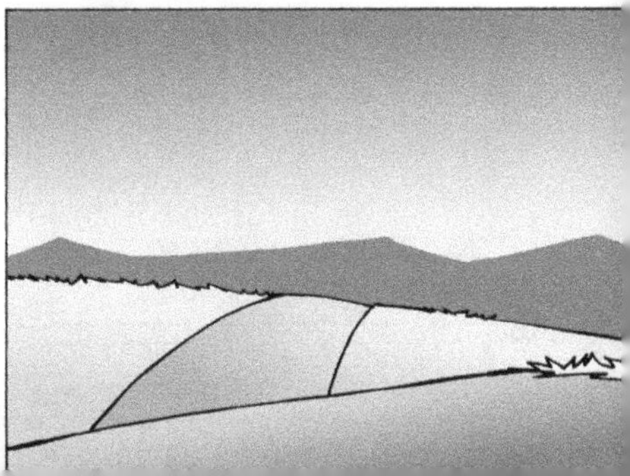

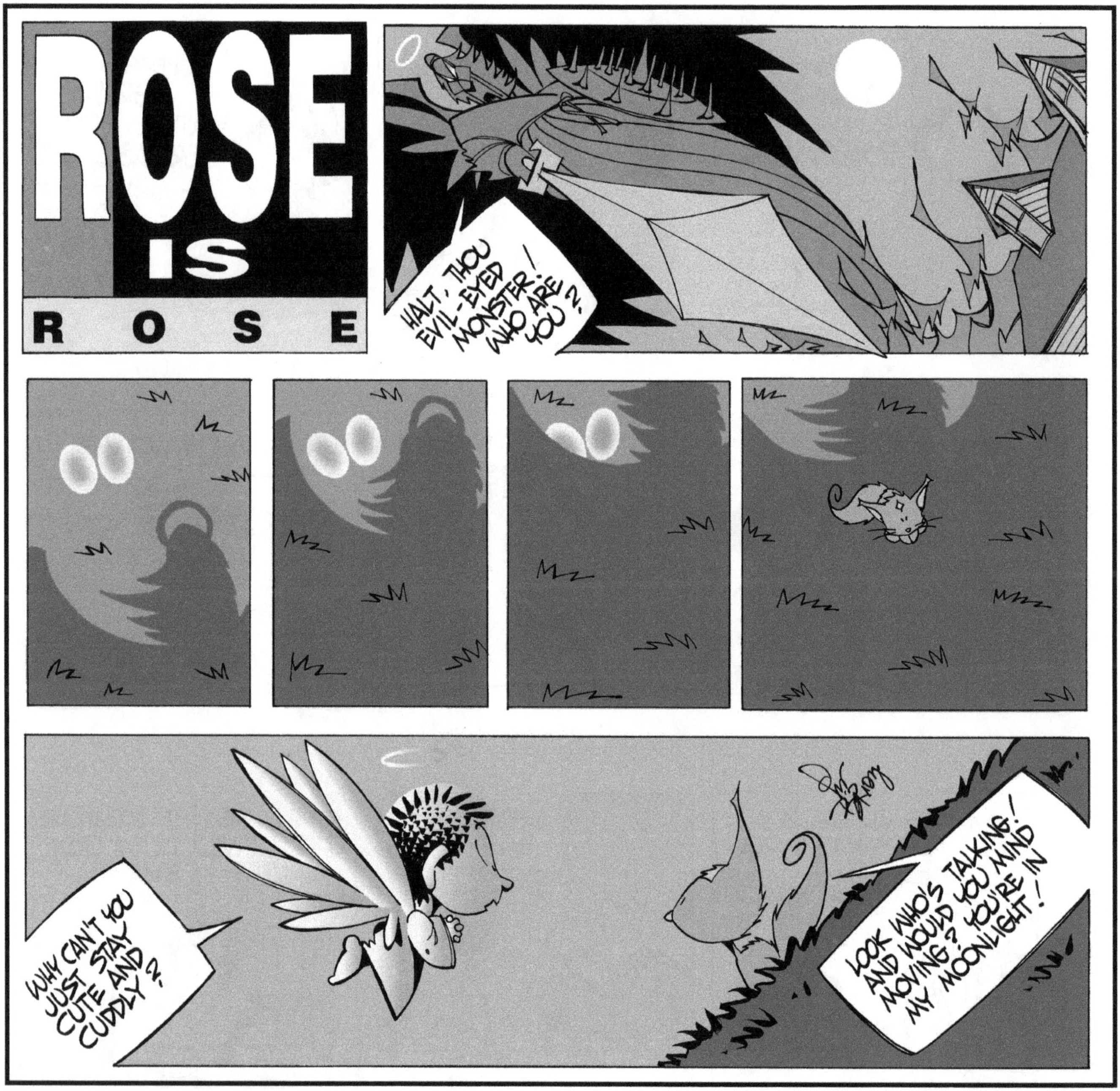
ROSE IS ROSE
HALT, THOU EVIL-EYED MONSTER! WHO ARE YOU?
WHY CAN'T YOU JUST STAY CUTE AND CUDDLY?
LOOK WHO'S TALKING! AND WOULD YOU MIND MOVING? YOU'RE IN MY MOONLIGHT!

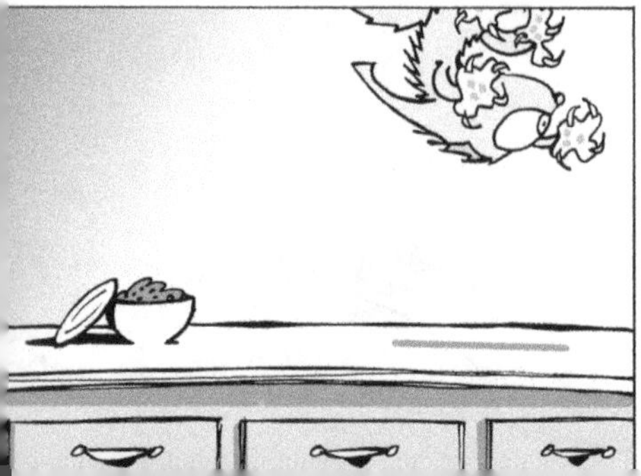

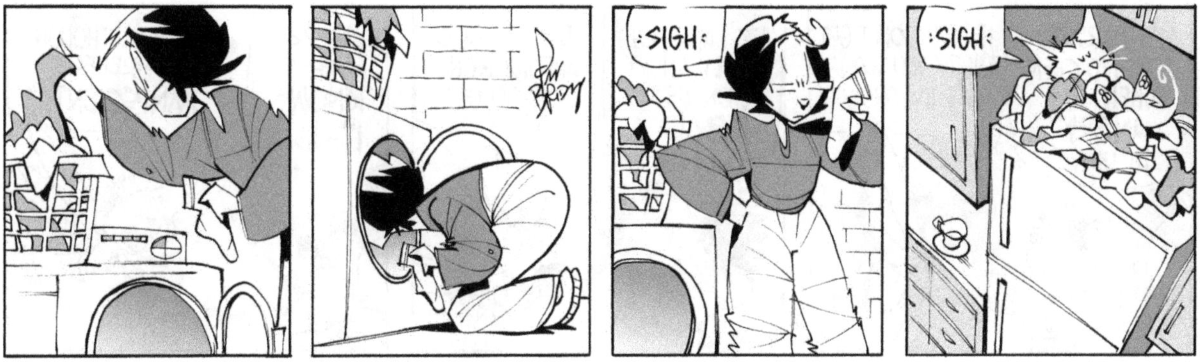
:SIGH:
:SIGH:

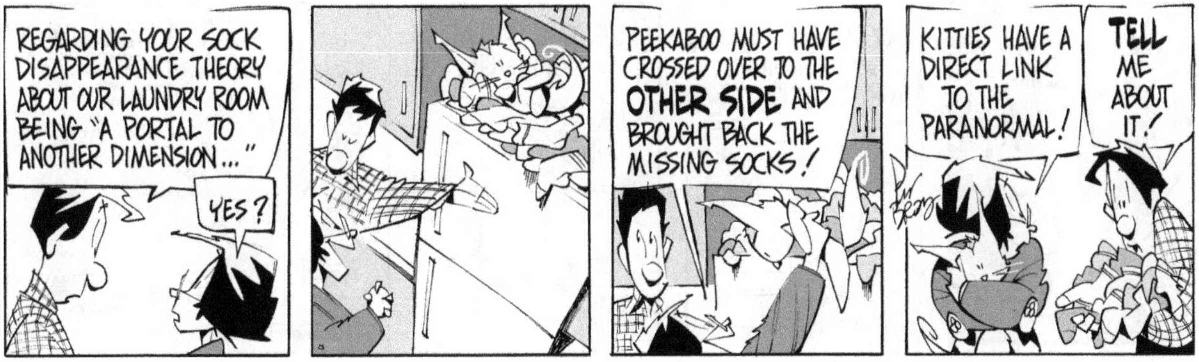
REGARDING YOUR SOCK DISAPPEARANCE THEORY ABOUT OUR LAUNDRY ROOM BEING "A PORTAL TO ANOTHER DIMENSION..."
YES?
PEEKABOO MUST HAVE CROSSED OVER TO THE OTHER SIDE AND BROUGHT BACK THE MISSING SOCKS!
KITTIES HAVE A DIRECT LINK TO THE PARANORMAL!
TELL ME ABOUT IT!

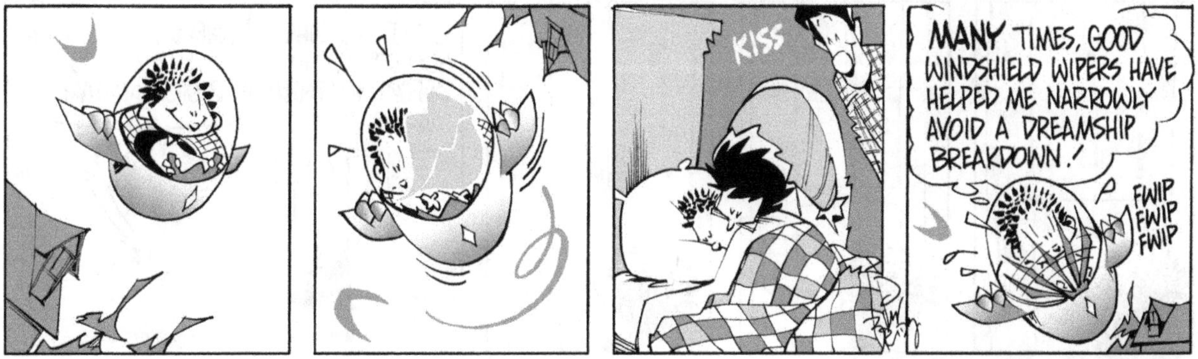
KISS
MANY TIMES, GOOD WINDSHIELD WIPERS HAVE HELPED ME NARROWLY AVOID A DREAMSHIP BREAKDOWN!
FWIP FWIP FWIP

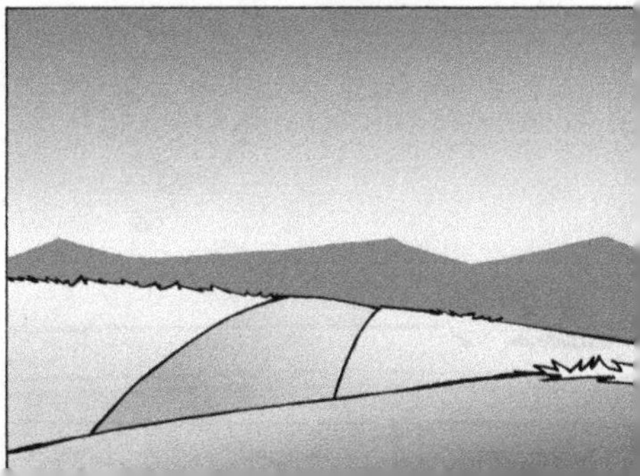

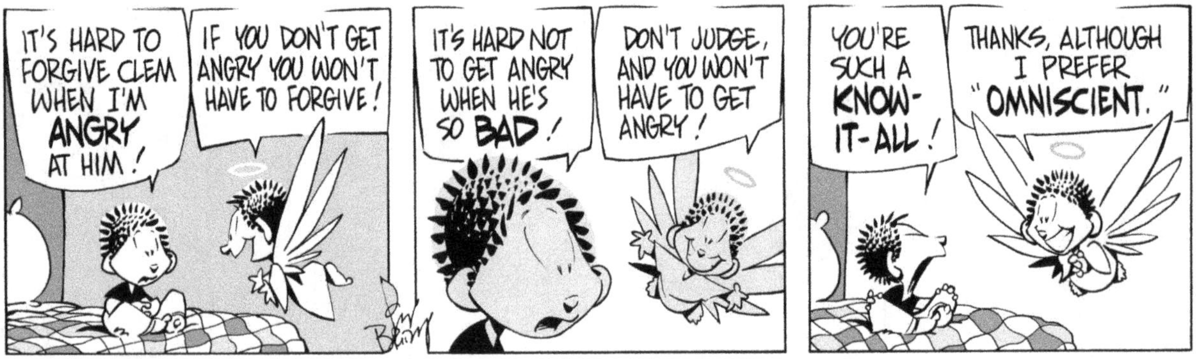
IT'S HARD TO FORGIVE CLEM WHEN I'M ANGRY AT HIM!
IF YOU DON'T GET ANGRY YOU WON'T HAVE TO FORGIVE!
IT'S HARD NOT TO GET ANGRY WHEN HE'S SO BAD!
DON'T JUDGE, AND YOU WON'T HAVE TO GET ANGRY!
YOU'RE SUCH A KNOW-IT-ALL!
THANKS, ALTHOUGH I PREFER "OMNISCIENT."

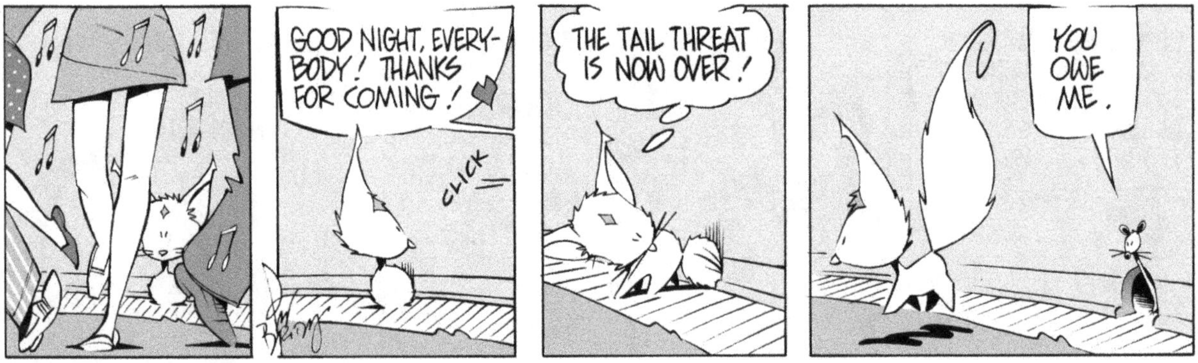
GOOD NIGHT, EVERY-BODY! THANKS FOR COMING!
CLICK
THE TAIL THREAT IS NOW OVER!
YOU OWE ME.

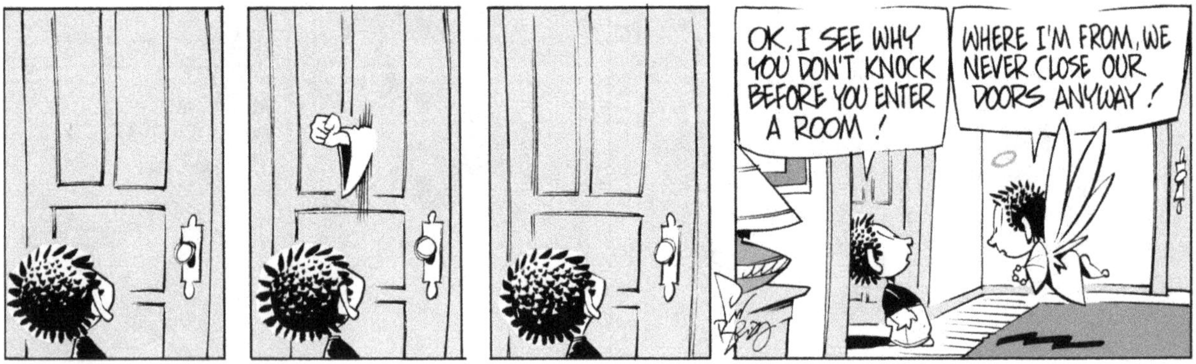
OK, I SEE WHY YOU DON'T KNOCK BEFORE YOU ENTER A ROOM!
WHERE I'M FROM, WE NEVER CLOSE OUR DOORS ANYWAY!

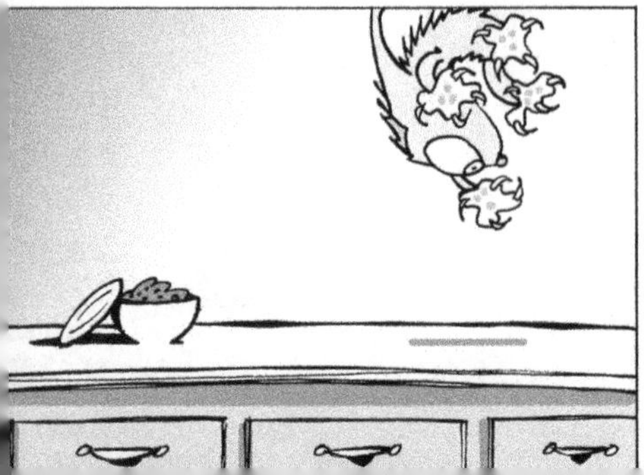

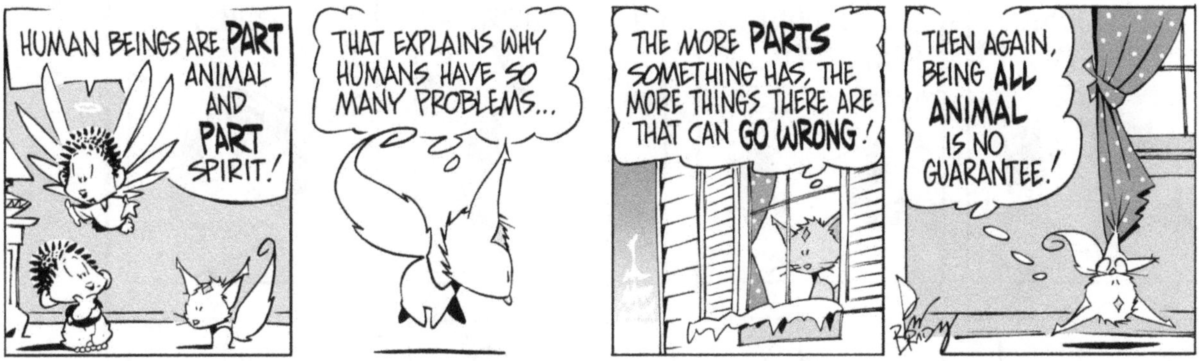
HUMAN BEINGS ARE PART ANIMAL AND PART SPIRIT!
THAT EXPLAINS WHY HUMANS HAVE SO MANY PROBLEMS...
THE MORE PARTS SOMETHING HAS, THE MORE THINGS THERE ARE THAT CAN GO WRONG!
THEN AGAIN, BEING ALL ANIMAL IS NO GUARANTEE!

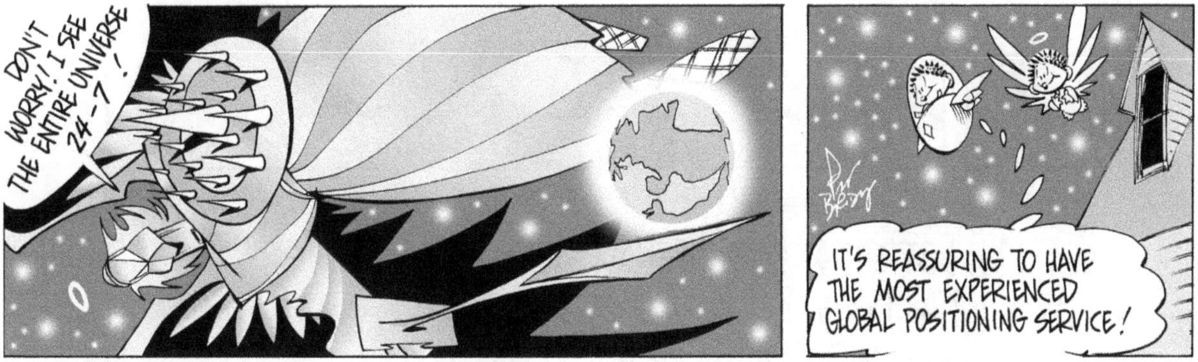
DON'T WORRY! I SEE THE ENTIRE UNIVERSE 24-7!
IT'S REASSURING TO HAVE THE MOST EXPERIENCED GLOBAL POSITIONING SERVICE!

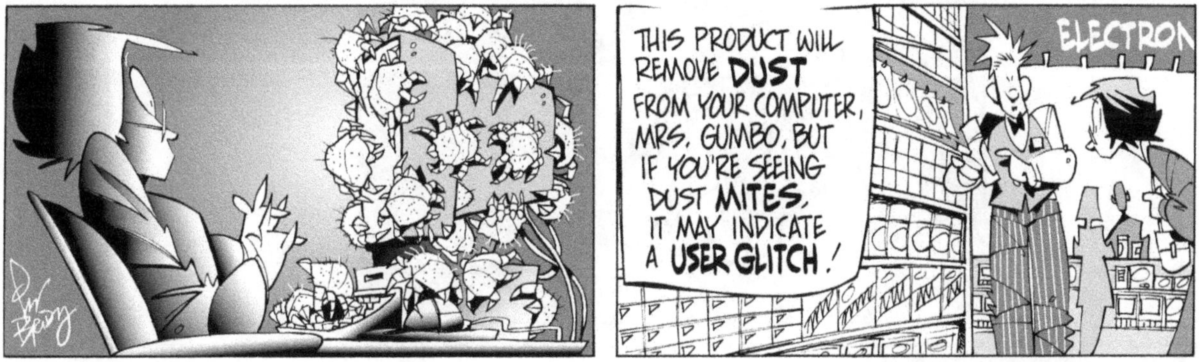
THIS PRODUCT WILL REMOVE DUST FROM YOUR COMPUTER, MRS. GUMBO, BUT IF YOU'RE SEEING DUST MITES, IT MAY INDICATE A USER GLITCH!
ELECTRON

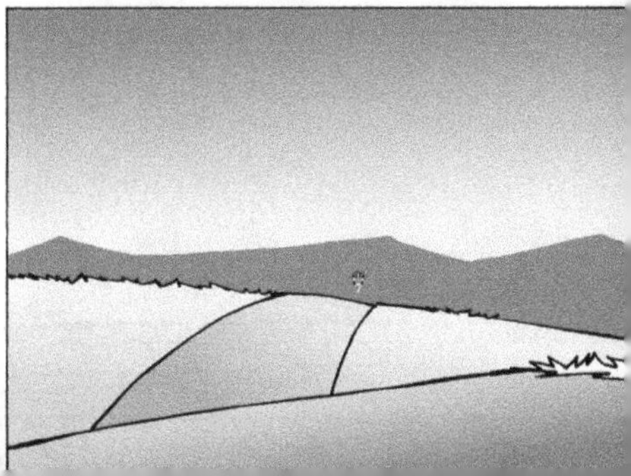

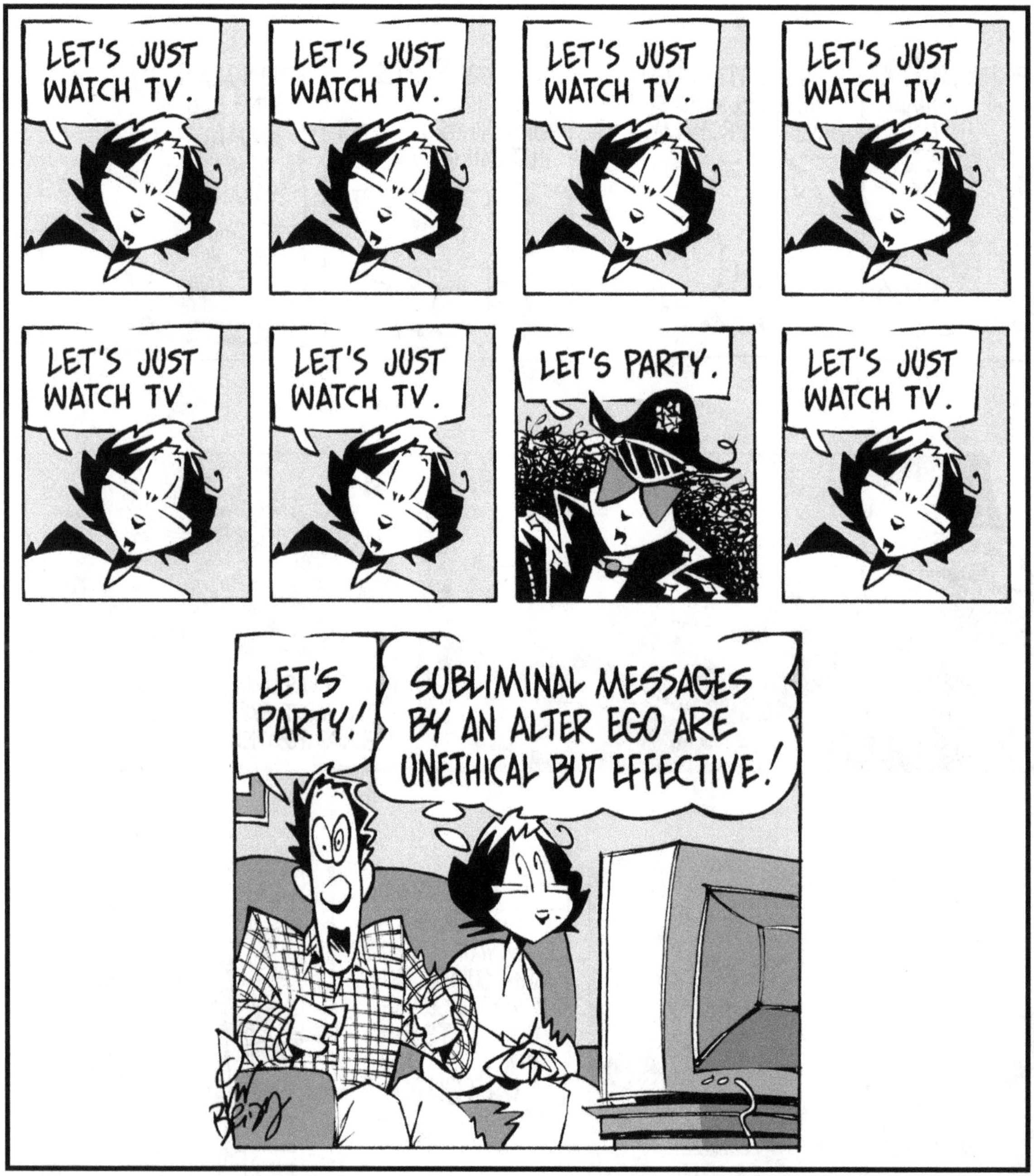
LET'S JUST WATCH TV.
LET'S JUST WATCH TV.
LET'S JUST WATCH TV.
LET'S JUST WATCH TV.
LET'S JUST WATCH TV.
LET'S JUST WATCH TV.
LET'S PARTY.
LET'S JUST WATCH TV.
LET'S PARTY!
SUBLIMINAL MESSAGES BY AN ALTER EGO ARE UNETHICAL BUT EFFECTIVE!

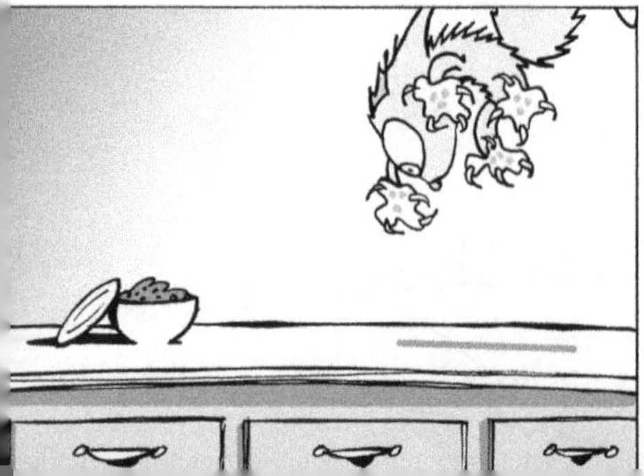

OATMEAL ?
OATMEAL ?
OATMEAL ?
OATMEAL ?
OATMEAL ?
OATMEAL ?
OATMEAL ?
JALAPEÑO OMELET ?
OATMEAL ?
I'M SORRY MY ALTER EGO USED SUBLIMINAL MESSAGES TO MAKE YOU WANT TO PARTY LAST NIGHT ! IT WON'T HAPPEN AGAIN !

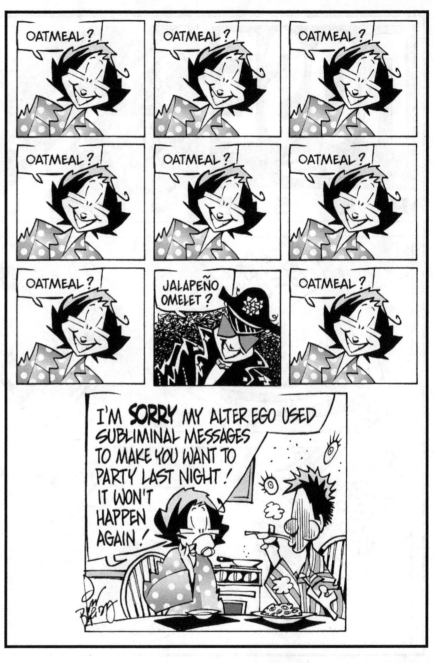

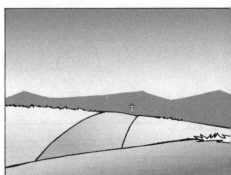

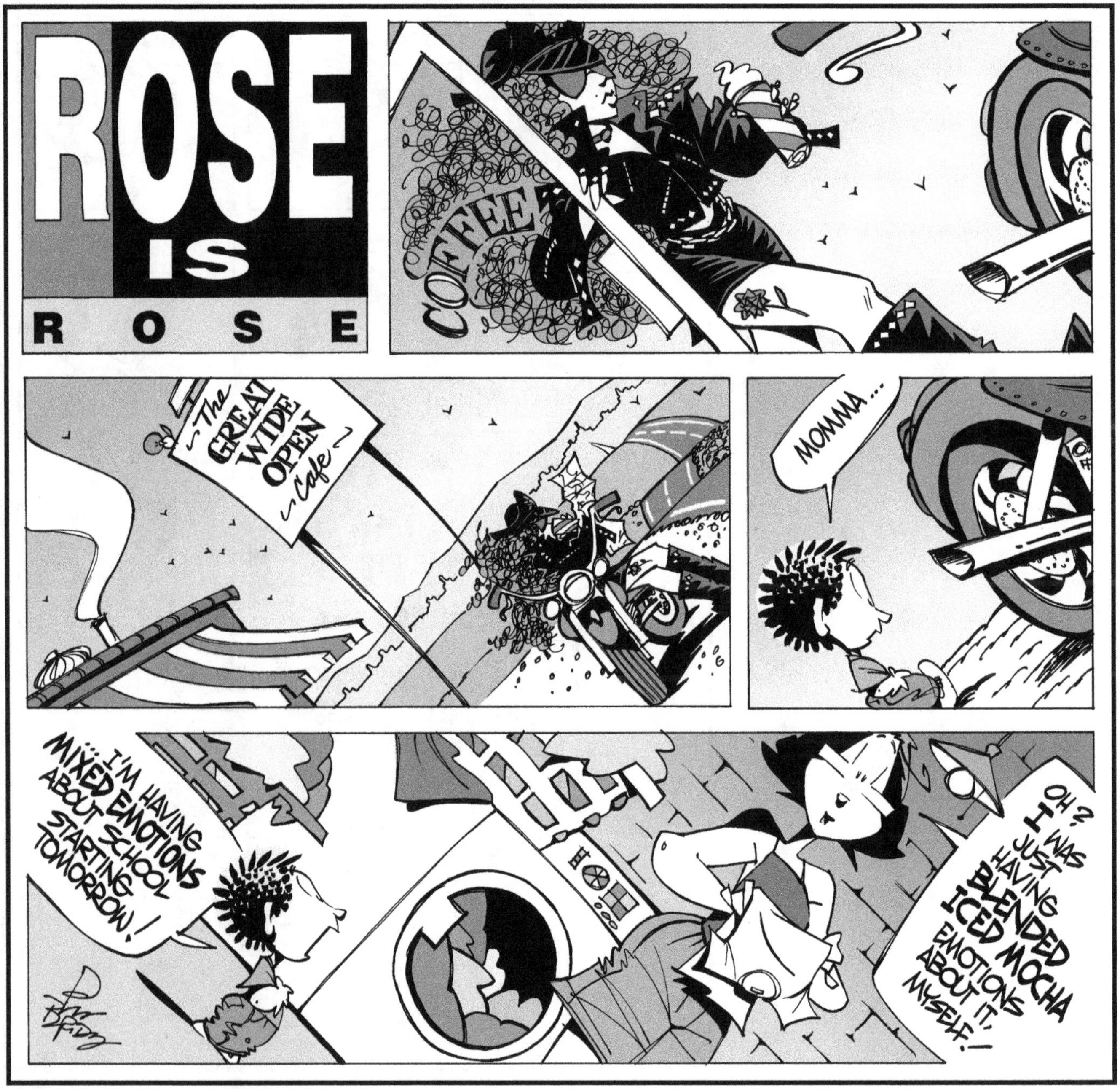
ROSE IS ROSE
COFFEE
The GREAT WIDE OPEN Cafe
MOMMA....
...I'M HAVING MIXED EMOTIONS ABOUT SCHOOL STARTING TOMORROW!
OH? I WAS JUST HAVING BLENDED ICED MOCHA EMOTIONS ABOUT IT, MYSELF!

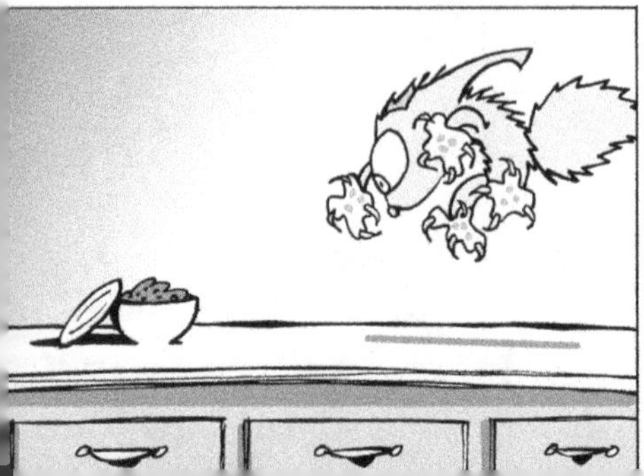

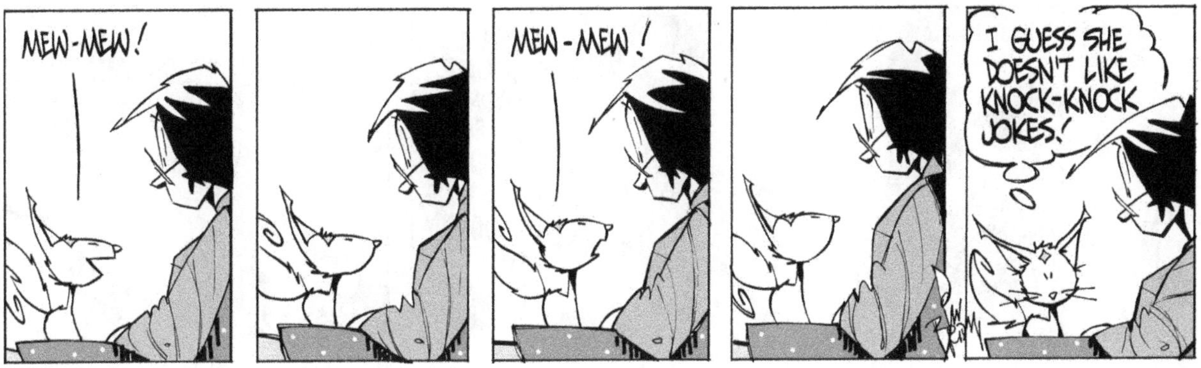
MEW-MEW!
MEW-MEW!
I GUESS SHE DOESN'T LIKE KNOCK-KNOCK JOKES!

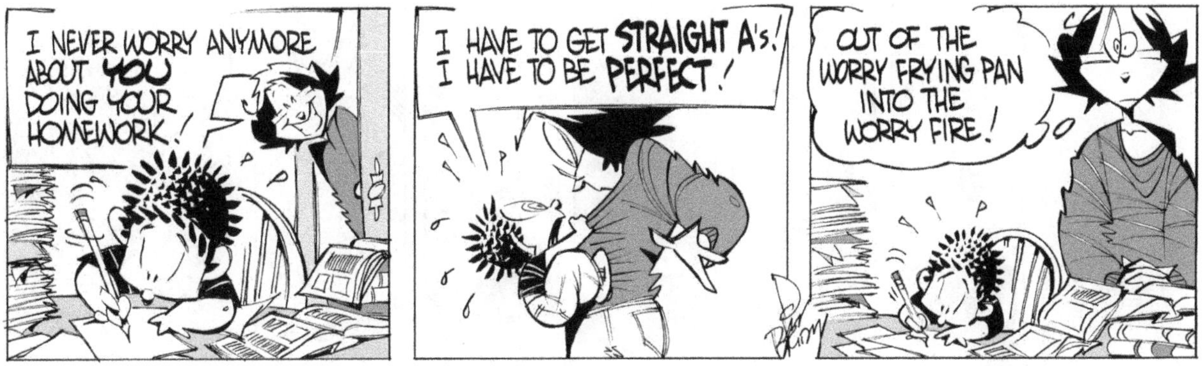
I NEVER WORRY ANYMORE ABOUT YOU DOING YOUR HOMEWORK!
I HAVE TO GET STRAIGHT A's! I HAVE TO BE PERFECT!
OUT OF THE WORRY FRYING PAN INTO THE WORRY FIRE!

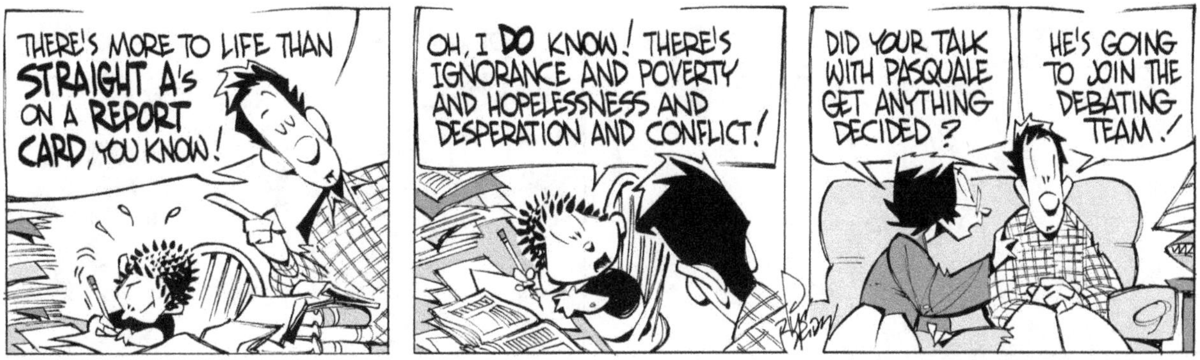
THERE'S MORE TO LIFE THAN STRAIGHT A's ON A REPORT CARD, YOU KNOW!
OH, I DO KNOW! THERE'S IGNORANCE AND POVERTY AND HOPELESSNESS AND DESPERATION AND CONFLICT!
DID YOUR TALK WITH PASQUALE GET ANYTHING DECIDED?
HE'S GOING TO JOIN THE DEBATING TEAM!

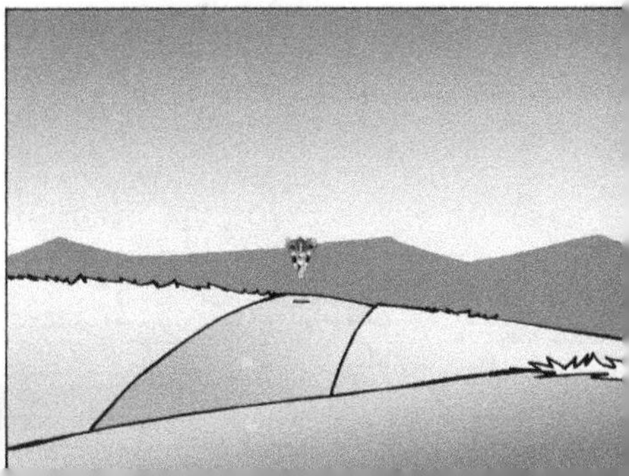

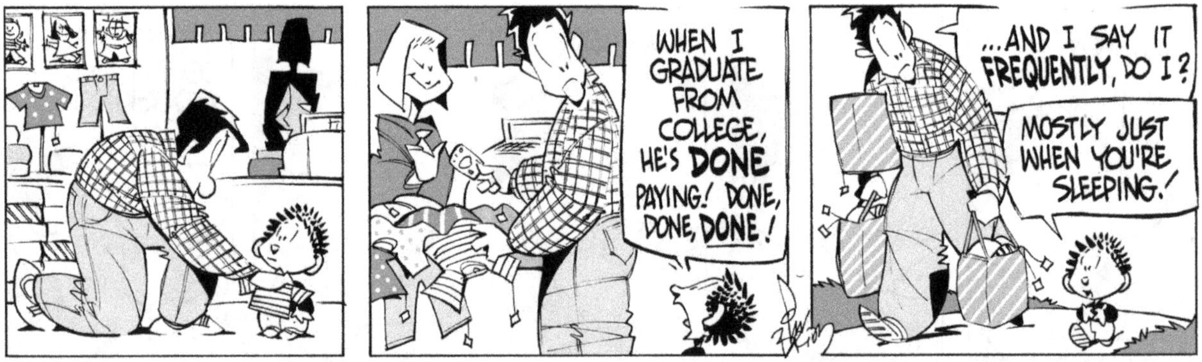
WHEN I GRADUATE FROM COLLEGE, HE'S **DONE** PAYING! DONE, DONE, **DONE**!
...AND I SAY IT **FREQUENTLY**, DO I?
MOSTLY JUST WHEN YOU'RE SLEEPING!

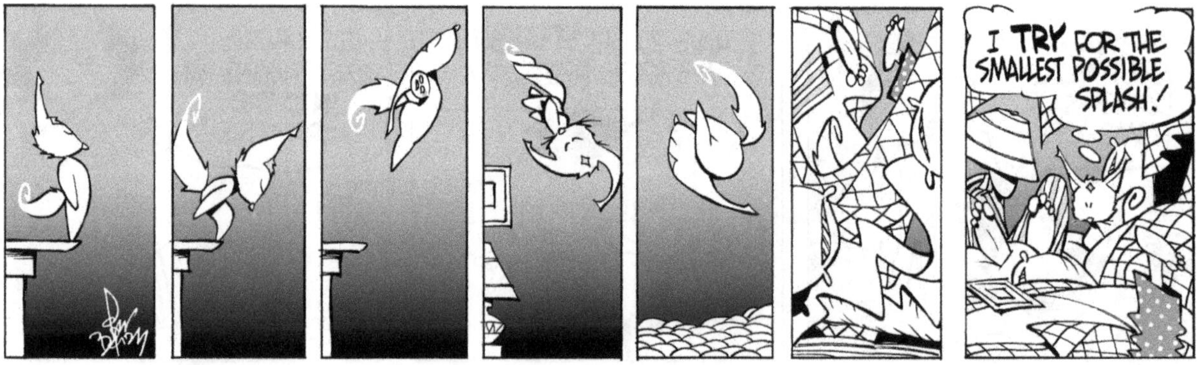
I **TRY** FOR THE SMALLEST POSSIBLE SPLASH!

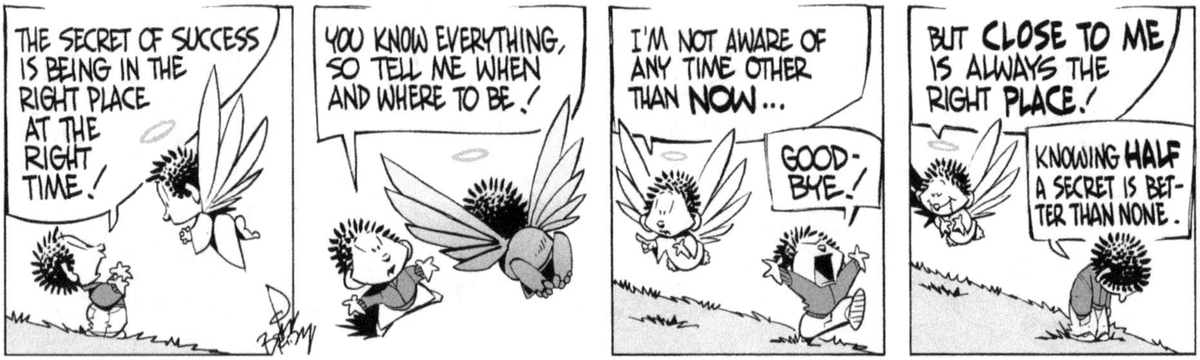
THE SECRET OF SUCCESS IS BEING IN THE RIGHT PLACE AT THE RIGHT TIME!
YOU KNOW EVERYTHING, SO TELL ME WHEN AND WHERE TO BE!
I'M NOT AWARE OF ANY TIME OTHER THAN **NOW**...
GOOD-BYE!
BUT **CLOSE TO ME** IS ALWAYS THE RIGHT **PLACE**!
KNOWING **HALF** A SECRET IS BETTER THAN NONE.

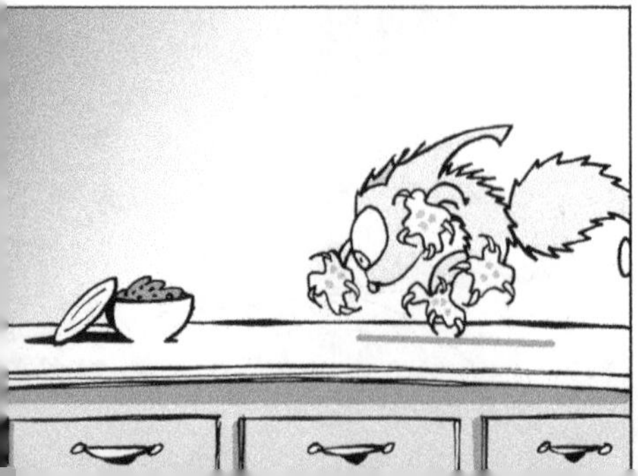

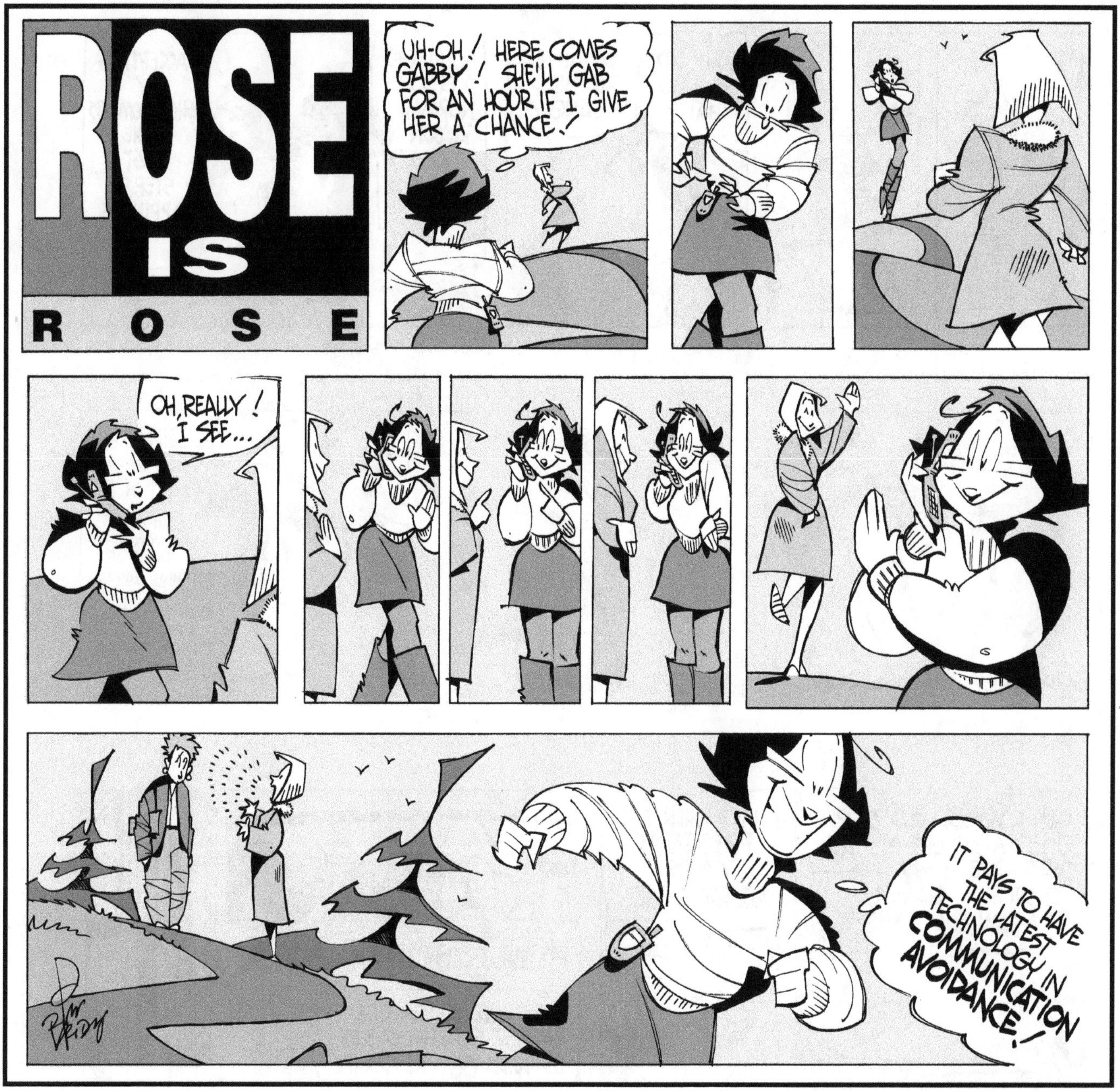
ROSE IS ROSE
UH-OH! HERE COMES GABBY! SHE'LL GAB FOR AN HOUR IF I GIVE HER A CHANCE!
OH, REALLY! I SEE...
IT PAYS TO HAVE THE LATEST TECHNOLOGY IN COMMUNICATION AVOIDANCE!

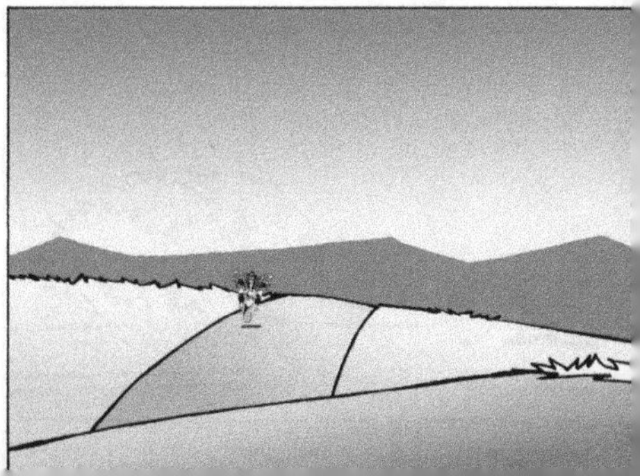

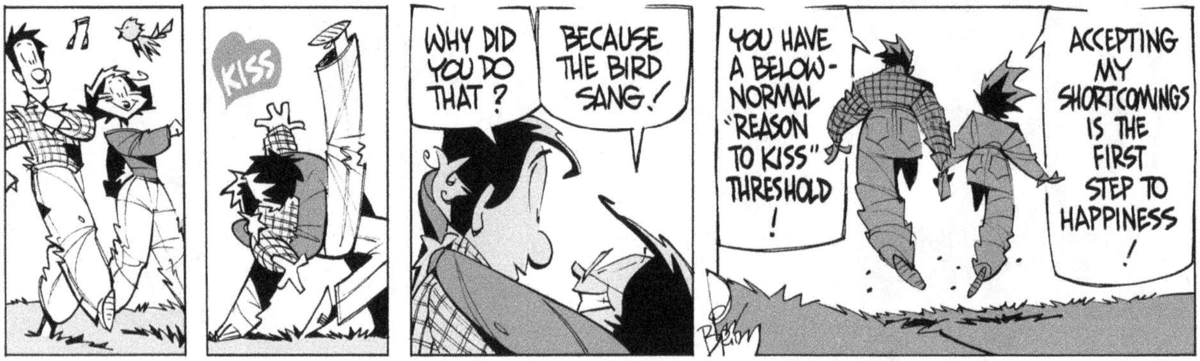
KISS
WHY DID YOU DO THAT ?
BECAUSE THE BIRD SANG!
YOU HAVE A BELOW-NORMAL "REASON TO KISS" THRESHOLD!
ACCEPTING MY SHORTCOMINGS IS THE FIRST STEP TO HAPPINESS!

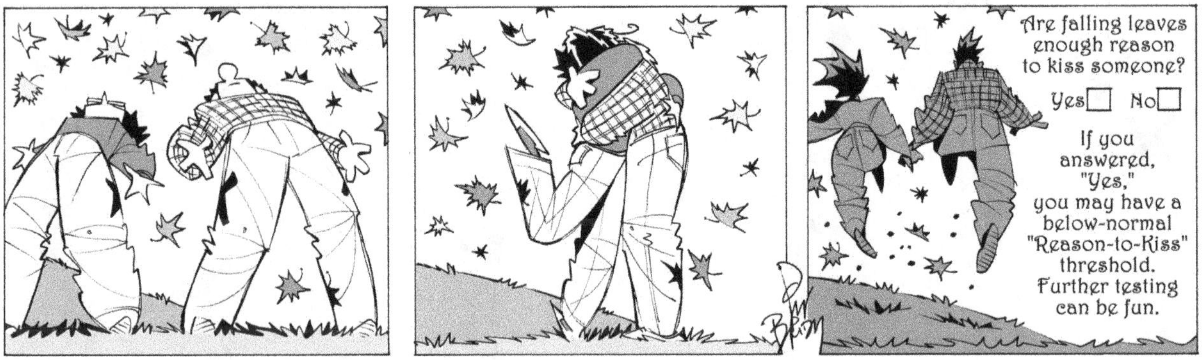
Are falling leaves enough reason to kiss someone?
Yes☐ No☐
If you answered, "Yes," you may have a below-normal "Reason-to-Kiss" threshold. Further testing can be fun.

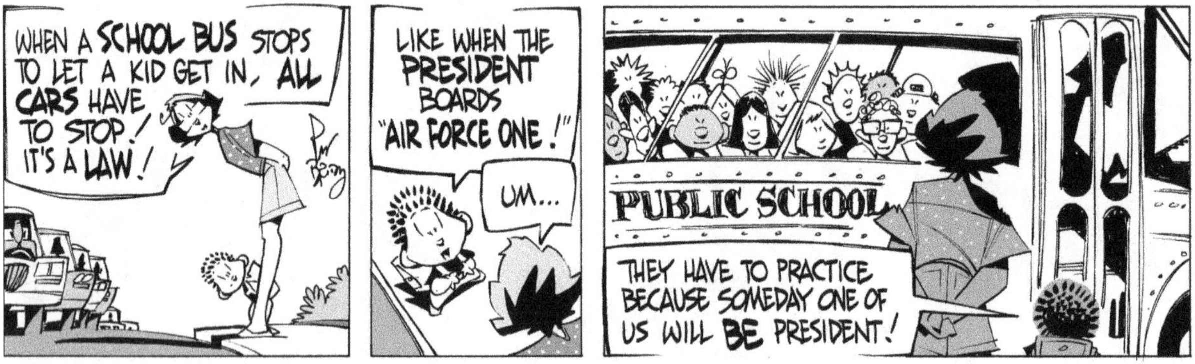
WHEN A SCHOOL BUS STOPS TO LET A KID GET IN, ALL CARS HAVE TO STOP! IT'S A LAW!
LIKE WHEN THE PRESIDENT BOARDS "AIR FORCE ONE!"
UM...
PUBLIC SCHOOL
THEY HAVE TO PRACTICE BECAUSE SOMEDAY ONE OF US WILL BE PRESIDENT!

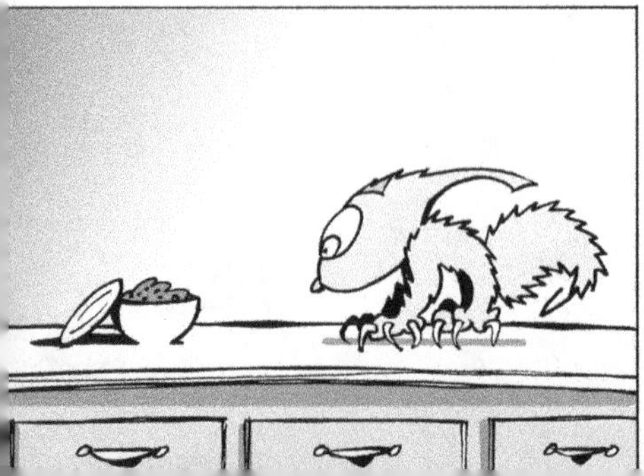

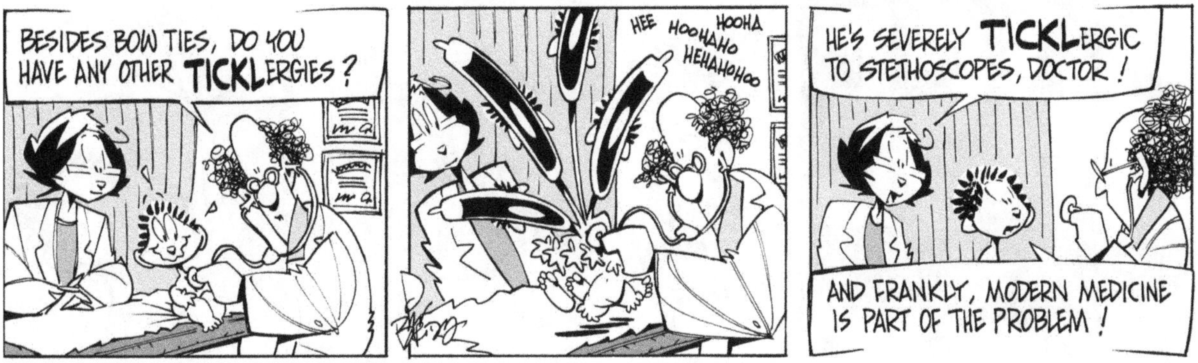
BESIDES BOW TIES, DO YOU HAVE ANY OTHER TICKLERGIES ?
HEE HOOHAHO HOOHA HEHAHOHOO
HE'S SEVERELY TICKLERGIC TO STETHOSCOPES, DOCTOR !
AND FRANKLY, MODERN MEDICINE IS PART OF THE PROBLEM !

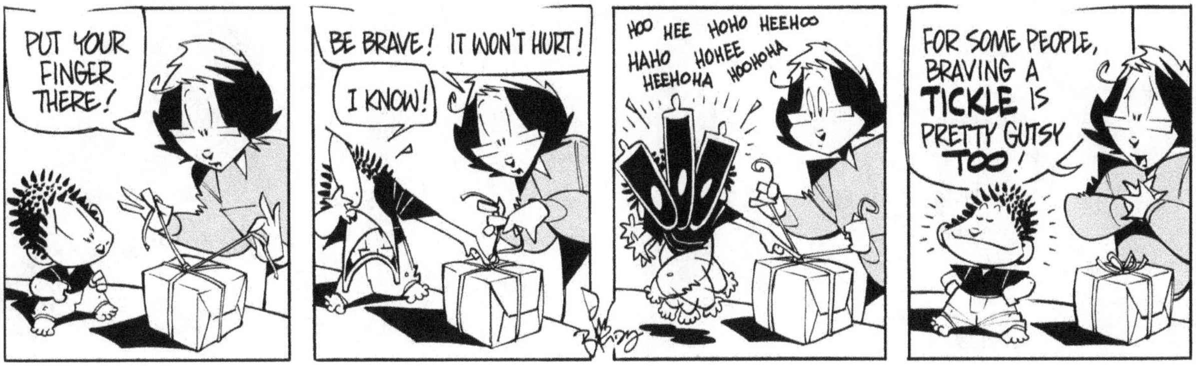
PUT YOUR FINGER THERE !
BE BRAVE ! IT WON'T HURT !
I KNOW !
HOO HEE HOHO HEEHOO
HAHO HOHEE
HEEHOHA HOOHOHA
FOR SOME PEOPLE, BRAVING A TICKLE IS PRETTY GUTSY TOO !

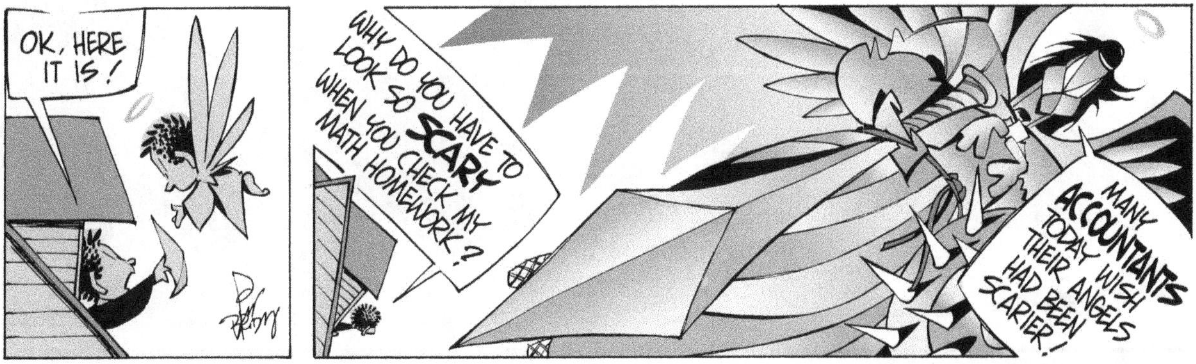
OK, HERE IT IS !
WHY DO YOU HAVE TO LOOK SO SCARY WHEN YOU CHECK MY MATH HOMEWORK ?
MANY ACCOUNTANTS TODAY WISH THEIR ANGELS HAD BEEN SCARIER !

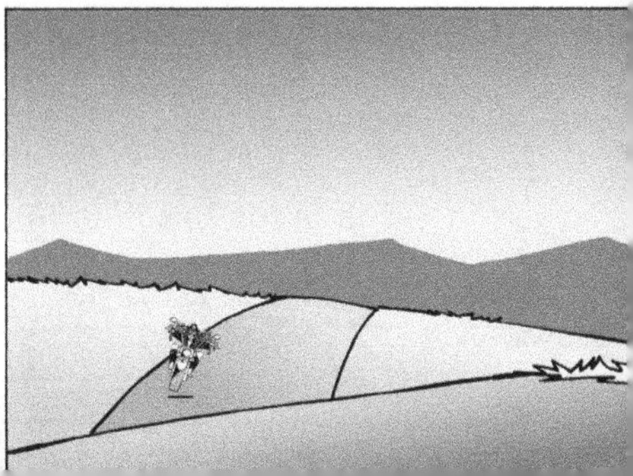

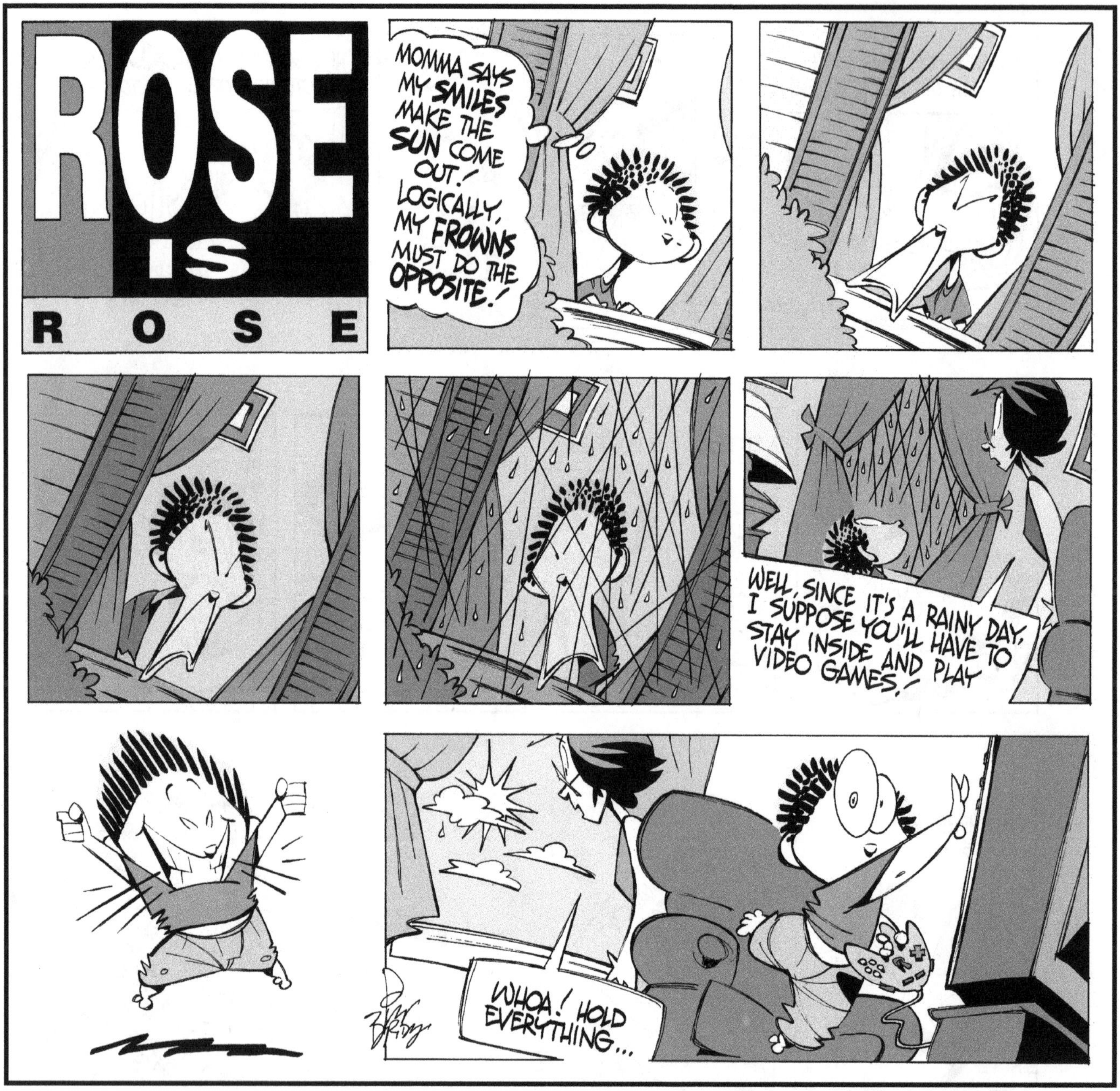
ROSE IS ROSE
MOMMA SAYS MY SMILES MAKE THE SUN COME OUT! LOGICALLY, MY FROWNS MUST DO THE OPPOSITE!
WELL, SINCE IT'S A RAINY DAY, I SUPPOSE YOU'LL HAVE TO STAY INSIDE AND PLAY VIDEO GAMES!
WHOA! HOLD EVERYTHING...

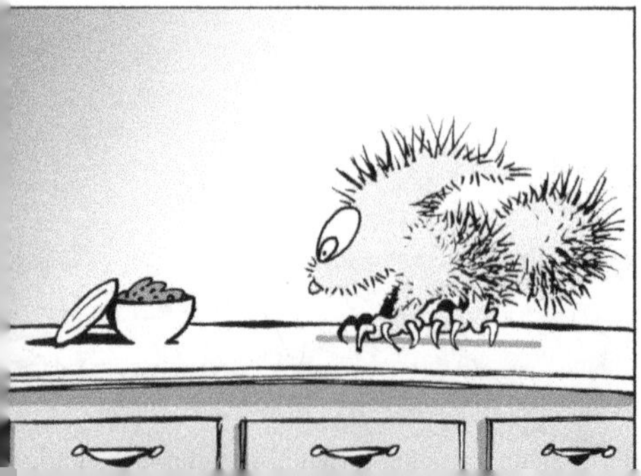

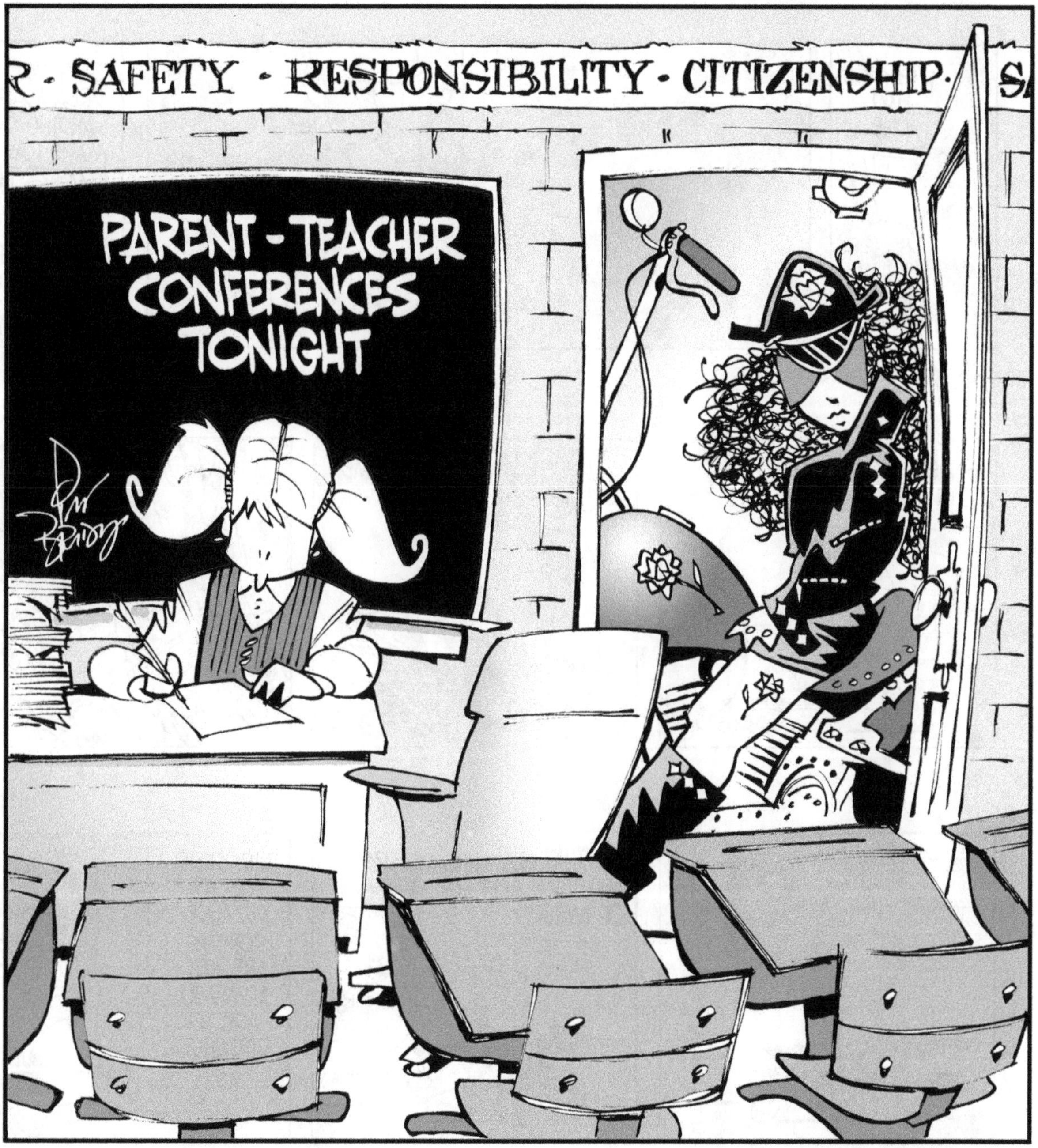
SAFETY · RESPONSIBILITY · CITIZENSHIP
PARENT - TEACHER CONFERENCES TONIGHT

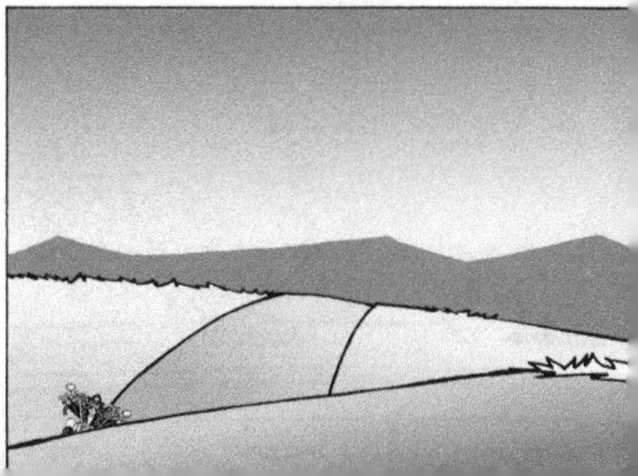

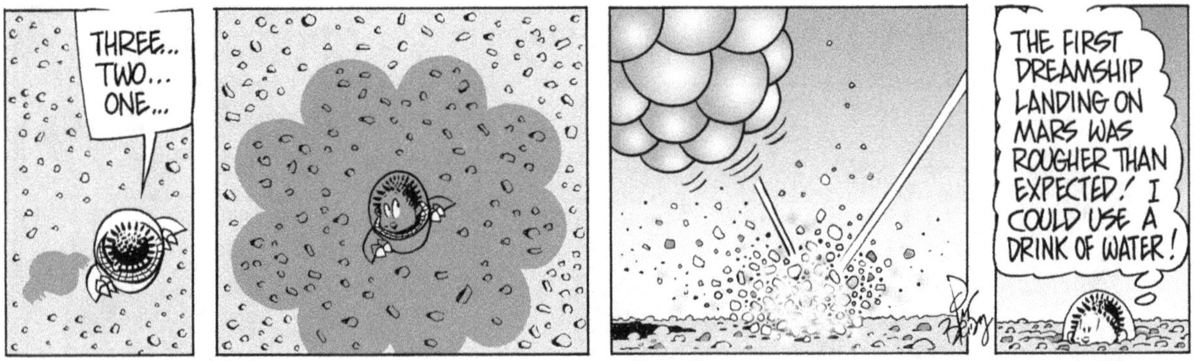
THREE... TWO... ONE...
THE FIRST DREAMSHIP LANDING ON MARS WAS ROUGHER THAN EXPECTED! I COULD USE A DRINK OF WATER!

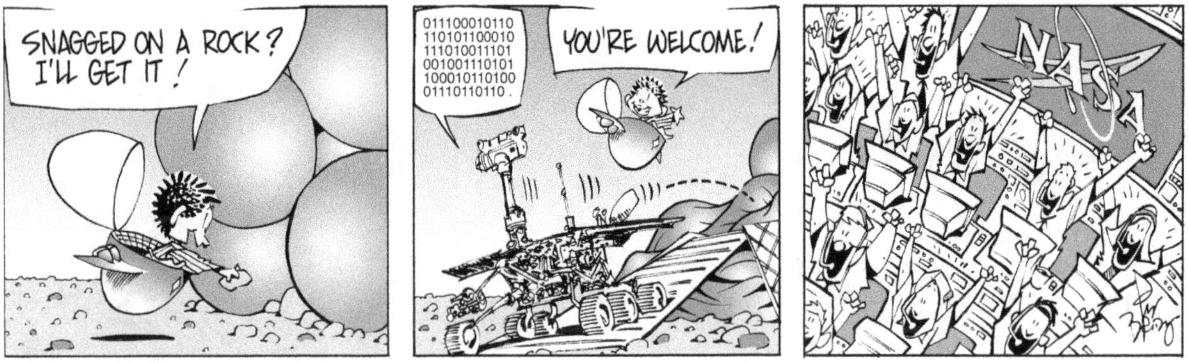
SNAGGED ON A ROCK? I'LL GET IT!
0111000101101101011000101110100111010010011101011000101101000111011010110.
YOU'RE WELCOME!
NASA

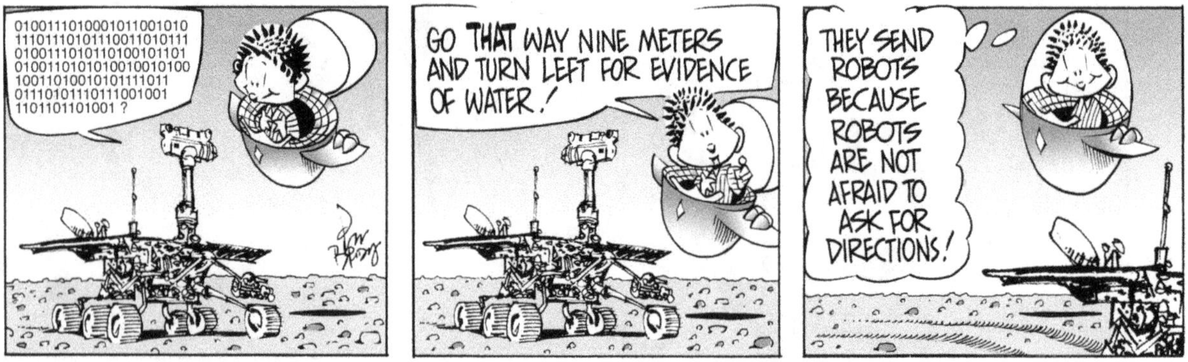
01001110100010110010101110111010111001101011101001110101101001011010100110101010010010100100110100101011110110111010111011100100111011011010 01 ?
GO THAT WAY NINE METERS AND TURN LEFT FOR EVIDENCE OF WATER!
THEY SEND ROBOTS BECAUSE ROBOTS ARE NOT AFRAID TO ASK FOR DIRECTIONS!

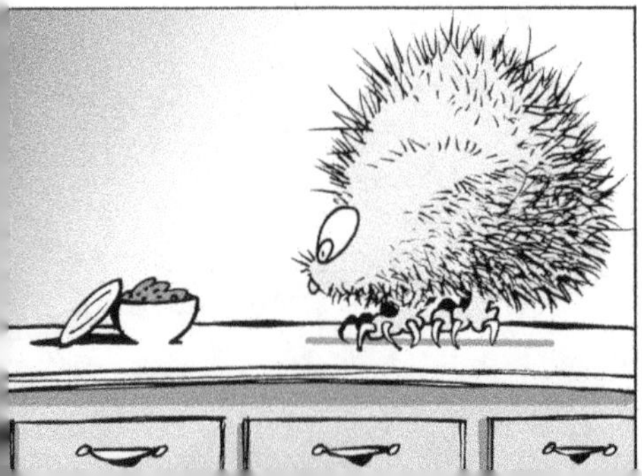

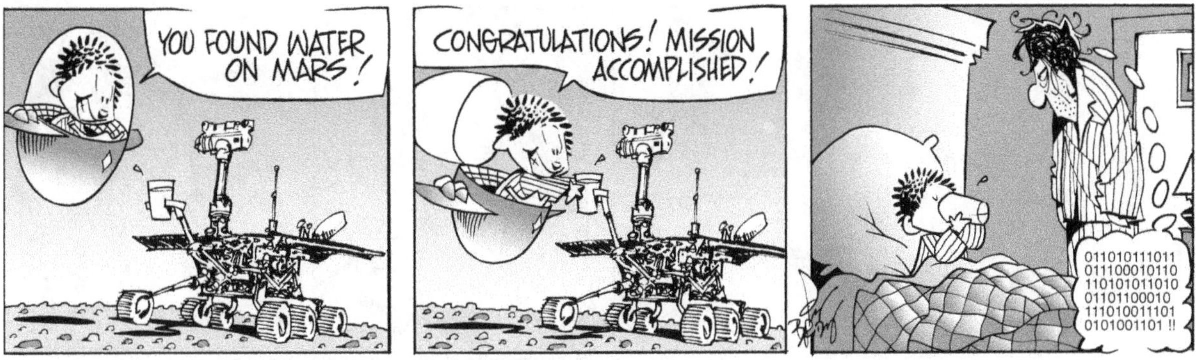
YOU FOUND WATER ON MARS!
CONGRATULATIONS! MISSION ACCOMPLISHED!
011010111011
011100010110
110101011010
01101100010
111010011101
0101001101 !!

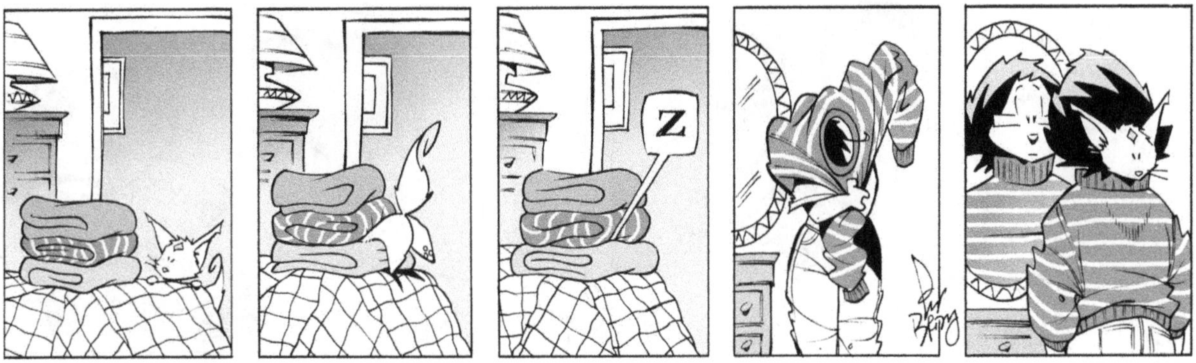
Z

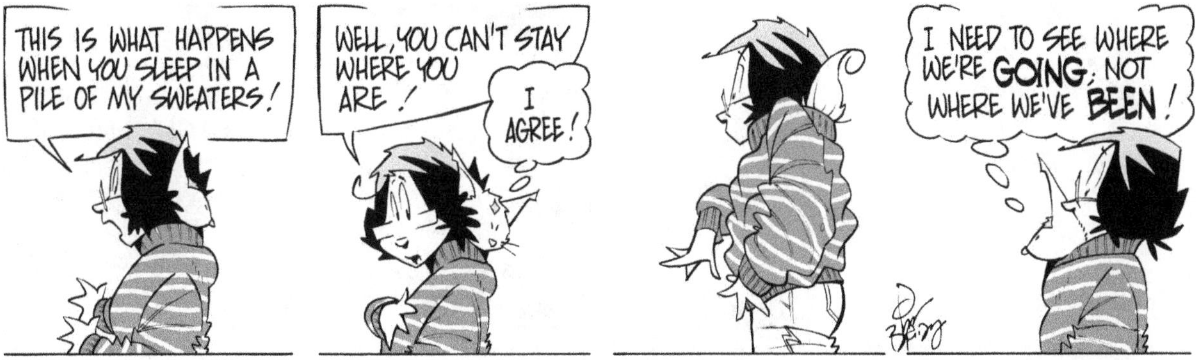
THIS IS WHAT HAPPENS WHEN YOU SLEEP IN A PILE OF MY SWEATERS!
WELL, YOU CAN'T STAY WHERE YOU ARE!
I AGREE!
I NEED TO SEE WHERE WE'RE GOING, NOT WHERE WE'VE BEEN!

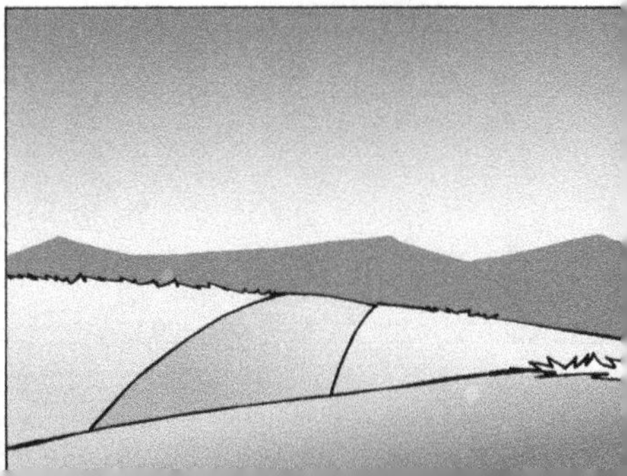

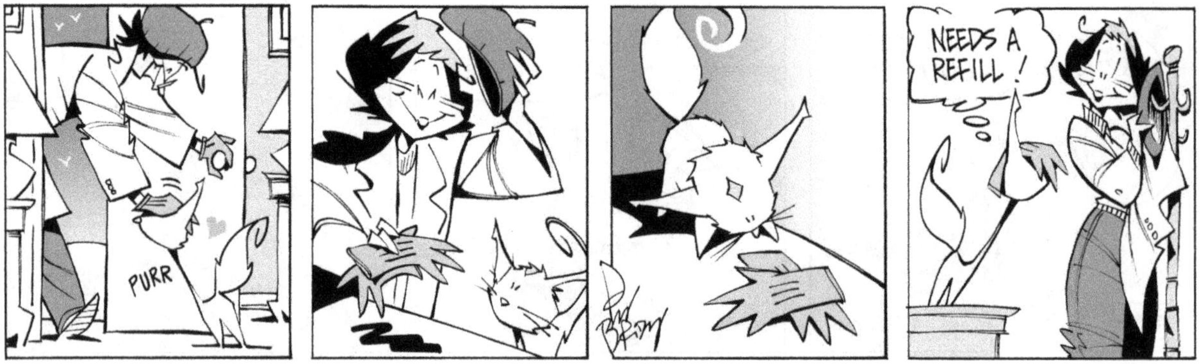
PURR
NEEDS A REFILL!

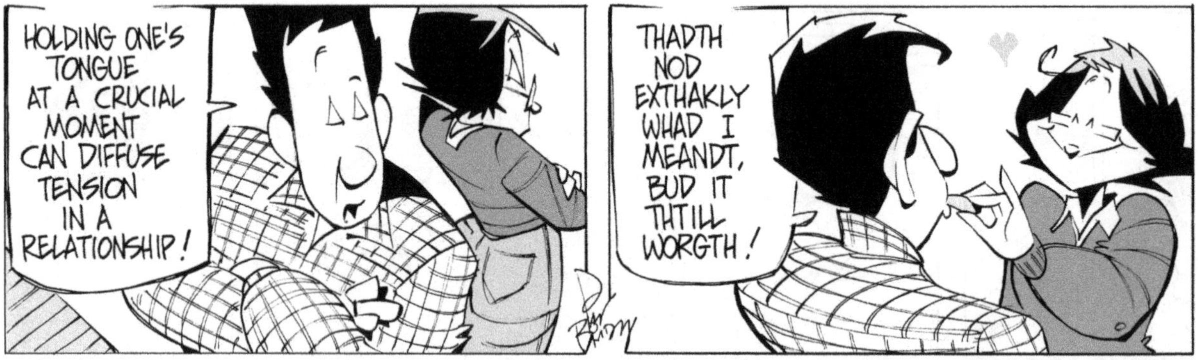
HOLDING ONE'S TONGUE AT A CRUCIAL MOMENT CAN DIFFUSE TENSION IN A RELATIONSHIP!
THADTH NOD EXTHAKLY WHAD I MEANDT, BUD IT THTILL WORGTH!

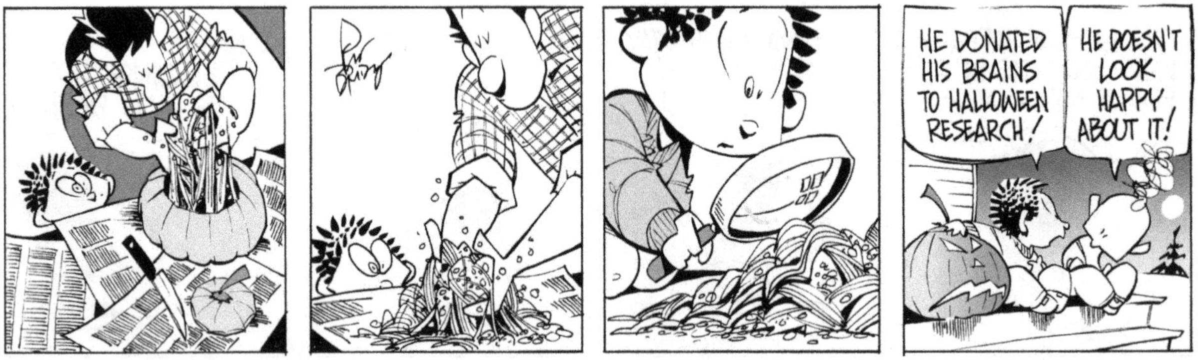
HE DONATED HIS BRAINS TO HALLOWEEN RESEARCH!
HE DOESN'T LOOK HAPPY ABOUT IT!

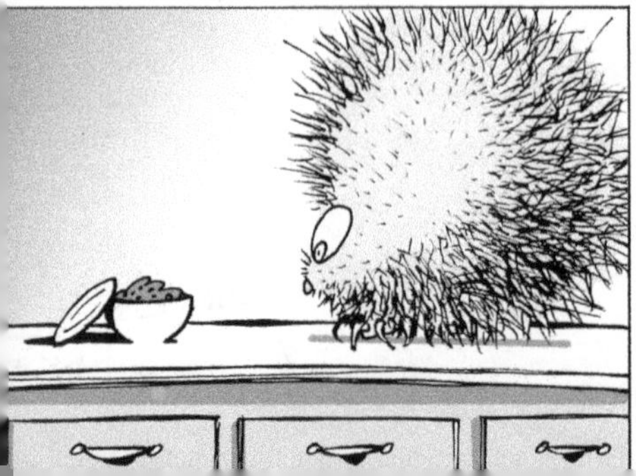

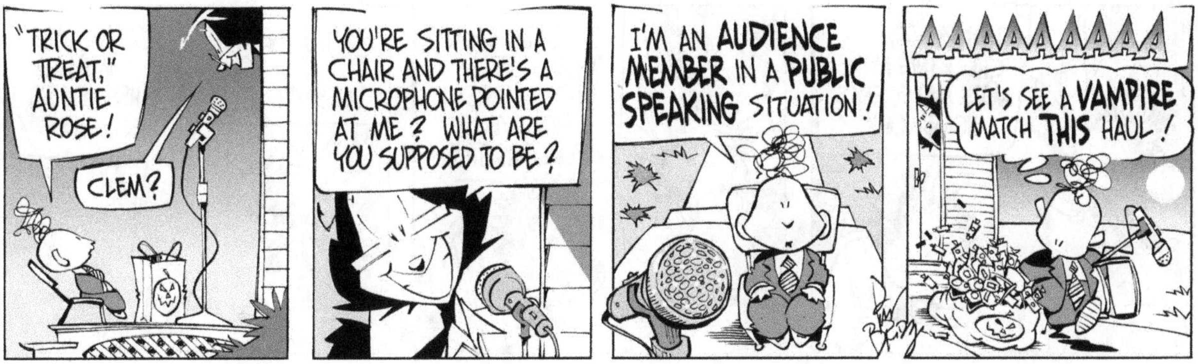
"TRICK OR TREAT," AUNTIE ROSE!
CLEM?
YOU'RE SITTING IN A CHAIR AND THERE'S A MICROPHONE POINTED AT ME? WHAT ARE YOU SUPPOSED TO BE?
I'M AN AUDIENCE MEMBER IN A PUBLIC SPEAKING SITUATION!
AAAAAAAAA
LET'S SEE A VAMPIRE MATCH THIS HAUL!

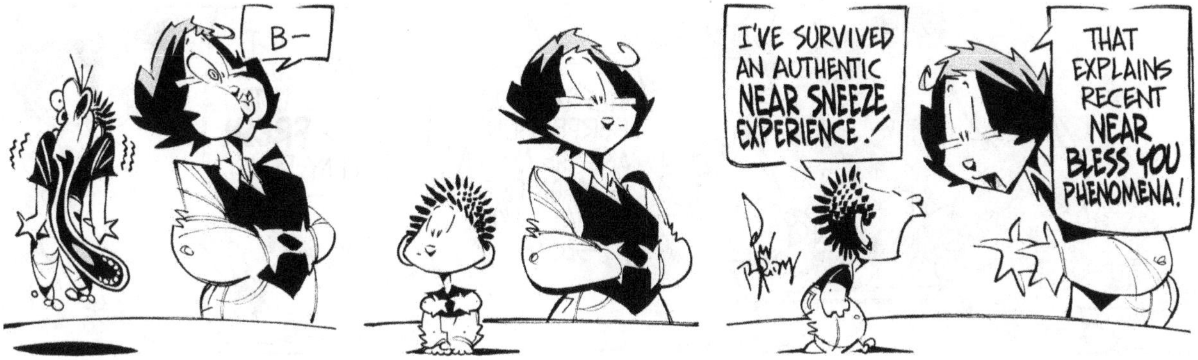
B—
I'VE SURVIVED AN AUTHENTIC NEAR SNEEZE EXPERIENCE!
THAT EXPLAINS RECENT NEAR BLESS YOU PHENOMENA!

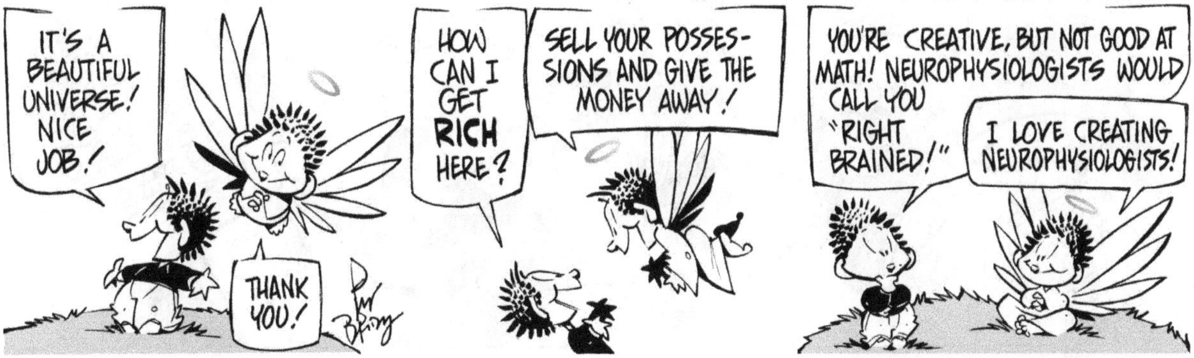
IT'S A BEAUTIFUL UNIVERSE! NICE JOB!
THANK YOU!
HOW CAN I GET RICH HERE?
SELL YOUR POSSESSIONS AND GIVE THE MONEY AWAY!
YOU'RE CREATIVE, BUT NOT GOOD AT MATH! NEUROPHYSIOLOGISTS WOULD CALL YOU "RIGHT BRAINED!"
I LOVE CREATING NEUROPHYSIOLOGISTS!

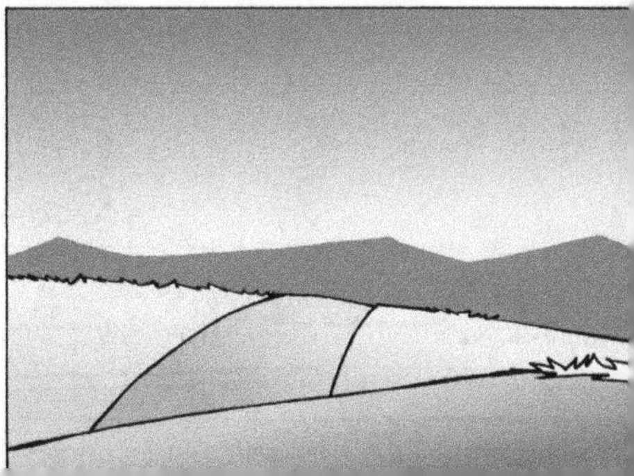

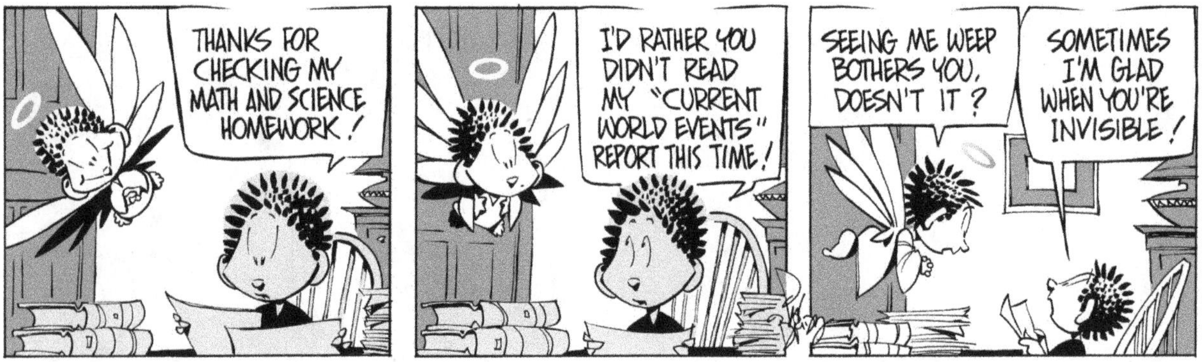
THANKS FOR CHECKING MY MATH AND SCIENCE HOMEWORK!
I'D RATHER YOU DIDN'T READ MY "CURRENT WORLD EVENTS" REPORT THIS TIME!
SEEING ME WEEP BOTHERS YOU, DOESN'T IT?
SOMETIMES I'M GLAD WHEN YOU'RE INVISIBLE!

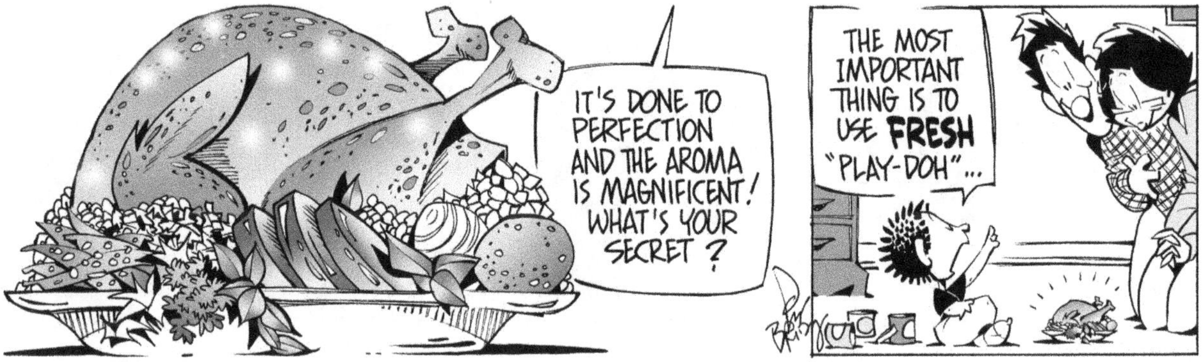
IT'S DONE TO PERFECTION AND THE AROMA IS MAGNIFICENT! WHAT'S YOUR SECRET?
THE MOST IMPORTANT THING IS TO USE FRESH "PLAY-DOH"...

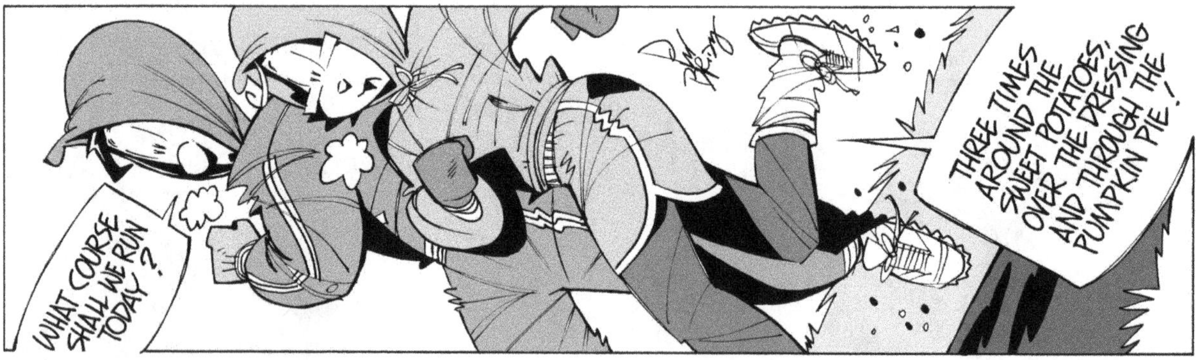
WHAT COURSE SHALL WE RUN TODAY?
THREE TIMES AROUND THE SWEET POTATOES, OVER THE DRESSING AND THROUGH THE PUMPKIN PIE!

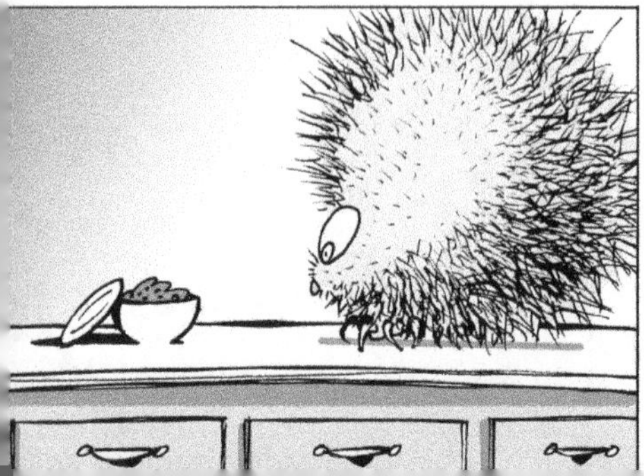

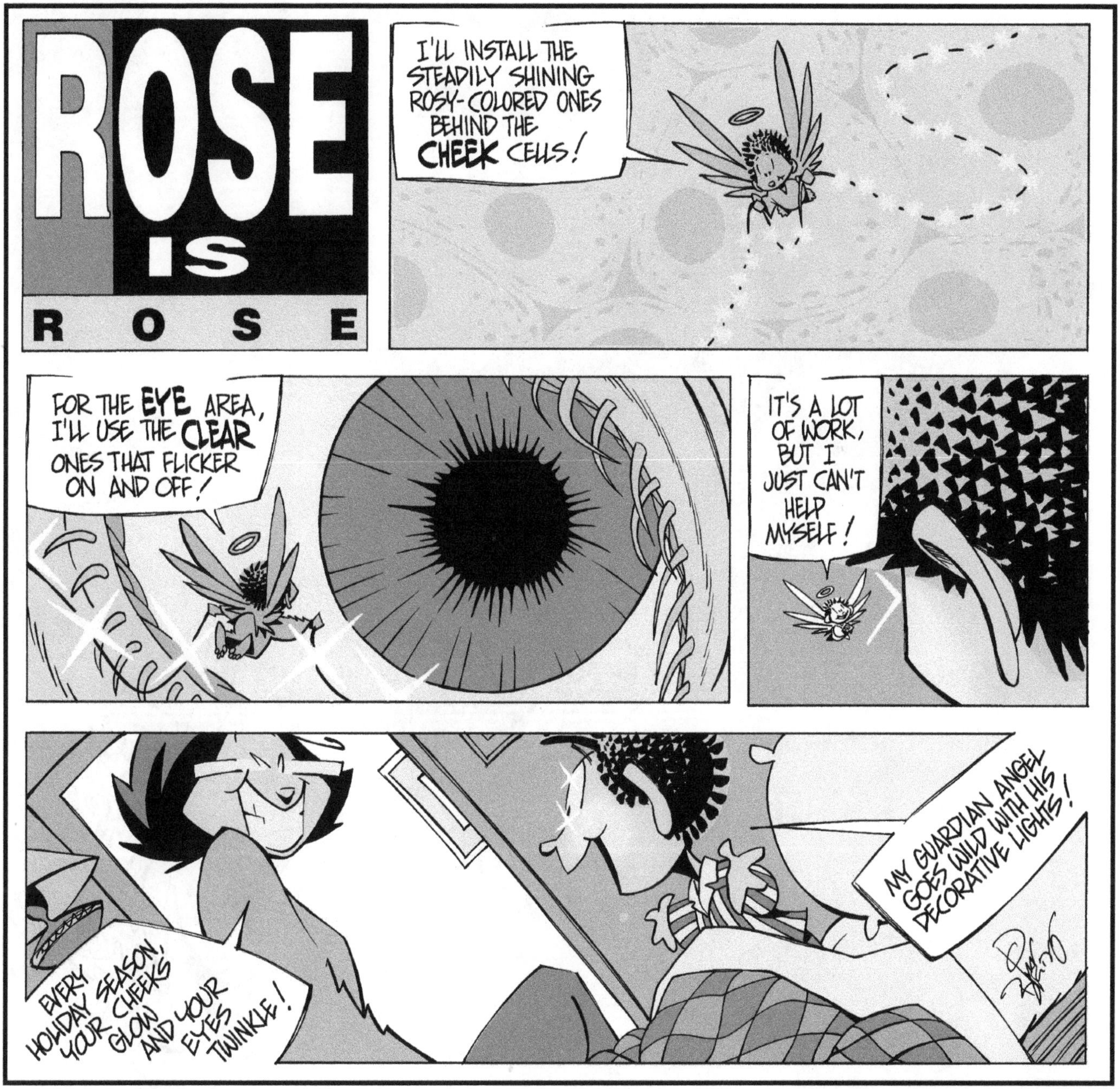
ROSE IS ROSE
I'LL INSTALL THE STEADILY SHINING ROSY-COLORED ONES BEHIND THE CHEEK CELLS!
FOR THE EYE AREA, I'LL USE THE CLEAR ONES THAT FLICKER ON AND OFF!
IT'S A LOT OF WORK, BUT I JUST CAN'T HELP MYSELF!
EVERY HOLIDAY SEASON, YOUR CHEEKS GLOW AND YOUR EYES TWINKLE!
MY GUARDIAN ANGEL GOES WILD WITH HIS DECORATIVE LIGHTS!

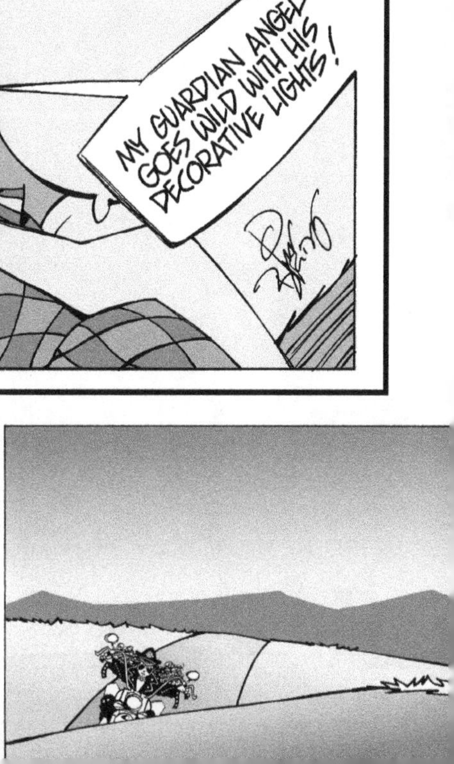

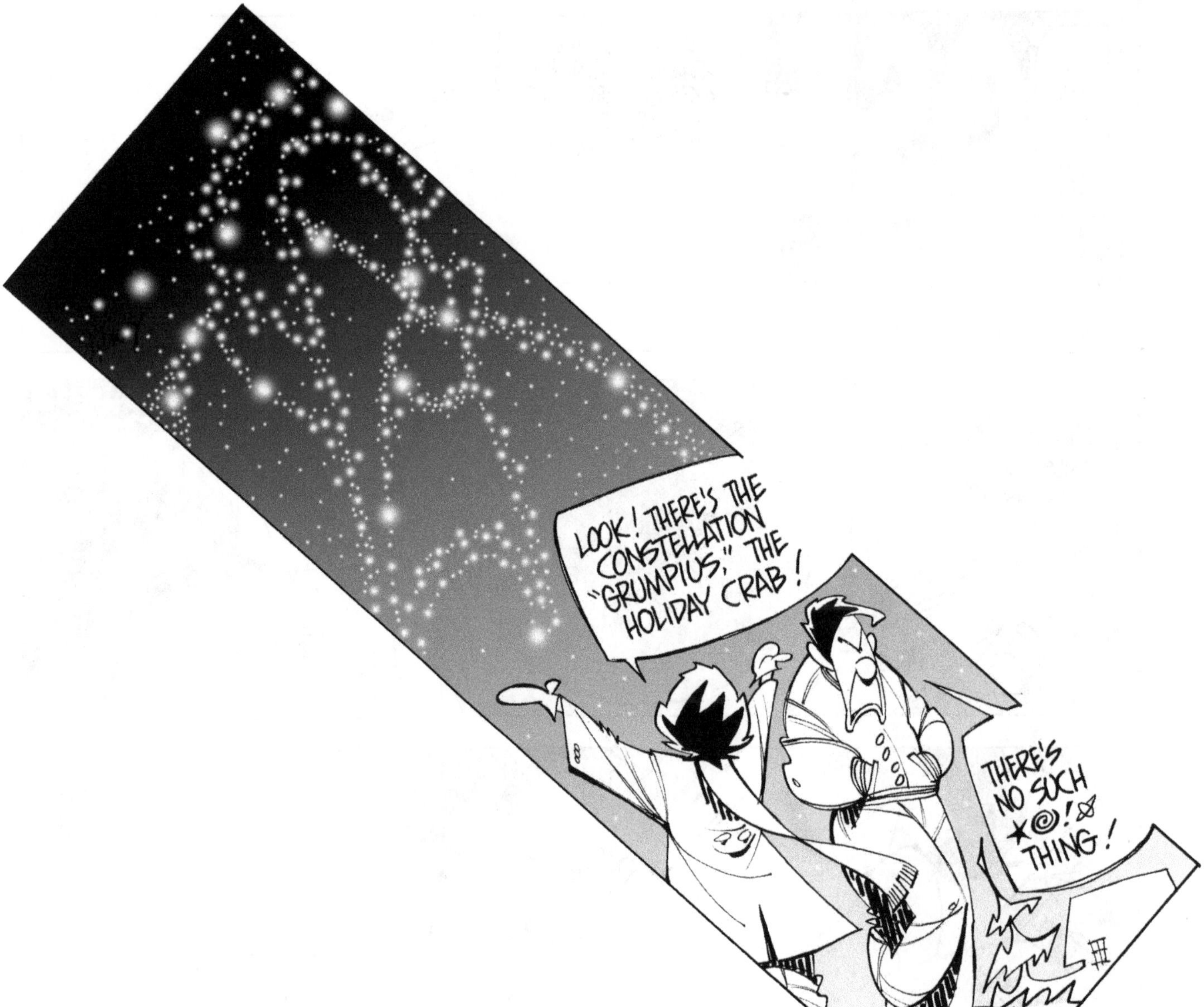
LOOK! THERE'S THE CONSTELLATION "GRUMPIUS," THE HOLIDAY CRAB!
THERE'S NO SUCH ★◎!✪ THING!

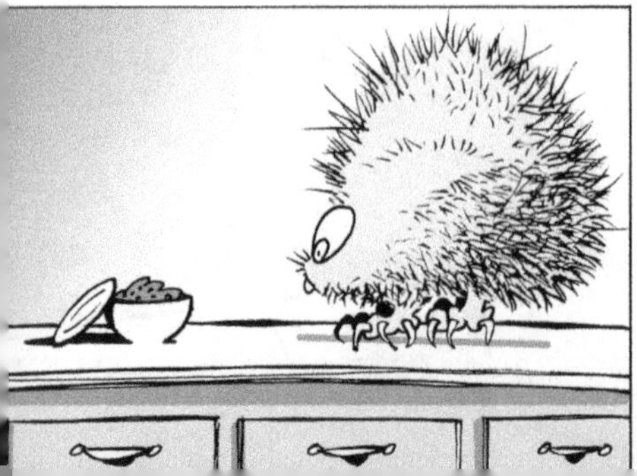

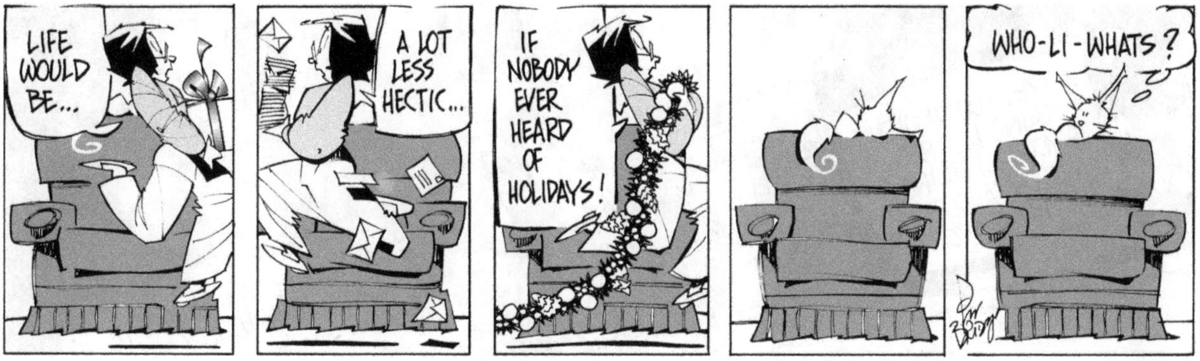
LIFE WOULD BE...
A LOT LESS HECTIC...
IF NOBODY EVER HEARD OF HOLIDAYS!
WHO-LI-WHATS?

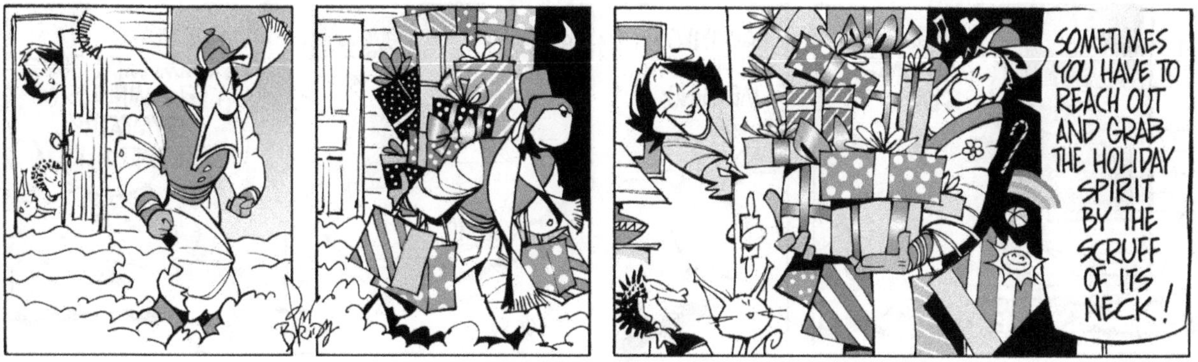
SOMETIMES YOU HAVE TO REACH OUT AND GRAB THE HOLIDAY SPIRIT BY THE SCRUFF OF ITS NECK!

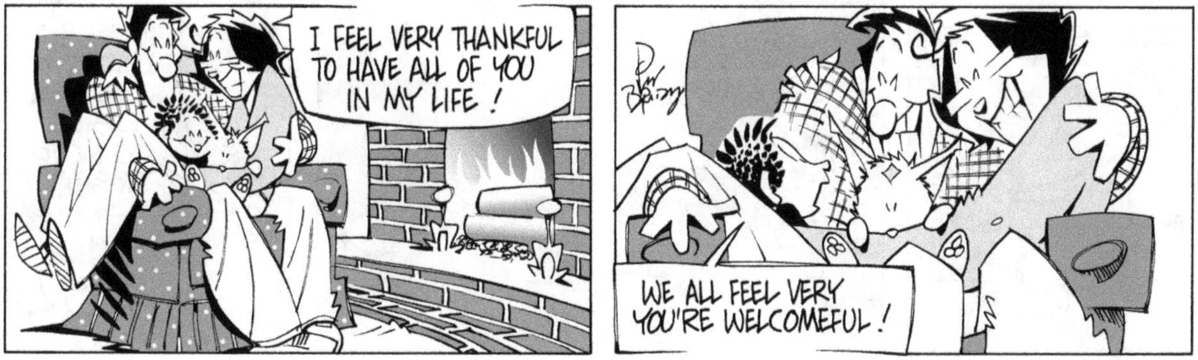
I FEEL VERY THANKFUL TO HAVE ALL OF YOU IN MY LIFE!
WE ALL FEEL VERY YOU'RE WELCOMEFUL!

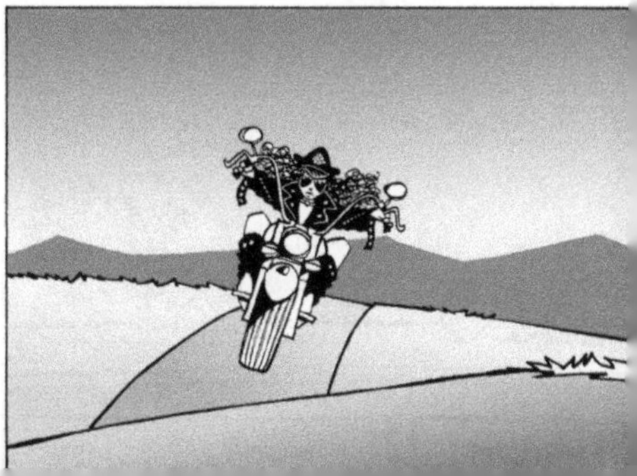

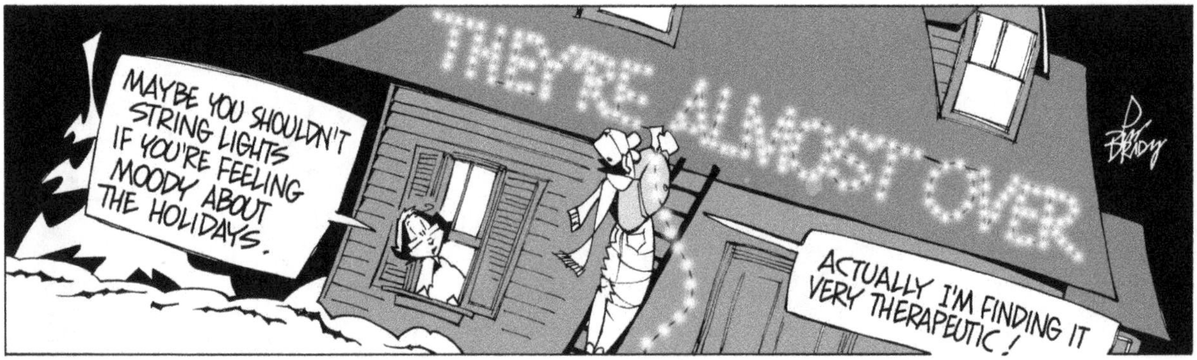
THEY'RE ALMOST OVER
MAYBE YOU SHOULDN'T STRING LIGHTS IF YOU'RE FEELING MOODY ABOUT THE HOLIDAYS.
ACTUALLY I'M FINDING IT VERY THERAPEUTIC!

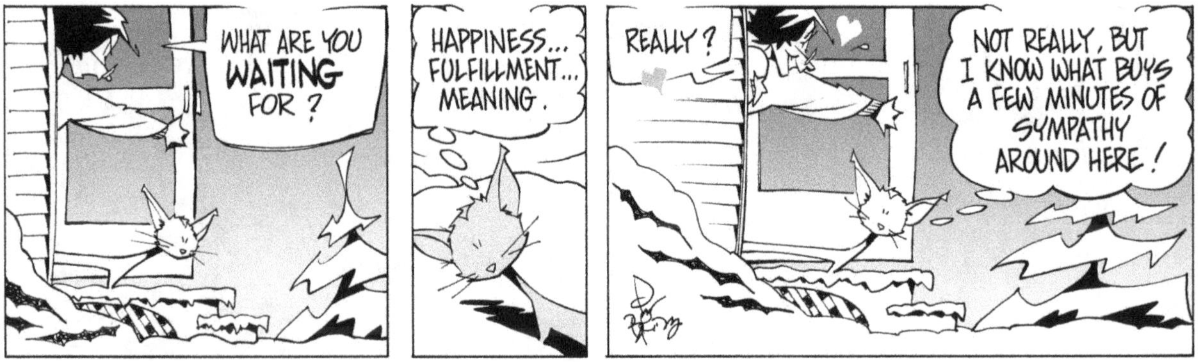
WHAT ARE YOU WAITING FOR?
HAPPINESS... FULFILLMENT... MEANING.
REALLY?
NOT REALLY, BUT I KNOW WHAT BUYS A FEW MINUTES OF SYMPATHY AROUND HERE!

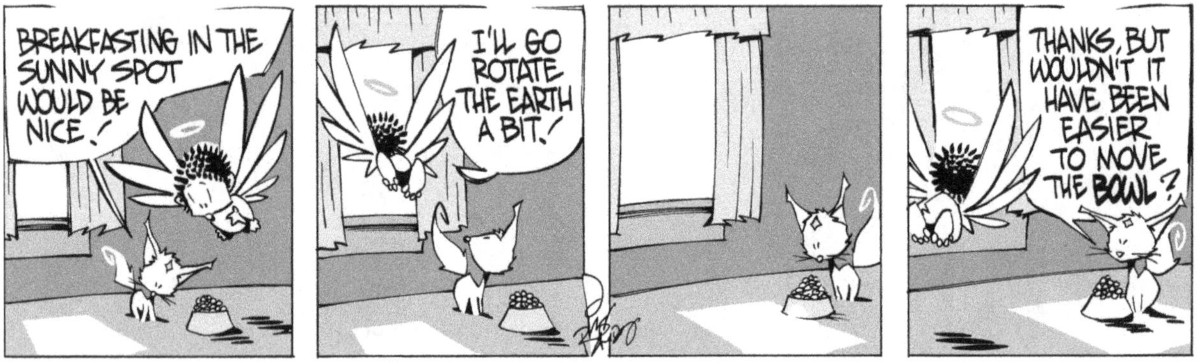
BREAKFASTING IN THE SUNNY SPOT WOULD BE NICE!
I'LL GO ROTATE THE EARTH A BIT!
THANKS, BUT WOULDN'T IT HAVE BEEN EASIER TO MOVE THE BOWL?

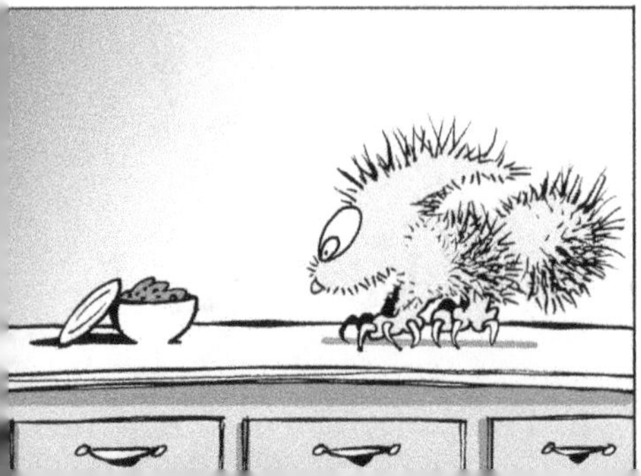

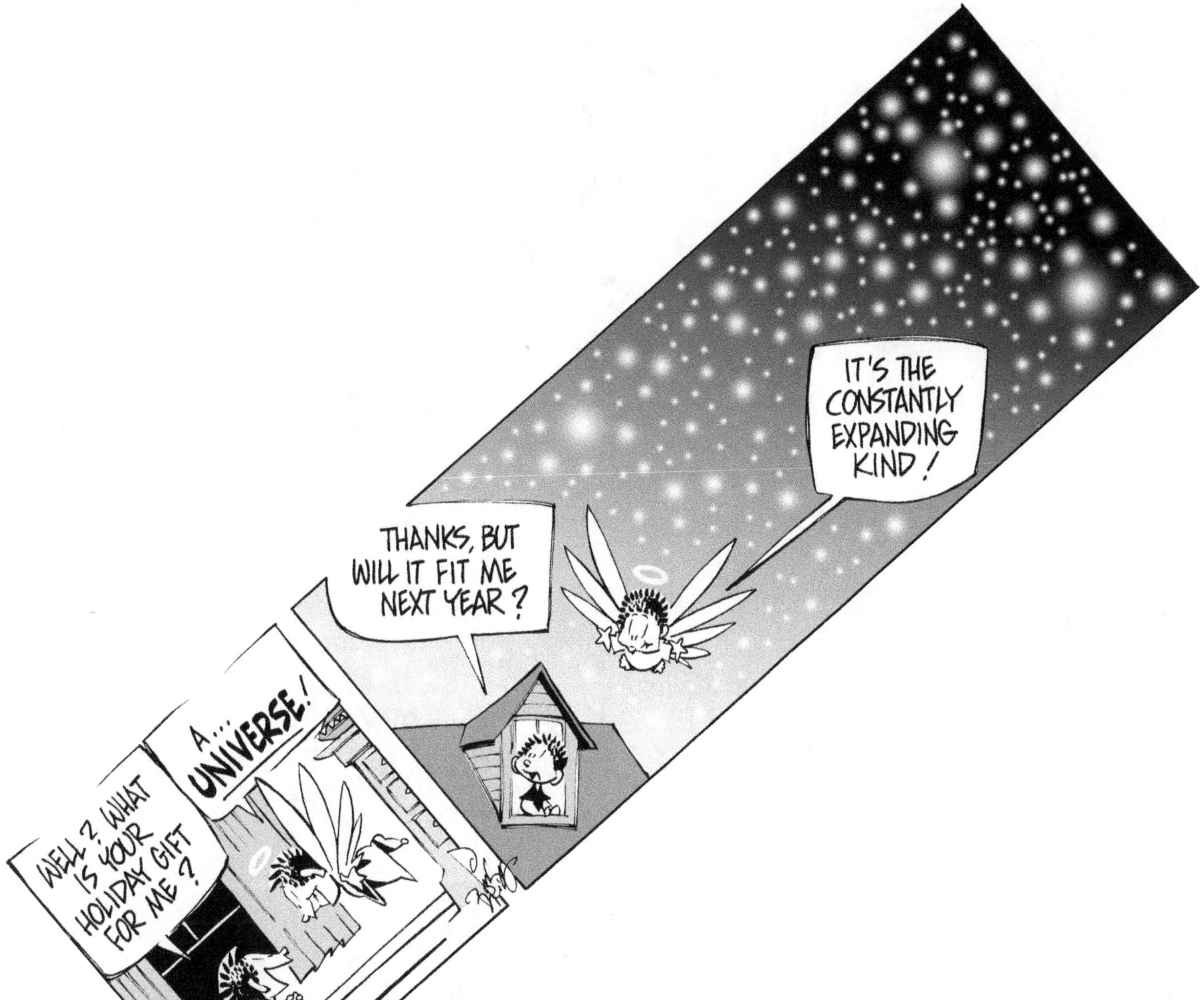
WELL? WHAT IS YOUR HOLIDAY GIFT FOR ME?
A... UNIVERSE!
THANKS, BUT WILL IT FIT ME NEXT YEAR?
IT'S THE CONSTANTLY EXPANDING KIND!

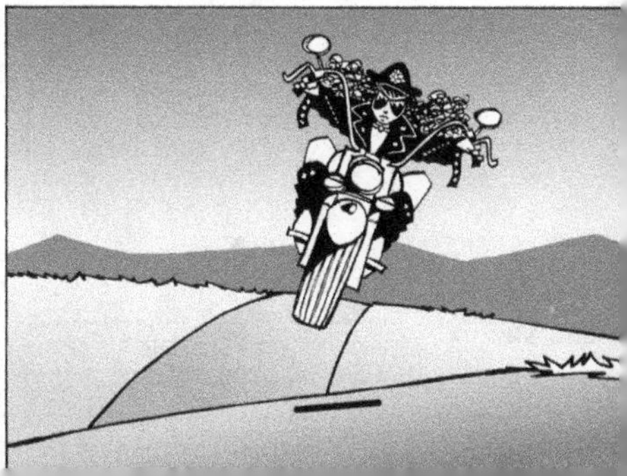

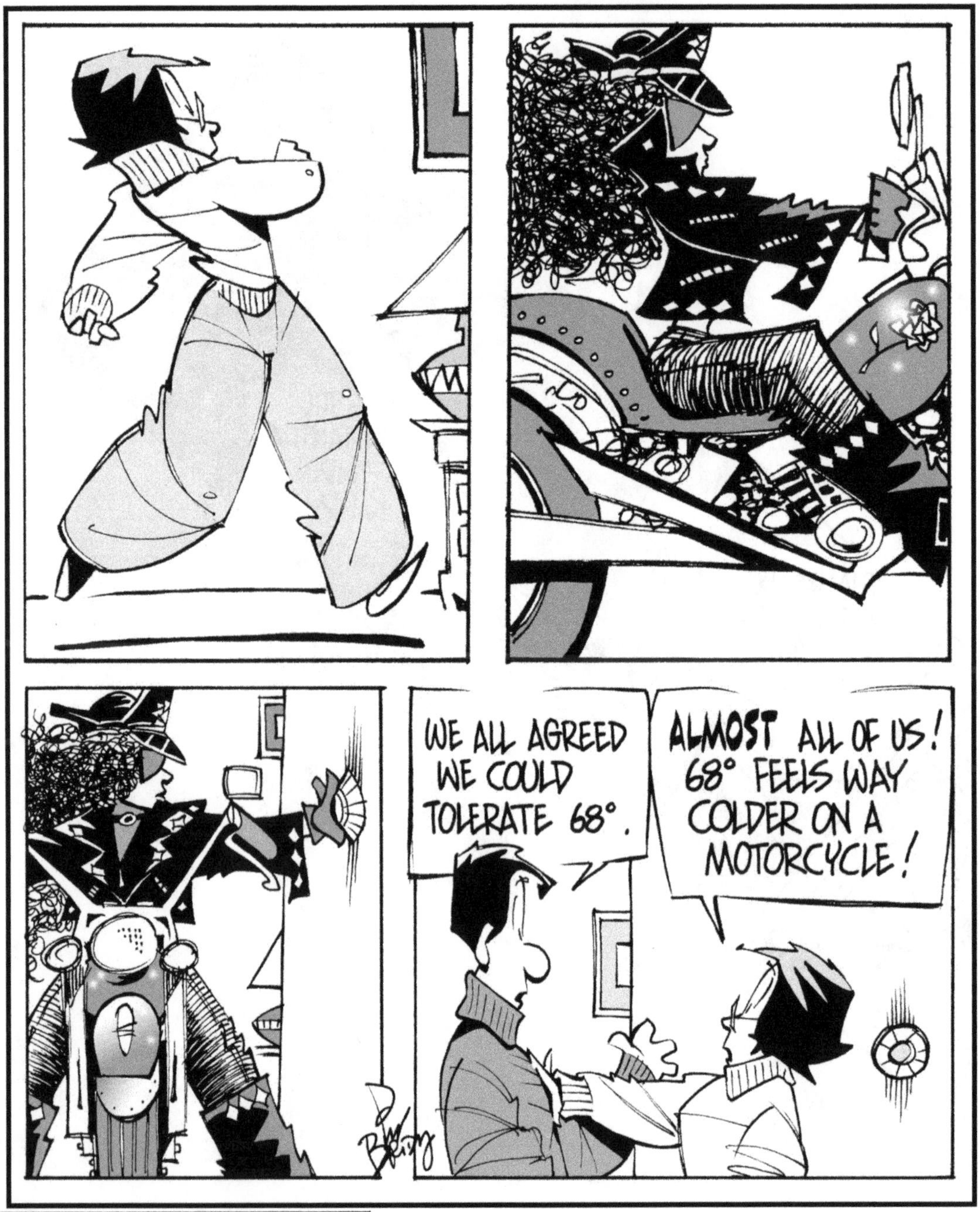
WE ALL AGREED WE COULD TOLERATE 68°.
ALMOST ALL OF US! 68° FEELS WAY COLDER ON A MOTORCYCLE!

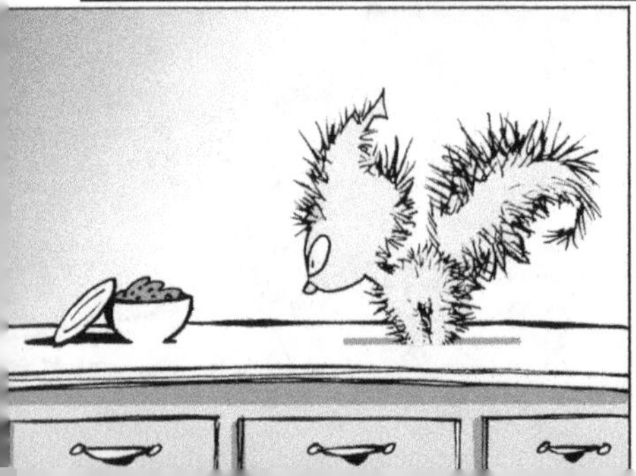

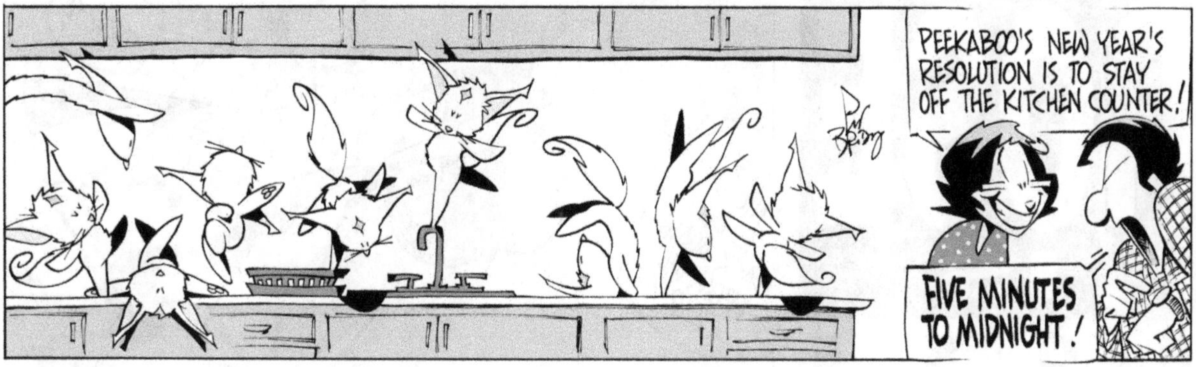
PEEKABOO'S NEW YEAR'S RESOLUTION IS TO STAY OFF THE KITCHEN COUNTER!
FIVE MINUTES TO MIDNIGHT!

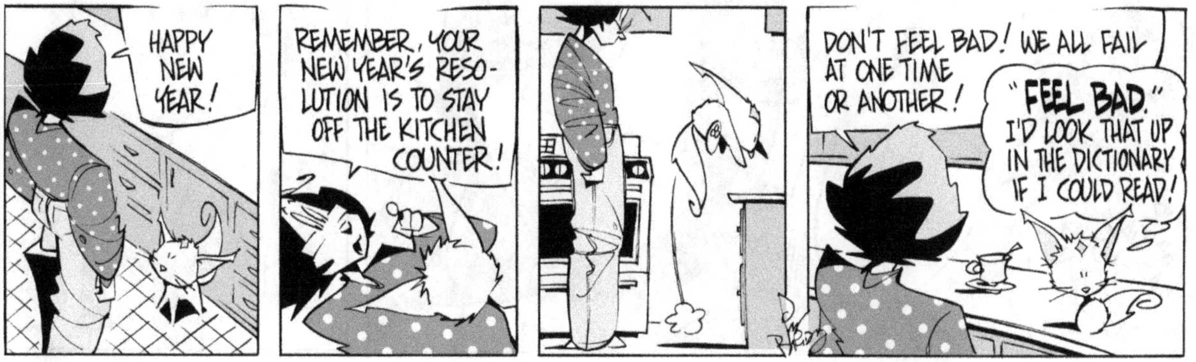
HAPPY NEW YEAR!
REMEMBER, YOUR NEW YEAR'S RESO-LUTION IS TO STAY OFF THE KITCHEN COUNTER!
DON'T FEEL BAD! WE ALL FAIL AT ONE TIME OR ANOTHER!
"FEEL BAD." I'D LOOK THAT UP IN THE DICTIONARY IF I COULD READ!

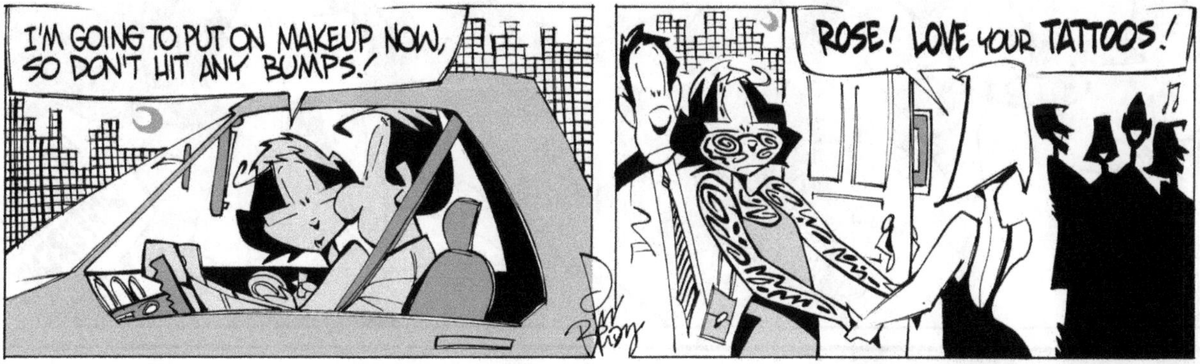
I'M GOING TO PUT ON MAKEUP NOW, SO DON'T HIT ANY BUMPS!
ROSE! LOVE YOUR TATTOOS!

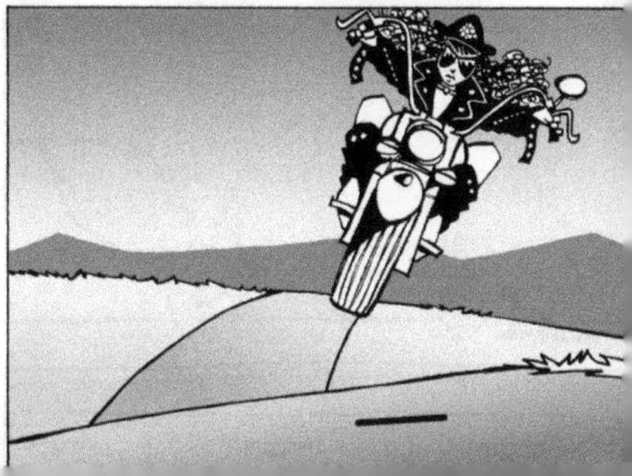

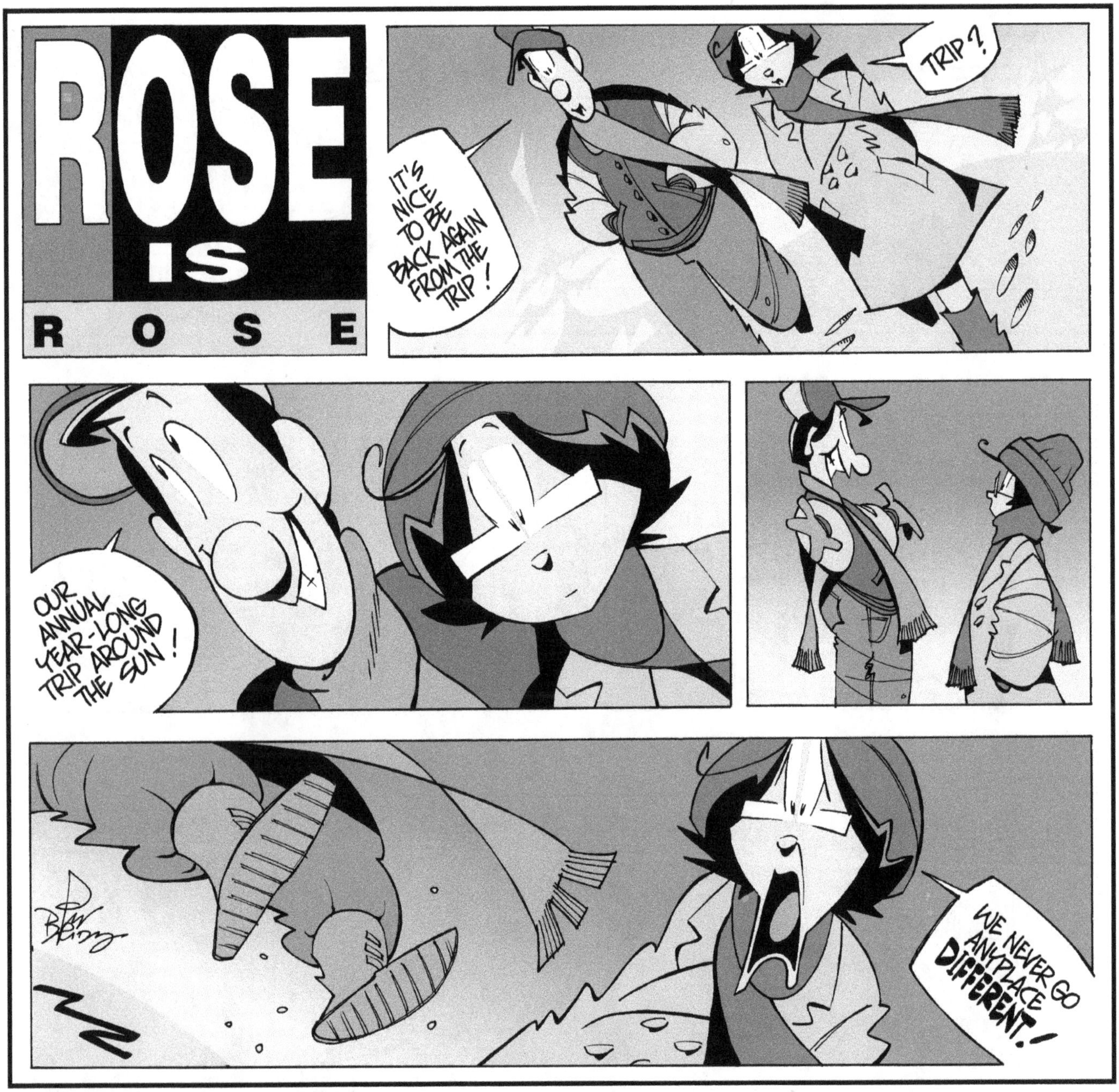
ROSE IS ROSE
IT'S NICE TO BE BACK AGAIN FROM THE TRIP!
TRIP?
OUR ANNUAL YEAR-LONG TRIP AROUND THE SUN!
WE NEVER GO ANYPLACE DIFFERENT!

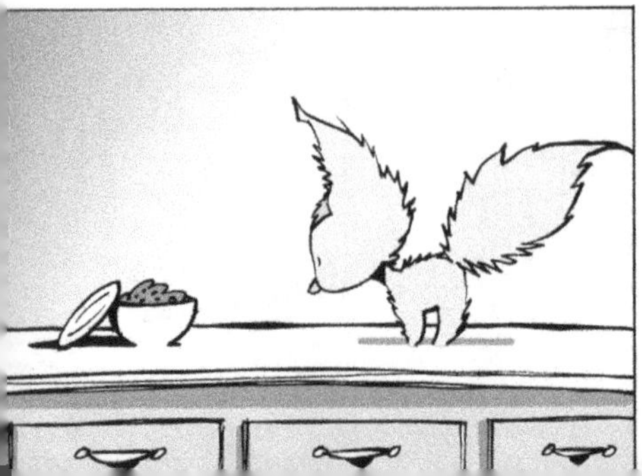

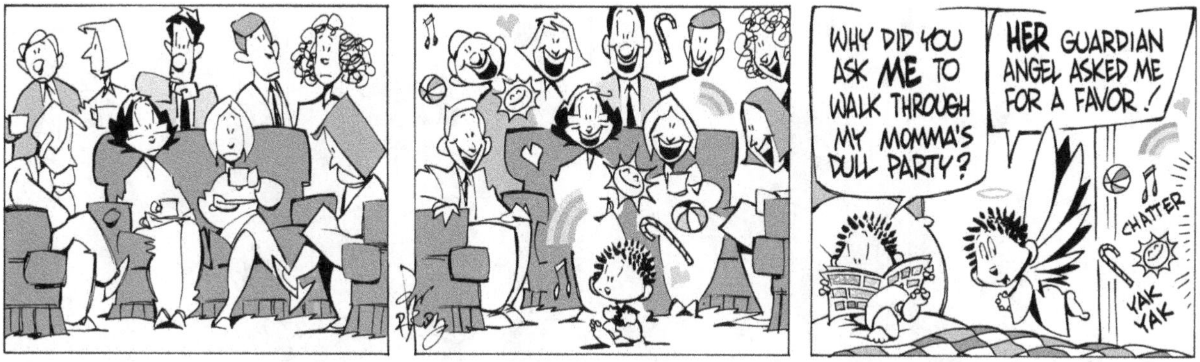
WHY DID YOU ASK ME TO WALK THROUGH MY MOMMA'S DULL PARTY?
HER GUARDIAN ANGEL ASKED ME FOR A FAVOR!
CHATTER
YAK YAK

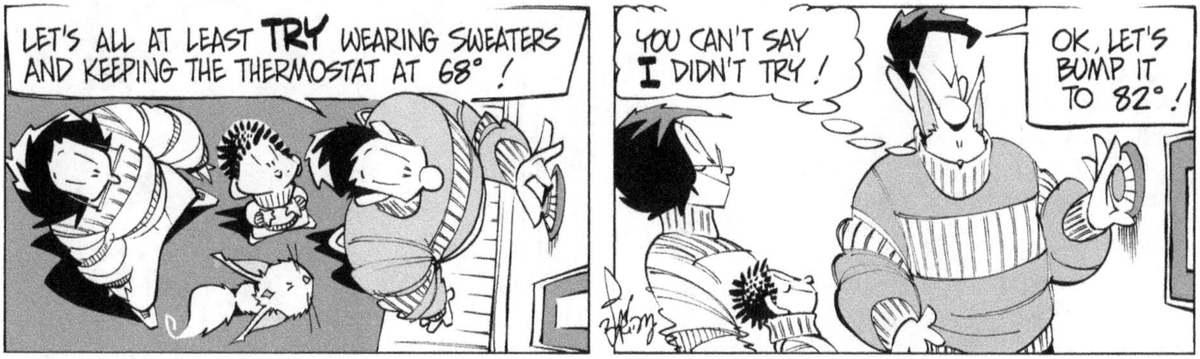
LET'S ALL AT LEAST TRY WEARING SWEATERS AND KEEPING THE THERMOSTAT AT 68°!
YOU CAN'T SAY I DIDN'T TRY!
OK, LET'S BUMP IT TO 82°!

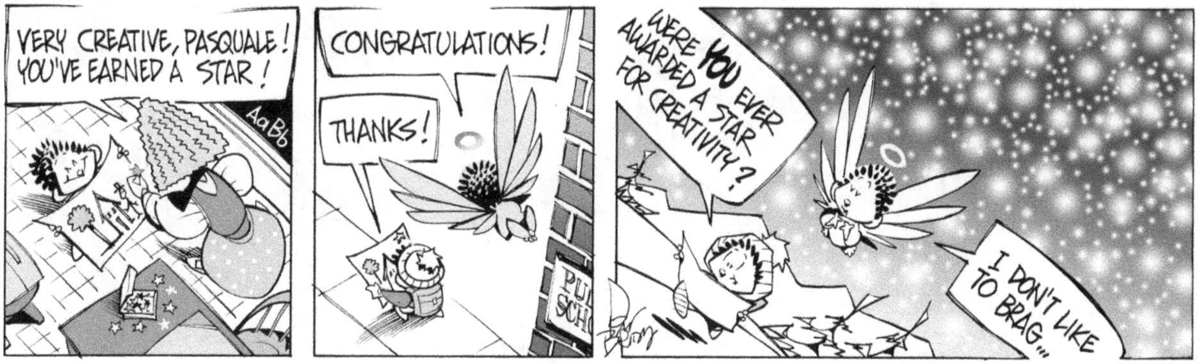
VERY CREATIVE, PASQUALE! YOU'VE EARNED A STAR!
AaBb
CONGRATULATIONS!
THANKS!
WERE YOU EVER AWARDED A STAR FOR CREATIVITY?
I DON'T LIKE TO BRAG...

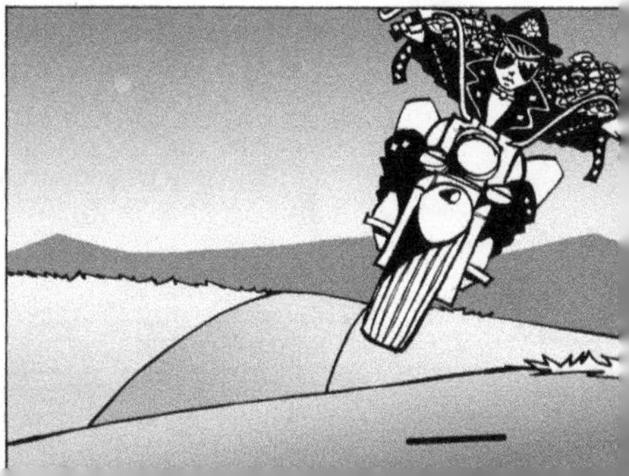

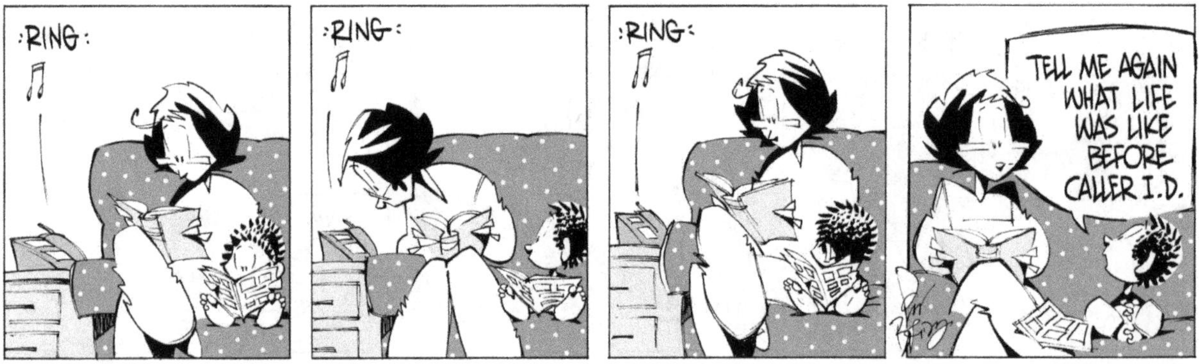
:RING:
:RING:
:RING:
TELL ME AGAIN WHAT LIFE WAS LIKE BEFORE CALLER I.D.

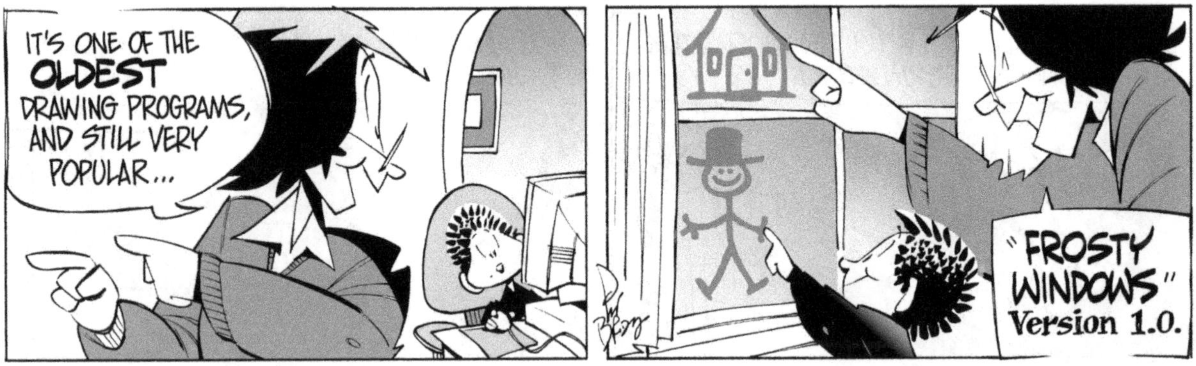
IT'S ONE OF THE OLDEST DRAWING PROGRAMS, AND STILL VERY POPULAR...
"FROSTY WINDOWS" Version 1.0.

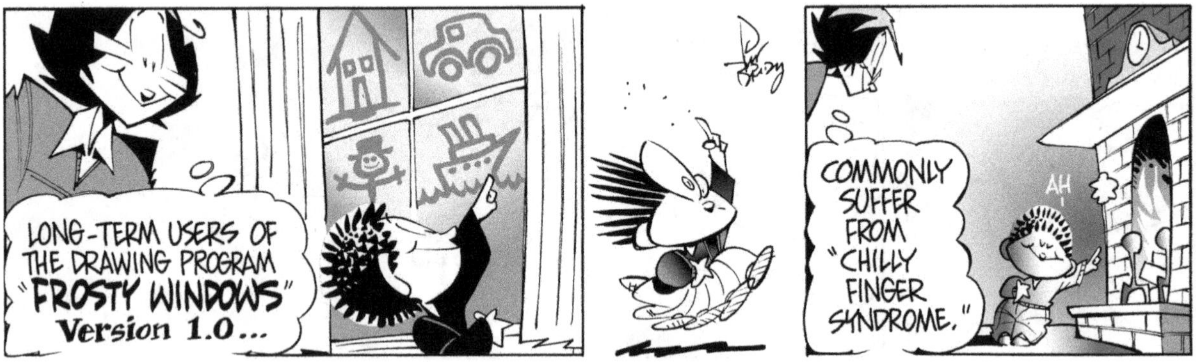
LONG-TERM USERS OF THE DRAWING PROGRAM "FROSTY WINDOWS" Version 1.0...
COMMONLY SUFFER FROM "CHILLY FINGER SYNDROME."
AH!

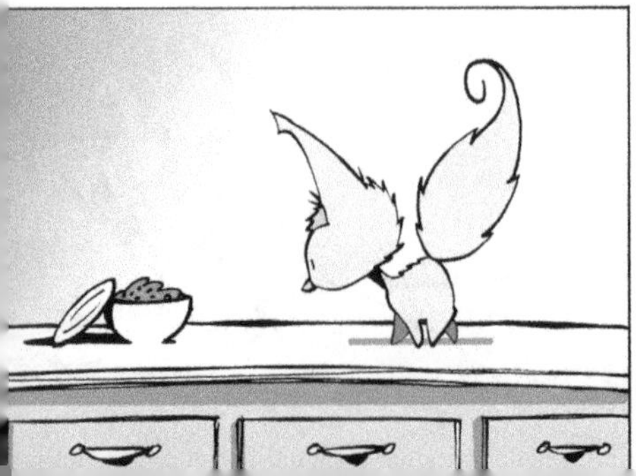

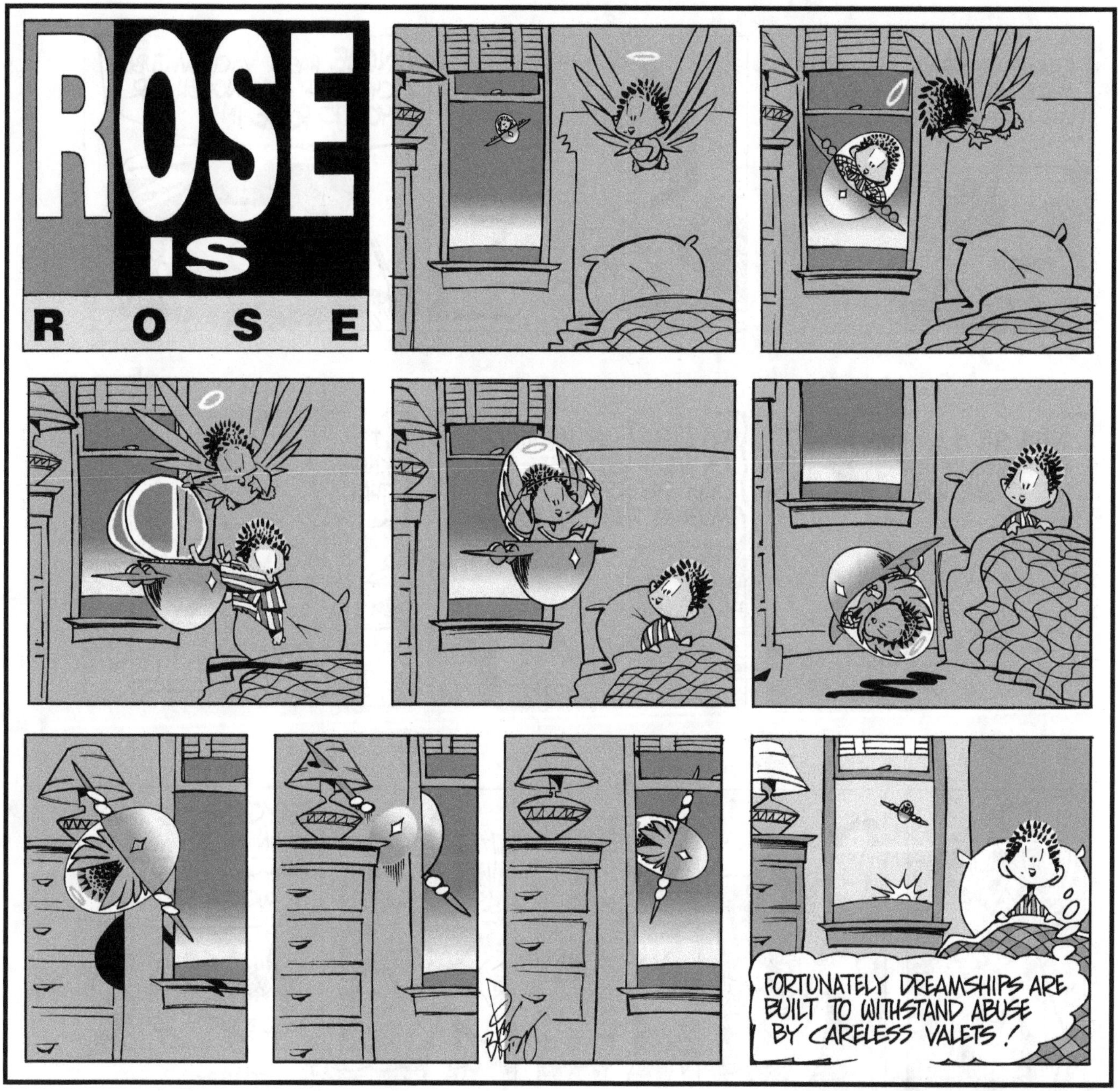
ROSE IS ROSE
FORTUNATELY DREAMSHIPS ARE BUILT TO WITHSTAND ABUSE BY CARELESS VALETS!

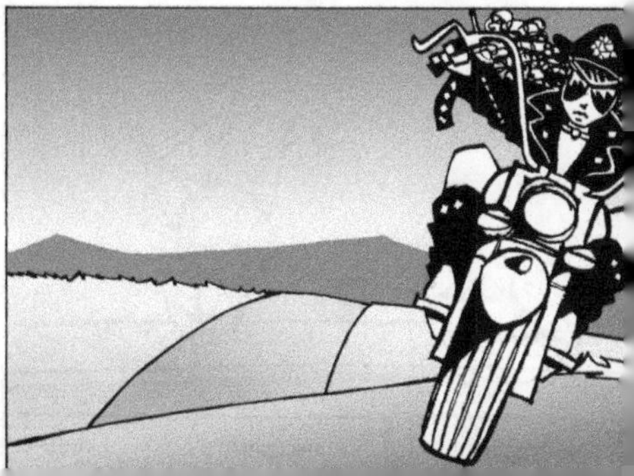

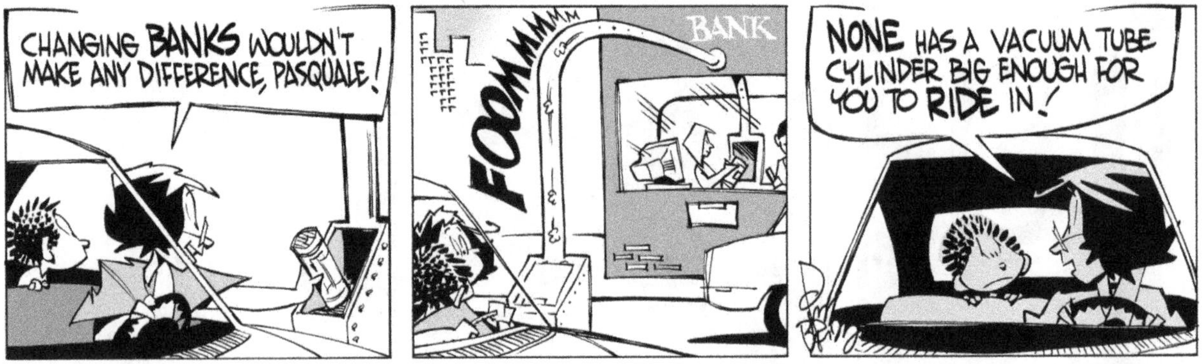
CHANGING BANKS WOULDN'T MAKE ANY DIFFERENCE, PASQUALE!
FOOMMMMMM
BANK
NONE HAS A VACUUM TUBE CYLINDER BIG ENOUGH FOR YOU TO RIDE IN!

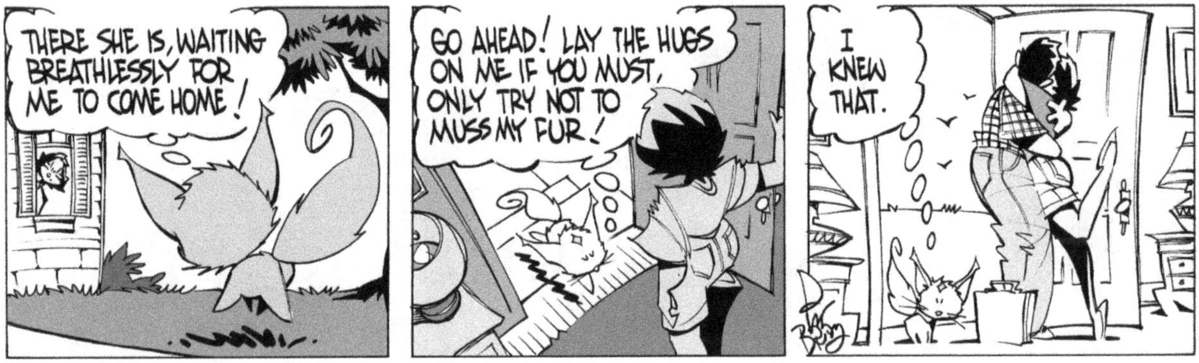
THERE SHE IS, WAITING BREATHLESSLY FOR ME TO COME HOME!
GO AHEAD! LAY THE HUGS ON ME IF YOU MUST, ONLY TRY NOT TO MUSS MY FUR!
I KNEW THAT.

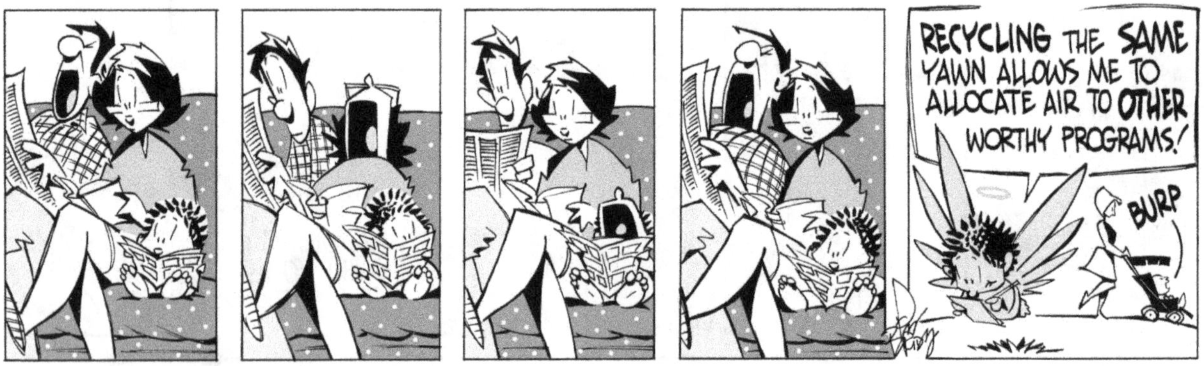
RECYCLING THE SAME YAWN ALLOWS ME TO ALLOCATE AIR TO OTHER WORTHY PROGRAMS!
BURP

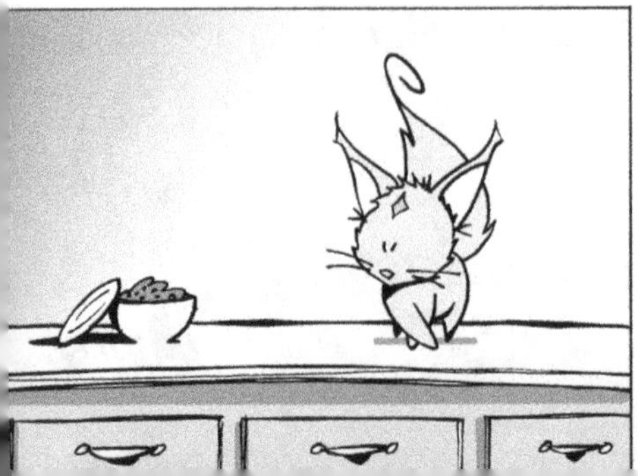

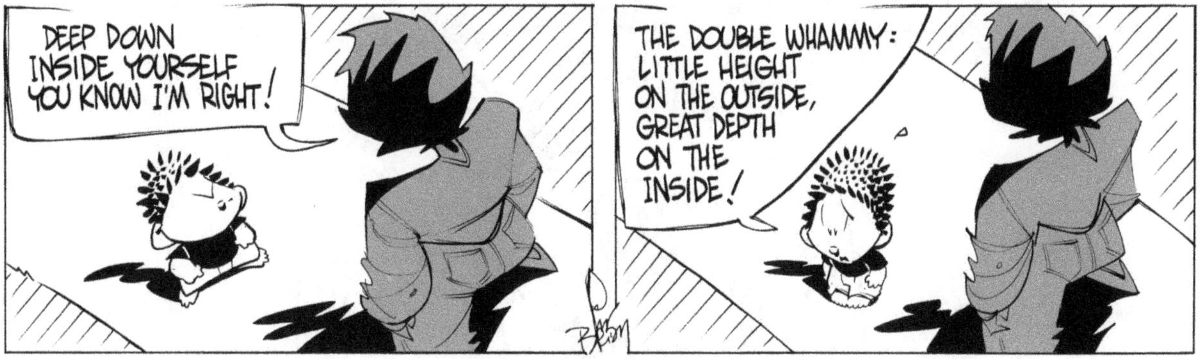
DEEP DOWN INSIDE YOURSELF YOU KNOW I'M RIGHT!
THE DOUBLE WHAMMY: LITTLE HEIGHT ON THE OUTSIDE, GREAT DEPTH ON THE INSIDE!

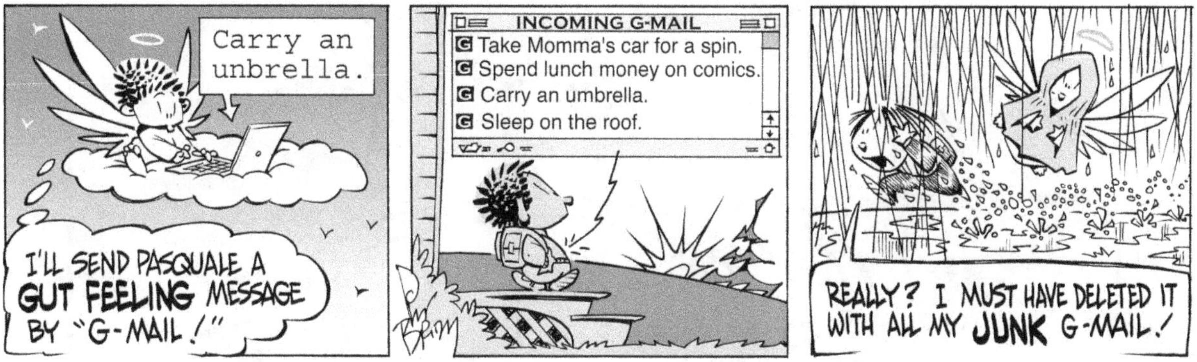
Carry an unbrella.
I'LL SEND PASQUALE A GUT FEELING MESSAGE BY "G-MAIL!"
INCOMING G-MAIL
Take Momma's car for a spin.
Spend lunch money on comics.
Carry an umbrella.
Sleep on the roof.
REALLY? I MUST HAVE DELETED IT WITH ALL MY JUNK G-MAIL!

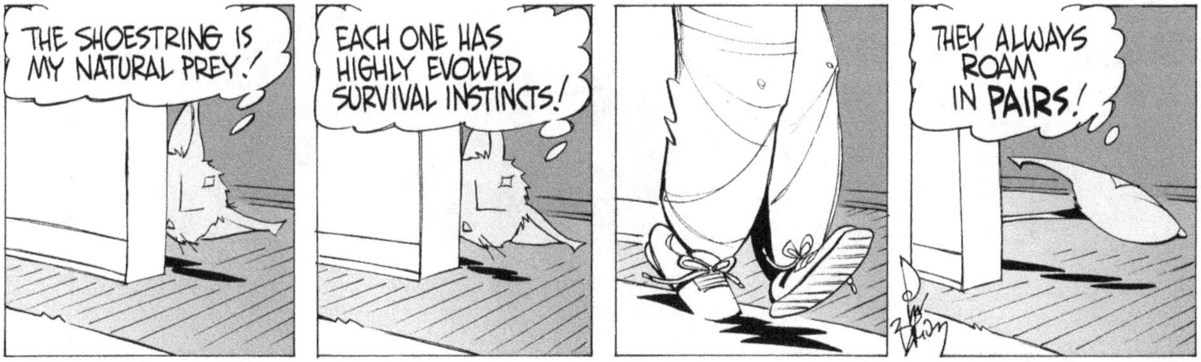
THE SHOESTRING IS MY NATURAL PREY!
EACH ONE HAS HIGHLY EVOLVED SURVIVAL INSTINCTS!
THEY ALWAYS ROAM IN PAIRS!

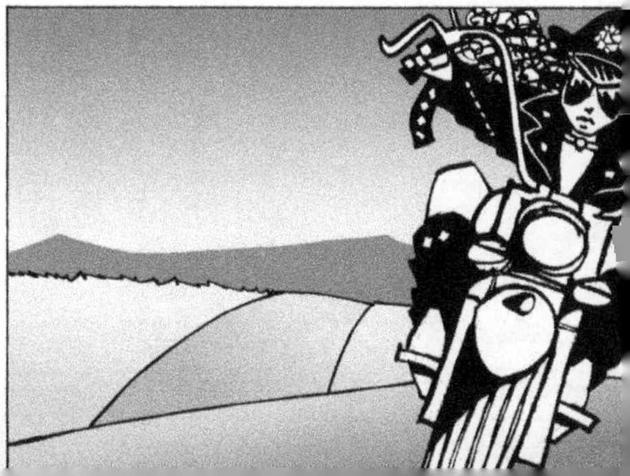

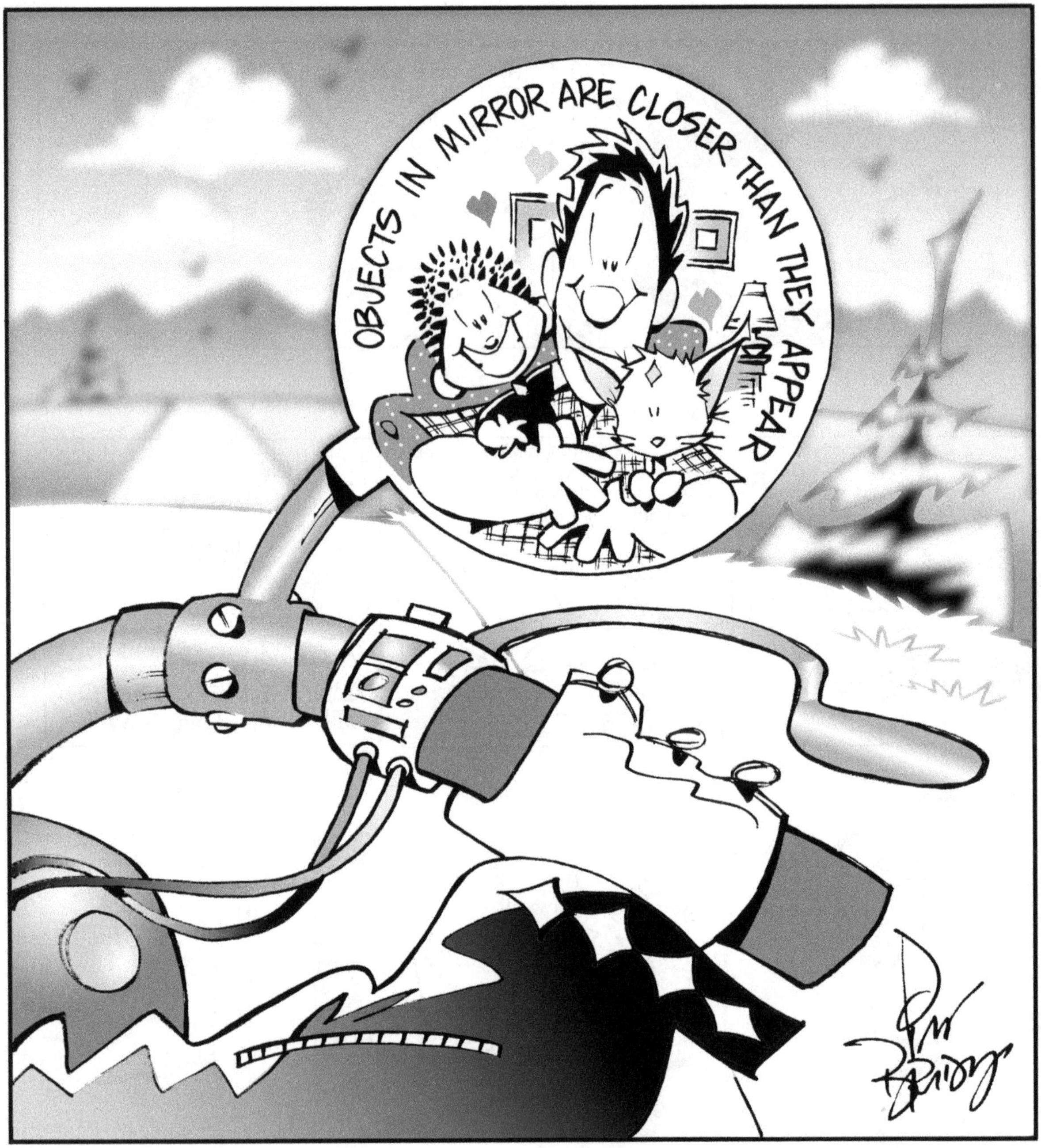
OBJECTS IN MIRROR ARE CLOSER THAN THEY APPEAR

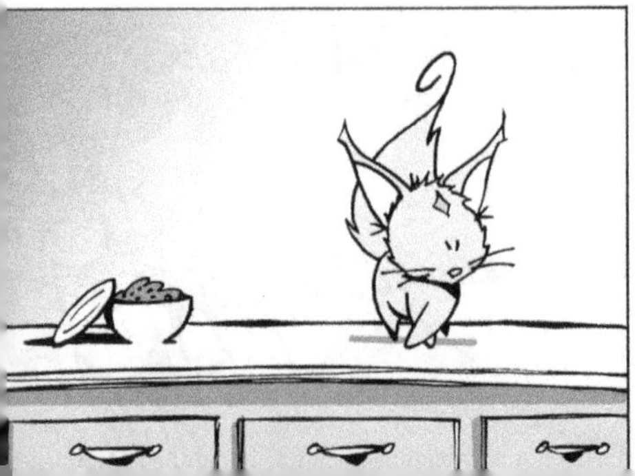

DON'T WORRY! HIS BARK IS WORSE THAN HIS BITE!
BARK! BARK! BARK! BARK!
HER YAWN IS WORSE YET!

WE'VE BEEN TOGETHER A LONG TIME...
AND I KNOW HOW YOU FEEL ABOUT ME...
STILL, IT'S IMPORTANT TO ME, TO HEAR YOU SAY IT!
PURRRR

HE WIPED HIS NOSE BEFORE COMING INSIDE. THAT'S A START!

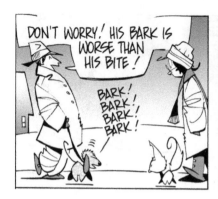

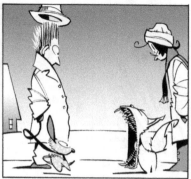

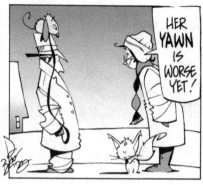

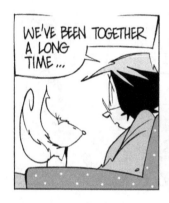

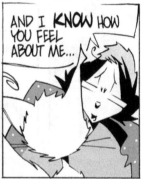

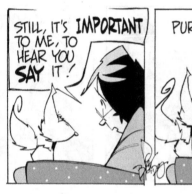

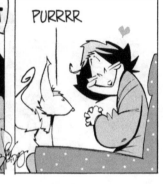

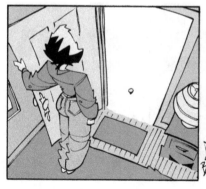

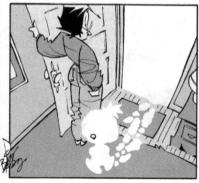

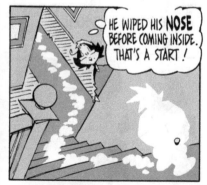

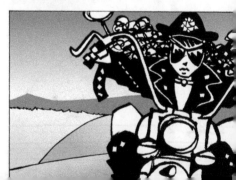

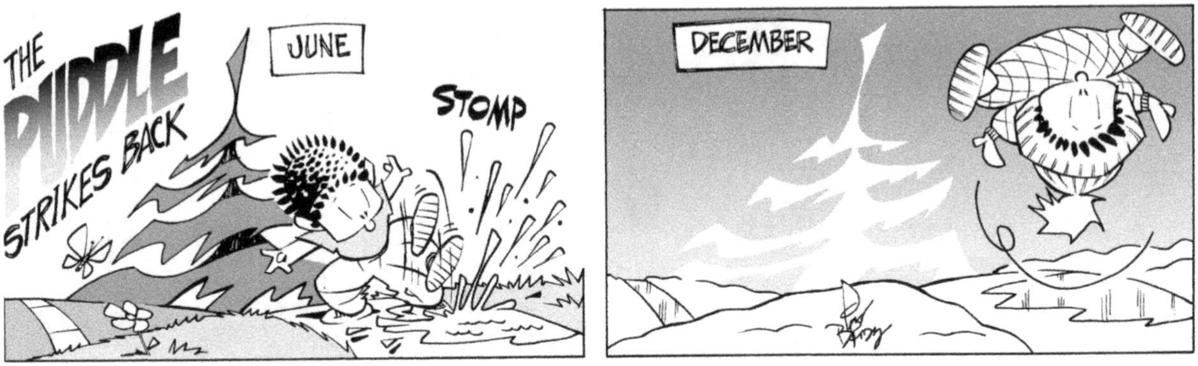
THE PUDDLE STRIKES BACK
JUNE
STOMP
DECEMBER

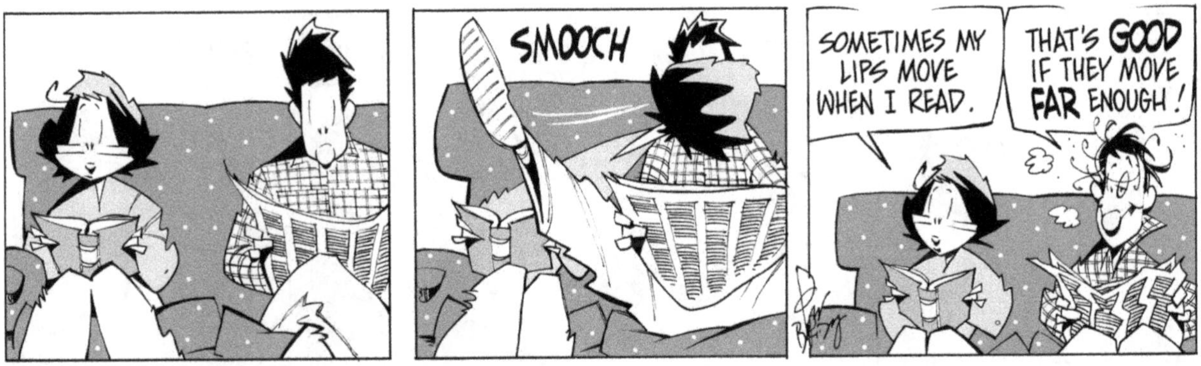
SMOOCH
SOMETIMES MY LIPS MOVE WHEN I READ.
THAT'S GOOD IF THEY MOVE FAR ENOUGH!

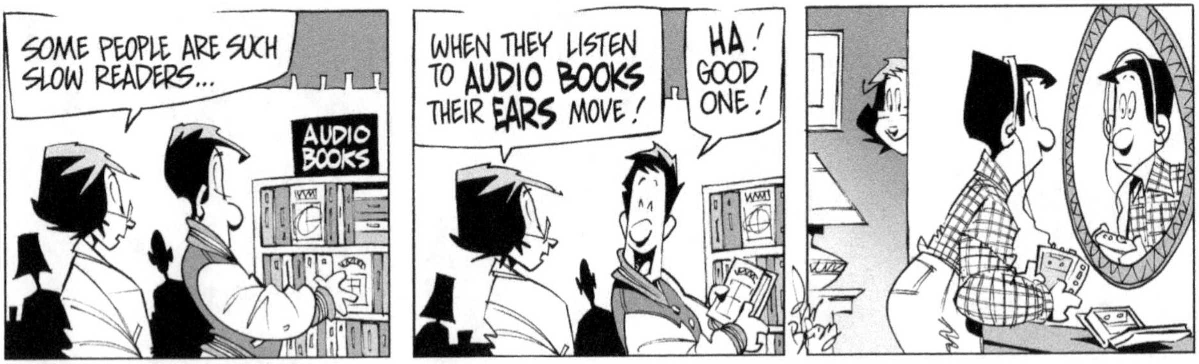
SOME PEOPLE ARE SUCH SLOW READERS...
AUDIO BOOKS
WHEN THEY LISTEN TO AUDIO BOOKS THEIR EARS MOVE!
HA! GOOD ONE!

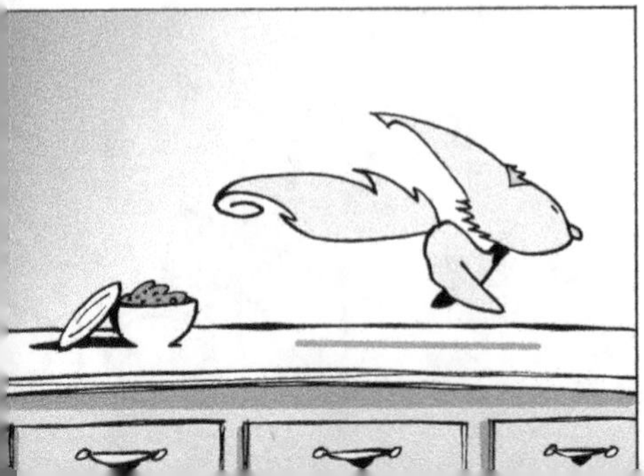

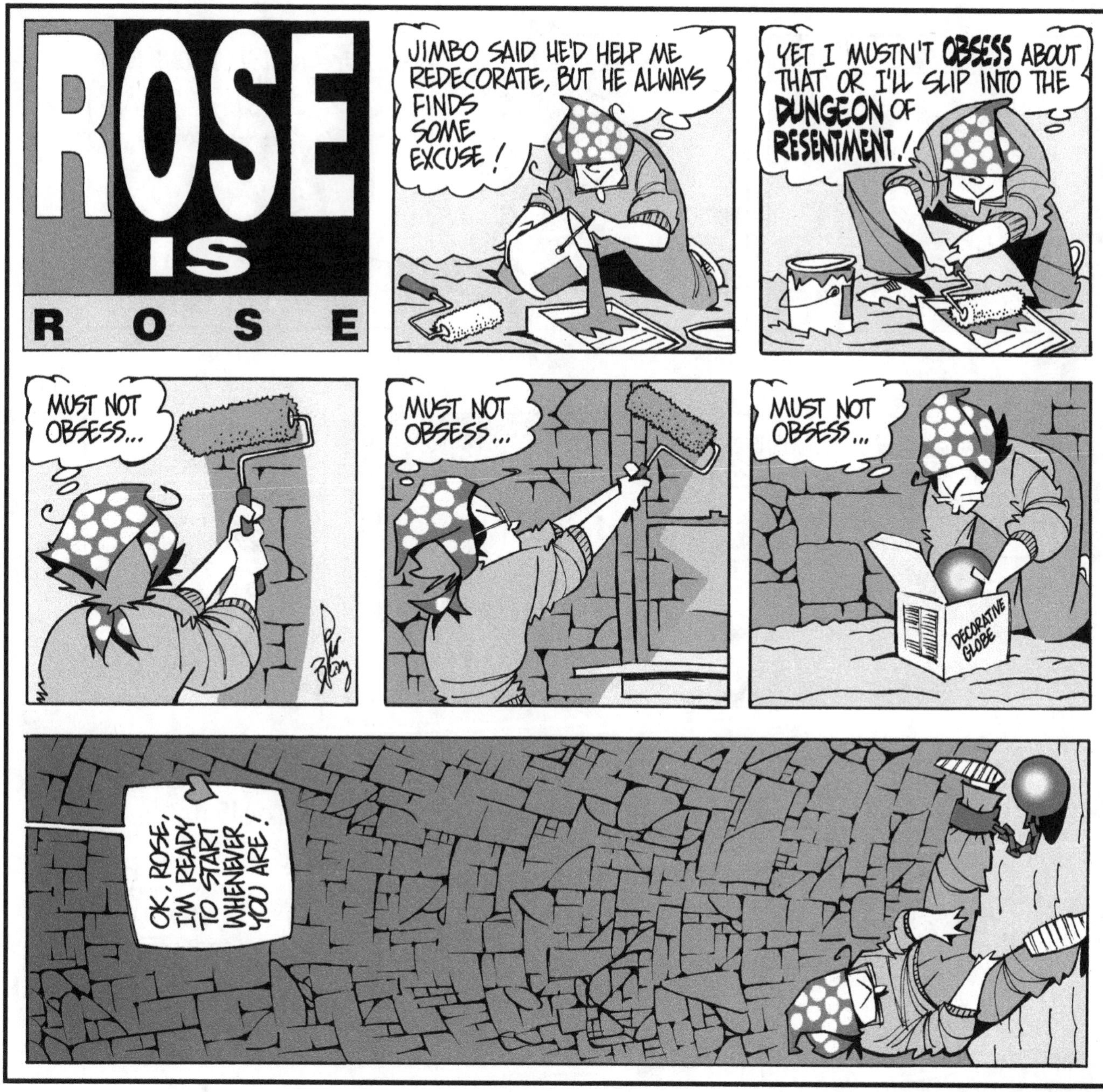
ROSE IS ROSE
JIMBO SAID HE'D HELP ME REDECORATE, BUT HE ALWAYS FINDS SOME EXCUSE!
YET I MUSTN'T OBSESS ABOUT THAT OR I'LL SLIP INTO THE DUNGEON OF RESENTMENT!
MUST NOT OBSESS...
MUST NOT OBSESS...
MUST NOT OBSESS...
DECORATIVE GLOBE
OK, ROSE, I'M READY TO START WHENEVER YOU ARE!

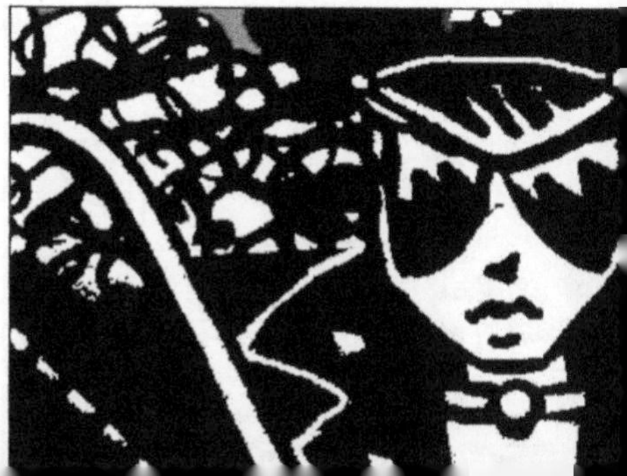

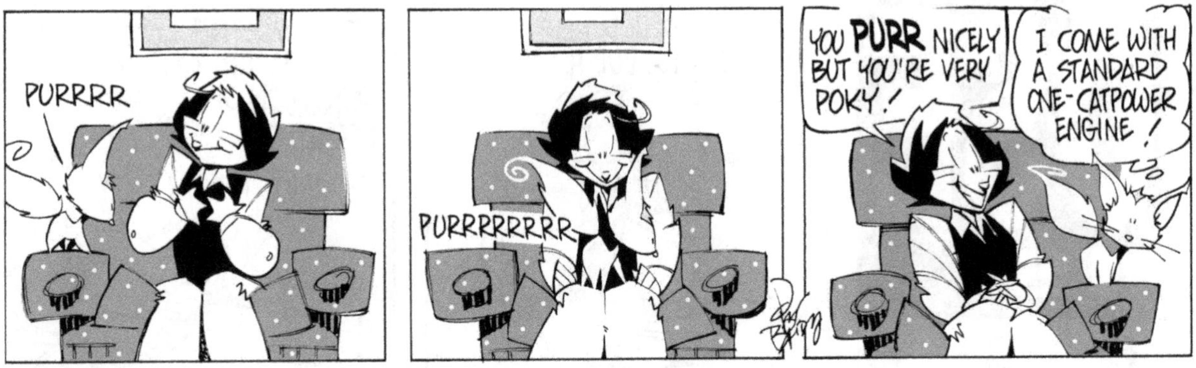
PURRRR
PURRRRRRRR
YOU **PURR** NICELY BUT YOU'RE VERY POKY!
I COME WITH A STANDARD ONE-CATPOWER ENGINE!

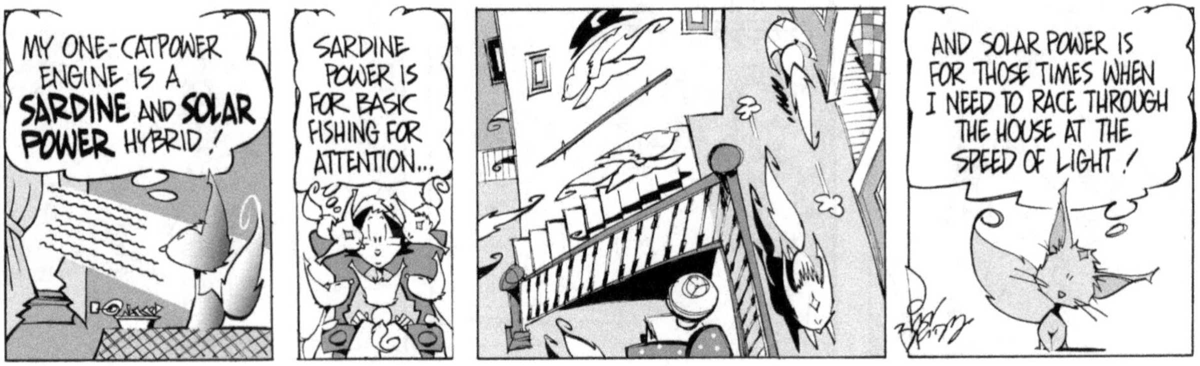
MY ONE-CATPOWER ENGINE IS A **SARDINE** AND **SOLAR POWER** HYBRID!
SARDINE POWER IS FOR BASIC FISHING FOR ATTENTION...
AND SOLAR POWER IS FOR THOSE TIMES WHEN I NEED TO RACE THROUGH THE HOUSE AT THE SPEED OF LIGHT!

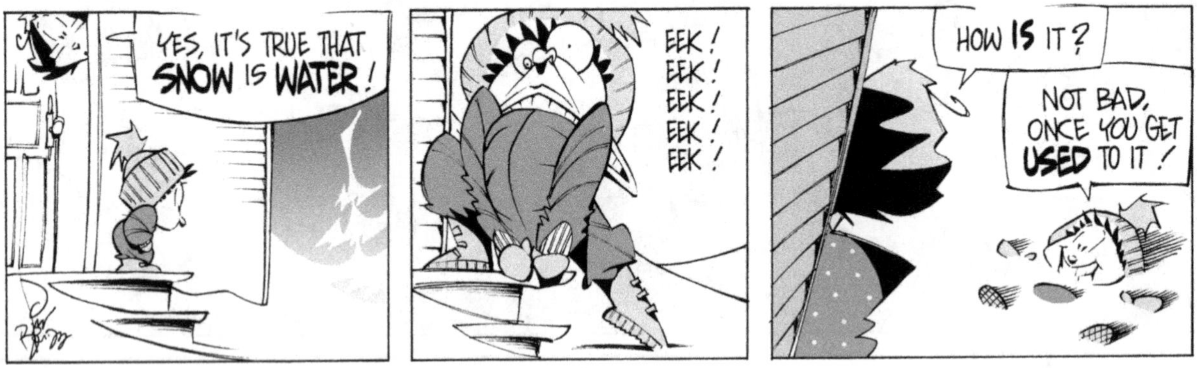
YES, IT'S TRUE THAT **SNOW** IS **WATER**!
EEK! EEK! EEK! EEK! EEK!
HOW **IS** IT?
NOT BAD, ONCE YOU GET **USED** TO IT!

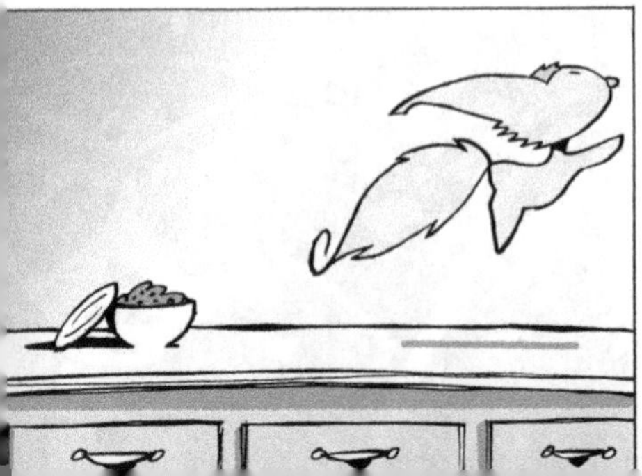

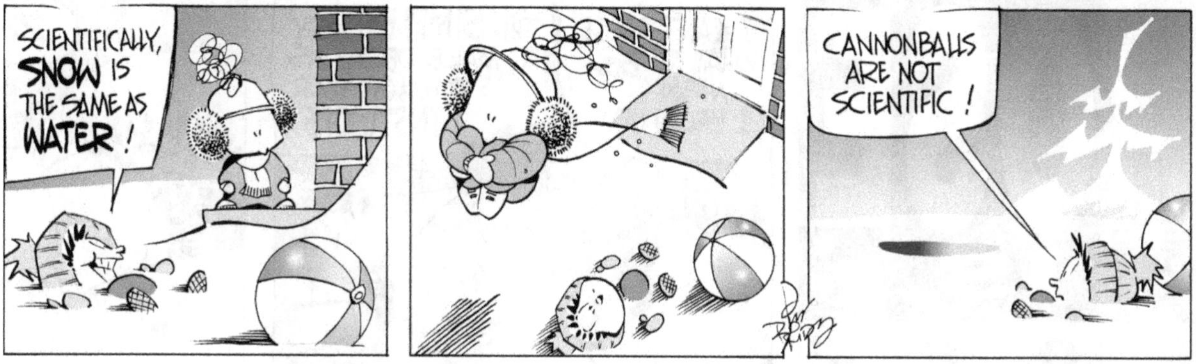
SCIENTIFICALLY, SNOW IS THE SAME AS WATER!
CANNONBALLS ARE NOT SCIENTIFIC!

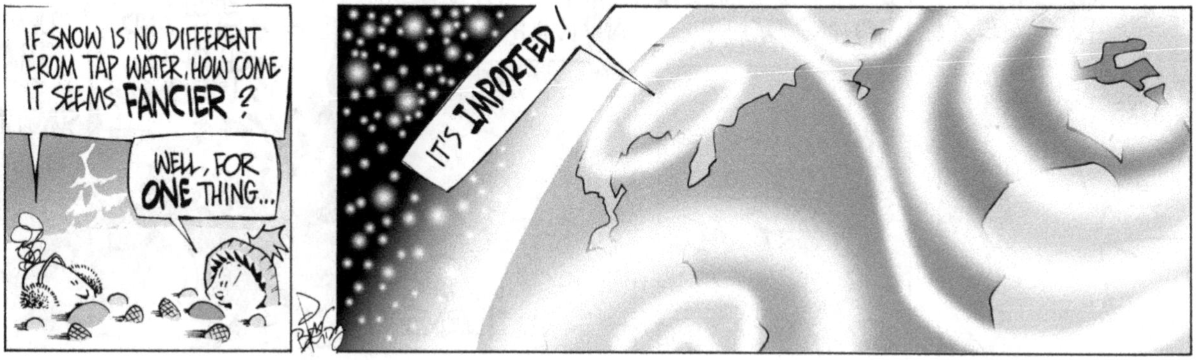
IF SNOW IS NO DIFFERENT FROM TAP WATER, HOW COME IT SEEMS FANCIER?
WELL, FOR ONE THING...
IT'S IMPORTED!

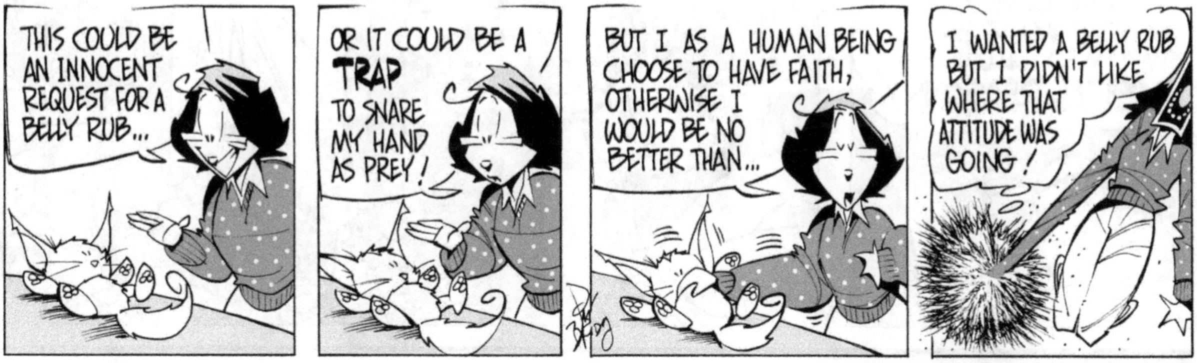
THIS COULD BE AN INNOCENT REQUEST FOR A BELLY RUB...
OR IT COULD BE A TRAP TO SNARE MY HAND AS PREY!
BUT I AS A HUMAN BEING CHOOSE TO HAVE FAITH, OTHERWISE I WOULD BE NO BETTER THAN...
I WANTED A BELLY RUB BUT I DIDN'T LIKE WHERE THAT ATTITUDE WAS GOING!

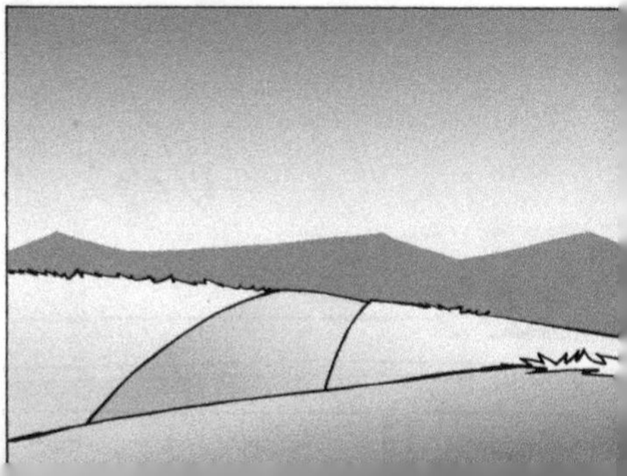

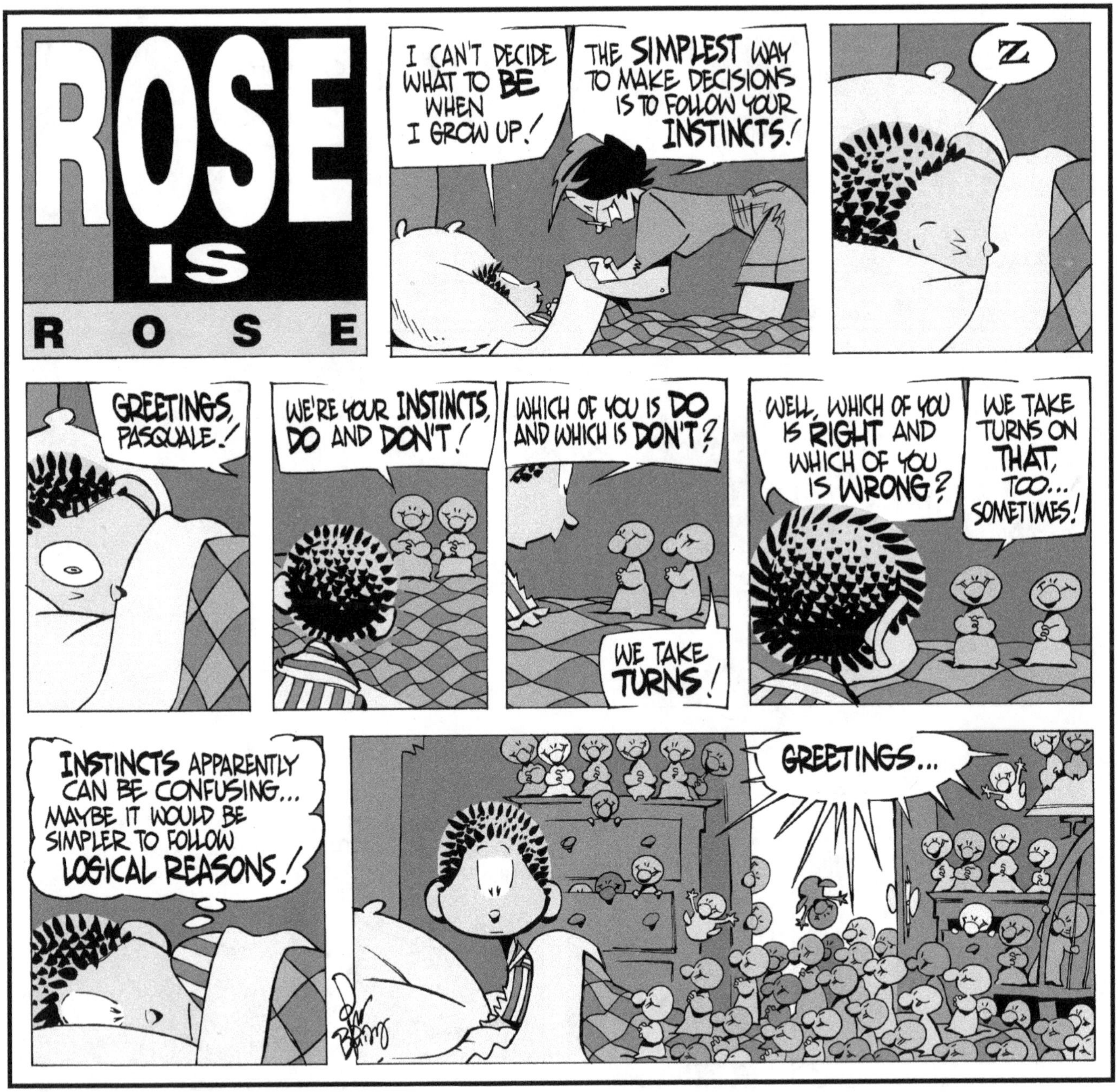
ROSE IS ROSE
I CAN'T DECIDE WHAT TO BE WHEN I GROW UP!
THE SIMPLEST WAY TO MAKE DECISIONS IS TO FOLLOW YOUR INSTINCTS!
Z
GREETINGS, PASQUALE!
WE'RE YOUR INSTINCTS, DO AND DON'T!
WHICH OF YOU IS DO AND WHICH IS DON'T?
WE TAKE TURNS!
WELL, WHICH OF YOU IS RIGHT AND WHICH OF YOU IS WRONG?
WE TAKE TURNS ON THAT, TOO... SOMETIMES!
INSTINCTS APPARENTLY CAN BE CONFUSING... MAYBE IT WOULD BE SIMPLER TO FOLLOW LOGICAL REASONS!
GREETINGS...

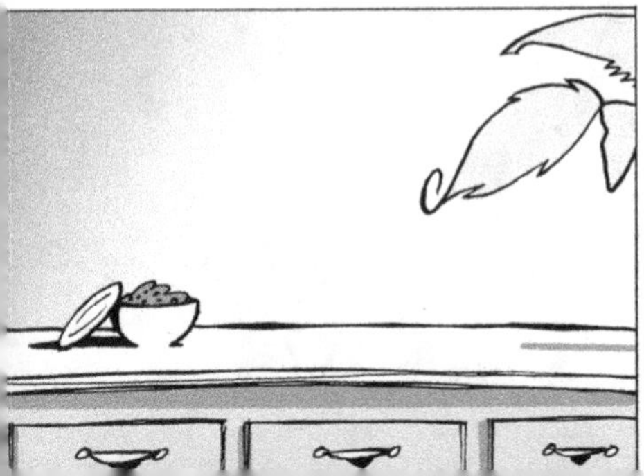

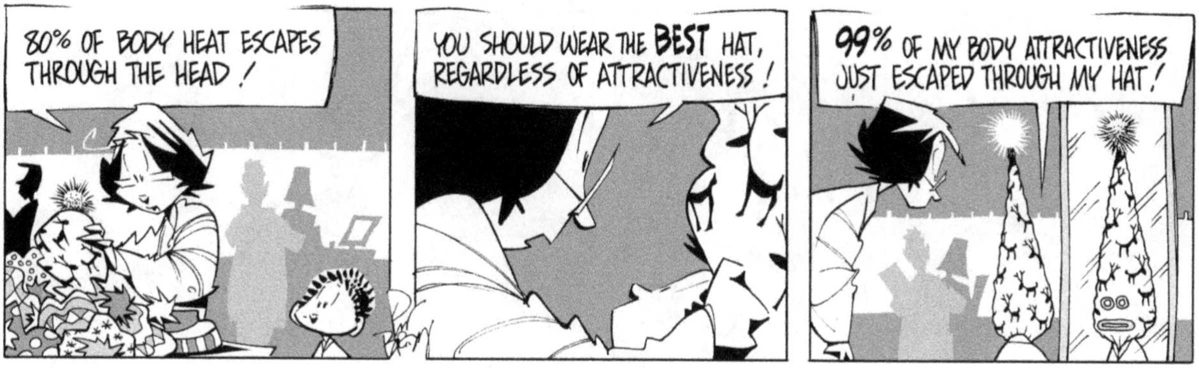
80% OF BODY HEAT ESCAPES THROUGH THE HEAD!
YOU SHOULD WEAR THE **BEST** HAT, REGARDLESS OF ATTRACTIVENESS!
99% OF MY BODY ATTRACTIVENESS JUST ESCAPED THROUGH MY HAT!

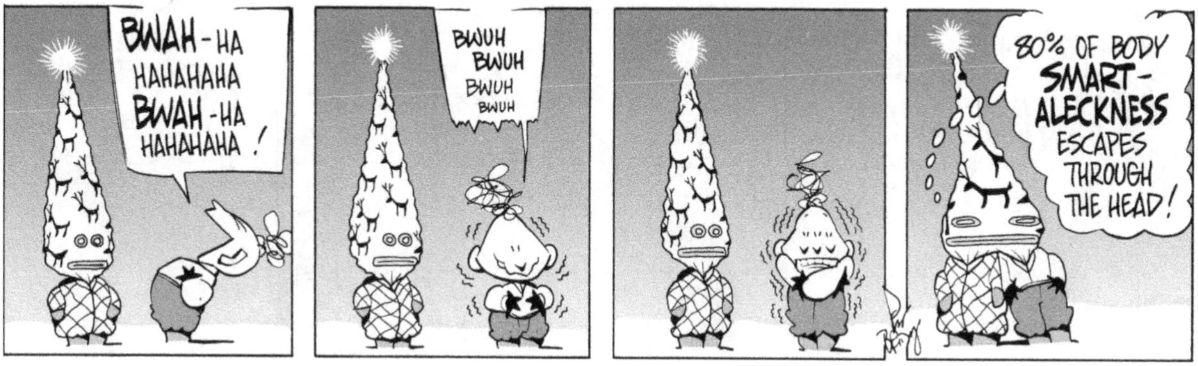
BWAH-HA HAHAHAHA **BWAH**-HA HAHAHAHA!
BWUH BWUH BWUH BWUH
80% OF BODY **SMART-ALECKNESS** ESCAPES THROUGH THE HEAD!

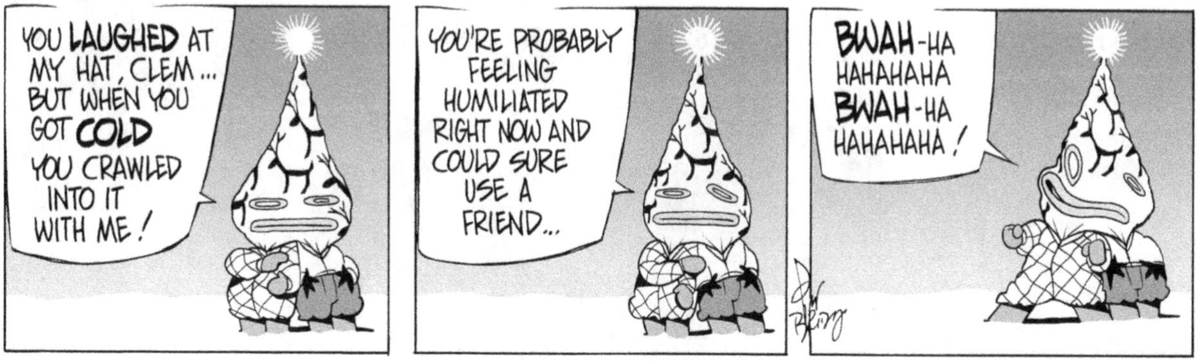
YOU **LAUGHED** AT MY HAT, CLEM... BUT WHEN YOU GOT **COLD** YOU CRAWLED INTO IT WITH ME!
YOU'RE PROBABLY FEELING HUMILIATED RIGHT NOW AND COULD SURE USE A FRIEND...
BWAH-HA HAHAHAHA **BWAH**-HA HAHAHAHA!

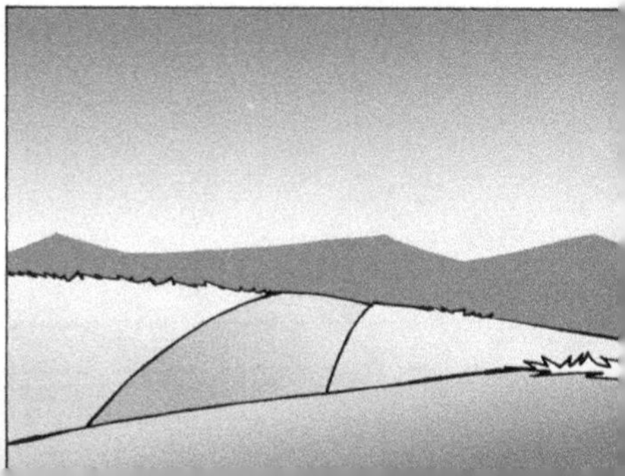

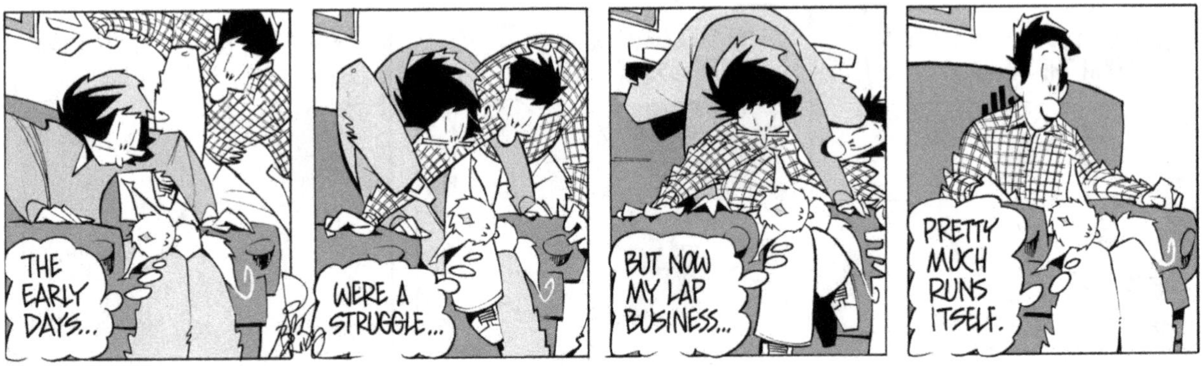
THE EARLY DAYS...
WERE A STRUGGLE...
BUT NOW MY LAP BUSINESS...
PRETTY MUCH RUNS ITSELF.

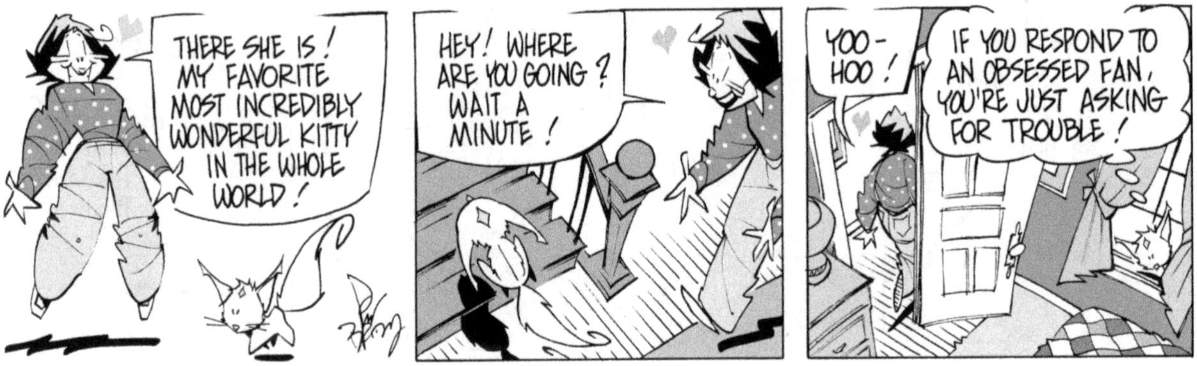
THERE SHE IS! MY FAVORITE MOST INCREDIBLY WONDERFUL KITTY IN THE WHOLE WORLD!
HEY! WHERE ARE YOU GOING? WAIT A MINUTE!
YOO-HOO!
IF YOU RESPOND TO AN OBSESSED FAN, YOU'RE JUST ASKING FOR TROUBLE!

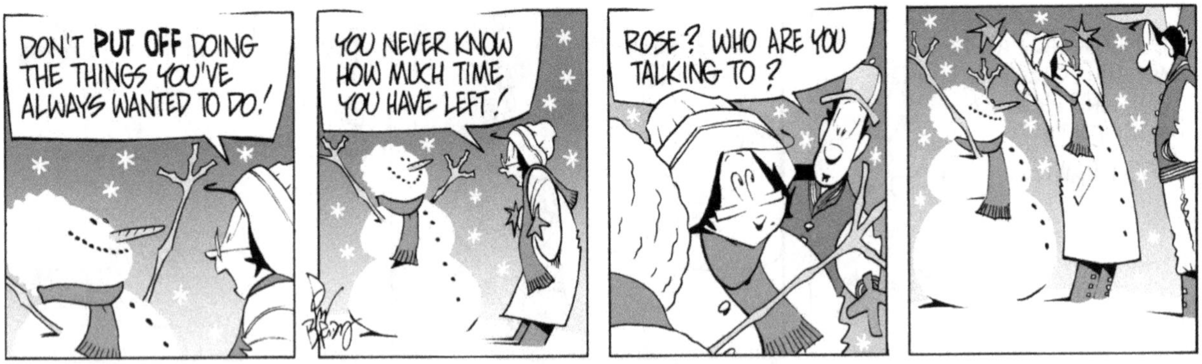
DON'T PUT OFF DOING THE THINGS YOU'VE ALWAYS WANTED TO DO!
YOU NEVER KNOW HOW MUCH TIME YOU HAVE LEFT!
ROSE? WHO ARE YOU TALKING TO?

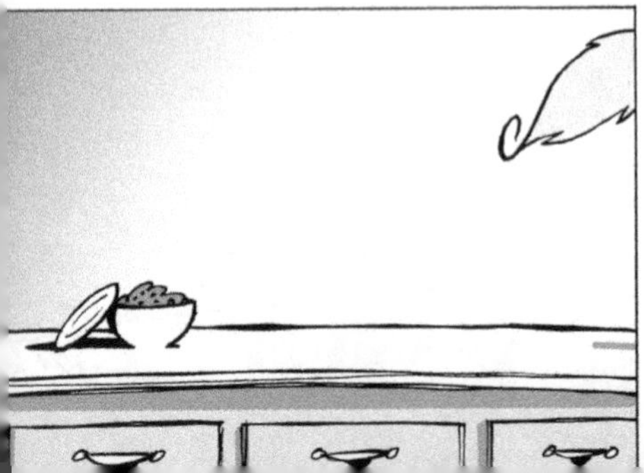

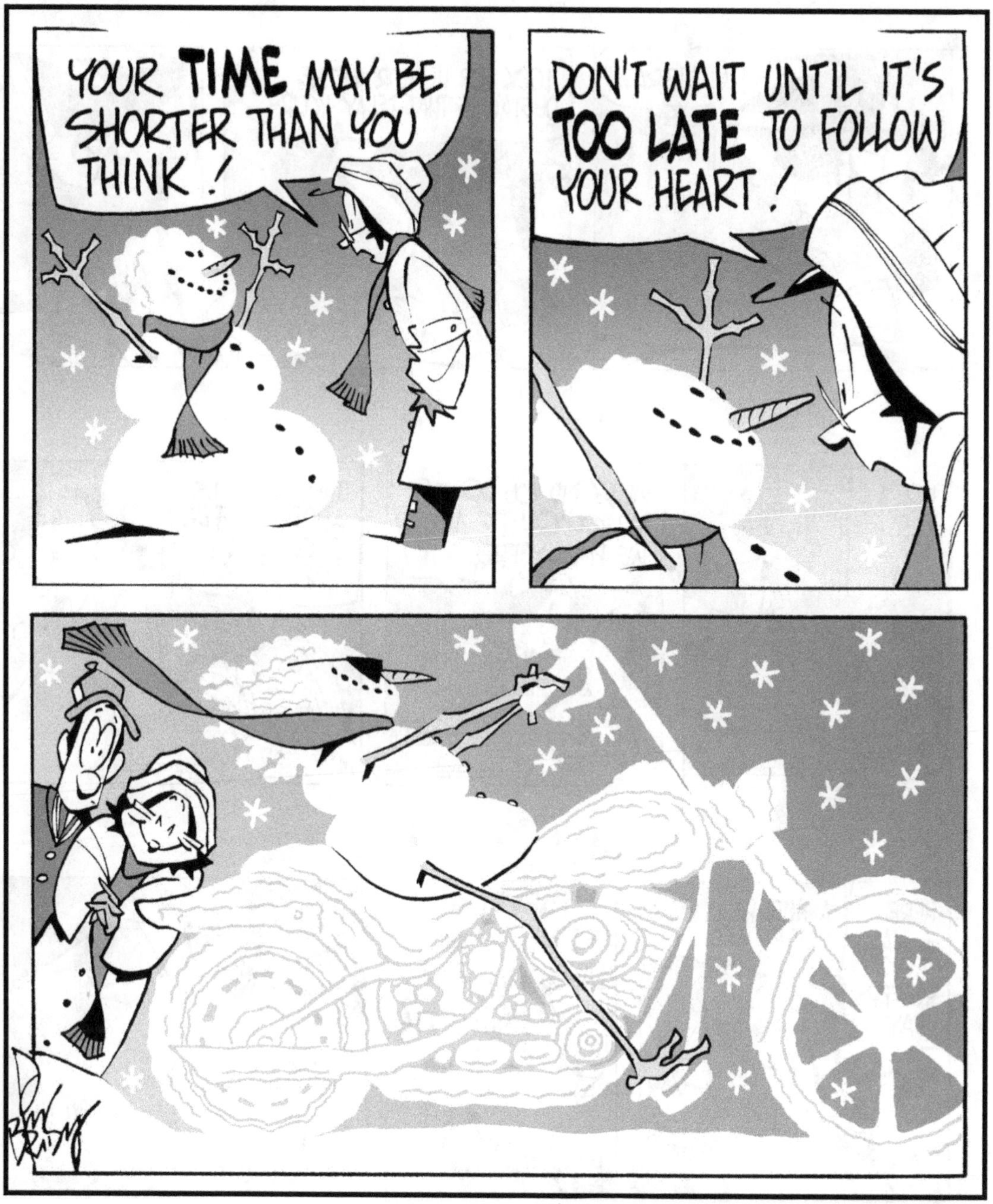

YOUR **TIME** MAY BE SHORTER THAN YOU THINK!
DON'T WAIT UNTIL IT'S **TOO LATE** TO FOLLOW YOUR HEART!

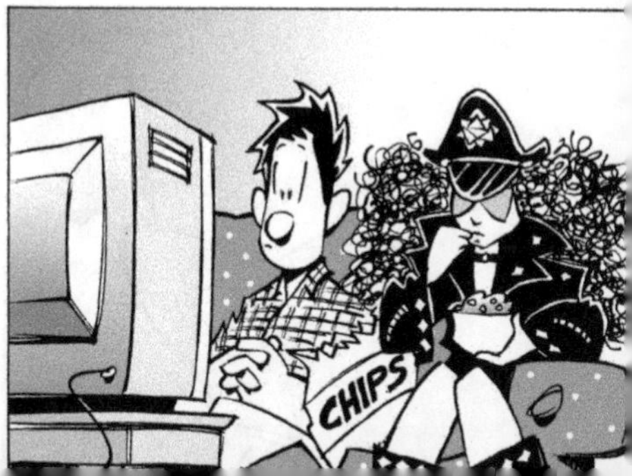

CHIPS

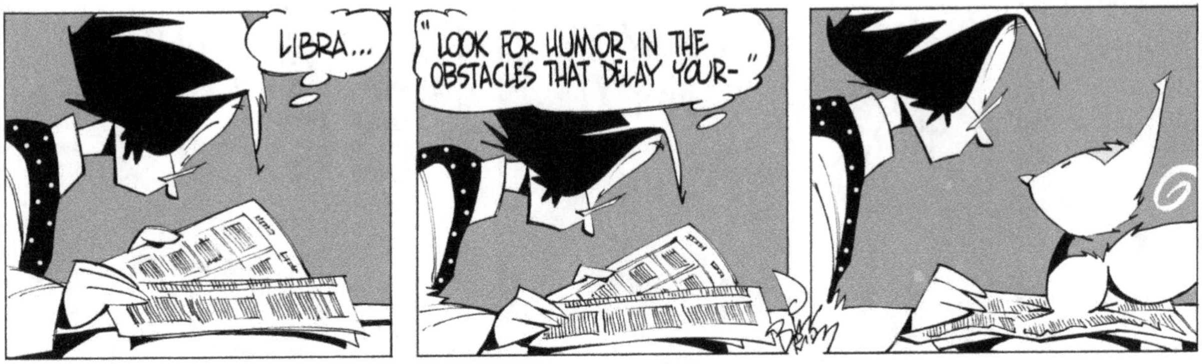
LIBRA...
"LOOK FOR HUMOR IN THE OBSTACLES THAT DELAY YOUR-"

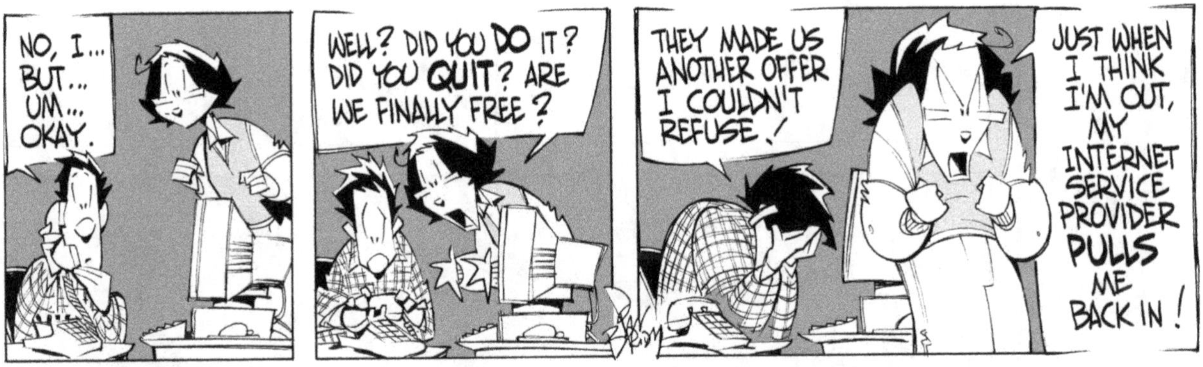
NO, I... BUT... UM... OKAY.
WELL? DID YOU DO IT? DID YOU QUIT? ARE WE FINALLY FREE?
THEY MADE US ANOTHER OFFER I COULDN'T REFUSE!
JUST WHEN I THINK I'M OUT, MY INTERNET SERVICE PROVIDER PULLS ME BACK IN!

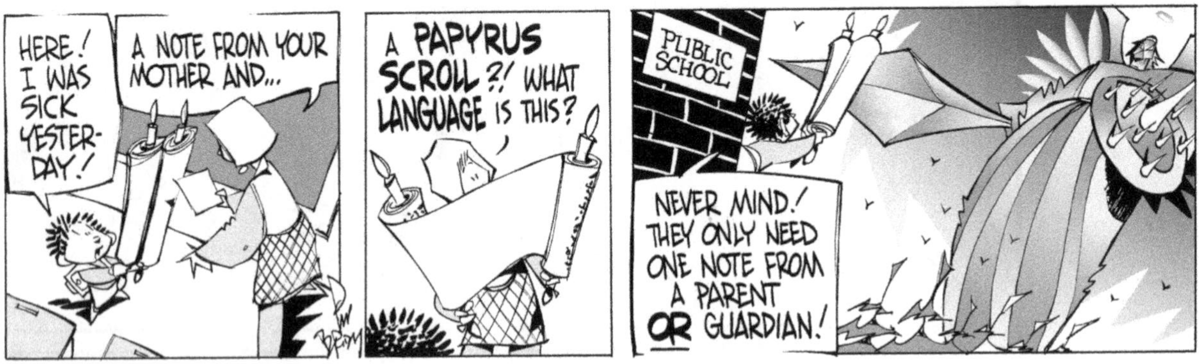
HERE! I WAS SICK YESTERDAY!
A NOTE FROM YOUR MOTHER AND...
A PAPYRUS SCROLL?! WHAT LANGUAGE IS THIS?
PUBLIC SCHOOL
NEVER MIND! THEY ONLY NEED ONE NOTE FROM A PARENT OR GUARDIAN!

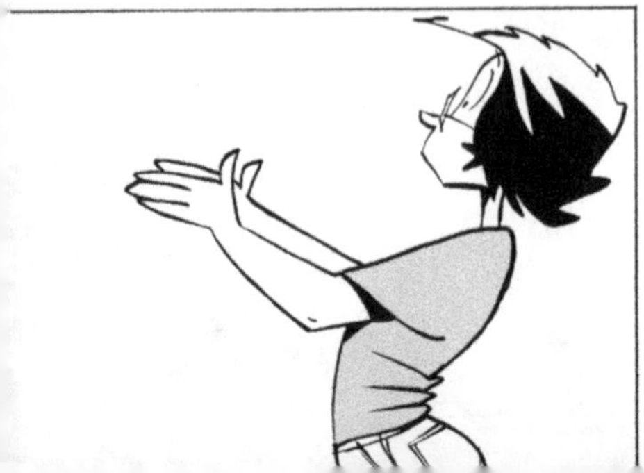

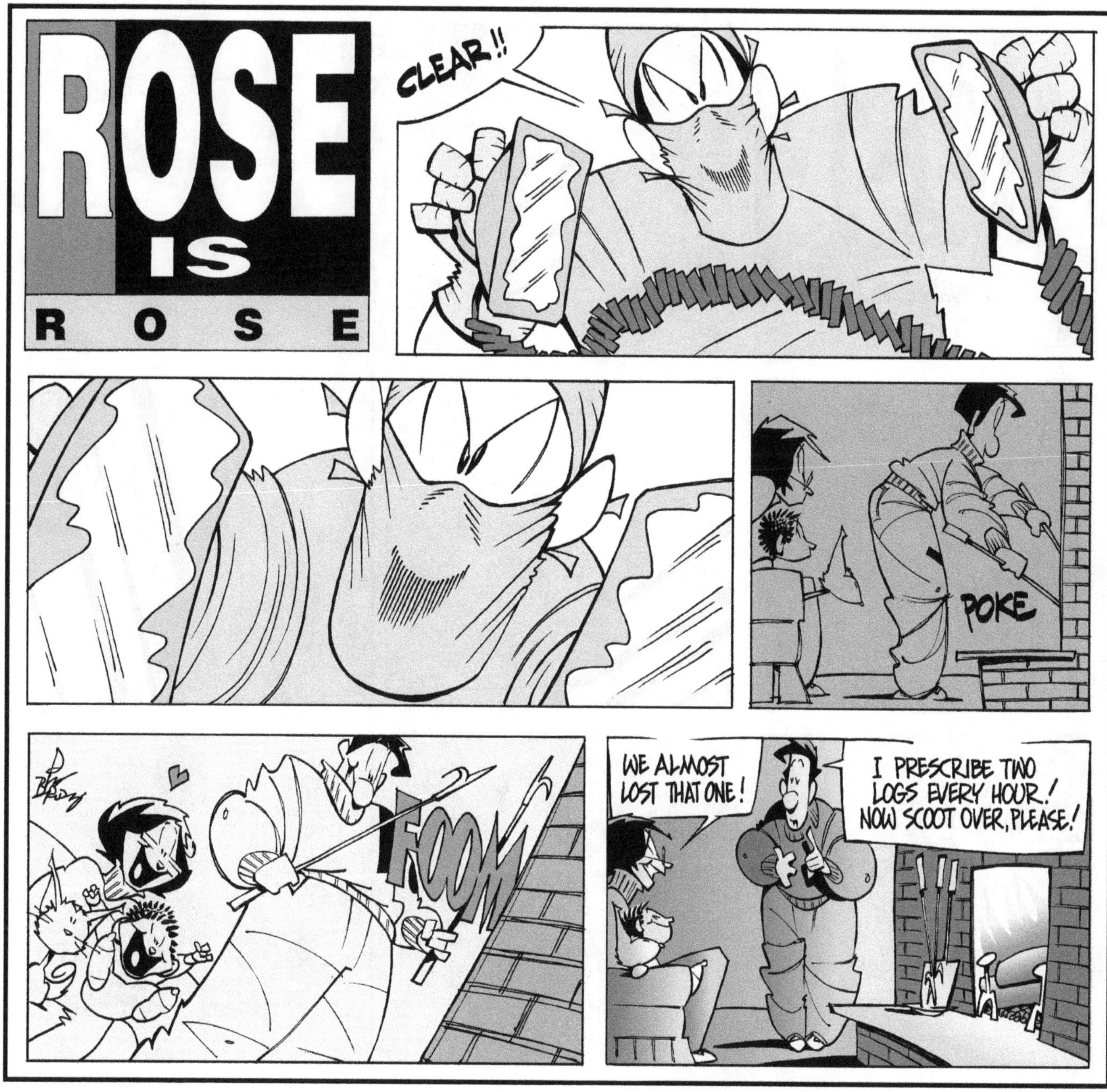
ROSE IS ROSE
CLEAR!!
POKE
FOOM
WE ALMOST LOST THAT ONE!
I PRESCRIBE TWO LOGS EVERY HOUR! NOW SCOOT OVER, PLEASE!

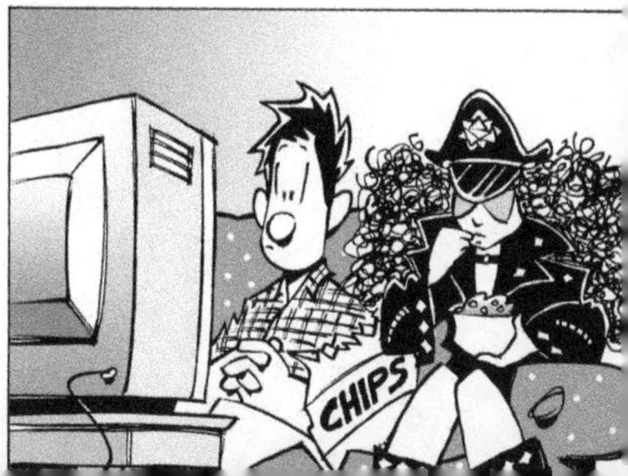
CHIPS

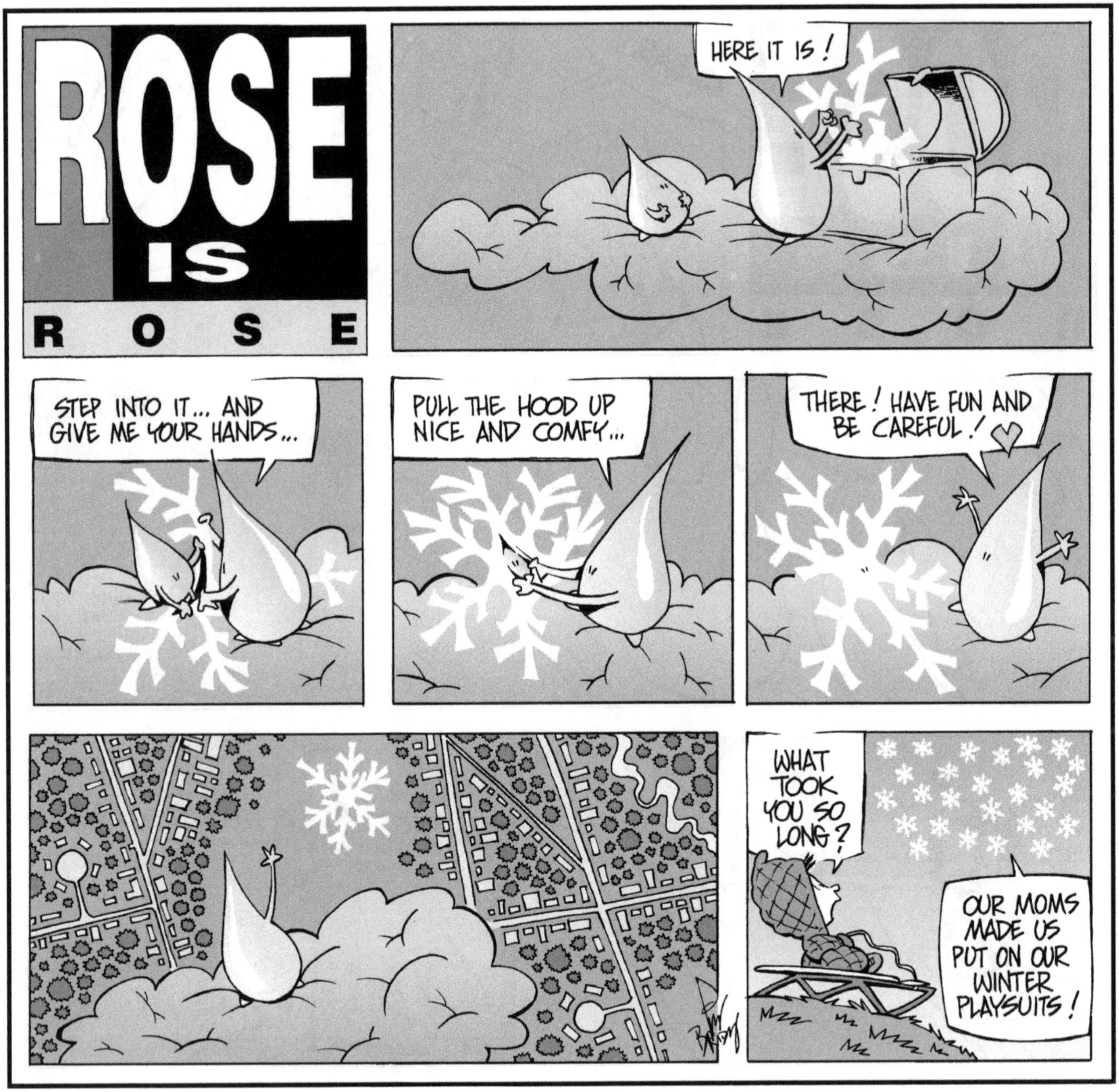
ROSE IS ROSE
HERE IT IS!
STEP INTO IT... AND GIVE ME YOUR HANDS...
PULL THE HOOD UP NICE AND COMFY...
THERE! HAVE FUN AND BE CAREFUL!
WHAT TOOK YOU SO LONG?
OUR MOMS MADE US PUT ON OUR WINTER PLAYSUITS!

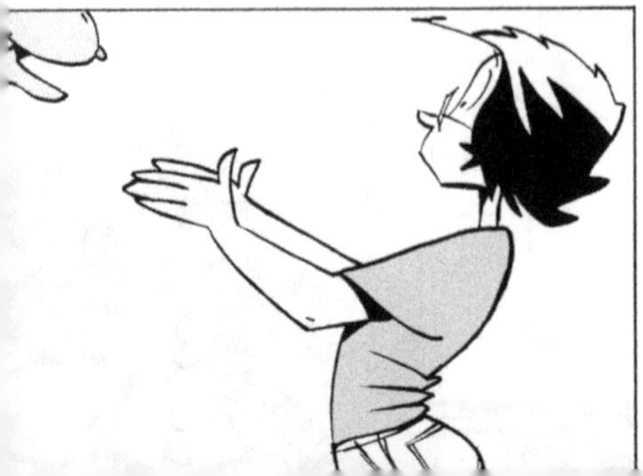

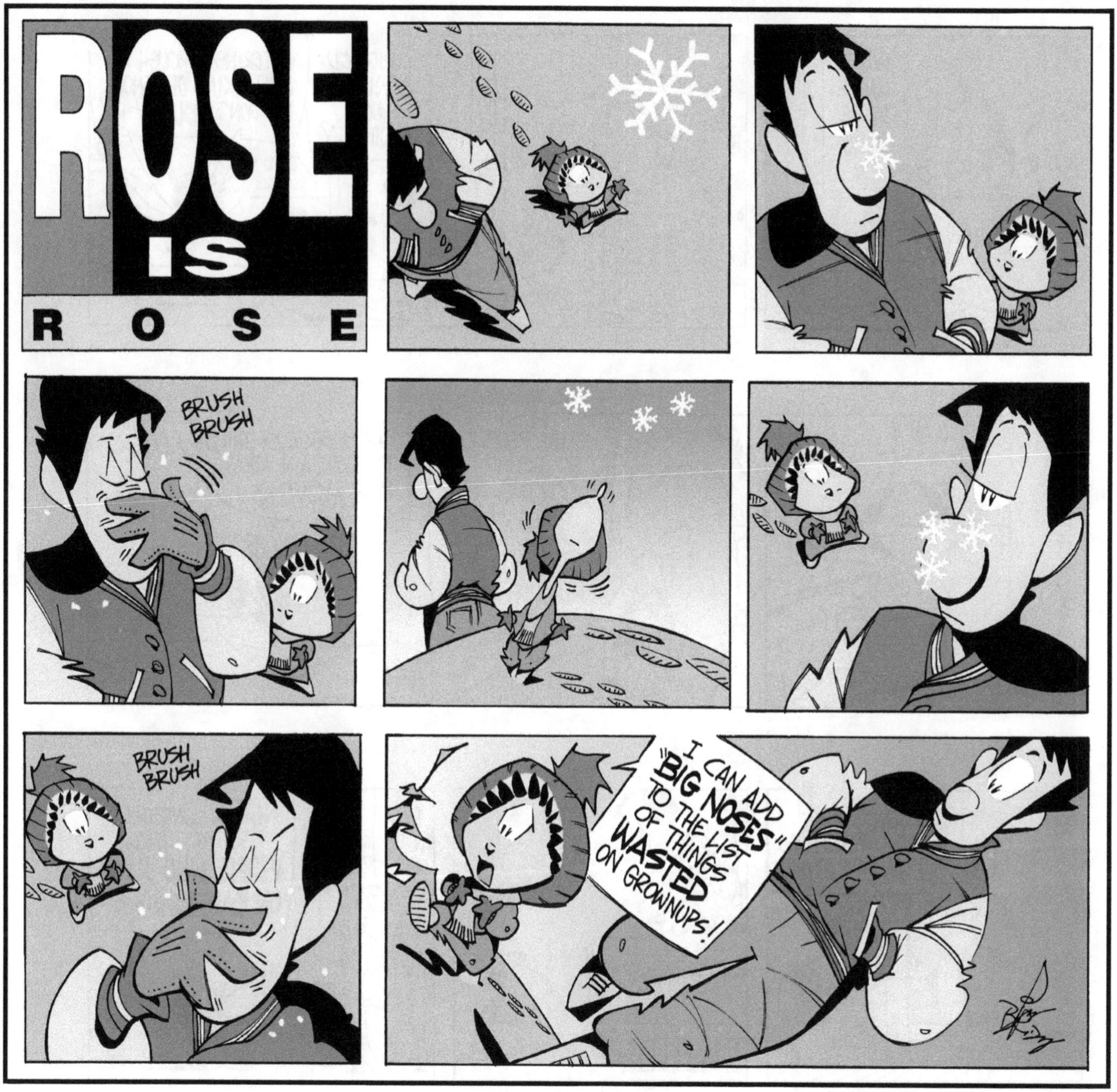
ROSE IS ROSE
BRUSH BRUSH
BRUSH BRUSH
I CAN ADD "BIG NOSES" TO THE LIST OF THINGS WASTED ON GROWNUPS!

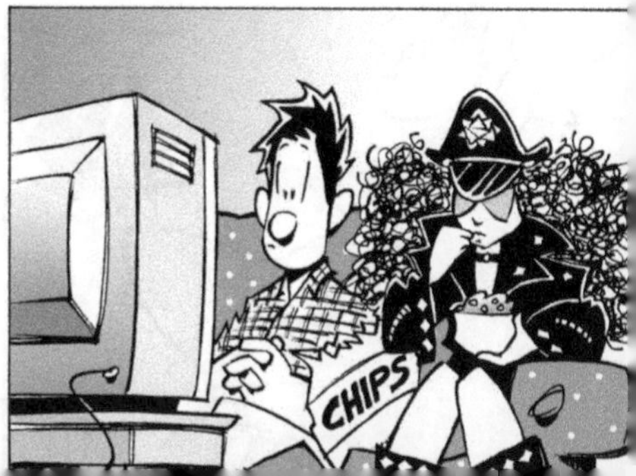
CHIPS

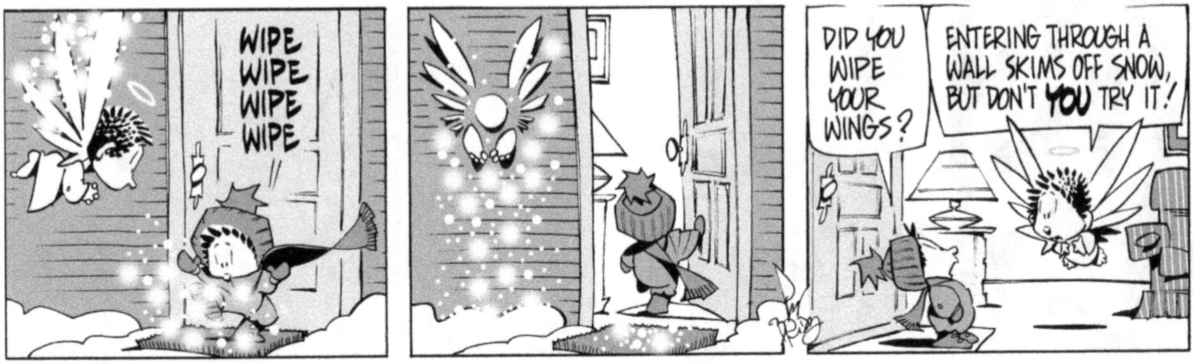
WIPE
WIPE
WIPE
WIPE
DID YOU WIPE YOUR WINGS?
ENTERING THROUGH A WALL SKIMS OFF SNOW, BUT DON'T YOU TRY IT!

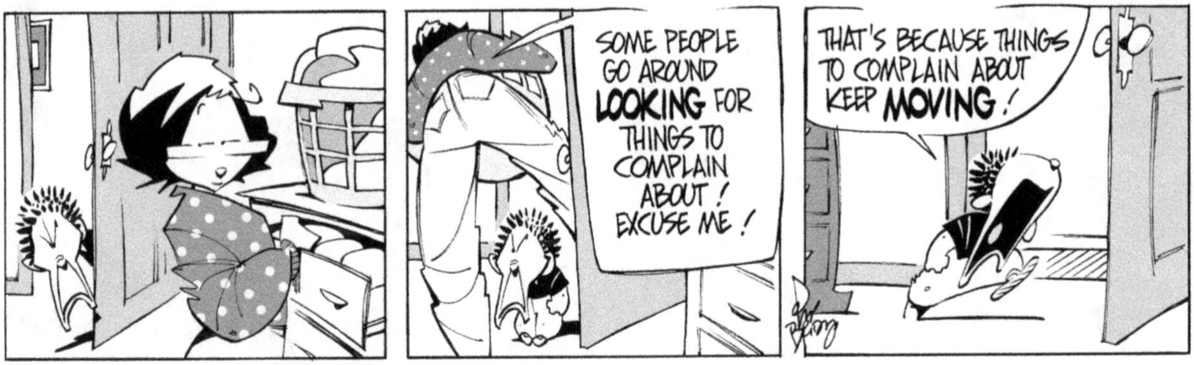
SOME PEOPLE GO AROUND LOOKING FOR THINGS TO COMPLAIN ABOUT! EXCUSE ME!
THAT'S BECAUSE THINGS TO COMPLAIN ABOUT KEEP MOVING!

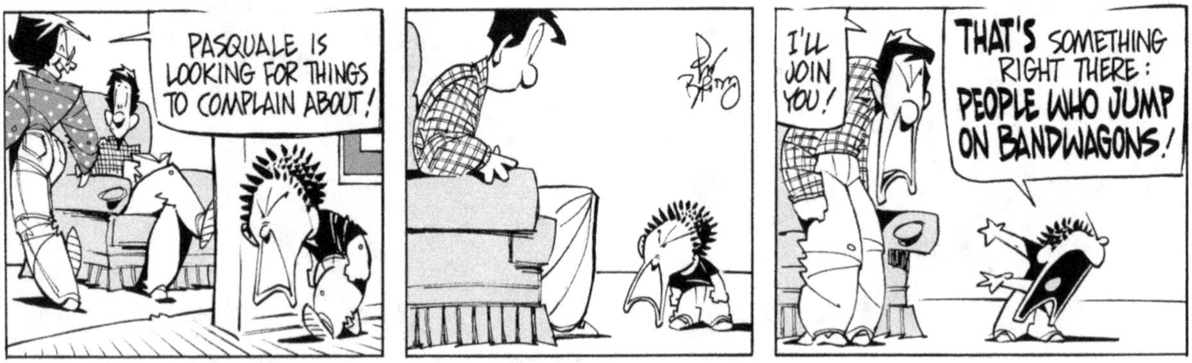
PASQUALE IS LOOKING FOR THINGS TO COMPLAIN ABOUT!
I'LL JOIN YOU!
THAT'S SOMETHING RIGHT THERE: PEOPLE WHO JUMP ON BANDWAGONS!

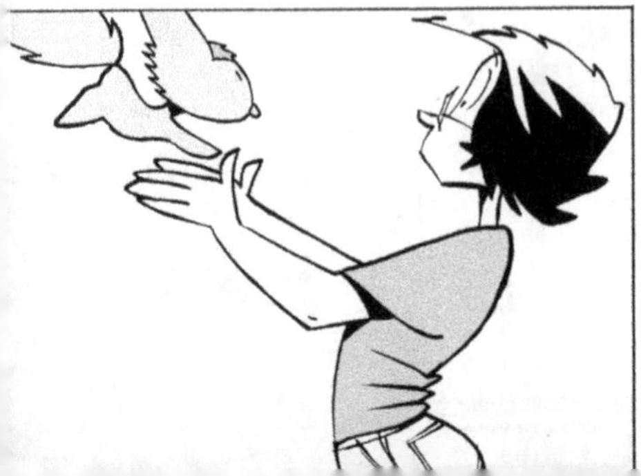

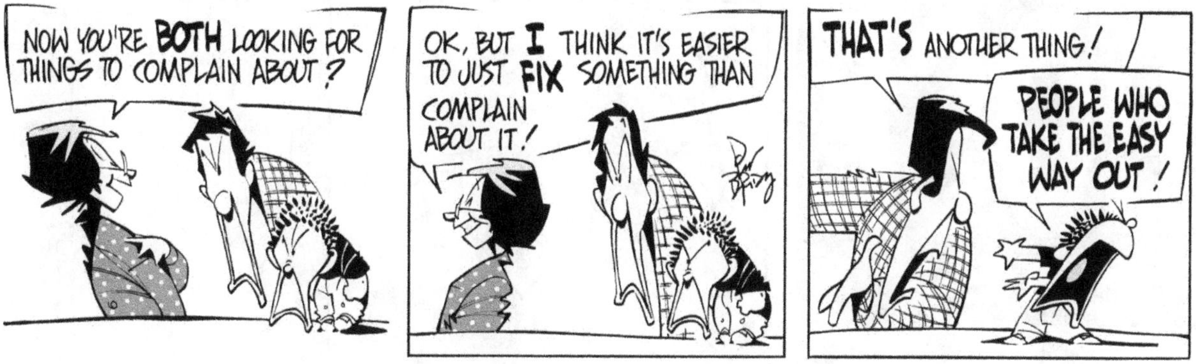
NOW YOU'RE BOTH LOOKING FOR THINGS TO COMPLAIN ABOUT?
OK, BUT I THINK IT'S EASIER TO JUST FIX SOMETHING THAN COMPLAIN ABOUT IT!
THAT'S ANOTHER THING!
PEOPLE WHO TAKE THE EASY WAY OUT!

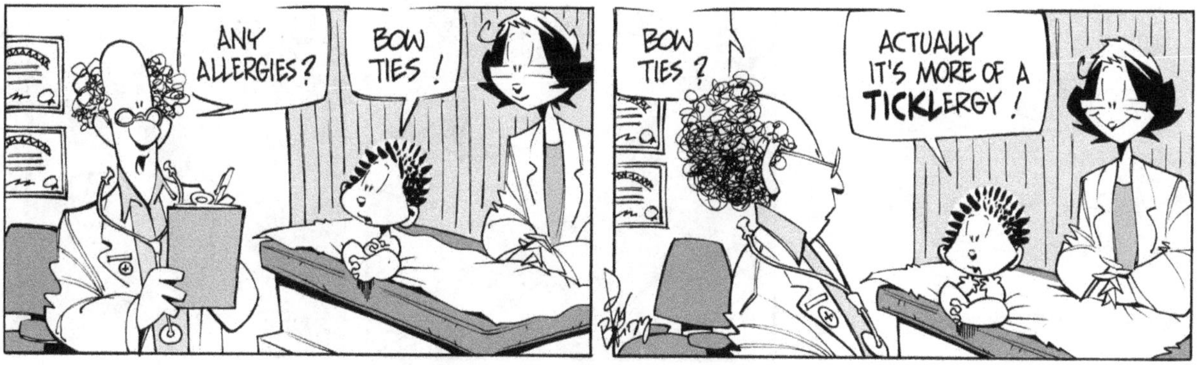
ANY ALLERGIES?
BOW TIES!
BOW TIES?
ACTUALLY IT'S MORE OF A TICKLERGY!

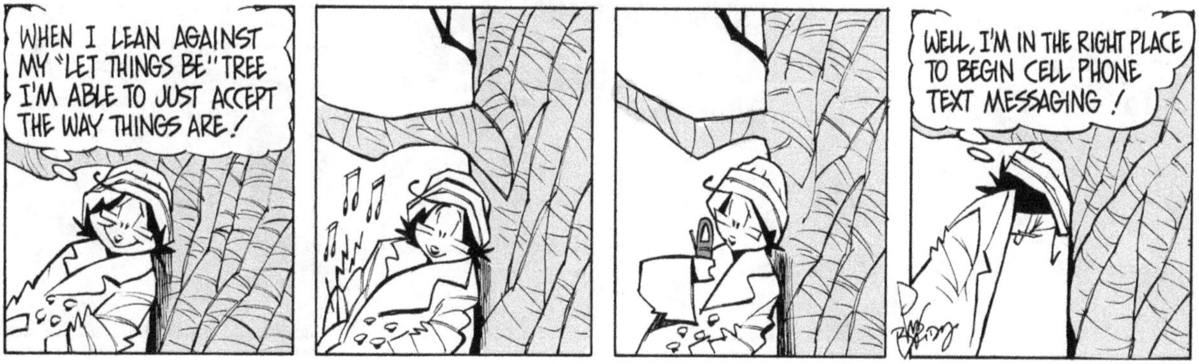
WHEN I LEAN AGAINST MY "LET THINGS BE" TREE I'M ABLE TO JUST ACCEPT THE WAY THINGS ARE!
WELL, I'M IN THE RIGHT PLACE TO BEGIN CELL PHONE TEXT MESSAGING!

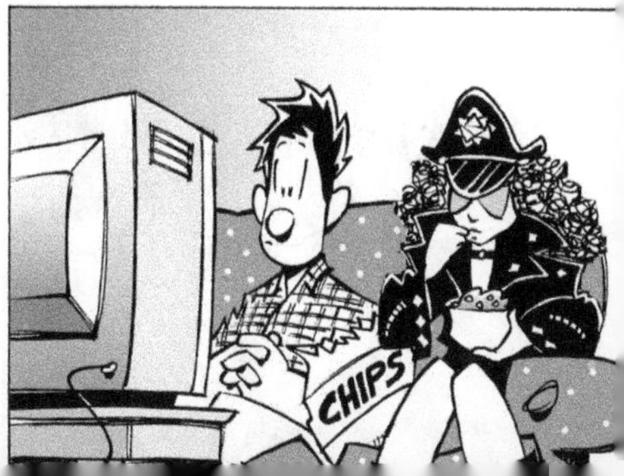
CHIPS

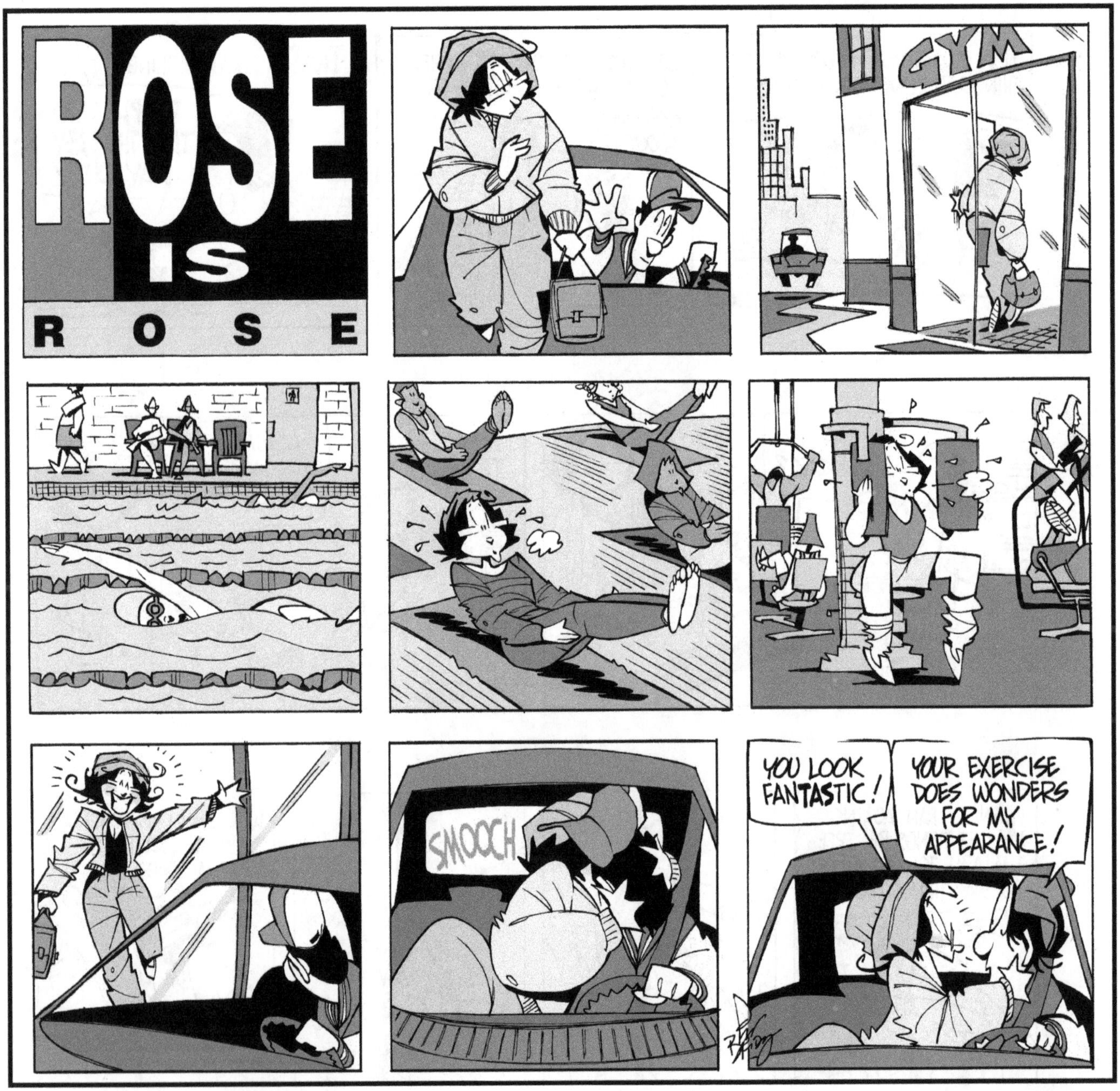
ROSE IS ROSE
GYM
SMOOCH
YOU LOOK FANTASTIC!
YOUR EXERCISE DOES WONDERS FOR MY APPEARANCE!

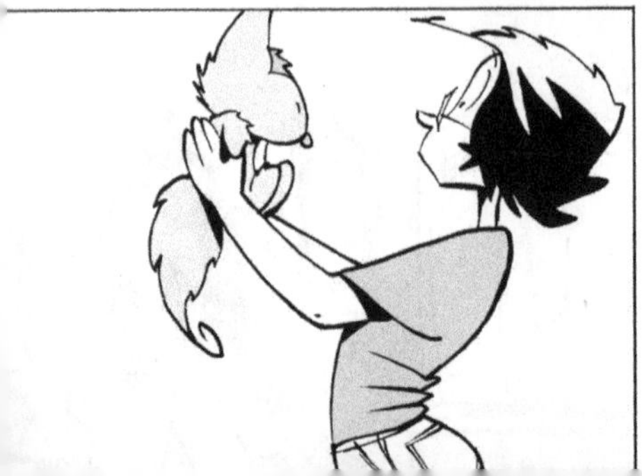

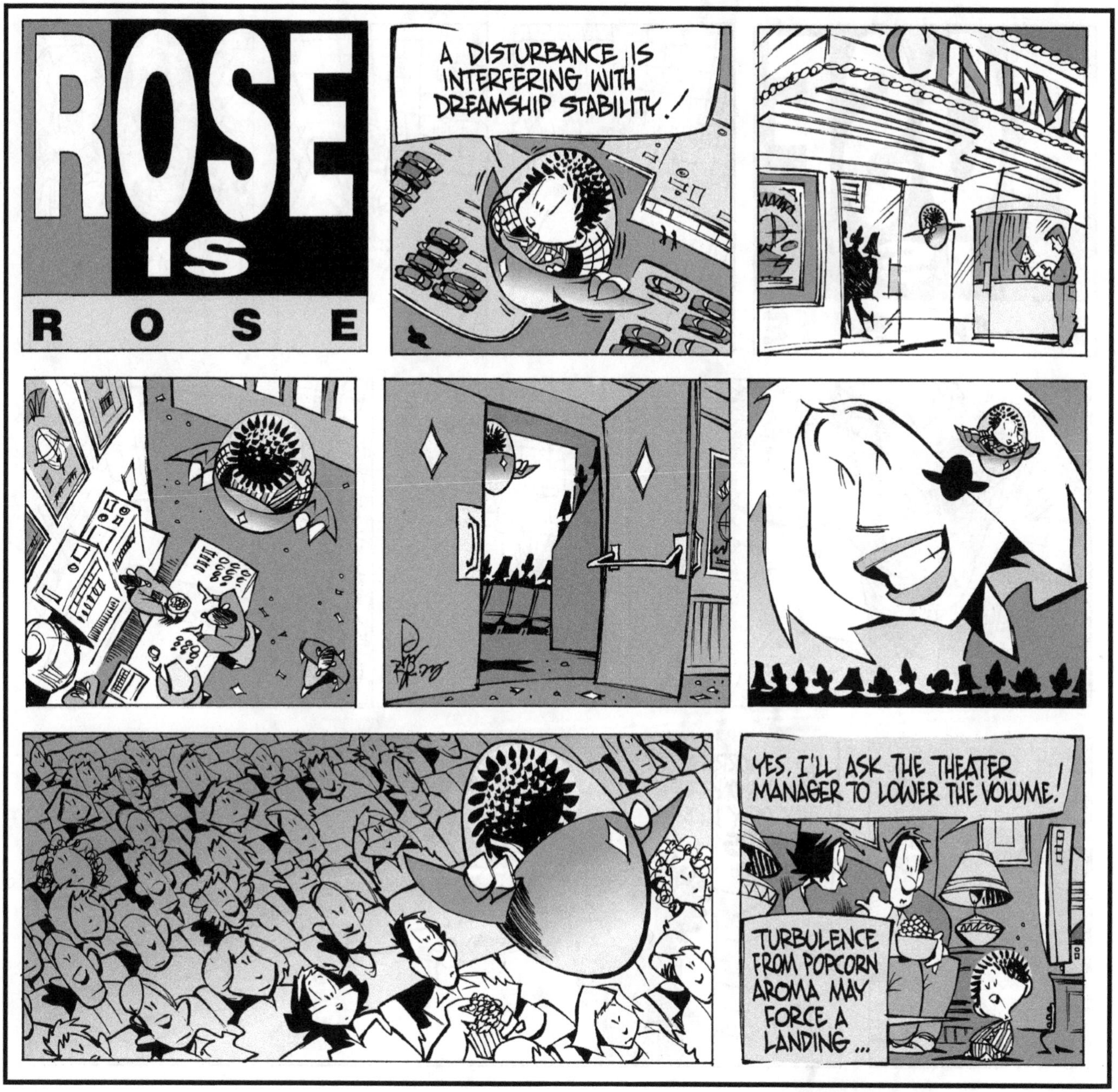
ROSE IS ROSE
A DISTURBANCE IS INTERFERING WITH DREAMSHIP STABILITY!
CINEMA
YES. I'LL ASK THE THEATER MANAGER TO LOWER THE VOLUME!
TURBULENCE FROM POPCORN AROMA MAY FORCE A LANDING...

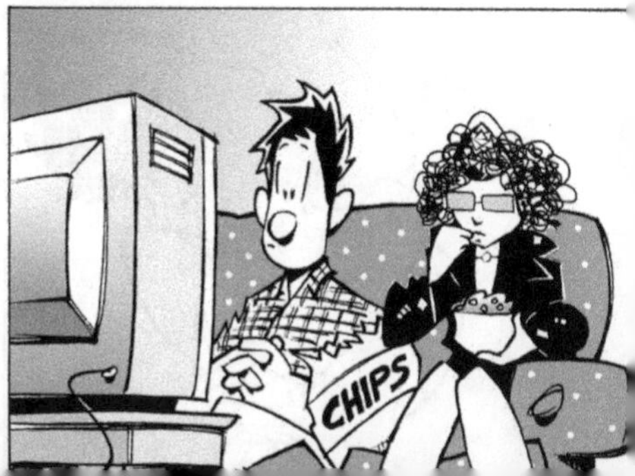
CHIPS

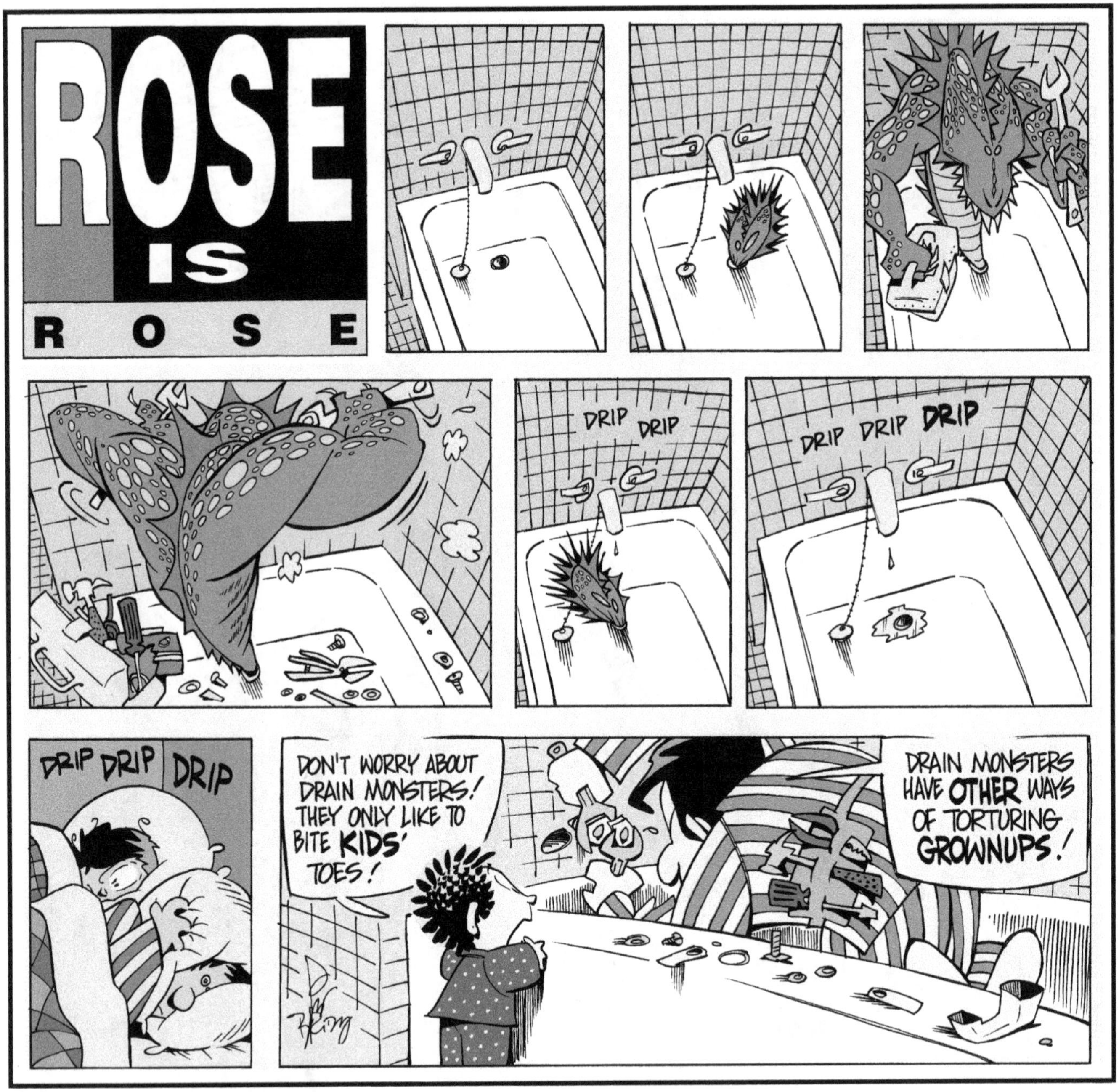
ROSE IS ROSE
DRIP DRIP
DRIP DRIP DRIP
DRIP DRIP DRIP
DON'T WORRY ABOUT DRAIN MONSTERS! THEY ONLY LIKE TO BITE KIDS' TOES!
DRAIN MONSTERS HAVE OTHER WAYS OF TORTURING GROWNUPS!

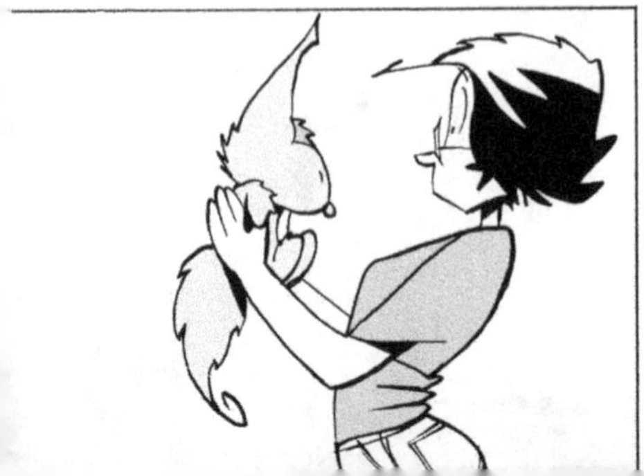

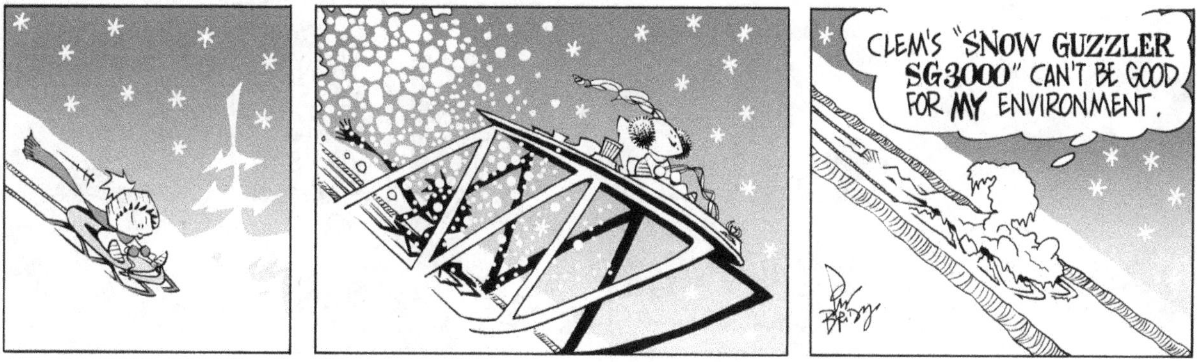

CLEM'S "SNOW GUZZLER SG3000" CAN'T BE GOOD FOR MY ENVIRONMENT.

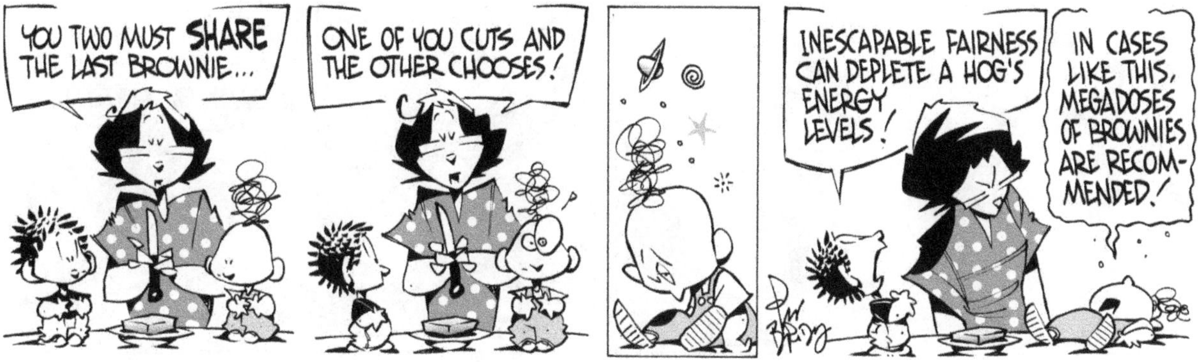

YOU TWO MUST SHARE THE LAST BROWNIE...
ONE OF YOU CUTS AND THE OTHER CHOOSES!
INESCAPABLE FAIRNESS CAN DEPLETE A HOG'S ENERGY LEVELS!
IN CASES LIKE THIS, MEGADOSES OF BROWNIES ARE RECOMMENDED!

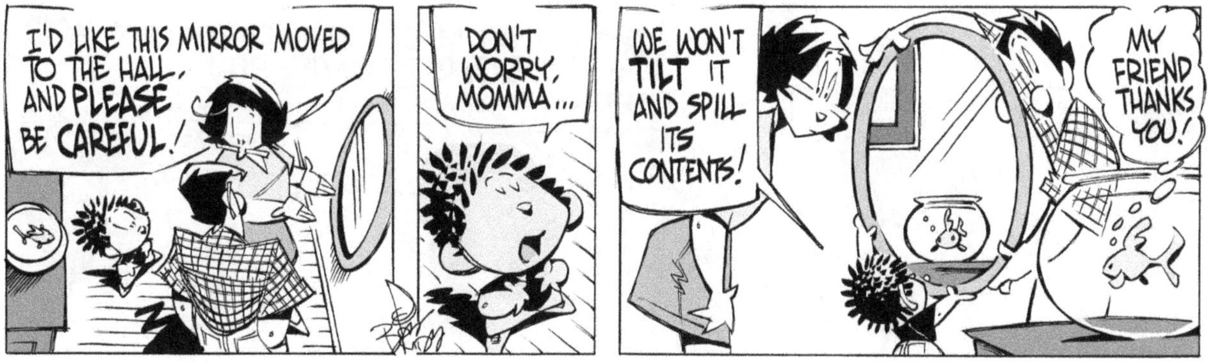

I'D LIKE THIS MIRROR MOVED TO THE HALL, AND PLEASE BE CAREFUL!
DON'T WORRY, MOMMA...
WE WON'T TILT IT AND SPILL ITS CONTENTS!
MY FRIEND THANKS YOU!

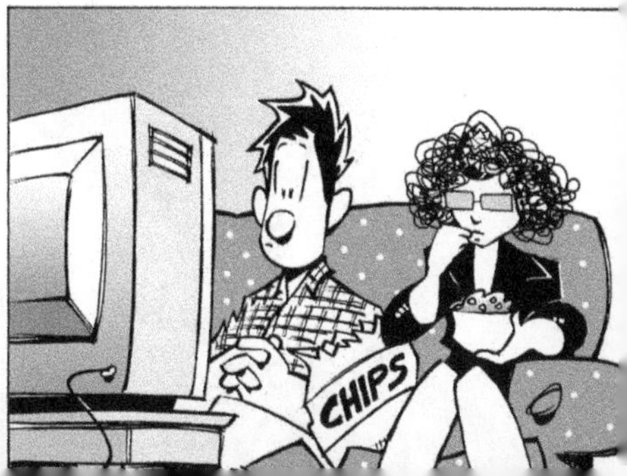

CHIPS

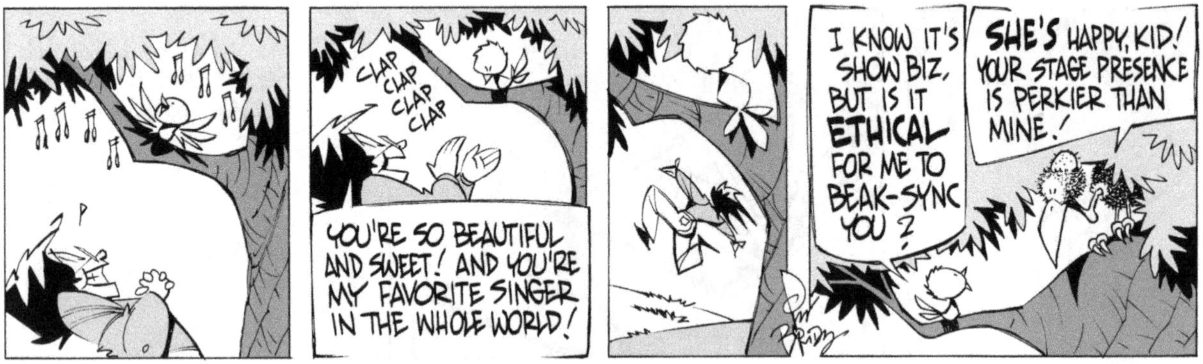
CLAP CLAP CLAP CLAP
YOU'RE SO BEAUTIFUL AND SWEET! AND YOU'RE MY FAVORITE SINGER IN THE WHOLE WORLD!
I KNOW IT'S SHOW BIZ, BUT IS IT ETHICAL FOR ME TO BEAK-SYNC YOU?
SHE'S HAPPY, KID! YOUR STAGE PRESENCE IS PERKIER THAN MINE!

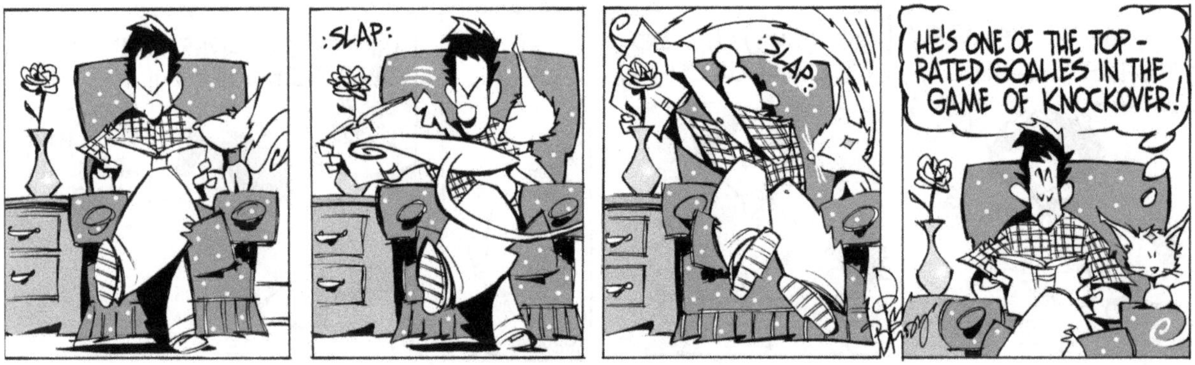
:SLAP:
:SLAP:
HE'S ONE OF THE TOP-RATED GOALIES IN THE GAME OF KNOCKOVER!

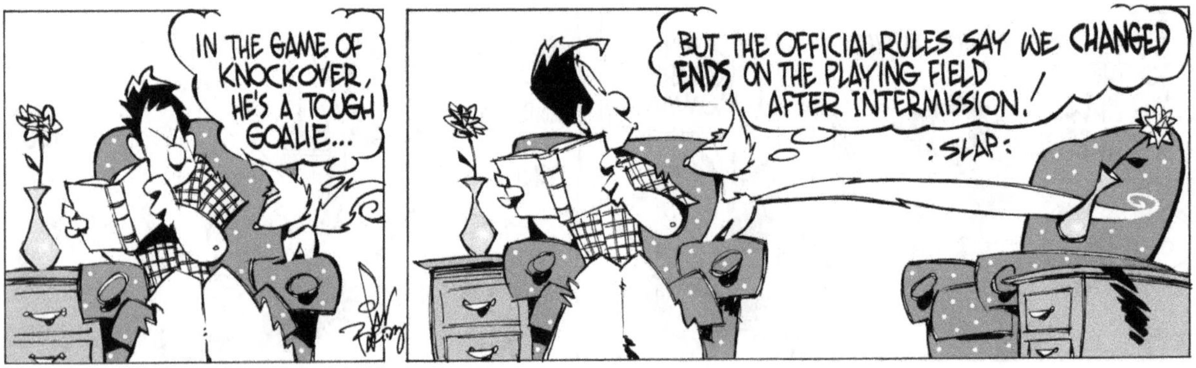
IN THE GAME OF KNOCKOVER, HE'S A TOUGH GOALIE...
BUT THE OFFICIAL RULES SAY WE CHANGED ENDS ON THE PLAYING FIELD AFTER INTERMISSION!
:SLAP:

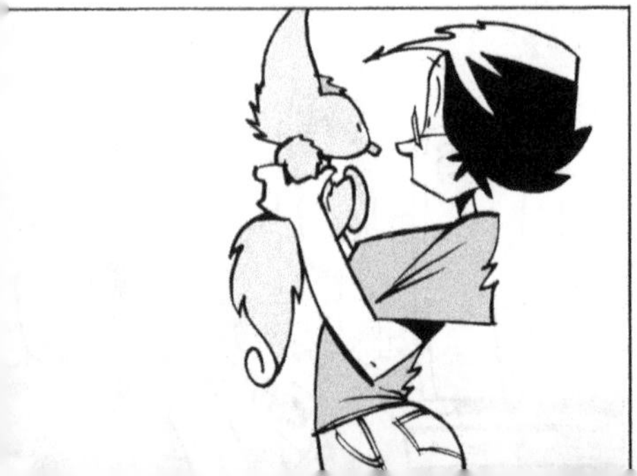

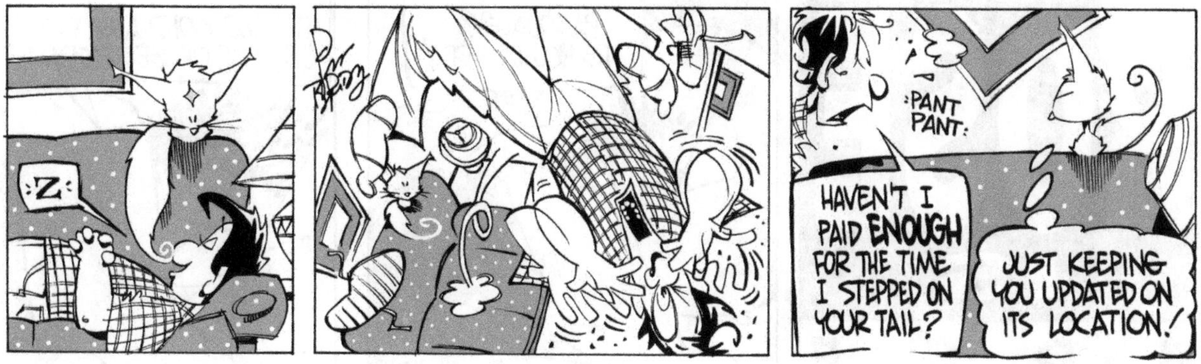
Z
PANT PANT
HAVEN'T I PAID ENOUGH FOR THE TIME I STEPPED ON YOUR TAIL?
JUST KEEPING YOU UPDATED ON ITS LOCATION!

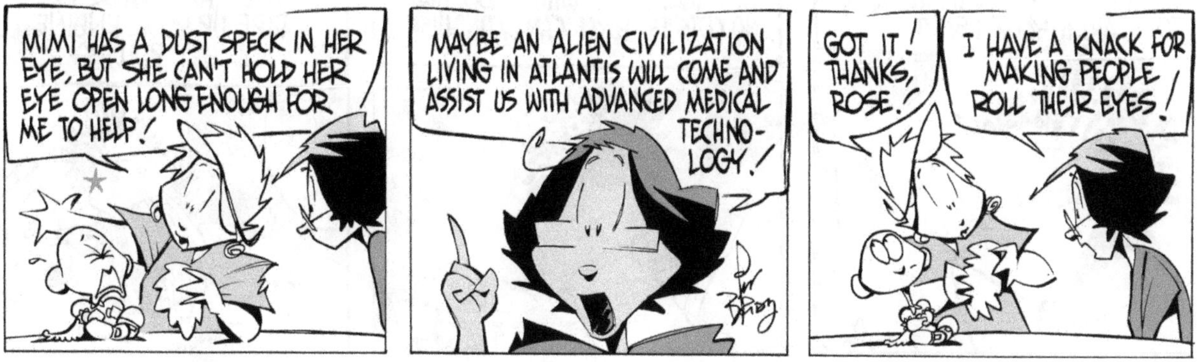
MIMI HAS A DUST SPECK IN HER EYE, BUT SHE CAN'T HOLD HER EYE OPEN LONG ENOUGH FOR ME TO HELP!
MAYBE AN ALIEN CIVILIZATION LIVING IN ATLANTIS WILL COME AND ASSIST US WITH ADVANCED MEDICAL TECHNOLOGY!
GOT IT! THANKS, ROSE.
I HAVE A KNACK FOR MAKING PEOPLE ROLL THEIR EYES!

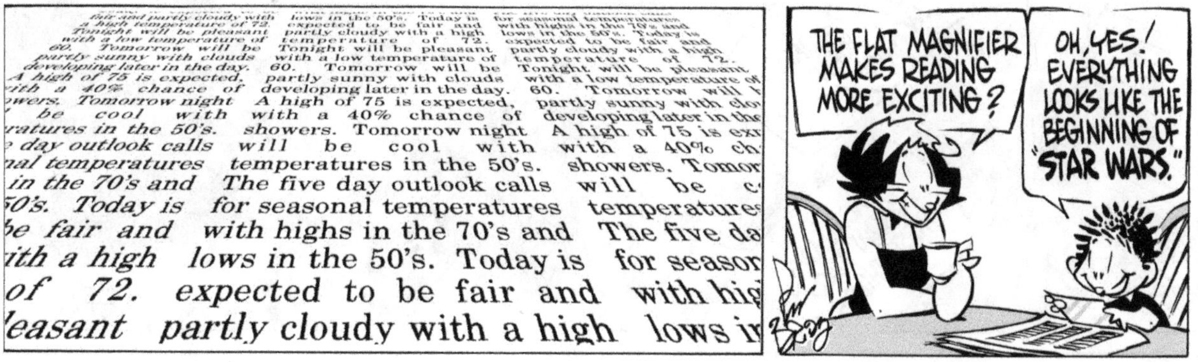
be fair and with highs in the 70's and The five da
ith a high lows in the 50's. Today is for seasor
of 72. expected to be fair and with hig
leasant partly cloudy with a high lows i
THE FLAT MAGNIFIER MAKES READING MORE EXCITING?
OH, YES! EVERYTHING LOOKS LIKE THE BEGINNING OF "STAR WARS."

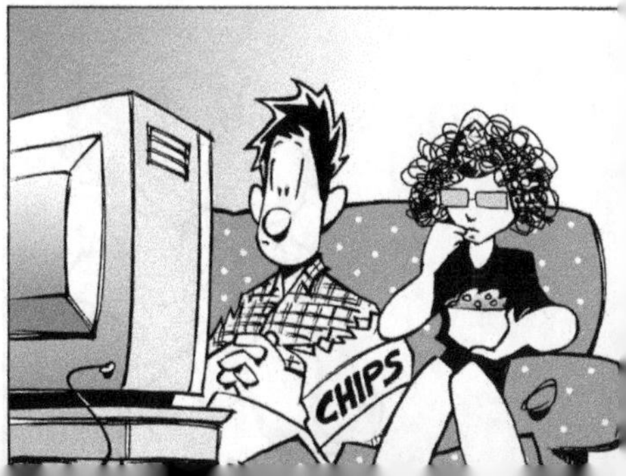
CHIPS

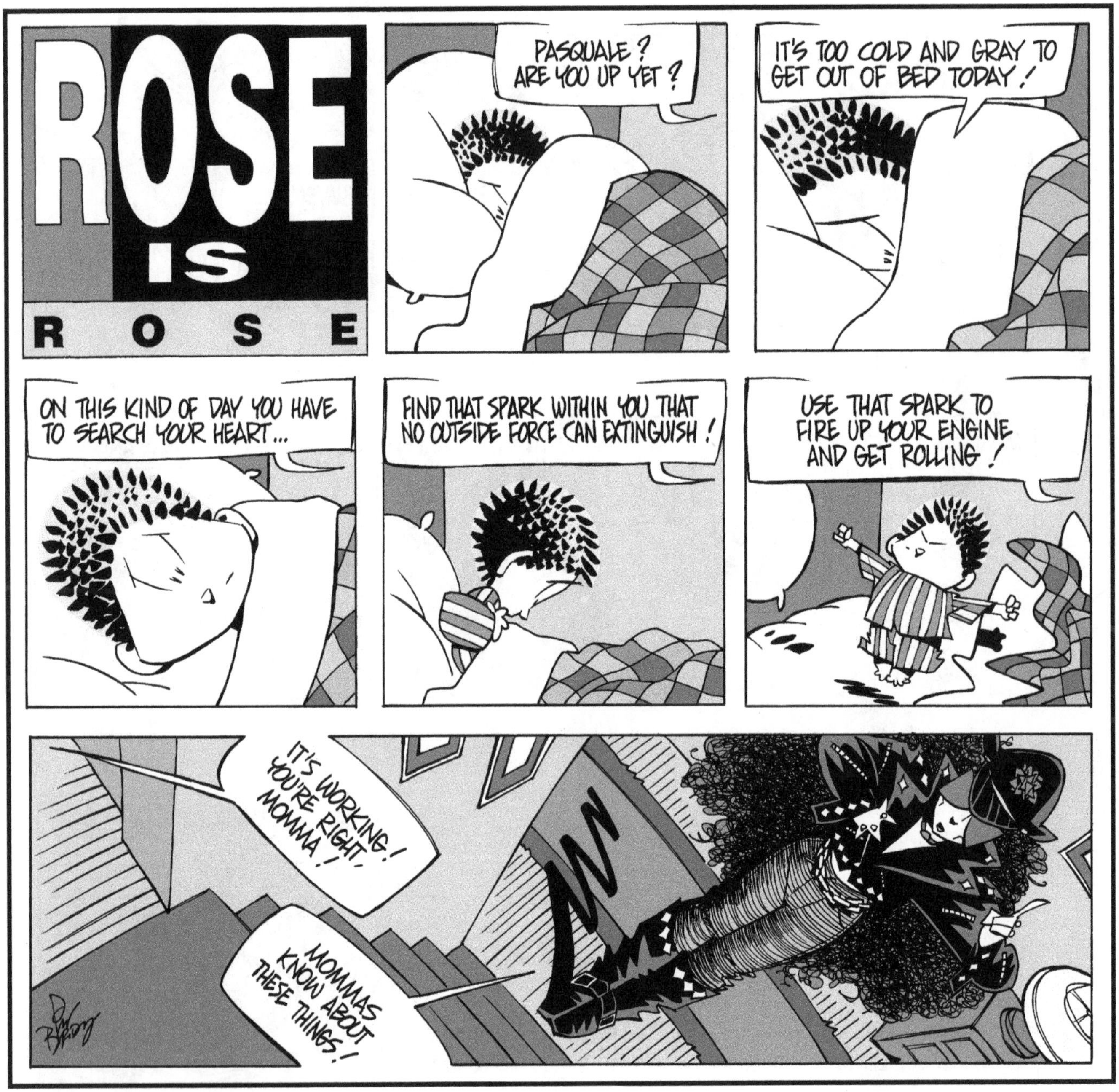
ROSE IS ROSE
PASQUALE? ARE YOU UP YET?
IT'S TOO COLD AND GRAY TO GET OUT OF BED TODAY!
ON THIS KIND OF DAY YOU HAVE TO SEARCH YOUR HEART...
FIND THAT SPARK WITHIN YOU THAT NO OUTSIDE FORCE CAN EXTINGUISH!
USE THAT SPARK TO FIRE UP YOUR ENGINE AND GET ROLLING!
IT'S WORKING! YOU'RE RIGHT, MOMMA!
MOMMAS KNOW ABOUT THESE THINGS!

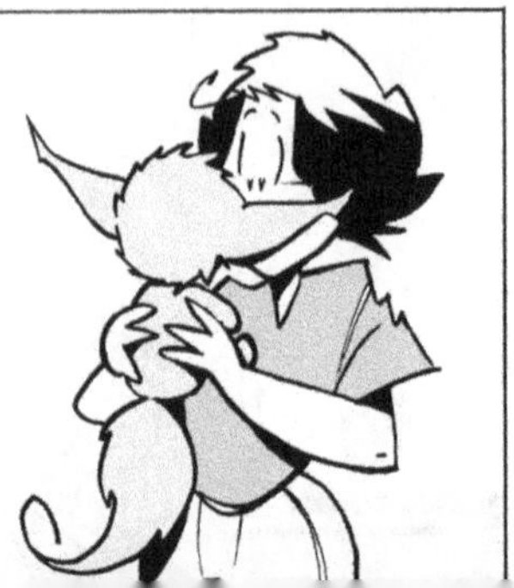

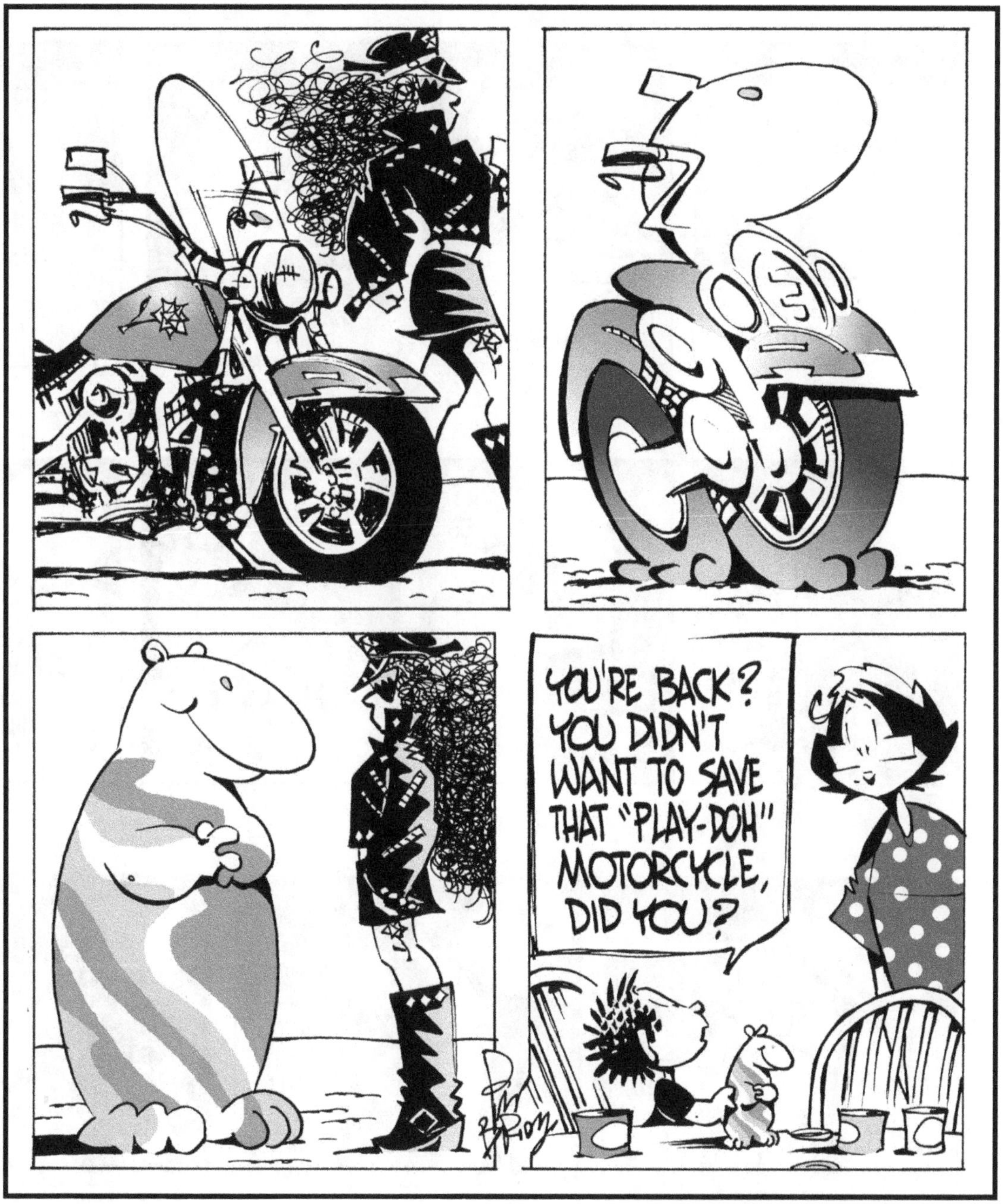
YOU'RE BACK? YOU DIDN'T WANT TO SAVE THAT "PLAY-DOH" MOTORCYCLE, DID YOU?

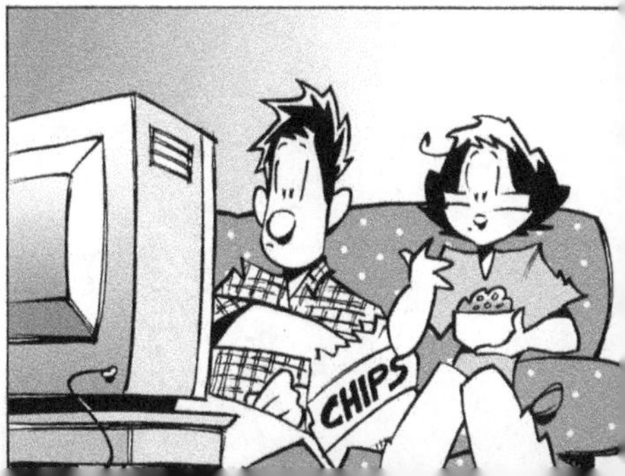
CHIPS

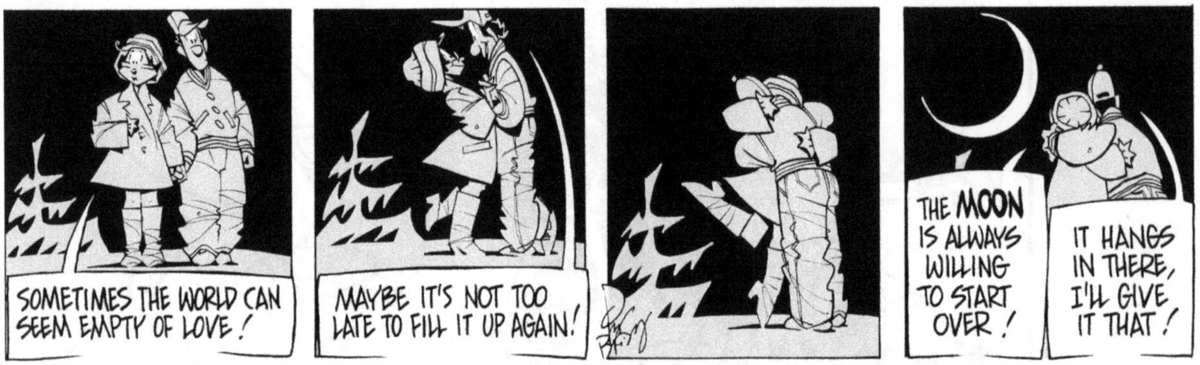

SOMETIMES THE WORLD CAN SEEM EMPTY OF LOVE!
MAYBE IT'S NOT TOO LATE TO FILL IT UP AGAIN!
THE MOON IS ALWAYS WILLING TO START OVER!
IT HANGS IN THERE, I'LL GIVE IT THAT!

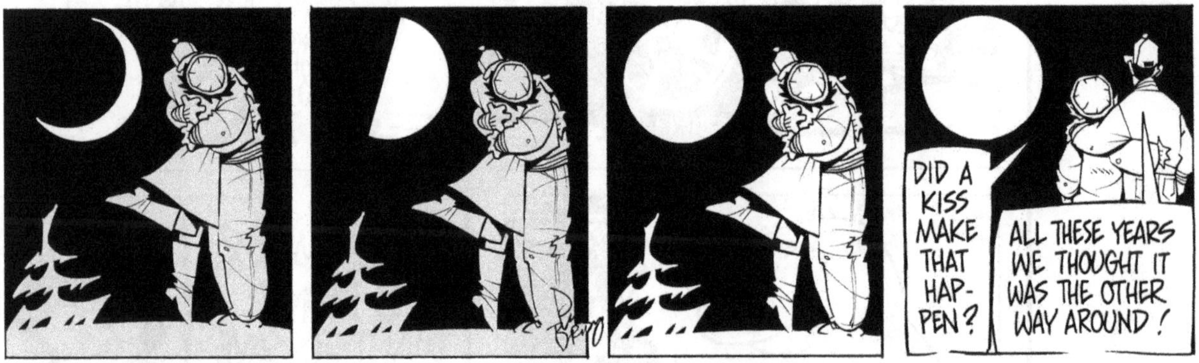

DID A KISS MAKE THAT HAP-PEN?
ALL THESE YEARS WE THOUGHT IT WAS THE OTHER WAY AROUND!

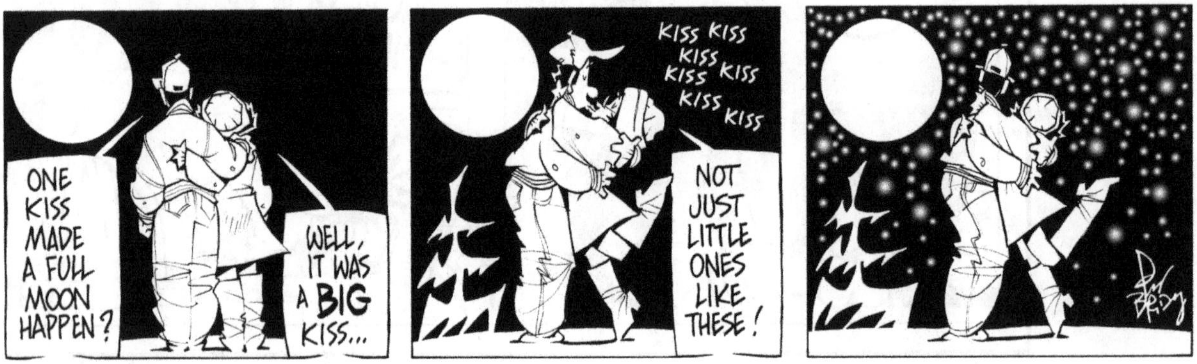

ONE KISS MADE A FULL MOON HAPPEN?
WELL, IT WAS A BIG KISS...
KISS KISS KISS KISS KISS KISS KISS
NOT JUST LITTLE ONES LIKE THESE!

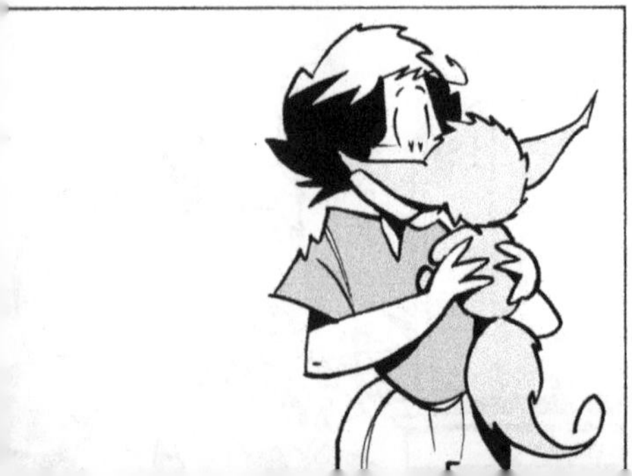

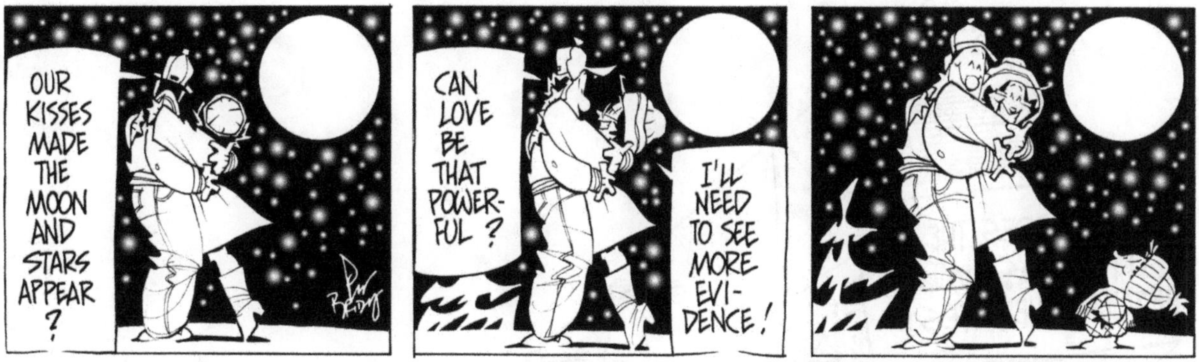
OUR KISSES MADE THE MOON AND STARS APPEAR ?
CAN LOVE BE THAT POWERFUL ?
I'LL NEED TO SEE MORE EVIDENCE !

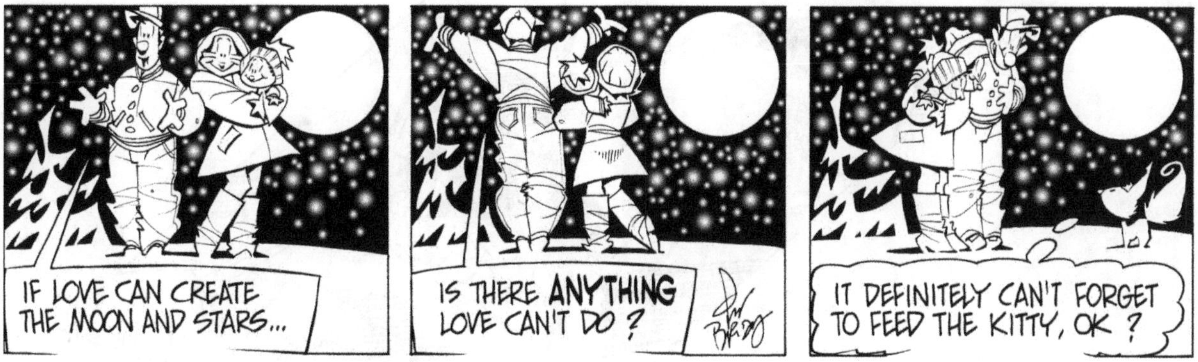
IF LOVE CAN CREATE THE MOON AND STARS...
IS THERE ANYTHING LOVE CAN'T DO ?
IT DEFINITELY CAN'T FORGET TO FEED THE KITTY, OK ?

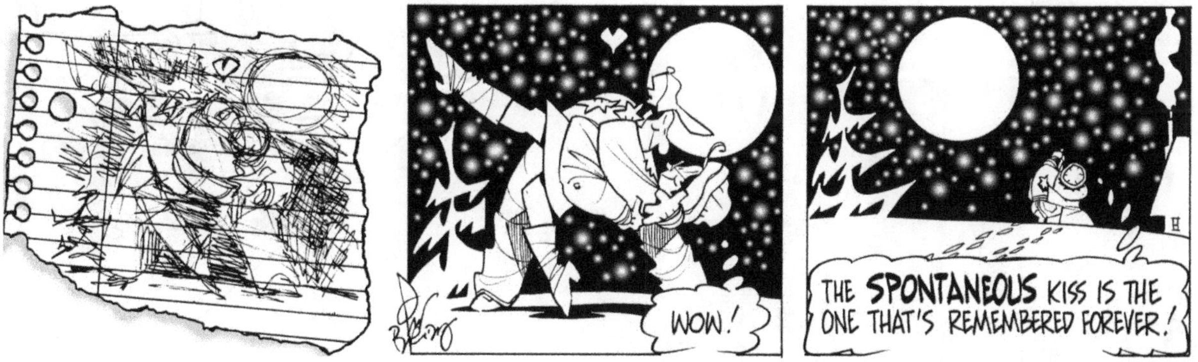
WOW !
THE SPONTANEOUS KISS IS THE ONE THAT'S REMEMBERED FOREVER !

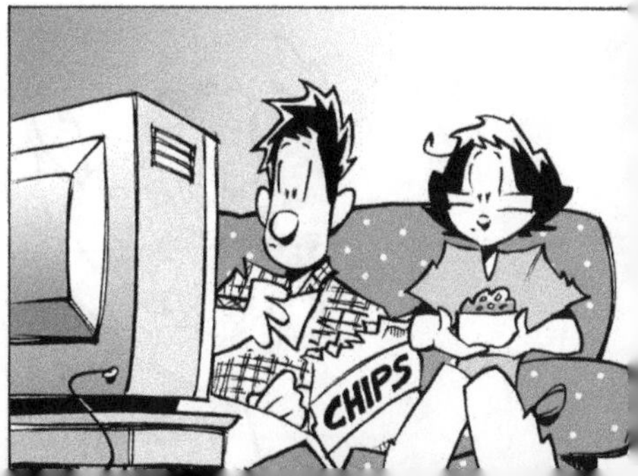
CHIPS

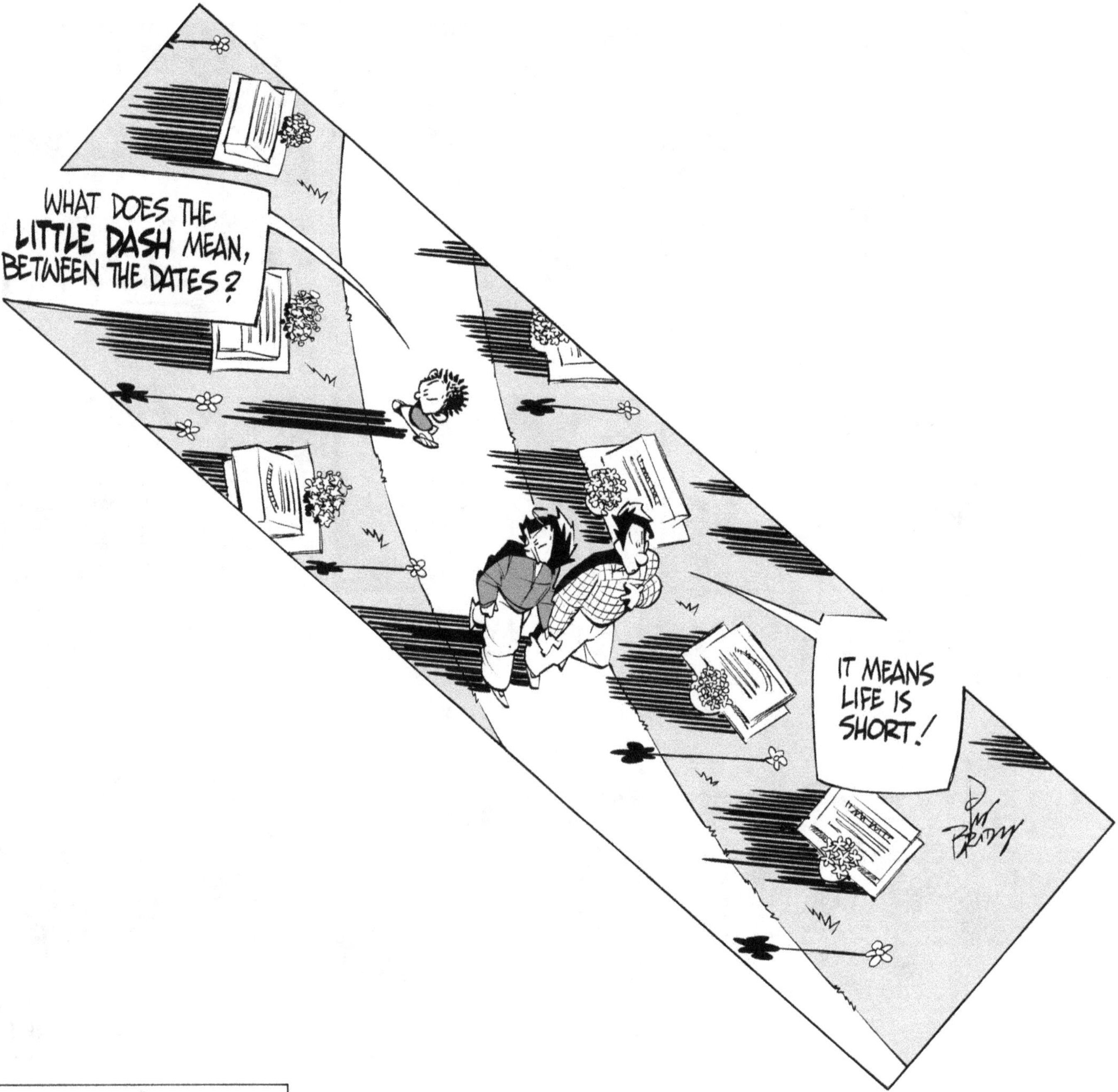
WHAT DOES THE LITTLE DASH MEAN, BETWEEN THE DATES?
IT MEANS LIFE IS SHORT!

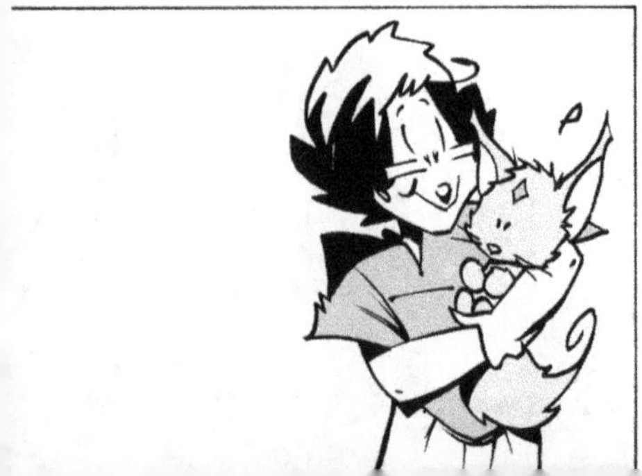

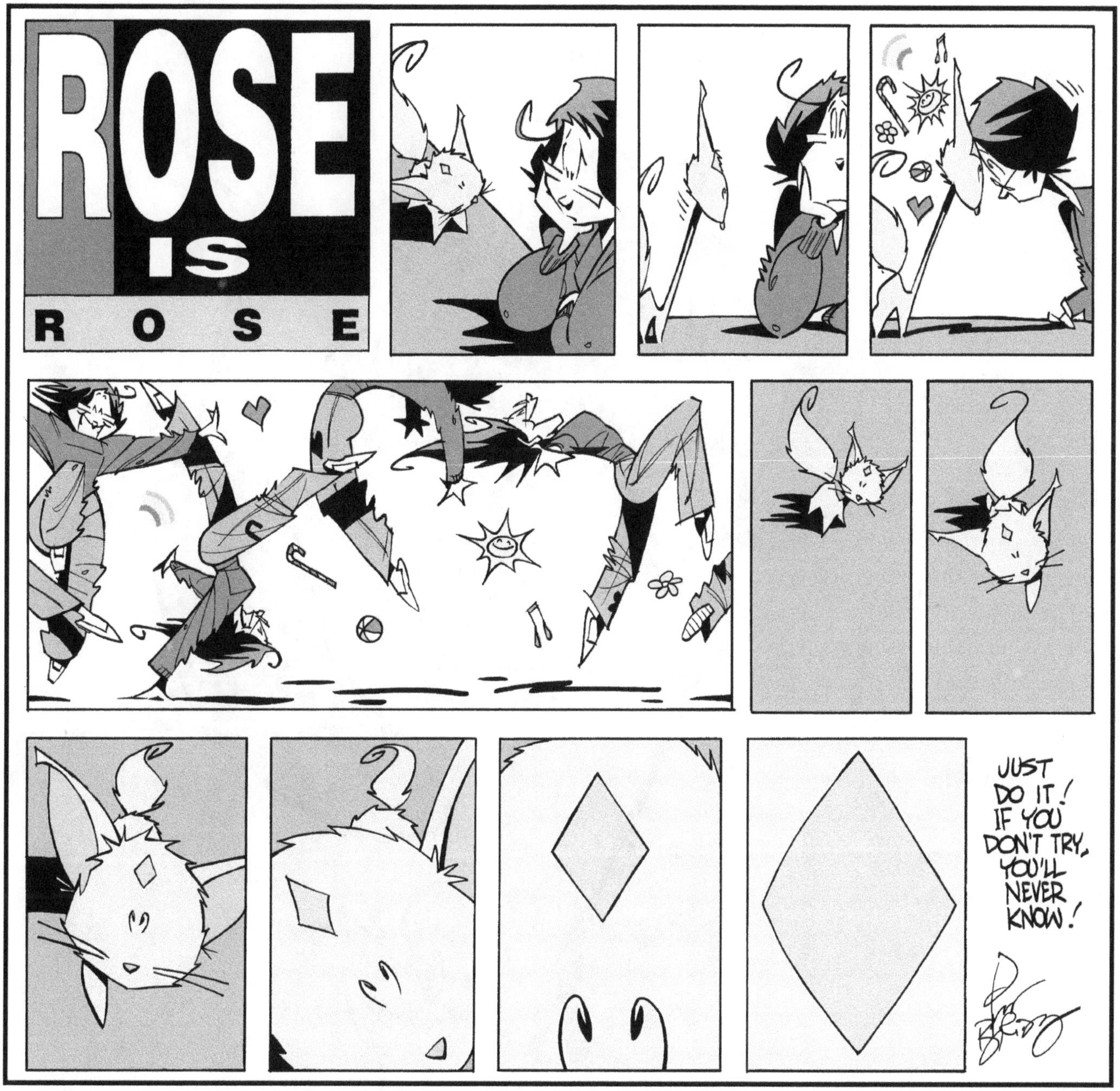
ROSE IS ROSE
JUST DO IT! IF YOU DON'T TRY, YOU'LL NEVER KNOW!

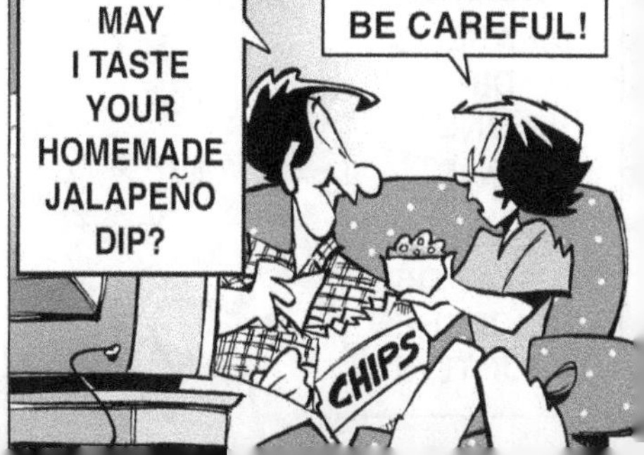
MAY I TASTE YOUR HOMEMADE JALAPEÑO DIP?
BE CAREFUL!
CHIPS

ROSE
IS
ROSE

JALAPEÑO
DIP
IS ONLY
ONE
REASON
TO STAY OFF
THE KITCHEN
COUNTER!